JEWISH ENTANGLEMENTS IN THE ATLANTIC WORLD

JEWISH ENTANGLEMENTS IN THE ATLANTIC WORLD

Edited by Aviva Ben-Ur and Wim Klooster

CORNELL UNIVERSITY PRESS
Ithaca and London

Copyright © 2023 by Aviva Ben-Ur and Wim Klooster

All rights reserved. Except for brief quotations in a review, this book, or parts thereof, must not be reproduced in any form without permission in writing from the publisher. For information, address Cornell University Press, Sage House, 512 East State Street, Ithaca, New York 14850. Visit our website at cornellpress.cornell.edu.

First published 2023 by Cornell University Press

Library of Congress Cataloging-in-Publication Data

Names: Klooster, Wim, editor. | Ben-Ur, Aviva, editor.
Title: Jewish entanglements in the Atlantic world / edited by Aviva Ben-Ur and Wim Klooster.
Description: Ithaca, NY : Cornell University Press, 2023. | "This book began its life as a workshop at Clark University in 2019, sponsored by the David and Edith Chaifetz Fund for Jewish Studies. The papers presented there became book chapters, which were supplemented by commissioned chapters"—CIP galley acknowledgments page. | Includes bibliographical references and index.
Identifiers: LCCN 2023023904 (print) | LCCN 2023023905 (ebook) | ISBN 9781501773143 (hardcover) | ISBN 9781501773150 (paperback) | ISBN 9781501773167 (pdf) | ISBN 9781501773174 (epub)
Subjects: LCSH: Jews—Atlantic Ocean Region—History. | Jews—Atlantic Ocean Region—Migrations—History. | Jewish diaspora. | Atlantic Ocean Region—History.
Classification: LCC DS135.A87 J49 2023 (print) | LCC DS135.A87 (ebook) | DDC 909/.04924—dc23/eng/20230815
LC record available at https://lccn.loc.gov/2023023904
LC ebook record available at https://lccn.loc.gov/2023023905

Contents

Acknowledgments vii

Note on Terminology ix

Introduction: The Revolutionary
Potential of Atlantic Jewish History   1
AVIVA BEN-UR AND WIM KLOOSTER

1. The U.S. and the Rest: Old and New
Paradigms of Early American Jewish
History   22
JOHN M. DIXON

2. Atlantic Commerce and Pragmatic
Tolerance: Portuguese Jewish
Participation in the Spanish
Navíos de Registro System in the
Seventeenth Century   42
OREN OKHOVAT

3. To Trade Is to Thrive: The Sephardic
Moment in Amsterdam's Atlantic
and Caribbean Sugar Trade in the
Seventeenth Century   62
YDA SCHREUDER

4. Trading Violence: Four Jewish
Soldiers between Atlantic Empires
(ca. 1600–1655)   78
VICTOR TIRIBÁS

5. Imperial Enterprise: The Franks
Family Network, Commerce, and
British Expansion   99
TONI PITOCK

6. Declarations of Interdependence: Understanding the Entanglement of Jewish Rights and Liberties in the Anglo-Atlantic, 1740–1830   116
HOLLY SNYDER

7. Jews and Free People of Color in Eighteenth-Century Jamaica: A Case Study in Experiential and Ethnic Entanglement   136
STANLEY MIRVIS

8. Jewish Involvement in the Age of Atlantic Revolutions: The Threat of Equality to the Jewish Way of Life   156
WIM KLOOSTER

9. Sex with Slaves and the Business of Governance: The Case of Barbados   177
AVIVA BEN-UR

10. Connecting Jewish Community: An Anglophone Journal, Rev. Isaac Leeser, and a Jewish Atlantic World   197
LAURA NEWMAN ECKSTEIN

Notes 215

Notes on Contributors 277

Index 279

Acknowledgments

This book began its life as a workshop at Clark University in 2019, sponsored by the David and Edith Chaifetz Fund for Jewish Studies. The papers presented there became chapters in this book, which were supplemented by commissioned chapters. We are grateful to Adam Mendelsohn and the two anonymous reviewers for their scholarly advice, and we thank Michael McGandy and Susan Specter at Cornell University Press and copy editor Deborah A. Oosterhouse for the smooth collaboration.

Note on Terminology

Contrary to the established practice, we emphasize that the term and concept "Sephardic" is ahistorical for the Atlantic world, whose temporal parameters overlap with early modernity. During that era, actors who self-identified as Sephardim—those of the Ottoman Empire—had yet to densely populate local Jewish communities.[1] Rather, Jews of Iberian origin in the Atlantic world called themselves—and were generally denoted by others—as "Portuguese Jews" and branded their congregations as "Spanish and Portuguese." They did so because they were part and parcel of the Iberian diaspora—a pan-Sephardic self-understanding had yet to emerge.[2] Although we prefer the term "Portuguese," most practitioners of Jewish studies continue to use "Sephardic," as do some of the authors in this volume.

Readers will note that a number of contributors have consciously chosen to use "slave" and "enslaved" interchangeably, with "slave" intentionally retained to communicate both legal status and the brutality of a system that combined unfree labor with rampant sexual exploitation. Some use "Africans" to denote unfree people arriving from Africa. Others prefer "Black" or "black" to refer to enslaved people of colonial or uncertain nativity. Some prefer "white" over "of European origin." Some use "free people of color," reflecting the legal language of colonial records, while other prefer "Eurafricans," to underscore the dual heritage of certain free or unfree people. Some use "Indigenous Americans" instead of "Indians" or "Native Americans." Echoing our policy on the terms "Portuguese Jews" vs. "Sephardic," we have decided to allow each author to retain their informed and deeply considered judgments on terminology.

Introduction
The Revolutionary Potential of Atlantic Jewish History

AVIVA BEN-UR AND WIM KLOOSTER

This volume is organized around the notion of entanglement. It stresses the close ties between Jews and non-Jews across imperial boundaries and the connections between Jews and other ethnic groups in their own environments. It aims to revolutionize the study of Jews in early American history. For more than a century, a parochial and ahistorical approach has prevailed that privileges events, developments, and institutions in the United States.[1] The standard narrative is linear and nationalistic and emphasizes U.S. exceptionalism. The long period prior to the foundation of the North American republic is presented in a trajectory that follows a route from the Spanish expulsion of 1492, the first synagogue in Brazil, and settlement in the Caribbean, to the arrival of Jews in New Amsterdam in 1654.

This funnel vision not only reduces the colonial era to the status of prehistory, it also obscures the fundamentally connective nature of early American Jewish history. Just like in American history at large, what is needed is a broader, Atlantic approach. Networks, transimperial connections and comparisons, actors across boundaries, and interactions with a wide array of non-Jewish actors deserve a place in the limelight. A deeper understanding of early modern Jewish history in the New World can be accomplished by using the tools and insights of Atlantic history.

This book invites historians of the early modern world to look beyond the borders of the United States in studying the interactions of Jews with others. As it turns out, these interactions were not limited to North America or non-Atlantic Europe, but extended to numerous places across the Atlantic world. Analysis on an Atlantic scale is therefore required to do justice to the lives of these Jews.[2] While some colleagues may prefer an even larger canvas, we believe that it would be a mistake to move from a North American scale to a global one. Although there were Jews who lived and worked in India—including two indigenous groups, a migrant group hailing mainly from Baghdad, and a few Anglo-Dutch colonies—their activities for the most part ran parallel to rather than intersected with Atlantic Jewish history. Moreover, since there were only episodic interactions between Atlantic and Asian Jews, a global Jewish history encompassing both world hemispheres would carry little self-justification.[3] The Atlantic world being broad enough as it is, we do not see it as our task to be exhaustive in covering early modern Jewry. The ten essays in this volume constitute the first collective attempt to self-consciously reframe the study of colonial and early American Jewry within an Atlantic paradigm.

The volume opens with John M. Dixon's chapter, which shows how the field of American Jewish history has ended up where it is today. Drawing on an array of scholarly conversations that challenge the national paradigm, many of them unearthed from arcane publications, Dixon argues that what has come to dominate the specialization is a linear and nationalistic metanarrative that celebrates American exceptionalism. Whereas late nineteenth-century scholars still conceived of the history of U.S. Jewry as part of a vaster world, a narrower conception that presented the United States as the culmination of Jewish civil and political freedom and commercial activity and prosperity gained the upper hand around the turn of the twentieth century. Dixon explains how writing about Jewish history in early America—by and large by practitioners who were themselves Jews—was purified of elements that were not North American. By the mid-twentieth century, demographic factors further worked against a more capacious view of the past, as most American Jews had been born in the United States at the same time that their community had become the largest Jewish population in the world. Instead of a more entangled vision, what historians continued to depict was a North American Jewish community marked by longevity and continuity.

Entanglement is prominently on display in Oren Okhovat's chapter, which follows the trajectories of Portuguese Jews in the early Spanish Empire. These men used the opportunities presented by local Spanish officials to simultaneously serve the Spanish Crown and engage in contraband trade with other empires. When their influence began to wane, they shifted to Amsterdam, which gradually attracted (former) New Christians from Portuguese and Spanish territories as well as France and nearby Antwerp. Portuguese Jews thus played crucial roles as intermediaries in the Spanish Empire before contributing to Amsterdam's commercial heyday. In this role, Portuguese Jews formed part of a broad trading network, which—like many other international trading networks—was characterized by religious diversity. Even after one branch of this network, headquartered in Amsterdam, evolved into a strictly Jewish community, Okhovat argues, it "continued to function as a de facto Iberian merchant nation."

One sector in which Portuguese Jews were well represented was the sugar business, as has been documented for the period before 1630, when Brazilian sugar dominated the European markets.[4] In her chapter, Yda Schreuder shows that Portuguese Jewish involvement in the international sugar trade continued in later decades, when Amsterdam connected Jewish and New Christian communities in Lisbon, Hamburg, London, Brazil, Barbados, Jamaica, and some French Caribbean colonies. The fall of Dutch Brazil and the sudden emergence of Barbados as the world's premier sugar producer encouraged Portuguese Jews to adapt quickly. Many intertwined themselves with the English Empire by receiving English denization papers and moving to London and the English Caribbean.

Past historians have shown that the men of the Portuguese Nation who became Jews in places such as Amsterdam maintained close cultural and commercial ties not only with other Jews but also with Catholics, some of them even returning to the Catholic faith. Conversion was not a purely religious affair, even if many genuinely adopted the Jewish faith when presented with the opportunity. Material considerations were important as well. The migration of Portuguese Jews back and forth between Protestant and Catholic lands, which Yosef Kaplan and other scholars have presented as a movement between public and secret Jewish identities, arguably should not be understood in Jewish terms, but rather in terms of the Portuguese Empire and the mandates of its imperial commerce. In his chapter, by contrast, Victor Tiribás pushes back against the notion that religious identity was the product of pragmatic considerations. His analysis of the vicissitudes of four Jews who served as soldiers in the ranks of the Dutch West India Company's army in the Americas tells a different story. What motivated them to face discrimination and defy death "was a deep sense of revenge against the tyranny of Catholics embodied in the Inquisition, their messianic expectations about the dispersion of the Jews across the globe, and the possibility of gaining prestige within the Jewish community itself. Willing to kill and die for Judaism, their religious commitment seems beyond doubt." Whatever their motives were, they connected their fate to the Dutch, who had their own, partly religious, reasons to fight their Spanish "hereditary" enemies. While this handful of Jews was not necessarily representative of the broader, interimperial Jewish community, Tiribás's case study is an important example of the ongoing relevance of microhistory to the emerging field of Atlantic Jewish history.

The next two chapters are focused on anglophone America. In her contribution, Toni Pitock writes about the Franks family, Ashkenazim who aided the expansion of Britain into the North American interior in the wake of the Seven Years' War. Through backcountry trade, army contracting, and land speculation, various members of this prominent family demonstrated their allegiance and commitment to the expanding empire. In contrast to their dedication to the British Empire, the Frankses' Jewishness is marginal and inconsequential, as Pitock shows. Their mercantile and class aspirations probably did not differ from those of the Christians with whom they traded. Their proximity to gentile colonists was underlined by the marriages that siblings David and Phila Franks entered into with Christians. Her argument challenges previous historiography, which continues to center the Jewishness of the Franks family and other North American coreligionists in their political entanglements and commercial pursuits.[5]

Holly Snyder's ensuing chapter analyzes the well-known but complex case of Ezekiel Hart, who was refused by Lower Canada's Legislative Assembly to take his seat in that body, not once, but twice (in 1807 and 1809), despite having been elected. His Jewishness ostensibly kept him out. But Snyder demonstrates that the outcome of the election was not purely an expression of attitudes about Jews and their status. In her telling, political allegiances and interpersonal alliances were also a significant force, making Jewishness a vulnerability, but not an initial deciding factor in disenfranchisement. Moreover, Snyder places the case in a broader perspective by framing it as part of the rights of Jews in

English political thought and legal practice. The legal status of Jews in English territories, she shows, remained unclear until the Naturalization Act of 1740, which allowed Jews to be naturalized, and even then, the position of Jews remained ambiguous. Their situation was, however, not unique. Snyder reveals the parallels and links between Jews and Catholics in the British Empire in the late eighteenth and early nineteenth centuries. Snyder's essay demonstrates that we should not solely look at Jews across the board, comparatively, but appreciate the idiosyncrasies of local history that made Jewishness arguably less consequential than existing scholarship would have it. The cases that tested Jewish enfranchisement throughout the colonies and in the metropole are so few and far between that the scholar must foreground the local situation.

If Snyder emphasizes the intertwined struggles of Catholics and Jews, Stanley Mirvis points to the remarkable connections on the island of Jamaica between the Jewish fight for rights and that of the free people of color. In urban environments, these groups—who were similarly disenfranchised—lived in the same neighborhoods and engaged in sexual relationships with each other, across a spectrum of what historians understand as mutually consenting, coerced, exploitative, and pragmatic. By the late eighteenth century, these relationships had given rise to a sizable group of Jews of color, to the extent that many Christians conflated Jews with free people of color. Colonial authorities approached the groups' simultaneous campaigns for more privileges by weighing their cases against each other. This bred conflict between the groups, as each sought to be the first to achieve certain civil and political entitlements. The struggle for parity, Mirvis demonstrates, was intertwined rather than parallel, and this interrelation long preceded the better-known lobby for suffrage of the 1820s.[6]

The quest for equality is also discussed in Wim Klooster's chapter, which makes a tour around the Atlantic world in order to retrieve Jewish thoughts and actions during the era of revolutions. While the scholarly literature discusses Jews as reacting to revolutionary changes, it largely ignores Jewish agency. The essay reveals that despite the age-old discriminatory laws against Jews everywhere, there was no generalized Jewish push for equality. Full individual equality meant the loss of Jewish self-rule, which many Jews felt would jeopardize the traditional Jewish way of life, centered around adherence to rabbinical culture. Others may have cherished autonomy because it was organized around the dispensation of charity to the numerous Jewish poor. On the other hand, there was no lack of Jews who fully submerged themselves in the ideas and politics of revolutionary regimes and to whom historians have paid scant attention.

As the age of revolutions left the British Caribbean largely untouched, slavery continued to underpin these colonies until its abolition by Parliament in 1833. In the Barbadian town of Bridgeport, slaves, free people of African descent, and poor white Christians dwelled in the same commercial district as Jews, most of whom struggled to eke out a living. In her chapter, Aviva Ben-Ur considers the sexual liaisons carried out within the framework of physical force, economic exploitation, or pragmatism. She shows that some Jews, notably the indigent synagogue functionaries involved in such relationships, incurred public condemnation by defying existing Jewish norms. Their wealthier coreligionists also engaged in extramarital sexual encounters, especially with women of African descent, but successfully shielded themselves from exposure until a communal rift forcefully exposed double standards within the Jewish community. Ben-Ur ends with a reflection on the relationships she brings to light, concluding that there was nothing uniquely Jewish about them. Thus, these cases are a rare opportunity to consider the sexual lives of the island's underclass and the integration of Jews into the heart of slave society.

The final chapter, by Laura Newman Eckstein, takes a look at the readership of *The Occident*, a thriving Anglo-Jewish journal in the period before the American Civil War. Eckstein argues that by using local agents, the journal's editor, Isaac Leeser, who immigrated in 1824, helped construct a communication network that connected Jews not only in the United States, but also across the Atlantic world. His concerns with Jewish communities in the Caribbean, evinced in his letters and sermons, suggest that he saw the fate of his community as bound up with theirs, reminding us that North American Jews were very aware of those living south of the border. They not only traded with them, but also exchanged letters and synagogue functionaries with them.[7] Leeser's adoption of the Portuguese Jewish rite, which included a distinctively Iberian pronunciation of Hebrew, is yet another indication of his immersion in the (by then waning) Atlantic Jewish world and stands in striking contrast to the national orientation of his younger rival, rabbi and journalist Isaac Mayer Wise, who arrived in the United States in 1846, just as Jewish emigration from central Europe was nearing its peak.[8] Leeser is well known to scholars as the United States' most important Jewish leader of the nineteenth century, but his awareness of and contacts with Caribbean Jews have so far remained largely unassessed. They do not fit the nationalistic metanarrative of American Jewish history to which John Dixon refers. It is time for that narrative to make way for a richer and more diverse understanding of the Jewish past, one that places Jews on the same plane as other historical actors.

One of the insights of an Atlantic approach is that across the Americas, hybrid societies were formed in the colonial era. In many places, the predominant character of the emergent culture may have been shaped by European settlers, but the distinctive regional nuances were formed by the interaction of all ethnic groups. Likewise, colonies belonging to different empires often enjoyed close ties. Discrete imperial spaces never existed, since mutual influence, commerce, boundary disputes, and wars were the norm. In border areas, but elsewhere, too, there was a constant interpenetration of colonial empires and the groups that inhabited them.[9] While Atlantic history centers mobility and links, it makes ample room for local studies of cities, countries, and colonies positioned within its broader framework. Moreover, it is a complement to—not a replacement of—traditional imperial, national, and regional approaches, such as Latin American studies and American history.[10]

The temporal bookends of Atlantic Jewish history, 1500-ca. 1850, should align with its parent field. Yet Jews had a distinctive historical genealogy within the Atlantic world. A diasporic people with roots in the historic Land of Israel, Jews had already established a communal presence under Roman rule in the Iberian Peninsula by the turn of the fourth century CE.[11] By the Middle Ages, they had also formed communities in England and France. A series of forced conversions, expulsions, and massacres in England, the Iberian Peninsula, and France, starting in 1290, rendered Europe's Atlantic coast devoid of publicly professing Jews by the late fifteenth century. But Christians of Iberian Jewish origin, some of whom secretly retained Jewish practice or identity, constituted part of the Atlantic world from its advent and were intertwined through family and business ties, as well as through cultural commonality, with publicly professing Jews, who began to carve out new communities in France and the Low Countries in the sixteenth century. On the North African coast, where indigenous Jews speaking Berber languages had already carved out numerous enclaves, small Jewish communities appeared in the seventeenth century under Spanish occupation. Slightly more than a thousand strong in their totality, all were expelled by 1707, including the few who had emerged on Morocco's Atlantic coast. Most of their trade relations were tied to Spain and the shores of the Mediterranean littoral. These communities, thus, did not play any major role within the Atlantic world.[12]

One might imagine that Atlantic Jewish history is simply Atlantic history with Jews and Iberian converts to Christianity tossed in. We propose that this not be the case. Rather, Atlantic Jewish history offers a conceptual reorientation by disengaging itself from conventional approaches to the Jewish past in Europe, Africa, and the Americas, with their presumption of the centrality of Jewishness as a category of analysis. By contrast, Atlantic Jewish history conceives of Jews as a constitutive force of their environment, and thus, paradoxically, aims to shed more light on broader history than on the Jewish past per se. In parting from scholarly tradition, Atlantic Jewish history augurs a sea change for its parent field no less than for the study of the Jewish past. By definition focused on early modernity, Atlantic Jewish history also has the potential of transforming its sister fields of American Jewish and Latin American Jewish history, both of which are heavily weighted in favor of the late nineteenth through twenty-first centuries.

No scholarly conversation has yet developed as to what constitutes the Atlantic world in a Jewish key, nor how specialists should approach it and the prodigious primary sources it produced.[13] Elsewhere, we have suggested that the presence of Jews and reputed crypto-Jews was too small and regionally confined to justify a distinctive periodization for Atlantic Jewish history.[14] However, some broad conceptual and thematic parameters have already crystallized. Atlantic Jewish history should endeavor to combine obvious religious and economic approaches with less apparent ethnic, racial, linguistic, and political perspectives. According to this scheme, there are four elements that might serve as the bedrock of Atlantic Jewish history: the demographic and economic centrality of Caribbean Jewry among hemispheric American Jewish communities; Portuguese Jewish hegemony among Jews in the Atlantic world; slavery; and the triad of privileges, disabilities, and Jewish Emancipation. These broad terms remind us that in the Atlantic Jewish age, the American Jewish epicenter was in the insular and circum-Caribbean (not in colonial North America or the United States); for centuries most Atlantic Jews were of Iberian, rather than central or eastern European, origins; most hemispheric American Jews lived in slave societies, and starting in the 1800s, legal equality was gradually extended to Jews for the first time, replacing an earlier system predicated upon an ancien régime of dispensations and restrictions.

The essays herein gathered comprise the first edited volume to self-consciously demonstrate the revolutionary potential of Atlantic Jewish history. *Jewish Entanglements in the Atlantic World* aligns itself with a scholarly trajectory born at the dawn of the twenty-first century that saw the publication of three influential edited collections. Each, in its own way, has striven to innovate Jewish historiography. *Jews and the Expansion of Europe to the West* (2001), coedited by Paolo Bernardini and Norman Fiering, applied concepts such as "port Jews" and "diasporas" to the vast world westward of central Europe and underscored the circulation in this space of New Christians and Jews of Iberian origin. As its title hints, this volume was still pre-Atlantic, anchored in the history of European expansion, but was nevertheless anticipatory of a trend to come.[15] Just under a decade later, *Atlantic Diasporas* (2009), coedited by Richard L. Kagan and Philip D. Morgan, heralded the emerging field as "Atlantic Jewry" and sought to explore "the role of Jews and crypto-Jews in the Atlantic world."[16] Finally, *The Sephardic Atlantic* (2018), coedited by Sina Rauschenbach and Jonathan Schorsch, used postcolonial studies as an organizing principle, privileged Jews of Iberian descent, and like its predecessors admitted disciplines in addition to history, notably literary studies.[17] Collectively, these three oft-cited volumes augur a burgeoning new area of study that has lifted some of the gravity of Jewish historiography away from Europe and the modern United States.

In contrast to the aforementioned collections, *Jewish Entanglements in the Atlantic World* is uncompromisingly Atlantic, tempering any approach that would give dominance to a European imperial perspective and holding at bay potentially limiting concepts like "Caribbean," "Old World," "New World," "(Vast) Early America," or "the Americas."[18] Rather than adopting Kagan and Morgan's "Atlantic Jewry," a term that allows for an interdisciplinary treatment of an ethno-religious group, the present volume underscores the importance of upholding the *history* of the Atlantic Jewish past. While studies on material culture and modern-day fiction related to the Jewish Atlantic world brush up against relevant themes, such as slavery and interimperial mobility, they are more concerned with contemporary memories, perspectives, or modes of literary analysis than with the past.

A handful of recent monographs have self-consciously adopted the Atlantic framework in ways that suggest the viability of the aforementioned parameters and its growing acceptability among specialists of the Jewish past. These include two volumes on Portuguese Jews in West Africa and Suriname, respectively, both of which incorporate "Atlantic World" into their subtitles, and a monograph on eighteenth-century Jamaican Jewry, which does the same on its very first page.[19] All three books do so not as verbiage, but rather as an organizing principle, in recognition of the intense mobility, exchange, and interconnectedness that characterized the colonies in question. Additional monographs and a sourcebook with Atlantic Jewries at their center allude to the Atlantic world but do not always fully recognize that it was a system, rather than a region.[20]

The reception of the Atlantic paradigm by Jewish historians noticeably lags behind other affined specialties, including the study of religion, notably Christianity, and the history of Latin America.[21] Undeniably, thinking and writing about the Atlantic Jewish past has been inherently fraught in multiple ways. First, the interdisciplinary nature of Jewish studies means that not all treatments have been grounded in methods of inquiry that are historically sound, even if they may reverberate strongly for scholars of literature, ethnic and racial studies, and critical race theory. Moreover, some practitioners working within a postmodern framework experience the historicist perspective as "narrow," and therefore apply an understanding of postcolonial studies that encompasses everything from the onset of expansionism to the era of dismantled colonialism. This capacious rubric potentially layers the present over the early modern past and vitiates the concept of the Atlantic world.[22] The application of multiple disciplinary ports of entry, whether literature, the study of ethnicity and race, material culture, or postmodernism, expands awareness of the Atlantic Jewish past among academics and the broader public, and undoubtedly enhances the impact of scholarly production. But disciplinary fluidity often shortchanges historical context, nuance, and depth. This is particularly true for works that presume certain ethical standards of human behavior that are both universal and timeless, posit a colonial world divided into victims and collaborators of imperial power, and insist that scholarship and activism cannot and should not be separated. Such approaches are in consonance with the pressures of our era and, increasingly, institutional demands, but they will not withstand the scrutiny of historicism, nor the passing of time. Their concern with the present diminishes their ability to take the past on its own terms.

Rather than advocate that scholars adhere to a pristine model of "Atlantic Jewish history" that upholds historicism and moral neutrality, a better solution would be to recognize an emerging trend of "Atlantic Jewish studies" that is a multidisciplinary spinoff of Jewish studies, applies contemporary standards of social justice as timeless and global, and whose temporal parameters unproblematically extend beyond the nineteenth century. As such, "Atlantic Jewish studies" is a field that takes shape around such concepts as Caribbean Jewry and early American Jewry and is separate from both the origins and concerns of Atlantic Jewish history. Its strengths lie not necessarily in enhancing understanding of the past, but rather in highlighting the legacies of the Atlantic Jewish world in contemporary literature, memory, and present-day social values.

The incorporation of social justice perspectives by writers of Atlantic Jewish history poses additional conundrums. Many writers make it a point to explicitly affirm a supposedly universal value system of equality and freedom, sprinkling their works with derogatory adjectives aimed at white slaveowners, the institution of slavery, and racialist legislation. Since the 1980s, a parallel leverage of ethical judgments has been deployed against Jews as historical actors and their present-day descendants, as the works of the Nation of Islam attest.[23] Rauschenbach and Schorsch refer to this latter manifestation as "the misuse of early modern Atlantic Sephardic-*converso* history by twentieth-century Afro-American scholarship," which draws on "Afrocentric perspectives influenced by postcolonial thought" and often displays "an anti-Semitic orientation."[24] From another perspective, however, the publications of the Nation of Islam (a corporate author) are the result of ahistorical research methods, including the application of contemporary social justice values, leveraged with the intention to defame an entire group of people. This undertaking is arguably the flip side of nationalist writing used to praise a group of people or a political entity. The most significant problem is not the Nation of Islam's output, but rather the fact that professional scholars—by engaging these writings in the first place—have responded to them as if they merit historiographical reflection.[25] This is not to censure these scholars' public responses, including condemnatory statements made in national publications and professional organizations, but rather to underscore that an anonymous, "vicious propaganda tract" should not be assessed using historical methods.[26] Its rightful place is under the microscope of organizations such as the Anti-Defamation League, which rightfully categorize these works along with other "histories of hate."[27] Alternatively, scholars may legitimately analyze the text as they might *The Protocols of the Elders of Zion*, that is, not by attempting to disprove the text's central argument, but rather by assessing the work as a piece of influential *antisemitica*.²⁸ From whichever direction it comes, the application of contemporary morals to Atlantic Jewish history makes living people personally liable for events of the past. It diminishes historicity by focusing on ethno-religious identity rather than overarching structures and human behavior.

Finally, the study of the Atlantic Jewish past demands a particular scholarly training or self-adaptation. Ideally, one must not only master historiographical methods, but also possess fluency in Portuguese, Spanish, Dutch, Hebrew, and Aramaic at the very least, not to mention paleographical skills to enable decipherment of seventeenth-century manuscripts in European languages and other sources produced in a variety of Semitic cursives.²⁹ Atlantic Jewish history can surely be written relying solely on secondary sources, material culture, and printed primary sources. But its revolutionary potential can only be achieved through the discovery and analysis of prodigious collections of archival documents, located on four continents and in large part unmined.

Like its parent field, Atlantic Jewish history has generated a fair amount of skepticism. Critics of Atlanticists quip that the new branch of scholarship is at once "everything and nothing," a passing fad with little revelatory or explanatory value. Or worse, that it constitutes the usual political, maritime, and economic history rebranded as something ostensibly new and more marketable. These naysayers fear an overemphasis on cities at the expense of rural regions (precisely the effect of applying the somewhat passé "port Jew" concept to the Americas) and the reinforcement of traditionalist narratives about Europe's impact on the Americas. At the time of this writing, edited collections are still seeking to "probe the legitimacy" of an Atlantic framework, while the field of American Jewish history still largely clings to a national model. The aforementioned edited collections, *Jews and the Expansion of Europe to the West*, *Atlantic Diasporas*, and *The Sephardic Atlantic*, suggest that such skepticism is not justified for Atlantic Jewish history. The essays herein assembled seek to further expand on those revelatory adumbrations.

Jewish Entanglements in the Atlantic World undertakes to make a bold statement, both a reflection of the current research of its contributors and as an effort to stimulate debate and move an emerging specialty forward. One might suspect that a particularist, ethnoreligious framework has little to offer as a signpost for scholars dealing with the broader Atlantic world. On the contrary, as the contributions to this volume collectively suggest, the revisionism of Atlantic Jewish history as a method upends some of the assumptions regarding the racial and religious hierarchies that informed the Atlantic world and were transmuted within it. A case in point pertains to the aforementioned elements that undergird Atlantic Jewish history, particularly Portuguese cultural and institutional hegemony among Atlantic Jewries.

First, the facts. In Spain and Portugal, in 1391 and 1497, respectively, thousands of Jews converted to Christianity under duress of the Catholic Church and popular violence. In both kingdoms by the end of the fifteenth century, Judaism was no longer a legal religion. The Inquisition, established in Spain in 1478 and in Portugal in 1536, sought to extirpate the practice of secret Judaism and in its first decades specifically targeted New Christians of Jewish descent, apprehending, trying, sentencing, reconciling, and occasionally burning at the stake. Despite the 1501 ban against immigrants of Jewish and Muslim origin in Spanish America, periodically reissued through the next three centuries, and occasional, halfhearted immigration restrictions promulgated by the Portuguese Crown, Iberians of Semitic ancestry continuously settled in the Iberian New World. The Inquisition was permanently established in Peru in 1570, one year before Mexico City received a tribunal, and four decades before Cartagena de Indias (in what is today Colombia). With the assistance of local lay collaborators (*familiares*), the Inquisition also became active in Brazil in the 1590s.

Most scholars who have studied these forced Jewish converts and their descendants in the peninsula and elsewhere in the Atlantic world have argued that Jewish identity and practices persisted through the centuries and were the major driving force for fleeing the Iberian Peninsula.[30] Others argue that the converts soon acculturated and that it was the Inquisition that through its targeted focus on people of Jewish origin (actual or not), stimulated faithful Christians to cultivate antinomian identity and practices. According to this view, most fully developed by Benzion Netanyahu and Antonio Saraiva, the Inquisition was primarily motivated by cupidity (since defendants were deprived of their wealth upon arrest) and functioned as a "marrano factory."[31] A third, more nuanced, position is offered by David L. Graizbord, who argues that those targeted by the Inquisition did not possess enduring doctrinal convictions and simply sought equanimity through the immediate approval of the local authorities of the territories in which they lived or through which they traveled on business. Their inner spiritual lives had less to do with religious conviction or ancestral fealty than with economic pragmatism and the yearning for social and religious stability.[32]

Graizbord thus far offers the most compelling assessment of the inner worlds of converted Jews and their legally Christian descendants, but his view has not been widely disseminated or accepted and the debate has thus reached an impasse. An Atlantic Jewish historical perspective helps to move the debate forward by underscoring two major flaws in the ongoing question "were they or were they not Judaizers?" First, the enduring dispute relies on the myth that New Christians were strictly endogamous. In fact, Jewish converts to Christianity did not refrain from sexually reproductive behavior with "Old Christians." Aside from the birth of children outside of wedlock, mixed-status progeny were also produced through marital alliances encouraged by the state, in part a consequence of a law promulgated in Portugal in 1498 that specifically prohibited unions between New Christian couples.

The two populations—"Old" and "New" Christians—became progressively intertwined over the centuries, as inquisitorial trials demonstrate. In 1630, a group of fifty-three New Christians volunteered themselves before the Lisbon inquisitors to confess their Judaizing. The genealogical investigation that followed revealed that only 13 percent of the defendants were fully New Christian, that is, of presumably indivisible Jewish ancestry. The remainder fell along a spectrum that officials variably described as one-eighth, three-fourths, one-half, three-eighths, one-fourth, or "part" New Christian. At an auto-da-fé celebrated in Lisbon a few years later, nearly 80 percent of the ninety-six New Christians burned at the stake for secret Judaism were "part" New Christian. If one calculates that the rate of exogamy among New Christians hovered around 20 percent in each generation, the result would have been a gradual decrease in the proportion of Portuguese who were of "pure" Jewish descent, and a concurrent rise in the proportion of those of partial Jewish descent, however diluted. Robert Rowland, who discusses these cases, estimates that in Portugal by the eighteenth century, those of "pure" Jewish descent comprised nearly 4 percent of the New Christian population, while Christians descended by any degree from Jews represented 34 percent, and over half of the urban dwellers.[33] In exile, too, publicly professing Portuguese Jewish communities in Amsterdam and Venice openly welcomed members whose parentage was only half "Hebrew."[34] If these cases are representative, as they surely are, the vast majority of the urban Portuguese population was of mixed ethno-religious origins as early as the seventeenth century.

The second conceptual flaw in the dominant historiography on New Christians relates to the presumed capacity of Judaism and Jewishness to prevail over competing identities and practices, which Bruno Feitler has critiqued as the notion of "Jewish indestructibility."[35] Scholars have uncritically accepted the ascribed New Christian identity of Portuguese men and women, which was imposed on them by inquisitors who presented them as Judaizers. Juan Ignacio Pulido Serrano has convincingly shown that centuries-old false—and often rhetorical—characterizations of New Christians continue to plague historians today. One key assumption is that early modern individuals in the Iberian Peninsula possessed only one "primary and principal affiliation," in this case, an affiliation with a secret Jewish community that supposedly trumped all other identities. Historians thus ignore the many additional identities that people had, as members of guilds and trades, as elite businessmen, or as migrants.[36] They also overlook the open and dynamic construction of such identities, which allowed a significant role for individual free will. The specific context and conditions in which Iberians found themselves helped shape their religious identities.[37]

Scholars of inquisitorial history tend to fixate on secret Jewish survivals to the exclusion of all other manifestations of ethnoreligious persistence, notably those of the descendant Muslim population. But if one foregrounds demographics, this stance is simply untenable. Jews constituted only 2 percent of the late medieval Iberian Jewish population (between two hundred thousand and three hundred thousand individuals), while Muslims, who also underwent several waves of forced conversions to Christianity and expulsions, vastly outnumbered both Jews and reputed crypto-Jews.[38] By around 1100, more than 80 percent of the indigenous population of the Iberian Peninsula had converted to Islam.[39] In the late fourteenth century, three centuries after the initiation of the *Reconquista* (the Christian reconquest of Muslim Iberia), two-thirds and one-third of the populations of Valencia and Aragon, respectively, were still Muslim, while 3 percent of Catalonia's residents espoused Islam.[40] The expulsion of the entire *morisco* population of Spain between 1609 and 1614, mandated by King Philip III, resulted in the ejection of some 350,000 forced converts to Christianity and their descendants, constituting the "largest removal of a civilian population in European history" until that time, even exceeding the Expulsion of the Jews in 1492.[41] And yet, no monarch could have possibly eradicated a group whose contours had been so blurry both before and during their expulsion. Aside from a small number of Moriscos who had obtained exemptions, surreptitiously remained behind, or returned to the Iberian Peninsula undetected, there remained an innumerable population of Muslim heritage who after generations of conversion had been accepted as Old Christians.[42]

The obsession with lineage among early modern Iberians, along with the will to conceal certain progenitors, has often been misinterpreted as an awareness of Jewish ancestry. In reality, official genealogical investigations triggered by accusations of heresy or a person's candidacy for noble status sought to uncover not Jewish ancestry solely, but either Jewish or Muslim ancestry. The following example illustrates this point. The lineage of the painter Diego Velázquez (1599–1660) came under public scrutiny in 1659, when King Philip IV of Spain informed him of his desire to grant the painter an honorary title of knighthood. The application process for admission to the Order of Santiago, initiated in 1658, obliged the artist to demonstrate not only his "purity of blood" (that is, the absence of Jewish or Muslim lineage) and that his family had been free of inquisitorial prosecution, but also that he was of noble descent and that none of his ancestors had been merchants or artisans. After the artist presented his genealogy to the Council of the Orders, official investigators spent several months gathering evidence on the candidate's background, including about one hundred oral testimonies and various ecclesiastical and government documents, such as birth and taxation records.[43] Historian Kevin Ingram has demonstrated through recently unearthed notarial documents that Velázquez lied about the identity of his paternal grandfather (who was apparently not Juan Velázquez, whose exemption from the meat tax implied nobility, but rather the merchant Juan Velázquez Moreno). He also misidentified his maternal grandmother, who was not Catalina Zayas, but Juana Mexía Aguilar. Ingram surmises that the investigators intentionally chose witnesses who were "disposed to corroborate the false genealogy."[44] He and a few other scholars argue that Velázquez was undoubtedly or probably of Jewish origin.[45]

This assertion rests on the same kind of evidence deployed by the seventeenth-century investigators: credulous supposition. While officials of the Council of the Orders seem to have slanted their investigation in accordance with the king's desire to knight Velázquez, the goal of some contemporary historians, by contrast, seems to be a quest for crypto-Jewish background and cultural practices. "I am led to believe," writes Ingram, "that Velázquez's family originated not from northwest Portugal, as the artist claimed, but rather from Portugal's eastern borderland, where according to one scholar the majority of the land's *conversos* lived."[46] For Ingram, Velázquez's literacy, his maternal grandfather's occupation as a maker of gentlemen's breeches, his occasional activity as a renter of property and moneylender, the occupation of his associates in the clothes trade and silversmithing, and the notarial profession of his friends from Seville are additional indicators of the painter's Jewish ancestry.[47] Another historian, Edgar Samuel, surmises that Velázquez was of Jewish ancestry because his parents chose most of their children's names in a fixed order to honor grandparents, which Samuel claims is an ancient Jewish practice, and because a man with the same name as Velázquez's father, Juan Rodriguez de Silva, was in 1596 condemned to death in absentia by the Mexican Inquisition for Judaizing.[48] For both Ingram and Samuel, this chain of logic serves as a platform from which to argue that Velázquez's *converso* background directly informed his artistic career. For Ingram, the artist's "New Christian background" provided "potential creative impulses" for his art and infused into it a subtle, "non-conformist message," while for Samuel, this lineage led Velázquez to paint for "New Christian clerical clients" and "might have increased his ambition to win approval and to attain success."[49]

Yet no concrete evidence has surfaced that any of Velázquez's ancestors were Jews who had been forcibly converted to Christianity in 1391, 1497, or any other year. The confirmation that Velázquez actively obfuscated the true identities of his biological ancestors, as did many Iberians, does not reveal his precise motivation.[50] The concoction and purchase of fictitious ancestors was a widespread phenomenon in medieval and early modern Spain, whose society constituted a cornucopia of ethnic groups and spiritual traditions, and where the two prevailing religions, Christianity and Islam, were engaged in a prolonged geopolitical struggle.[51] The acquisition of membership in certain orders demanded not only *limpieza de sangre*, but also the absence of ancestors who had engaged in certain types of nonnoble labor. In other words, the efforts of candidates to verify a pure lineage was not only racial/religious, but also class based. Moreover, the application process Velázquez underwent to establish his noble lineage relied heavily on public reputation and hearsay. Such evidence, like birth and other municipal records, was not only falsifiable, but also frequently falsified in medieval and early modern Iberia as a means to an end.[52] As Jane Gerber has recently demonstrated, the forging of ancestral documents in the peninsula was not necessarily connected to Christians' desire to conceal their Jewish heritage. Indeed, it predated the forced conversion of Jews to Christianity in 1391.⁵³

Related is the case of the father and three brothers of Santa Teresa de Ávila (1515–82). After municipal authorities in the parish of Majalbálago, a town near Ávila in Spain, demanded payment of one hundred maravedís in obligatory tribute in 1519, the four men filed a lawsuit to accredit their nobility and affirm that they were thus exempt from paying taxes. Their claim triggered a genealogical inquest, which turned up a paternal grandfather who had run afoul of the Inquisition in Toledo and subsequently relocated to Ávila. Locals in the latter town alleged that the Toledo-born children of this man were "conversos" descended patrilineally from Jews.⁵⁴ On that basis, many scholars have affirmed that Santa Teresa was of (agnate) Jewish descent.⁵⁵ The problem with this assessment goes beyond the "indivisible Jewishness" problem, namely the cognitive error that one quarter of Teresa's ancestry determined her true essence. What is also key is that these genealogical inquiries were dependent on witnesses, reputation, and memory, rather than the kind of evidence that would historically verify unambiguous belonging in a publicly professing Jewish community, such as an old circumcision book or documentation of a Hebrew name, preserved from the era prior to mass Jewish conversion to Christianity.

The flimsiness on which allegations of converso status were based (and, in turn, some scholars' assumption that allegations of converso lineage denoted Jewish ancestry) become ever more problematic in the context of the Atlantic world. Demographic complexity was magnified in the Americas, owing to the large presence of multiple indigenous and forcibly transported African populations. By overlooking these groups, studies that interrogate lingering crypto-Jewish praxis or identity—to the exclusion of other spiritual legacies in the Americas—implicitly downplay Indian and African cultures as ephemeral. Notably, this approach is entirely out of touch with the scholarly debate, now three quarters of a century old, on African survivals in the United States, the Caribbean, and Brazil, and a more recent, parallel discussion on indigenous endurance in the Caribbean.⁵⁶ In short, implicit assumptions about "indivisible Jewishness" and "indestructible Jewishness" ignore the fundamental processes characteristic of the Atlantic world, at whose heart lies the intensive interaction of people originating from four different continents. In such an interlinked environment, the conviction that a particular practice was the exclusive domain of one group is logically unsustainable.

Recent historians working within an Atlantic framework understand this point well. As María Elena Martínez has demonstrated for colonial Mexico, the results of ancestral investigations did not necessarily denote particular ethnoreligious origins, which were based largely on reputation, memory, and negotiation. Disagreements on whether officials should rely more on oral testimonies of reputation or written records, and how far back they should search into family trees, remained unresolved through the centuries.[57] Martínez's analysis shows that when a person's ancestry was researched, the real discussion was not about actual origins, but rather access to a particular status or privilege. Not surprisingly, the motivation undergirding genealogical research also stimulated a burgeoning practice of falsifying or purchasing family trees, purity of blood certificates, and copies of baptismal and marriage records.[58] These "genealogical fictions," as Martínez characterizes them, were magnified in the Iberian Americas, but first emerged and continued on the peninsula. This is not to say that examiners of the heritage of inquisitorial defendants and nobility candidates in the Iberian Peninsula and abroad were uninterested in actual Jewish (or any other) lineage, but rather that the process of inquest was shaped by many other concerns.

Tamar Herzog's research on Iberian and Iberian American citizenship, another implicitly Atlantic project, can also deepen our understanding of so-called New Christians. In *Defining Nations*, an analysis of early modern citizenship in the Iberian Peninsula and its American possessions, Herzog fixes precisely on the gap between theory and practice.[59] She argues that the process of obtaining citizenship was focused less on legislation and more on the local reputation and behavior of foreign individuals and families and their degree of integration into a local community. Inspired by Herzog's insights, we might go a step further and posit that inquisitorial and municipal investigations into allegedly Jewish lineage in both the Iberian metropole and its American colonies acted as a kind of citizenship qualification assessment, dependent not on (allegedly) verifiable Jewish ancestry alone, but more on "performance, reputation, local relations," and "interests at stake," and principally motivated not by the presence of actual Jewish lineage, but rather by whether or not the individual in question was deemed meritorious of privileges or, contrarily, deserving of punitive legal disabilities or taxation. The analyses of María Elena Martínez and Tamar Herzog offer compelling alternatives to a century-old historiographical paradigm that revolves around the assumption that verifiable Jewish ancestry, belief, or practices were the only matters at stake.[60]

In much professional writing on conversos, the guiding research question concerning the tenacity of cryptic Judaism has not fundamentally departed from the nationalist-idealist Jewish scholarship initiated by formative scholars like Cecil Roth and Yitzhak Baer who, beginning in the 1930s, imagined an indestructible Judaism and indivisible Jewishness. An Atlantic history approach proposes a more realistic understanding of this past, one that places persons of alleged or verified Jewish ancestry on the same plane as the rest of the population. If we have dwelled inordinately on the first century of Atlantic Jewish history, that is a reflection of the deep cognitive work that needs to be carried out for this foundational period. Similar types of foundational turns in thinking about the Atlantic Jewish past are warranted for later centuries as well. Collectively, the essays herein collated suggest some promising new directions.

Atlantic Jewish history is a practice, not a vision or recipe. It will write itself as increasing numbers of historians begin to embrace its methodology, which demands new, multilingual archival work, consideration of diachronic (continuous) sources, attention to an interconnected quadricontinental region, and the decentering of Jewishness. The essays herein gathered undertake to model participation in that historiographical practice, rather than to showcase sea-changing research. Moreover, Atlantic Jewish history seeks not to replace the national model with a regional one, nor disqualify local studies. But this new subfield of Atlantic history does aspire to conceive of the American Jewish past as part of a tightly interconnected region of four continents and to reorient the field away from the modern era, modern eastern European Ashkenazim, and the themes of survival and assimilation.

While previous American Jewish historians strove to demonstrate the contributions of Jews to what would become the United States, the contemporary field rejects that goal as apologetic, and instead strives to explore the "uniqueness" or "impact" of Jews and their communities. The main goal of Jewish history writ large and the Judaic studies archival collections that inform much of the writing on the Jewish past is by definition to illuminate the history of a specific ethnoreligious group.[61] By contrast, Atlantic Jewish history takes for granted that certain aspects of Jewish lives and institutional life (such as the use of Hebrew and Jewish Aramaic and legal status as non-Christian) are distinctive. But that distinctiveness is not the end goal of historical inquiry about the Jewish past.

Recent calls by scholars to provisionally abandon a Jewish frame suggest that the field of Jewish history is ripe for such a paradigm shift. Anne Oravetz Albert urges scholars to understand New Christians who transitioned to public Judaism in Amsterdam as a variety of converts, rather than as "returnees" to Judaism. By examining their experience as conversion rather than return (and hence as "exceptional, problematic, and even miraculous"), Albert proposes that their embrace of public Judaism "can be subjected to analysis along the lines of gendered, legal, and political hegemony; of syncretism, acculturation, and colonization; and of determinative social and psychological factors . . . as one example of a wider phenomenon."[62]

Even more provocatively, in an essay titled "Jewish History beyond the Jewish People," Lila Corwin Berman pinpoints the first act of Jewish historiography—the identification of something or someone as Jewish—as the field's very problem. Instead of posing a "foundational question," Berman explains, the first act of the Jewish historian is to categorize their subject matter as Jewish, deploying an "ahistorical foundation for historical questions."[63] This act of categorization at the outset overlooks Jews as moving targets of intersectionality, who might alternately be approached—to cite examples meaningful to an Atlantic context—as among the general population of indigent migrants, colonial entrepreneurs, shopkeepers, merchants, slave traders, slaves, or women subject to sexual violence. Atlantic Jewish history is driven by the motivation to foreground entanglement, placing Jews on the same plane as other historical actors, as a means to shed light on broader society.

Chapter 1

The U.S. and the Rest

Old and New Paradigms of Early American Jewish History

JOHN M. DIXON

In December 1859, at a monthly meeting of the New-York Historical Society, Rabbi Arnold Fischel of Congregation Shearith Israel delivered a seminal presentation, "The History of the Jews in America," that anticipated and influenced the development of American Jewish history as a field of historical study.[1] Though the full body of Fischel's paper no longer exists, its skeleton can be recovered from contemporary newspaper and magazine accounts. On December 7, 1859, the *New York Times* reported:

> Dr. Fischell commenced the record of his investigations from the year 1492, when, by royal edict, the Jews were banished from Spain. Following the unhappy nation from Spain to Brazil, from Brazil to the West Indies, and thence to New-Amsterdam, he gave his testimony to the joy they felt when they set foot upon a free shore. The bravery and patriotism of the Jews, in connection with the American nation, were both presented. In conclusion he read a letter from Gen. Washington to the Jews in Newport, Rhode Island, in which he (Gen. Washington) lauded their patriotism.[2]

Later, an article published in *The Historical Magazine* recounted:

> [Fischel] traced the fortunes of a band of his countrymen from Spain, whence they were banished, about the time of the discovery of America, to Brazil, thence to the West Indies, and thence to New Amsterdam, where they were received with coldness under the administration of Peter Stuyvesant, and again compelled to depart. He spoke handsomely of the condition of the Jews at Newport, and in conclusion read the letter (apparently from the original) of General Washington, in reply to an address from that body.[3]

The subsequent monthly issue of *The Historical Magazine* contained Fischel's "Chronological Notes," a related set of jottings that extended American Jewish history deep into the nineteenth century. Its final entry read, "1859—Two hundred thousand Israelites in the United States, thirty thousand of whom reside in New York."[4]

In many ways, these journalistic summaries and historical notes are the ancestral fossils of current early American Jewish historiography. They predate the 1892 founding of the American Jewish Historical Society (AJHS) by over three decades. Yet their contours are eminently recognizable today. Like Fischel's sketch, general narratives of early American Jewish history published throughout the twentieth century routinely move from Spain to Brazil to the Caribbean to New Amsterdam to British North America and, ultimately, to the United States. In doing so, they reduce a vast transatlantic story down to a geographically narrower national tale, affirm the longevity and continuity of a relatively monolithic North American Jewish community, and assert the ethnic diversity, inclusivity, and exceptionalism of the United States.

This chapter explores why the study of Jews in early America became stuck in such a nationalist narrative rut. How did a linear, centralistic, and United States–oriented framing of early American Jewish history gain dominance during the nineteenth and twentieth centuries? And why did it face relatively few challenges given that twentieth-century scholars were quite aware of the wider history of Jews throughout the Western Hemisphere?

To answer these questions, this chapter revisits some of the substantial nineteenth-century and twentieth-century cultural work that welded early American Jewish history to the history of the United States, and consequently marginalized early modern Caribbean and South American Jewish history. Other scholars have examined how commemorative events and museums constructed and disseminated national versions of early American Jewish history.[5] Because it is primarily concerned with the academic field of American Jewish history, this chapter foregrounds historical writing and scholarly debates within the AJHS. It identifies two distinct historiographical phases: first, the 1890s and early decades of the twentieth century, when the Fischel paradigm, as it were, took hold despite the fact that some founders of the AJHS preferred a hemispheric or even global definition of American Jewish history; and, second, the period between the 1940s and 1990s when the Fischel paradigm gained further institutional backing as the field of America Jewish history became an established part of the academic profession.

The final section of this chapter juxtaposes three scholarly reflections on the Atlantic Jewish history published between 2009 and 2014, showing that historians reacted to the emergence of Atlantic Jewish history as a new area of study in the early 2000s with a mix of enthusiasm, caution, and frustration. That initial wave of scholarship on Atlantic Jewish history opened new pathways for research but failed to displace the traditional, national paradigm of early American Jewish history. With a few years of hindsight, we can now see that conceptual blurriness about the scope and purpose of Atlantic Jewish history was a major hindrance at the beginning of the twenty-first century. Scholars established a starting platform for overhauling early American Jewish history, but they did not articulate a coherent and compelling Atlantic alternative to Fischel's nation-oriented framework. Problems within the wider field of Atlantic history were largely to blame. Atlantic history rose quickly to prominence in the early 2000s as a part of a broad-based turn toward transnational methods and agendas in the social sciences and humanities. However, by 2010 the first burst of enthusiasm for the field had started to wane. Voices of criticism had grown louder. Other forms of supranational history, particularly global history, had assumed priority for many scholars and academic institutions. Also, the distinctive temporal and geographical identity of Atlantic history had become harder to discern as transnational and oceanic histories flourished. While the initial success of Atlantic history as a field had sparked a strong desire in the early 2000s for a new Atlantic-oriented conception of early American Jewish history, the subsequent diminishing and questioning of Atlantic history obstructed the growth of a new Atlantic Jewish history paradigm.

The field of American Jewish history took formal shape in the final years of the nineteenth century, coincidentally around the time that Fischel died in 1894. It has been pointed out elsewhere that educated and well-established Jews organized the AJHS in 1892 largely in response to the mass immigration of impoverished European Jews to North America, as well as growing antisemitism on both sides of the Atlantic Ocean. Academic and community leaders envisioned the AJHS as a way to demonstrate publicly that Jews had been present in North America ever since the colonial era and, furthermore, that Jews had contributed significantly to the founding and eventual success of the American nation.[6] Public interest in the four-hundredth anniversary of Christopher Columbus's first arrival in the Americas provided another motivation for the founding of the AJHS, as did sister developments on the other side of the Atlantic, where an Anglo-Jewish Historical Exhibition held in London in 1887, the initiation of the *Jewish Quarterly Review* in 1888, and the launch of the Jewish Historical Society of England in 1893 created an institutional footing for Jewish historical scholarship in Britain.[7]

The founders of the AJHS were aware of Fischel's earlier contribution. Writing in the 1890s, lawyer and historian Max J. Kohler, one of the most active early members of the AJHS, highlighted Fischel's 1859 lecture and "Chronological Notes" on more than one occasion.[8] Still, the Fischel paradigm was not the only grand vision of American Jewish history circulating at that time. In fact, at the initial planning meeting of the AJHS held in New York in June 1892, several delegates spoke against restricting the study of American Jewish history to the traditional confines of U.S. history. Advocating alternative hemispheric and global approaches, they argued that the field of American Jewish history would lack relevancy if it was construed narrowly in North American terms. In response, and seeking to carve out ground for a compromise, Harvard historian Charles Gross proposed that the AJHS might prioritize the history of Jews in the United States while simultaneously welcoming supplemental research on South America, the Caribbean, and elsewhere. Gross additionally suggested the AJHS could function on this provisional basis until enough archival research had been completed for a clear, overall picture of the field to emerge.[9] The AJHS founders settled on this strategy of deferment and defined their mission in June 1892 as "the collection, preservation and publication of material having reference to the settlement and history of the Jews on the American Continent." In so doing, they launched the AJHS with a nebulous research agenda and ambiguous geographical identity.[10]

This situation was perhaps unavoidable. National history dominated the academic discipline of history as it emerged in Europe and the United States in the nineteenth century.[11] Yet any full rejection of Atlantic and hemispheric aspects of American Jewish history would have cut against the grain of the Columbia quadricentennial celebrations of the late 1880s and early 1890s. From the perspective of American Jewish history, three entangled events of 1492 demanded consideration—and none of them directly concerned North America. Christian conquest of the entire Iberian Peninsula was the earliest. On January 2, 1492, the Catholic Monarchs, Ferdinand and Isabella, who had unified the Crowns of Aragon and Castile through their marriage, entered Granada and took formal control of the last remnant of Muslim Iberia. After almost eight hundred years of partial (and sometimes nearly complete) Islamic domination, the whole peninsula, now divided into the kingdoms of Portugal, Castile, Aragon, and Navarre, came under Christian rule once more. The second major act of 1492—Jewish expulsion from Castile, Aragon, and the Spanish-controlled islands of Sicily and Sardinia—followed months later. On March 31, 1492, Ferdinand and Isabella issued an edict ordering the removal of all Jews who would not submit to Christian conversion from these Spanish territories by the end of July. Finally, Europe commenced its expansion into the Americas. On August 3, a Spanish-sponsored Italian navigator departed the Andalusian port of Palos with the misguided intention of sailing west to Asia. Christopher Columbus and his cosmopolitan crew, among them several Jewish converts to Christianity, made landfall in the Bahamas that October, commencing centuries of European and Euro-descendant colonization, settlement, and slaving in the Caribbean islands and American continents.

The intersection of these three episodes understandably preoccupied scholars of American Jewish history at the time of the Columbus quadricentennial and therefore kept the Caribbean islands and South American continent in their gaze. In 1894 Meyer Kayserling, author of a pioneering study, *Christopher Columbus and the Participation of the Jews in the Spanish and Portuguese Discoveries*, commissioned and published roughly in parallel with the founding of the AJHS and translated from German into English by Charles Gross, declared, "Where the history of the Jews in Spain ends, that of the Jews in America begins."[12] Such claims for the importance of 1492 invited scholarly consideration of Caribbean and South American facets of American Jewish history just as the AJHS gathered momentum.

Although Fischel had similarly accepted 1492 as the starting point for American Jewish history and still managed to leap from Columbus's landing in the Bahamas to European settlement in North America, two additional factors hindered the AJHS founders from performing the same trick in the 1890s. First, overseas corresponding members, including Pinkus Hilfman, a Dutch Jew and religious teacher living in Suriname, insisted on the historical importance of early modern Caribbean and South American Jews. Second, the earliest and most prominent members of the AJHS favored inductive over deductive reasoning. In 1892, at the first annual meeting of the AJHS, society president Oscar Straus projected a "scientific" or "modern" undertaking designed "to bring out the facts" of "early American history."[13] Combined with Gross's strategy of deferment, the AJHS's commitment to empiricism discouraged the setting of hard-and-fast rules about the geography and chronology of American Jewish history. Consequently, papers on South American, Central American, and Caribbean topics featured regularly at the annual "scientific" meetings of the AJHS and in the society's journal, *Publications of the American Jewish Historical Society*.[14]

Hilfman ensured Suriname received particular attention. In 1907 he published information about that Dutch colony and announced his intention to produce an English translation of *Essai historique sur la colonie de Surinam* (*Historical Essay on the Colony of Surinam*), an important 1788 Surinamese-Jewish contribution to the Enlightenment and, arguably, the first major study of American Jewish history.[15] At the same time, other scholars promoted research on the Mexican Inquisition. Cyrus Adler, the chief organizer of the AJHS and one of several scholars who, in his own words, "yielded" to the "fascination" of American territory beyond the boundaries of the United States, published a lengthy assessment and extracted transcription of an alleged Judaizer's Mexican trial in the *Publications* in 1896.[16] Three years later, Adler's edited manuscript of another Mexican Inquisition trial filled the journal's entire 1899 issue.[17]

Notwithstanding the AJHS's initial commitment to empiricism and reluctance toward imposing a paradigm for American Jewish history, certain underlying themes and threads soon emerged in the historiography in these years. The perceived cruelty of the Mexican Inquisition was one. Starting in the early twentieth century, historians of American Jewry labeled the Jews who arrived in New Amsterdam in 1654 as "Jewish Pilgrim Fathers" who escaped South American persecution.[18] The significance of Jewish maritime commerce constituted a second major theme. Kohler was among the scholars who sought to generate an overview of American Jewish history. In several important pieces published between 1894 and 1902, he documented a Jewish trade network spanning

"Spain, Portugal, Italy and the Levant, Holland, England, Brazil, Spanish America, Curaçao, Jamaica and the West Indies, Surinam and New York." Decades before the term "trading diaspora" entered academic discourse, he affirmed that in an age "when people were in the habit of dealing largely with their immediate neighbors," Jews had the advantage of being able to conduct overseas trade through webs of trusted coreligionists based in regions with different commercial products and needs.[19]

During the 1890s, and somewhat paradoxically, themes of inquisitional persecution in Ibero-America and economic opportunity in the early modern Atlantic combined to organize the field of American Jewish history in ways that prioritized the United States and separated out historically entangled Iberian, Dutch, and English maritime empires. As early as 1894, Oscar Straus directly connected the "persecution of the Jews in Spain and Portugal and their dispersion to the four corners of the earth" to the development of Dutch, English, and North American "international commerce." Following Kohler's argument, he claimed Jewish networks advanced "the trade of the Italian republics with the Levant, and of Holland, England and New England with Surinam, Barbados, Jamaica and Brazil."[20] These statements gave an early hint of a periodization and thematic framing of early American Jewish history that sharply contrasted the suffering of Iberian crypto-Jews with the commercial success and religious freedoms of Jewish merchants in Dutch and English America and, particularly, the United States. In the 1894 issue of the *Publications*, Kayserling further confirmed this schema by projecting the history of colonial American Jewry as a narrative of persecuted crypto-Jews and Judeoconversos in Spanish and Portuguese America, and tolerated Sephardic Jews in Dutch and British territories.[21]

From the mid-1890s onward, the field of American Jewish history relied on the twin themes of progressive commercialization and liberty to justify closing an initial Atlantic-wide aperture down to the United States. To be sure, this trend did not go entirely unquestioned. In 1908, having succeeded Straus as AJHS president, Adler bluntly recognized that "no university or college has established a chair of American Jewish history, nor even a regular or systematic course of lectures on the subject." He urged scholars of American Jewry to look beyond the United States and embrace some form of transatlantic or even global Jewish history.[22] Soon afterwards, the AJHS restated its mission in a way that gave additional prominence to international movements and events, while reaffirming its primary interest as "the settlement and history of Jews on the American continent."[23] Even so, the field of American Jewish history continued to consolidate around a United States–centric framework. Without a coherent alternative on offer, early twentieth-century practitioners of American Jewish historiography effectively ignored Adler's concerns and adopted a new version of the Fischel paradigm.

The publication of journalist Peter Wiernik's popular survey, *The History of the Jews in America*, in 1912 marked the completion of this process. A book usually remembered for its assertion that Jews migrated to the United States in distinctive Sephardic, German, and east European waves, Wiernik's *History* is equally notable for its division (à la Fischel) of early American Jewish history into successive Iberian, Dutch-British, and United States phases. Through these nationalized containers, Wiernik traced a stadial progression from Iberian persecution and medievalism to United States tolerance, enlightenment, and modernity.[24] Wiernik thus played a key role in establishing an expanded version of the Fischel paradigm in popular and academic memory by the second decade of the twentieth century.

In many ways, the middle decades of the twentieth century were as critical to the development of American Jewish history as the 1890s. The situation of Jews in the United States changed dramatically after 1924, when the Immigration (or Johnson-Reed) Act passed by Congress amid a climate of growing antisemitism in America abruptly ended a century of Jewish mass migration that had bought approximately 3 million European Jews to the United States since 1820, with over 2.5 million of them landing after 1880. By the start of the Second World War, the majority of the Jews of the United States were American born. Moreover, as a group, they had broadly achieved middle-class status.[25] The mass slaughter of European Jews during the Second World War meant that United States Jewry became the largest Jewish population in the world. Burdened with new global responsibility, Jewish community leaders in the United States, fretting about cultural assimilation during the prosperous postwar years, increasingly saw American Jewish history as a means to elevate Jewish identity. In 1947 the Hebrew Union College in Cincinnati organized the American Jewish Archives under the leadership of historian Jacob Rader Marcus. Scholarship on American Jewish history that appeared in the 1950s and 1960s emphasized that American Jewry remained a distinct ethnic and religious entity even as American Jews embraced the mainstream culture of the United States.[26]

One illustrative feature of this period was the unprecedented national attention thrust upon the Jews of colonial Newport, Rhode Island, whom President George Washington had met and corresponded with in 1790. Even prior to the 1940s, the public knew Washington's letter to Newport's Jewry. Indeed, Fischel had brought the original copy, then in private hands, with him to the New-York Historical Society in 1859. Its text had later appeared, along with that of all Washington's correspondence with Jewish American congregations, in the 1895 issue of the AJHS's *Publications* and in Wiernik's 1912 *History*.[27] Also, during the 1930s, Rabbi Lee Levinger had included extracts of these presidential exchanges in his textbook of American Jewish history, and Rabbi Morris Gutstein had added a facsimile of Washington's 1790 letter to his history of Jews in Newport.[28] All the same, a series of events pushed Washington's Newport correspondence further into the limelight in the 1940s. First, in 1940, a national radio broadcast and a special service at Newport's Touro Synagogue marked the 150th anniversary of Washington's visit to Rhode Island.[29] Two years later, Lee Friedman's *Jewish Pioneers and Patriots* asserted Washington's 1790 letters to Jewish American congregations "gave point to the theory of American democracy which, finally and expressly embodied in 1791 in the Bill of Rights, struck from the Jews of the United States the shackles of disabilities."[30] In 1944, the American Jewish Committee reproduced Washington's Newport letter at the front of a pamphlet on antisemitism that derived its title, *To Bigotry No Sanction*, from the most famous phrase in Washington's exchange with Newport Jewry.[31] In 1946, the Touro Synagogue gained official recognition as a national historic site. Subsequently, in 1947–48, Washington's Newport letter reached millions of Americans as part of the Freedom Train, a travelling exhibit of national historical documents that displayed Washington's missive alongside such documents as the Mayflower Compact, the Bill of Rights, and Lincoln's Gettysburg Address.[32]

The reputation of Washington's Newport letter as a crucial founding expression of U.S. religious tolerance and liberalism only continued to rise as U.S. Jewry adjusted to its new status as the largest Jewish population in the world. Simultaneously, the factors that boosted the standing of this document pushed non–North American aspects of early American Jewish history deeper into the background. In 1947, Hyman Grinstein pronounced in a review published in the *William and Mary Quarterly* that "strictly speaking, only elements in American civilization which were directly affected by the impact of Jews living in the United States may be considered within the province of American Jewish history."[33] Historians worked in broad agreement with this statement for the subsequent three or four decades, turning the vitality of North American Jewish communal life and the persistence of Jewish culture in North America into central themes of American Jewish historiography.[34] As president of the AJHS, Friedman declared to the 1950 annual meeting of the society, "American Jewish history has come of age," and urged his audience to demonstrate that Jews participated in American history "naturally and as natively as any other elements of our citizenry," while preserving their Jewish identity. Ethnic and political diversity was America's strength, Friedman asserted. "Culture rebels at uniformity."[35] The following year, he told a meeting of the New-York Historical Society that "cultural pluralism is upon what American democracy feeds."[36] Evidently, he regarded cultural pluralism as the coexistence of distinct, compartmentalized cultures within the United States, rather than an entangling or intermixing of cultures.

The centralizing and nationalistic trends established earlier in the twentieth century therefore flourished in the second half of the twentieth century. Building on the work of their predecessors, mid-century scholars of early American Jewry described the Dutch and, more especially, British North American colonies as sanctuaries of religious tolerance that presaged the liberalism of the United States. Emphasizing the exceptionalism of America, they asserted that Jews of the United States did not experience the protracted and tortuous emancipation process that marked the start of modern European Jewish history, but rather benefited (with relatively little effort on their part) from the inclusivity and tolerance afforded all white ethnic groups in North America. In 1947, Abram Goodman characterized the colonial era as an "overture" and "era of gestation . . . rich in promise of the America that was to be."[37] Three years later, Salo Baron observed that colonial Jews were "as a rule, incorporated in the American body politic, so to say, in complete absentmindedness."[38] In 1954 Oscar Handlin remarked, "the Revolution and independence completed the process begun in the American colonial past."[39] Henry Feingold, in his 1974 survey of American Jewish history, *Zion in America*, in a chapter titled "The Genesis of American Religious Tolerance," wrote, "it was during the Colonial period that the basic outlines of the American-Jewish relationship were established . . . that relationship was even for its time remarkably free from religious bigotry."[40]

As the exceptional tolerance and liberalism of the United States became guiding themes of early American Jewish historiography in the second half of the twentieth century, historians broadly concurred that Jewish men enjoyed many civil and some political rights in the North American colonies, and that Jewish men, along with other white male citizens, gained full political rights under the Constitution of the United States. They left some room for disagreement within this consensus. Most notably, historians differed on the importance of the revolutionary and founding eras as turning points, though this quarrel was more an issue of emphasis than a clash of opposing viewpoints. The scholarship most concerned with the attainment of formal citizenship status and full political rights tended to perceive the Revolution as transformative rather than a continuation of colonial trends, but it also recognized that Jews enjoyed a remarkable degree of religious and economic liberty in the colonial era.

Jacob Rader Marcus, the founding director of the American Jewish Archives in Cincinnati and the preeminent scholar of American Jewish history at that time, confirmed the ascendancy of this nationalistic model with his 1958 article, "The Periodization of American Jewish History," originally an address to the AJHS annual meeting, which recommended widespread adoption of Wiernik's "natural and correct" 1912 division of American Jewish history into "three 'successive strata of immigration.'" In that light, and with the assertion that Sephardim dominated Jewish communal life in North America until 1840, notwithstanding the fact that Ashkenazim outnumbered Sephardim in North America from the 1720s, he proposed a quadripartite schema of Sephardic (1654–1840), German (1841–1920), east European (1852–1920), and American (1921–) epochs. Paralleling Wiernik even further, Marcus subdivided the Sephardic stage into colonial Dutch (1654–64), colonial English (1664–1776), and early national (1776–1840) phases. By assuming 1654 as his starting point, he bypassed the complications and entanglements of Caribbean and South American history. However, he imbued his schema with progressive momentum by characterizing Peter Stuyvesant's Dutch New Netherland as "medieval—in the worse sense of the term." According to Marcus, then, the seeds of modernity only sprouted in the British era, when "mercantilists" granted "economic opportunities, adequate civil and religious rights, and ample scope for cultural advancement," but not political liberties, to Jewish settlers. Full Jewish Emancipation in North America later arrived under the auspices of the United States, "first on the Federal level through the new Federal Constitution," and then on the state level.[41]

Between 1958 and his death in 1995, Marcus filled out this periodization in exhaustive detail in his three-volume study, *The Colonial American Jew, 1492–1776* (1970), the four-volume *United States Jewry, 1776–1985* (1989–93), and the comparatively bite-sized, single-volume narrative history, *The American Jew, 1585–1990* (1995).[42] In this way, he confirmed the national trajectory of early American Jewish history. The first of these works, for instance, opened with a preliminary section on South America, Central America, and the insular Caribbean, and then a section on Dutch New Netherland, before concentrating extensively on British North America. As Marcus explained in his preface, he emphasized colonial North American Jewry fully aware that "it was of lesser contemporary importance than the Jewries to the south," but believing that the longer history of American Jewry centered on the United States.[43] Moving beyond the colonial era, Marcus divided *United States Jewry* into "The Sephardic Period" (1776–1840; volume 1), "The Germanic Period" (1841–1920; volumes 2 and 3), and "The East European Period" (1852–1920; volume 4), with an epilogue on the "Emergence of the American Jew." Marcus subsequently repeated this pattern in *The American Jew*, which condensed the colonial period (dated as 1500–1776) into 41.5 pages of text, 4.5 of which covered the ancient and medieval European backstory. The early national period (1776–1840) received 43 pages of text and opened with a chapter titled "Jews Become Citizens."

Besides raising the evidential standard and confirming a preexisting periodization, strict North American focus, and underlying narrative of progressive Emancipation, Marcus's several tomes consolidated the writing of early American Jewish history around five core avenues of investigation: Jewish settlement; Jewish legal and political status; Jewish economic activity; Jewish religion and charity; and Jewish-Gentile relations. These strands, which can be traced back to the work of Adler, Kohler, and other historians working in the 1890s and early 1900s, undergirded *The Colonial American Jew*, volume one of *United States Jewry*, and *The American Jew*. To illustrate this point, we might consider a section titled "The English Period in North American Jewish History" that appeared in *The American Jew*. Its ten subheadings—"Where They Settled," "Rights and Disabilities," "How They Made a Living," "Religious Life and Organization," "What Did These Jews Believe?," "Charity," "Jewish Education and Culture," "Rejection," "America Accepts the Jews," and "The Jews Accept America"—map neatly onto Marcus's five main lines of inquiry.[44]

Marcus's conception of early American Jewish history as a prelim to the history of Jews and Judaism in the United States meant that Caribbean and South American topics could only be partially incorporated even though Marcus was well aware of their historical significance. In fact, as director of the American Jewish Archives, he was closely involved around this time in an English translation of *Essai historique sur la colonie de Surinam*.⁴⁵ Furthermore, in 1952 he led an "expedition" to the insular Caribbean and South America with the primary goal of securing "copies of all Jewish manuscript materials up to the year 1800."⁴⁶ Also, he actively supported the completion and publication of Isaac Emmanuel and Suzanne Emmanuel's impressive and important two-volume study, *A History of the Jews of the Netherlands Antilles* (1970). The "history of the Jews of Curaçao forms an integral part of American Jewish history," Isaac Emmanuel affirmed in his preface to that work, before adding with some exaggeration, "Small wonder Dr. Jacob R. Marcus devotes considerable space to Curaçao in his forthcoming book, *The Colonial American Jew*."⁴⁷

The Emmanuels' deeply researched and chronologically organized study focused heavily on local and congregational matters on Curaçao and, albeit to a much lesser extent, other Dutch Caribbean islands. Like Marcus's work, it emphasized the themes of settlement, rights, economics, religion, and Jewish–Gentile relations. However, it implied a radically different understanding of American Jewish history because it situated North America at the margins of the Caribbean, rather than vice versa. By asserting Curaçao's mid-eighteenth-century role as the "mother community" of Caribbean Jewry, it quietly recentered early American Jewish history. Still, the primary concern of the Emmanuels in 1970 was not inventing a new historiographical paradigm, but addressing a contemporary decline of Sephardic Jewry on their island. Guiding their book was a strong desire to bring the "oldest [Sephardic] community in the Western Hemisphere" back to something like its mid-eighteenth-century heyday.⁴⁸

Meanwhile, Marcus struggled to accommodate the Caribbean region in his *Colonial American Jew*, which sought to combine comprehensive coverage of all aspects of early American Jewish history within a framework that looked ahead to the history of Jews in the United States. The limitations of the Fischel paradigm and the classic Wiernikian periodization of American Jewish history were exposed when the colonial era was considered by itself. Marcus knew that the Jewish Caribbean communities remained vital and important well beyond 1654, the standard starting point for histories of Jews in North America. And so, having decided to provide full coverage of the insular Caribbean and South American Jewish communities, he could not simply invoke the settlement of Jews in New Amsterdam in 1654 as justification for pivoting away from Spanish-Portuguese America toward Dutch-British North America and, eventually, the United States. Instead, he opted for a transparent North American–centrism and declared at the outset of his book that his primary mission was to tell the history of Jews in North America, "notwithstanding the fact that the seventeenth century Dutch and English dependencies in Brazil, Surinam, and the West Indies were far more noteworthy than the North American mainland colonies."[49] On this basis, he drew only passing comparisons between the Caribbean and North American Jewish communities. Tellingly, he also concluded his seven-chapter discussion of "Spain, South America, Mexico, and the West Indian Islands" with a section, "The Road to New Amsterdam," focused on 1654. In other words, having veered into unusual territory for general narratives of American Jewish history, he circled back to rejoin the traditional narrative track.[50]

Historian Moses Rischin immediately pointed out the limitations of Marcus's approach. As one of the first Harvard University graduate students to focus on American Jewish history, as well as the author of a landmark 1962 study, *The Promised City: New York's Jews, 1870–1914*, Rischin was at the vanguard of a new generation of professional scholars who greatly advanced American Jewish history as an academic field between the 1960s and the 1980s.[51] In a 1973 review of *The Colonial American Jew* written for the *William and Mary Quarterly*, he delivered a sharp, penetrating assessment of the field of pre-1820 American Jewish history. He bemoaned how Marcus and other scholars had become lost in the "obscure, episodic, and inconsequential" history of Jews on the North American continent. Noting that "the Jews of the English and Dutch [Caribbean] islands outnumbered their coreligionists of North America by five to one and may have equaled the Jews of England" in the mid-eighteenth century, Rischin recommended something like an Atlantic or hemispheric turn in early American Jewish history. Significantly, he saw this shift as opening up an entirely new research agenda. The history of the Jewish Caribbean reveals the essential "paradoxes of Atlantic civilization," Rischin contended. A year earlier, Edmund Morgan had identified the contemporaneous development of liberty and slavery in Virginia to be "the central paradox of American history."[52] Without mentioning Morgan, Rischin now identified a parallel phenomenon whereby Caribbean "slave islands" provided Jews with a degree of "personal and corporate dignity never before imagined in Christian Europe." He recommended careful examination of Jews in "the Caribbean borderlands of warring empires," essentially proposing a new synthesis of early American Jewish history that by taking the insular Caribbean as its focal point, would both expand "the horizons of American colonial history" and enlarge our "understanding of an emergent multi-national and multi-racial world."[53]

Unfortunately, Rischin's 1973 opposition to the nationalistic impulse of most early American Jewish historical writing fell on deaf ears. At that time, the field of American Jewish history was not only becoming more professionalized but also more focused on the nineteenth-century and twentieth-century United States. Ironically, Rischin had himself encouraged this trend away from the colonial era through his influential work, *The Promised City*.[54] By the 1970s, the presence of Jews in colonial America and the contribution of Jews to the founding of the United States no longer demanded the attention they had received earlier in the twentieth century. This shift in research interests discouraged a large-scale reevaluation of early American Jewish history in the last decades of the twentieth century. Instead, surveys of American Jewish history continued to espouse narratives of the early modern period that echoed Fischel and Wiernik. Most ran as follows: expelled from Spain in 1492 (and having endured forced mass conversion to Christianity in Portugal in 1497), Jews arrived in North America following the fall of Dutch Brazil in 1654, forged lasting synagogue communities, generally prospered, and incrementally won civil and political rights under Dutch then English rule; full citizenship status duly arrived after the American Revolution; and, as Washington acknowledged in 1790, Jews were recognized as an integral part of the United States from the founding era onward.

A Time for Planting, Eli Faber's 1992 survey of early American Jewish history, still the standard single-volume study of the period, repeated a version of this storyline even as it incorporated Atlantic aspects of Jewish history. As the first volume in a five-volume series on what was essentially the history of Jews in the United States, it performed the traditional task of reducing a geographically vast transatlantic scope down to the level of five or so colonial North American cities. Admittedly, in a chapter titled "The Atlantic World of Colonial Jewry," as well as elsewhere in his book, Faber located North American Jews within Atlantic commercial and religious contexts. Overwhelmingly, however, *A Time for Planting* identified American Jewish history as a North American phenomenon. Its opening lines even proclaimed the landing of twenty-three Jews in New Amsterdam in 1654 as the beginning of American Jewish history.[55]

Concerted scholarly efforts to foreground Atlantic elements of early American Jewish history, as well as to establish Atlantic Jewish history as a new area of study, erupted around the turn of the millennium as part of a wider proliferation in Atlantic history scholarship and, more broadly, in transnational research across the social sciences and humanities.[56] Two colloquia-inspired edited works on Atlantic Jewry appeared in 2001 and 2009 respectively.[57] Another volume on Jews in the Caribbean was published in 2014.[58] The essay collection *The Sephardic Atlantic*, which foregrounded postcolonial approaches to Jewish Atlantic studies, arrived in 2018.[59] Meanwhile, several studies of the so-called "western Sephardic diaspora," including Jonathan Israel's mammoth *Diasporas within a Diaspora*, issued in 2002, engaged extensively with Atlantic and American themes.[60] Research on Jews and the Atlantic slave trade, as well as on Jews and race in America, similarly flourished in and after the 1990s.[61]

Discussions of the "Port Jew"—a heuristic invention of the late 1990s—heightened academic interest in Jewish communities around the Atlantic littoral.[62] By 2001, David Cesarani, director of the AHRB Parkes Research Centre for the Study of Jewish/non-Jewish Relations (now the Parkes Institute) at the University of Southampton, England, had instigated a five-year research project on Port Jews. In partnership with the Kaplan Centre for Jewish Studies at the University of Cape Town, Cesarani organized three international symposia, each of which produced separate collections of papers between 2002 and 2009.[63] Meanwhile, the journal *Jewish History* devoted an issue to Port Jews in 2006,[64] and a sizeable number of books and articles mentioned or discussed, sometimes critically, the Port Jew concept.[65]

Regrettably, these scholarly efforts of the late 1990s and early 2000s, while considerable and often insightful in their own way, failed to generate a comprehensive and cohesive Atlantic-oriented alternative to the traditional narratives of early American Jewish history. To a large degree, the underlying problem lay with the field of Atlantic history as a whole, rather than Atlantic Jewish history specifically. As David Armitage reflected in 2018, Atlantic history peaked as "a distinct field of study" in the early 2000s when "what was good for Atlantic history seemed to be good for oceanic history more generally, and even for transnational history *tout court*."[66] But these opening boom years did not produce a settled definition of Atlantic history as a field simultaneously connected to and distinctive from other supranational histories. Consequently, and in quite short order, "oceanic history and global history engulfed [Atlantic history] once more."[67]

Adam Sutcliffe's important historiographical contribution to the 2009 volume *Atlantic Diasporas* usefully illustrates how this broader issue within Atlantic history impacted discussions of Atlantic Jewish history during the early 2000s. Sutcliffe asserted the centrality of nation-oriented issues of rights, integration, and patriotism to early modern European Jewish life. He welcomed Atlantic history's "power to destabilize traditional nation-based narratives of the past," as well as to "challenge . . . the imagined fixity of all social categories." Yet he simultaneously advised that Atlantic history was a Cold War artifice that had lost relevancy as globalization assumed popular and academic attention at the start of the twenty-first century. Atlantic history, Sutcliffe further warned, could preserve false West-East binaries and hinder "the study of global interconnections." Additionally, "overemphasis on transnational flows of contact and exchange" could distract academics from the peculiarities of nations such as the United States.[68] Overall, then, Sutcliffe judged the relative merits of national, Atlantic, and global perspectives of early modern Jewish history on the grounds of their contemporary political and intellectual appeal rather than, say, their ability to recover and explain the past on its own terms. Holly Snyder dismissed Sutcliffe's piece in 2014 as "a historiographical apologetic for the sloth with which practitioners of Jewish history have approached the Atlantic paradigm."[69] While that assessment is fair, it should also be noted that Sutcliffe's hesitancy was in keeping with a general scholarly "weariness" toward Atlantic history that emerged around 2009.[70]

The field of Atlantic history, we might now reflect, was a product more of the post–Cold War era than, as Sutcliffe indicated, the Cold War itself.[71] Along with global history, Atlantic history marked a strong academic reaction that took hold in the 1990s and early 2000s against the nationalist methods and narratives that had dominated the social sciences and humanities in the United States and Europe since the nineteenth century.[72] In line with that trend, scholars of early American Jewish history pressed the importance of both Atlantic and global approaches at the start of the twenty-first century, weakening the grip of the traditional national paradigm. Contributing to the 2014 volume on *Jews in the Caribbean*, Eli Faber lamented that almost all studies of early American Jewry are "limited to five congregations on the North American mainland—New York, Newport, Philadelphia, Charleston, and Savannah—as well as a handful of settlers in the interior, and, later, joining the original five in the late eighteenth century, Richmond and Baltimore." Faber then optimistically predicted "a new historiography, one that paints a far broader picture of early American Jewish history."[73]

One logical outcome of global history, he explained, was a "shift among historians of American Jewish history away from their traditional isolationist perspective to viewing and analysing the settlements in North America, the Caribbean, the eastern Atlantic (the Canaries and Madeira), the north-eastern coast of South America (Suriname), and western Europe as an integrated entity spanning the Atlantic region."[74] Faber did not say exactly how, why, and when this region was "integrated" beyond asserting that commercial, religious, and kinship networks linked North American colonial Jews to other parts of the Atlantic basin. The main thrust of his chapter was to recommend rather than effect a "thorough rewriting of early American Jewish history" from an undefined Atlantic perspective.[75]

Rather than looking forward expectantly as Faber did, Holly Snyder expressed frustration in 2014 at the lack of interest shown by scholars of Jewish history in Atlantic approaches and urged more concerted action. In a sharp state-of-the-field assessment, she exposed "a self-reflexive defense of Jewish historiography as it is presently practiced, against the suspicion that an Atlantic Jewish paradigm might undermine the very premises on which more traditional forms of Jewish history writing have relied for several generations now." Snyder faulted the methodological conservatism and defensive insularity of early modern Jewish historiography. Furthermore, she criticized persistence of traditional nationalist agendas and frameworks in the research and writing of Jewish history generally. "To date," she wrote, "very few studies have actually approached Jewish history, in any degree, from an Atlanticist perspective."[76]

Published in a five-year span, the essays of Sutcliffe, Faber, and Snyder collectively encapsulated a historiographical moment when, first, the study of Atlantic Jewish history was gathering pace but also struggling to get off the ground and, second, when Atlantic history was losing its predominance as a transnational and oceanic field. Practitioners of Atlantic Jewish history faced the daunting prospect of having to establish their own area of study while simultaneously helping to reenergize the parent field of Atlantic history. Fortunately, a valuable new methodology was in the works.

Like Atlantic history, entangled history emerged after the Cold War amid rising interest in transnational and global scales of history. It was one of several related historical approaches (including *histoire croisée*, connected history, and shared history) that appeared in Europe and the United States during the late 1990s and early 2000s. In the United

States especially, entangled history also intersected with borderland history.[77] These affiliated approaches all sought to move beyond traditional national frameworks without resorting to comparative history, which oftentimes preserves national entities even as it seeks to transcend them through comparison. Put simply, entangled history crosses borders and straddles boundaries. It prioritizes the intersections, interconnections, and intermingling of national and imperial spaces. Similarly, it views social and cultural categories as dynamic, permeable, and intersecting. It therefore decries the sort of neat historical compartmentalization, fixed religious identities, clear through-lines, and North American exceptionalism that underpin both older and newer surveys of early American Jewish history.

Can entangled history produce the sort of coherent and historically precise Atlantic paradigm required to dislodge early American Jewish history from its old nationalist assumptions and narratives? To achieve that goal, historians will need to do more than provide microstudies and vague allusions to Atlantic scales of analysis. A more rigorous Atlantic framework will need to be constructed. Toward this end, Aviva Ben-Ur's important 2020 study of Jews in Suriname made a critical intervention by expressly naming four cardinal principles of Atlantic Jewish history: "the demographic and economic centrality of Caribbean Jewry among hemispheric American Jewries; Portuguese Jewish hegemony among Jews in the Atlantic World; the era of slavery; and the triad of privileges, disabilities, and Jewish Emancipation."[78] By restating these core elements of Atlantic Jewish history in the introduction to this book, Ben-Ur and Klooster have rightly brought them further to the fore.

One of the core advantages of entangled history is its ability to interconnect such framing principles with particular sites where social, political, and cultural negotiations, accommodations, and contingencies are most palpable. Micro and macro scales are interactive in entangled history. Discarding predefined containers or units of study (such as isolated nations), practitioners of entangled history emphasize the shared processes by which short-term actions on the ground shaped long-term expansive structures, and vice versa.[79] For this reason, entangled history can help to address some of the foundational methodological and interpretative challenges of American Jewish history as a field. As we have seen, the question of how to balance general and empirical approaches to history occupied the founders of the AJHS. They postponed setting the geographical and chronological boundaries of American Jewish history in the name of "scientific" research. Unfortunately, their strategy of deferment only served to silence Atlantic and hemispheric impulses and entrench a nationalist approach. It is time to restart the conversation about the Atlantic parameters and master narratives of American Jewish history that was put on hold one century ago. And entangled history needs to be part of that discussion.

CHAPTER 2

Atlantic Commerce and Pragmatic Tolerance

Portuguese Jewish Participation in the Spanish Navíos de Registro *System in the Seventeenth Century*

OREN OKHOVAT

This chapter explores how Portuguese Jewish merchants participated in transimperial commercial networks during the second half of the seventeenth century, not only as intermediaries but as equal partners in an increasingly liberalized Atlantic economic system. The observations made here build on earlier studies of Portuguese Jews as Iberian intermediaries to explore how Portuguese Jewish merchants functioned not only as cultural or religious go-betweens but as integral members of a European culture of international commerce and colonialism. Economic historians have explored how Portuguese Jewish merchants functioned as intermediaries between the Sephardic diaspora and Christian European merchants and state actors.[1] Cultural and religious historians have considered how Iberian precedents impacted the way that Portuguese Jews organized their community in Dutch realms.[2] This scholarship has examined how the community's leaders sought to present themselves as culturally European, even as they remained anxious about their status as religious others in the Dutch Republic.

More recent studies have shown that Portuguese Jewish communities across the Dutch Atlantic were diverse, with many impoverished members, and governed by a merchant elite firmly rooted in the wider Iberian merchant diaspora.[3] This chapter specifically seeks to advance the study of Portuguese Jewish merchants, who also composed the community's leadership. It argues that Portuguese Jewish merchants sought to present themselves as culturally European because they were deeply embedded in early modern imperial systems as fully European actors.[4] This approach departs from previous studies by seeking to use the case of Portuguese Jewish merchants not only for the study of a unique Jewish community but to examine the way that early modern empires functioned. In particular their integration into Spanish commercial networks and imperial institutions suggests that even religious decrees prohibiting the participation of non-Catholics and those of "impure blood" (New Christians and Moriscos) in Spanish state- and empire-building were subordinate to the immediate economic needs of both the Crown and colonial actors.[5] Studying the social impact of Portuguese Jewish merchant activity in Spanish imperial networks can therefore further illuminate our understanding of early modern policies of tolerance (or intolerance) in relation to individual acts of toleration.[6]

The Inquisition remained strong throughout the early modern period and vehemently prosecuted baptized individuals suspected of practicing any form of Islam, Judaism, or Protestant religion.[7] Nevertheless, as Stuart Schwartz has demonstrated, plural religious ideas held sway across the early modern Iberian Atlantic world due to a long history of forced conversions that incorporated a variety of ideas into a nominally uniform Iberian Catholic empire. As a result, the intolerance of inquisitors and high church officials often clashed with popular notions of religious pluralism in the Iberian Atlantic, leading to pragmatic toleration on the local level that disregarded state or church policies.[8] The present chapter expands upon Schwartz's analysis to demonstrate how the toleration of others by Spanish and Portuguese actors was further entangled with pragmatic economic decision-making that broke down political and social barriers across imperial divides. Tolerance is not the same as acceptance, but when driven by mutually beneficial commercial interest it resulted in dynamic and cosmopolitan spaces. This was especially true in the Caribbean where imperial control sometimes wavered and where local actors made decisions based on local necessity.

European merchants of a variety of religious and cultural backgrounds partnered to advance overseas commercial ventures, and European imperial governments fostered interimperial relationships for the same reason. The extent to which Portuguese Jewish merchants remained integral participants in Spanish imperial culture can be examined through their roles in a Spanish institution that became quintessential to the seventeenth-century Atlantic economy: the *navíos de registro* (registry ships) licensing system. This system was established by the Spanish Crown to sell royal permits to private merchants who could ship supplies and goods to Spanish American ports off the official galleon route. It also permitted license holders to fund their voyages by purchasing goods in Spanish America to sell in Cádiz. This essay proposes that the cosmopolitan nature of this institution helped to create an Atlantic culture of pragmatic toleration that fostered the emergence of regional, and often clandestine, transimperial markets in the Caribbean. Although designed as a monopolistic institution, it became defined by often clandestine private trade enterprises that at times undermined Spanish imperial prerogatives but also offered solutions to logistical issues, particularly given the economic and political turmoil that plagued Iberian imperial metropoles in mid-century.

As Jack P. Greene has argued, in the early modern period, in contrast to the later centralized state empires of the nineteenth century, European monarchies were forced to negotiate authority with local officials in American colonies because of vast physical distances and the Crown's lack of familiarity with realities on the ground. Colonial officials often took legal matters into their own hands and reevaluated royal decrees to suit local needs, frequently in consort with the residents of a colony.[9] J. H. Elliott has further emphasized that the Spanish monarchy under the Habsburgs was an extended patchwork of subject territories spread across great distances, each with a set of laws and customs rooted in various cultural settings that the monarch was "sworn to protect."[10] The Spanish Empire was thus constructed to support what historians have recently called a "polycentric monarchy"—a system whereby the monarch shared power with local political elites and royal administrators who maintained a degree of autonomy, sometimes substantial, to make pragmatic decisions within their jurisdiction. This led to the creation of multiple centers of authority across the Spanish Empire that interacted and participated in the creation and circulation of ideas and models of authority and thus the making of empire. Although the system could become unstable, it was tied together by a culture of loyalty to the king and the Catholic Church. Competition for royal favor between various branches of the Spanish imperial bureaucracy was therefore encouraged to maintain loyalty and cohesion.[11]

The *navíos de registro* system inadvertently allowed a broad array of non-Spanish and non-Catholic merchants to access Spanish markets on both sides of the Atlantic, essentially eroding mercantilist policies and religious restrictions. It nevertheless followed the Spanish monarchy's pattern of imperial rule, which often acted pragmatically to maintain imperial priorities even at the cost of absolute royal authority and religious uniformity. People from diverse economic classes were required to make this system function, including nonmerchant residents of the Spanish Caribbean, from indigenous laborers to royal governors. Portuguese Jews and Dutch Protestants also participated as equal partners, highlighting the extent to which pragmatism dominated the function of the Spanish Empire.

Economic Pragmatism and the Entangled Atlantic World

When the Spanish Crown continued to patronize individuals that the Inquisition identified as having "impure blood" (i.e., New Christians) along with openly Jewish merchants over the course of the seventeenth century it was acting on pragmatic considerations for the expansion of imperial interests overseas. The Crown also turned a blind eye to Dutch contraband trade with Spanish American ports despite its own mercantilist rhetoric denouncing both non-Catholics and non-Spanish participation in Spanish trade networks. Contradictions between idealistic rhetoric and popular practice further explain how Portuguese Jews and other non-Catholics were able to build such extensive extralegal trading relationships with Spaniards across the Atlantic World despite obvious religious and political differences.

At the highest echelons of government, King Philip IV of Spain and his procommerce prime minister, the Count-Duke of Olivares, favored pragmatic economic relationships at the expense of religious precedents that permitted only Old Christians to participate in royal institutions when they began courting Portuguese banking families, many of them New Christians, to serve as royal financiers in Madrid in the early 1620s. Unlike the Genoese, the Portuguese bankers had been subjects of the Habsburg Crown and thus could be considered insiders. Royal authorities regularly overlooked any degree of New Christian heritage that many of the Portuguese banking families had. The bankers themselves actively sought to conceal their New Christian ancestors by purchasing certificates of "purity of blood," bribing their way into military orders, marrying their children into the Spanish nobility, and grooming second sons to become religious and lay priests. At the same time, however, these families apparently saw no conflict in continuing to use their openly Jewish relatives and acquaintances in Amsterdam as correspondents. The Crown took notice that its principal financiers expanded their operations into what was enemy territory, since the Dutch Republic would remain at war with Spain until 1648.[12]

Rumors that the Portuguese correspondents in Amsterdam were openly apostatizing from the Catholic Church were set aside in the quest to tap into Dutch markets. As merchant nations from across Europe were flocking to Amsterdam at the end of the sixteenth century, the Castilian merchants who had been active in both Bruges and Antwerp were restricted from continuing to do so due to the ongoing war. This was not true for the Portuguese New Christian merchants who embraced Judaism, as they were capable of bypassing the commercial restrictions that other Catholic Iberian merchant groups faced. Rather than shun them for their apostasy, the Crown apparently began to take advantage of the opportunities of this potential foothold. The relationship that the later Spanish Habsburgs built with the Portuguese Jewish nation reflects the pragmatism that defined their imperial policies overseas.

This pragmatism was in evidence even after the Count-Duke of Olivares fell from grace after Portugal and Catalonia rebelled against Habsburg rule in 1640. Philip IV, and subsequently the regency governments of his son Charles II, continued to patronize Portuguese Jews living in Dutch territories. As New Christians, Portuguese Jewish merchants had been Habsburg subjects under the Iberian Union. Spanish royal patronage thus offered them opportunities to continue operating in the Spanish networks they were already familiar with, even though some Portuguese Jewish merchants focused on supporting the new Braganza dynasty in Portugal where they retained interests. For all intents and purposes, the Portuguese Jewish nation in Amsterdam functioned as both a Portuguese and Spanish merchant nation.

Iberian royal patronage manifested in the appointment of Portuguese Jews as royal agents, starting with Duarte Nunes da Costa (Jacob Curiel) and his son Jeronimo (Mosseh Curiel) as agents of the Portuguese Crown in Hamburg (1644) and Amsterdam (1645), respectively. In 1666 Manuel Belmonte (Ishac Nunes Belmonte) began regular correspondence with various Spanish royal agents, principal among them Juan José de Austria who was Philip IV's illegitimate son and later regent for his brother, Charles II.[13] Belmonte essentially functioned as a Spanish factor in Amsterdam even though he was not officially named a *residente* of the Crown until 1679. Manuel not only reported regularly to Spanish royal officials on political developments in the Netherlands but also was instrumental in securing slave asiento contracts for the Coymans merchant house in the 1680s and actively worked to realize the Habsburg claim to the Spanish throne during the War of the Spanish Succession (1701–14).[14]

The appointment of Jewish royal agents by the Iberian Crowns coincided with increasing Iberian royal interests in expanding trade with the Dutch Republic as Spain made peace with its former territories in 1648, followed by Portugal in 1661. Dutch merchants also started taking advantage of Spanish networks after peace was signed in 1648, allowing them to compete with their Flemish counterparts who had been part of Iberian Atlantic trade networks since the fourteenth century. By 1668 Spain and Portugal made peace with one another, and regular trade between Portuguese residing in the Dutch Atlantic and the Spanish and Portuguese Empires resumed. By this time the Dutch had become a leading maritime power in the Atlantic, actively undermining both Spanish and Portuguese trade monopolies in Africa and the Americas.

Ironically, this dominance was coupled with widespread territorial loss in the Atlantic. In 1654 the Dutch lost their colony in northeastern

FIGURE 2.1. Manuel Belmonte's house in Amsterdam. Print by Romeyn de Hooghe, 1693–ca. 1695. Rijksmuseum, Amsterdam.

Brazil to Luso-Brazilian insurgents. Most of their efforts to gain a territorial foothold in Spanish America, mainly in Chile and Peru, had also failed. These failures left them with only their Caribbean possessions and the large North American colony of New Netherland with its capital, New Amsterdam, on Manhattan Island. Suriname was conquered after the loss of New Netherland in 1664. In Africa, the West India Company (WIC) founded a colony at the Cape of Good Hope in 1652, but in 1648 the Portuguese retook Luanda in Angola, which the Dutch had held since 1641. They managed to hold on to the castle at Elmina on the African Gold Coast, which they captured in 1637 and retained until 1871.

The WIC had been created in 1621 to wage war on the Iberians. After Curaçao was captured in 1634 it became a base from which to raid the nearby Spanish mainland. Following peace with Spain in 1648, however, this strategy and the WIC itself essentially became obsolete. The company had tried its best to retain its role as a disruptor of Iberian Atlantic profits by restricting Dutch Atlantic trade only to areas not colonized by Spain and Portugal. Despite these efforts Dutch illicit trade with Spanish and Portuguese America had proved too difficult to control; by 1657 even WIC administrators in Curaçao engaged in it. By 1674 the WIC had collapsed and was reborn as a company focused on Atlantic trade, especially out of Curaçao, and on administering the remaining Dutch American colonies and the African trading posts.[15]

The fate of Dutch Atlantic trade, however, was not tied to the WIC, and in fact the Amsterdam chamber of the company typically favored supporting free trade over company monopolies. Private Dutch traders were also very familiar with Atlantic transit routes through their long history of participation in Spanish, Portuguese, English, and French networks, and smuggling accounted for many Dutch American trading ventures.[16] The only successful monopoly that the WIC was able to maintain after 1633 was the transfer of slaves from the Slave Coast and the Loango coastal area to the Caribbean.[17] In 1675, a year after the WIC was reorganized into a more trade-focused company, it designated Curaçao as a free port. The colony's inhabitants prospered from intercolonial trade, which became legal under Dutch law but remained illicit for non-Dutch imperial territories.[18]

The watershed moment of 1675 was the culmination of years of effort on the part of Dutch merchants to integrate into broader Atlantic markets, especially Spanish ones after 1648.[19] Despite initial protests from WIC directors, Portuguese Jewish merchants also used Curaçao as a base for expanding family company interests to Spanish America, often in cooperation with Dutch and Spanish business partners. Most of these ventures involved extralegal mechanisms using correspondents in Spain and Spanish America. As Spanish American markets expanded, new opportunities emerged that allowed the direct participation of a variety of Atlantic traders and entrepreneurs. One of the principal avenues through which this was possible was via the *navíos de registro* system.[20]

The *Navíos de Registro* Trade

Dutch manipulation of the *navíos de registro* trade in cooperation with Spanish accomplices became so widespread by the 1660s that the second Spanish ambassador to The Hague, Don Esteban de Gamarra, was tasked by the Council of Castile to begin compiling intelligence reports on illegal Dutch operations in the Indies in 1663. His spy operation uncovered dozens of *registro* trade ventures undertaken in the course of hundreds of voyages between 1663 and 1667 that were used to trade contraband.[21] As an Iberian diaspora community, and one with long-standing ties to Iberian merchants and the Spanish Crown, the Portuguese Jews were in a prime position to take advantage of the trail that Dutch merchants had blazed into the Spanish Atlantic through the *registro* trade. To understand the role of Portuguese Jewish merchants in Dutch contraband operations it is necessary to know how the Dutch were able to manipulate the *registros*.

Contraband trade with the Spanish Indies had become so widespread by the time the 1648 Peace of Münster was signed that even the Crown was forced to find ways to benefit from it rather than either ignoring its ubiquity or outlawing illegal ventures. Zacharias Moutoukias has demonstrated how the Crown financed elements of its military and administrative apparatus in the Río de la Plata through illegal commerce. Buenos Aires was established as the principal port of the region for one reason: the export of the Crown's most coveted commodity for the duration of the colonial period, silver. With a growing number of rival European colonies in the Caribbean, whence silver had previously been exported via Panama, the Crown sought to secure Buenos Aires for the export of Potosí silver. In order to pay for the salaries and supplies of a garrison and administrative-military structure the Crown created the *situado*, which was an annual subsidy that the royal treasury of Potosí was ordered to make by remitting coined silver to merchant-suppliers and high officials in Buenos Aires.[22]

The exponential growth of contraband in the Río de la Plata region over the course of the seventeenth century correlates with the establishment of an imperial apparatus to oversee the *situado* there. Buenos Aires was one of many ports lying off the official route for Spain's armed treasure fleet convoys known as the *Carrera de Indias*. Although notoriously unreliable, their purpose was to escort supplies and precious cargo to and from Spain and key ports in the Spanish Caribbean (Santo Domingo, Cartagena de Indias, Veracruz, and Havana). Supplying regions lying outside of the official *carrera* route therefore proved logistically difficult to regulate and protect. During the Iberian Union (1580–1640), the Crown tried to remedy this for Buenos Aires by permitting direct trade with Portuguese Brazil and Guinea.[23] After Portuguese independence in 1640 the Crown began promoting the sale of *licencias*, or royal permits to private merchants to trade with ports off the *carrera* (galleon) route and to supplement uncompleted *carrera* voyages. The merchant ships participating in this trade came to be known as the *navíos de registro* (registry ships) and slowly began to dominate imperial trade in the second half of the seventeenth century.

Moutoukias found that the silver coins of the *situado* rarely made it into the pockets of soldiers, but rather went mostly to merchant-suppliers contracted by a *registro* license and to some high officials who in turn supplied the garrison with provisions and paid them on credit. This created a situation whereby merchants and high local officials supplied basic commodities through the *navíos de registro* system to a relatively isolated port on the south Atlantic American coast. In order to supply and support this regime properly, the Crown was forced to ignore unsanctioned commercial activities in the Río de la Plata, where individuals seeking riches in the Indies otherwise had little to gain from participation in the limited royal supply trades under a royal license. Those who purchased a license entered into an asiento (contract) with the Crown that calculated the value of the license based on the tonnage being shipped as well as the rendering of extra services to the Crown, such as the transportation of officials and soldiers or the shipment of arms and supplies to the Indies.[24]

The dispatch of *navíos de registro* was a royal prerogative, meaning that it was a privilege maintained at the pleasure of the Crown despite complaints by officials who argued that they harmed royal monopolies. Private merchants also complained that since the *registro* trade was highly regulated as a royal prerogative, it harmed the expansion of private markets. The Crown itself enjoyed its benefits and could manipulate the system at will. The *registro* trade quickly became associated with smuggling as license holders regularly underreported the tonnage of their cargo. Rather than abandoning the system, however, the Crown merely increased the cost of licenses and fines for violations. It essentially turned a blind eye to contraband so long as fines were paid to the royal treasury. This loophole opened an avenue for a semi-illegal free trade to the Indies that simultaneously alleviated the Crown's fear of losing its monopoly in the Indies trade and solved the Crown's supply issues to far-off yet important regions such as the Río de la Plata.[25]

This shift in practice created a new avenue by which Portuguese Jewish merchants could reinforce their roles as imperial go-betweens after the financial influence of the Portuguese bankers in Madrid waned. The licenses to enter into a royal contract were usually sold publicly to the highest bidder in Seville, although private shipowners sometimes solicited them through an agent at court in Madrid. Portuguese Jews retained associates not only in Seville and Cádiz but also in Madrid, and their relationship with old Lisbon- and Porto-based private enterprises that tied the Iberian Peninsula to West Africa, Brazil, and the Caribbean still functioned.[26] Most of the commercial activities of Dutch Portuguese Jews involved trade with Portugal and its colonies in the period 1595–1648. From 1648 onward, however, there was a sudden shift among the community toward markets in Spain and Morocco.[27] Even Jeronimo Nunes da Costa (Mosseh Curiel), agent of the Portuguese Crown in Amsterdam, retained correspondents in San Sebastián and Alicante.[28] The *navíos de registro* trade was a critical factor in the shifting participation of Portuguese Jews in Spanish imperial trade networks.

At the same time, the *registro* trade was also becoming associated with Dutch merchants more generally. After the Peace of Münster of 1648, prominent Dutch merchant companies wasted no time incorporating both Seville and Cádiz into their trade networks, raising important questions about the presence of Protestants at the heart of the Spanish imperial system.[29] Dutch trade out of Cádiz became so important that in 1661 the Crown abolished the oppressive *almirantazgo* tax that imposed hefty fees on northern European, and specifically Dutch, ships trading with the Iberian Peninsula.[30] Even with this victory, however, participation of merchants based out of the United Provinces in the Indies trade was still legally limited.

It is no wonder, then, that the second half of the seventeenth century saw a massive increase in the number of pardons and fines (*indultos*) issued for the violations committed by license holders or their associates trading with the Indies, generally through the *navíos de registro* system. A survey of the fines issued between 1601 and 1728 reveals that only seven were issued between 1601 and 1647. This does not indicate an absence of contraband trade, since the Crown had been fighting to maintain its monopolies in the Indies from at least the mid-sixteenth century, if not earlier.[31] These early *indultos* were mostly issued to royal officials who committed financial violations. The only fine issued in 1647, for example, was for a captain of the galleon fleet who "forgot" to pay his taxes in New Spain during the fleet's visit there.[32]

In the first decade after the Peace of Münster there was a gradual but exponential growth in the number of *indultos* issued for license violations, or for sailing without a license at all. In 1650 a single *indulto* was issued for an English-Spanish smuggling operation that operated between England and Santo Domingo in the 1640s.[33] From then until 1659, twenty-five pardons were issued for license violations or the embezzlement of funds compared to the seven issued over the previous forty-six years. The value of the fines collected in the *indultos* for this decade alone equaled about 174,376 pesos. Between 1660 and 1665 there were twice as many *indultos*, totaling fifty. Although the data for the total value of contraband cargo are incomplete, the fees and punishments for participating in contraband trade with the Indies seem lenient at first glance. Between 1650 and 1699 only one person was imprisoned, and one royal official was banned from holding office for four years. The highest fee for license violation was for 27,852 pesos in 1650; the next highest was for 18,000 pesos in 1654. Most fees fell between 450 pesos and 6,000 pesos, mostly for license violations, with one case in which a full pardon was offered without a fee.[34]

Compared to the value of some of the cargo, however, one wonders if the risk for illegal trading ventures was worth the investment. However, as Moutoukias found for Buenos Aires, cargoes were generally underreported, and the ratio of cargo value to fees in the records can be deceiving. Moutoukias gives the example of a captain Ignacio Maleo, who in 1663 transported two hundred infantrymen, forty tons of arms, the *oidores* and the president of the Audiencia of Buenos Aires, and the governor of Chile under a legal *navío de registro* license. In total he paid 15,000 pesos for his permit and declared that he carried merchandise worth 43,500 pesos.[35] Moutoukias argues that 15,000 pesos for the permit was too high in relation to the supposed value of the commercial operation, demonstrating that it was through Maleo's illegal transactions, which he did not report to the Crown, that he made his true profit. It was also highly likely that royal officials adjusted fees for possible contraband tonnage.

The practice of underreporting cargo value was quite common for both licensed and unlicensed ships and remained one of the arguments against the continuation of the *registro* trade. In light of the volume of *indultos* issued by the Council of the Indies and signed by the king throughout the seventeenth century, the Crown clearly saw value in ignoring contraband as long as it benefited financially and logistically. One Juan de Pantaleón, for example, was apparently welcomed with open arms upon arriving in Cartagena de Indias in May 1657 with a cargo of wine and lamp oil without a license. The galleon fleet had not made it to the port for three consecutive years, and the port authorities were desperate to receive a fresh shipment of wine for celebrations and oil for lamps. They consulted the attorney general of the city about allowing Pantaleón to sell his cargo without a license. He in turn proposed to the town's cabildo that a request for a license be made to Pedro Zapata, governor and captain general of Cartagena. The governor agreed to request both a license and a pardon for Pantaleón. The Council of the Indies, for its part, ruled that the cargo was small enough that it did not compete with official supply lines. Since it was owned by a *natural* of Castile and the journey was undertaken "without malice," it was judged to pose no threat to the royal monopoly. Furthermore, the council argued, if ships such as these were refused entry, they could be seized by "English enemies and others that infest those coasts," or they could simply find another port where they could sell their merchandise clandestinely.[36]

For the Crown Pantaleón's journey, and others like his, offered logistical relief at a time when it was stretched thin financially. Not only was Spain at war with England in 1657, but it was preparing to reinvade Portugal and fighting a war against France in the Spanish Netherlands. The war with the English had begun with their capture of Jamaica, which created panic in the Caribbean and established a new base from which the English could harass the heart of the Spanish Empire. A single ship supplying necessary commodities to one of Spanish America's principal ports was of little consequence during such a tumultuous time, even if it was smuggling in more goods than anticipated.

Informal Trade Networks as Spaces of Sociocultural, Religious, and Political Entanglement

Both Zacharias Moutoukias and Wim Klooster have demonstrated the extent to which the *navíos de registro* trade became synonymous with contraband trade in Atlantic networks, particularly in relation to Dutch contraband in Spanish networks. Klooster's work presents smuggling as a relationship between people who were legally not supposed to be in contact with one another. Although he calls those who initiated smuggling "interlopers," he also recognizes the importance of the relationships they built with locals in the places where they made exchanges, which had long-term implications for commercial and social trends.[37] Local demand was a driving force behind the construction of private informal trade networks, but the actual act of trade could not be sustained without a system of trust to secure exchanges.

The *navíos de registro* provided the basis for such a system, and the turmoil that the Spanish Crown faced in the 1650s offered a window of opportunity to expand it into a complex vehicle for clandestine private international trade. To function, this system required the coordination of Dutch, Spanish, Portuguese, English, French, and other "interloping" merchants active in Europe, the Atlantic islands, West Africa, and the Americas. Portuguese Jewish merchants, who continued to function as a de facto Iberian merchant nation, were in an ideal position to take advantage of such a system and to serve as a fulcrum for potential collaborations between various commercial actors. Such intricate arrangements, however, required the cooperation of a broad group of actors who made it possible to bypass the registration of ships and cargo in Seville or Cádiz and to access ports in the Indies.

An excellent example of how Portuguese Jews helped coordinate and execute *registro* voyages can be seen in a 1664 expedition headed by the Dutch merchant Jacobus Alexander Beni (who used the alias Diego). Beni and his business partner Balthasar Besalaar were Dutch associates attached to the Grillos' trading house established in Cádiz. The city, like Seville and Lisbon, was a rather cosmopolitan space as a variety of merchants attached to Spanish institutions congregated in what became Spain's central port for importing American colonial goods by the mid-seventeenth century. Only Spanish merchants were legally allowed to purchase royal contracts, but this did not stop foreign investors and merchants from organizing contraband trade under the guise of a legal license. Beni and Besalaar thus partnered with two Spanish *vecinos* of Sanlúcar, another major port near Cádiz, in 1664 to carry out just such a venture.

These Spaniards were Francisco de Orejón and his friend Antonio Rodriguez Lodeño, who had worked with Beni and Besalaar since the 1650s. The venture in 1664 was organized after Orejón was appointed governor and captain-general of Havana, a post he would hold from

1664 until 1670.[38] The Spanish-Dutch associates conceived a plan to use the governorship to set up a regional trade network to export goods directly from Cuba to northern Europe. To accomplish this, they partnered with merchants resident in the Dutch Republic and in France who would fund the venture and supply goods to be sold throughout the Caribbean. These included the company of Francisco Cañete in Spanish Antwerp and the company of a French merchant resident in Amsterdam named Guillaume Belin de la Garde. It also included two Portuguese Jewish merchants whose role went beyond that of mere investors. They would be crucial to organizing the final stages of the venture using their correspondents and agents located in the principal European ports where Beni would eventually bring his Caribbean goods to sell.[39]

The first of these Portuguese Jewish partners was Balthasar Álvares Nogueira, who traded under the Dutch alias of Alberto Dirksen den Jonghen.[40] Since Beni's plan was to sell the bulk of his goods in France, Álvares Nogeuira's partnership was of great value. He had contacts in France and the French Caribbean where he conducted regular trade, sometimes in partnership with the Portuguese Jewish aristocracy like Abraam Pereyra, Antonio Lopes Suasso, and Jeronimo Nunes da Costa.[41] Beni's French contacts were undoubtedly important too, but Álvares Nogueira had access to the chain of Portuguese merchant communities located along the French Atlantic and in Martinique as well as to Portuguese Jewish merchants in Amsterdam who traded in French networks.[42] He also retained contacts in Cádiz, where his wealthy and influential relative Jacob Rodrigues Isidro resided. He was the son of Manuel Rodrigues Isidro, who used the alias Manuel Dirksen and collected payment from Álvares Nogueira's creditors in Hamburg when he and his sons resided there as Jews in the 1650s.[43] Álvares Nogueira, in short, offered Beni access to the extended international network of the Jewish and New Christian Portuguese merchant nation.

The other Portuguese Jewish partner was Diego Mendes de Brito, who had lived in Bayonne before arriving in Amsterdam, used the alias Jacques Alberto, and traded in both French and Spanish Atlantic networks.[44] In his intelligence report Ambassador Gamarra referred to a "French associate" of the group named Jacques Alberto who was in Cádiz when Beni arrived from France, whom he suspected of carrying out the final sale of goods there. Gamarra notes that this Alberto was a relative of the merchants in France who outfitted Beni for the final leg of his journey.[45] Mendes de Brito would have had no trouble passing as a French merchant since he spoke French and regularly used a

French alias for trade. It is very likely that he and Álvares Nogueira placed Beni in contact with family members or associates in one of the several Portuguese trading settlements there before Beni first embarked on his journey.

In June 1664 the group loaded three ships in Rotterdam with 6,000 florins (about 3,000 pesos) worth of Dutch goods and had the Spaniard Lodeño acquire a license to sail them directly to the island of Trinidad in the southern Caribbean, then part of the Venezuelan province of Guayana.[46] Lodeño sold the goods of one ship in Trinidad in exchange for cacao and then returned with the cargo to Cádiz, where Besalaar was to sell the cacao and use the proceeds to buy olive oil in Mallorca to sell in Holland. Beni, who sailed with Lodeño out of Rotterdam, took the other two ships along the coast of Venezuela to sell its cargo from Cumaná to Maracaibo and then stopped at Curaçao. There he sold the contents of one ship to the factors of the Grillo slave asiento, who paid for them in silver that Beni remitted to Amsterdam on the ship *San Jacob*. Beni then sailed the remaining ship to Havana where his friend and associate, the governor and captain-general Francisco de Orejón, organized a royal license for Beni to continue trading regionally. From Havana he sailed to Campeche, in Yucatán, where he loaded his ship with various goods. Upon completing his business along the Campeche coast, he returned to Havana where he organized the last leg of his voyage. Because of the ongoing Second Anglo-Dutch War, sailing directly to Holland with a large cargo under a Dutch flag would have been extremely risky. He therefore hired a smaller ship to remit eighty *cueros* (cases) of Campeche dyewood directly to Holland from Havana.[47] A direct shipment of Spanish American products from Havana to Holland was an extreme breach of Spanish mercantilist policies, but evidently it was possible because the highest government official in Havana himself found it beneficial to support an extralegal trading expedition with agents across various imperial and religious boundaries.

With his larger ship Beni organized another voyage from Havana to La Guaira, on the coast near Caracas. He kept most of his cargo from Yucatán for continued regional trade, which included 400 crates of tobacco, 3,500 more quintals of Campeche dyewood, 4,000 cowhide sacks of cochineal (a prized dye derived from an insect native to Mexico), and an undisclosed amount of American silver. Beni thus found it as profitable to sell his goods in regional markets as he did in European ones. In Caracas he negotiated a deal with a Spaniard there to remit another four hundred crates of tobacco, seemingly on credit, to Balthasar Besalaar in

Cádiz but that Beni would instead take to La Rochelle in France.[48] There he met one of the association's agents, Godefrois de Belaronda, who, together with a group of local merchants possibly tied to the Portuguese Jewish merchant Balthasar Álvares Nogueira, purchased Beni's remaining Caribbean merchandise and refitted his ship for a new voyage back to the Caribbean.[49]

All that remained to complete the journey was for Beni to return to Cádiz to fulfill his *registro* license obligations. These required the licensed vessel to return to Spain with goods from the American territories to which their license permitted them to sail. Since the original license was for a voyage to the Venezuelan coast the group needed to return with Venezuelan goods. Beni, however, sold all his Venezuelan goods in France, undoubtedly for a larger profit since normally French merchants would have to import such goods through Cádiz or organize a similar clandestine voyage to the Caribbean.

The Portuguese Jewish partners, Balthasar Álvares Nogueira (Alberto Dirksen) and Diego Mendes de Brito (Jacques Alberto), played a critical role in resolving this issue. Beni could have returned to Cádiz with Venezuelan goods, or with products similar enough that they could pass as being Venezuelan. He therefore returned to Amsterdam from France where he loaded his ship with barley purchased by Belin de la Garde. He then embarked for Lisbon where the barley was sold in exchange for Brazilian tobacco. This final leg of the journey was undoubtedly organized by Álvares Nogueira and Mendes de Brito. The pair had extensive contacts with experience in smuggling contraband between Portugal and Andalusia and who would have been able to help sell a cargo of Brazilian tobacco as Venezuelan tobacco.

Álvares Nogueira, for example, counted among his creditors the brothers Simão and Luis Rodrigues da Sousa and Francisco Lopes de Azevedo (Abraham Farrar). The former were major importers to Amsterdam of sugar from Oporto and olive oil from Andalusia during this time, and the latter had extensive contacts in both Faro in the Algarve and in Cádiz. Faro became an important port during Portugal's long war for independence (1640–68) as it was used to bypass Spanish blockades on Lisbon and Oporto. Dutch ships were often used by Portuguese merchants to smuggle Portuguese and Spanish products, including American silver, in and out of Cádiz. Lopes de Azevedo was one of these merchants and occasionally partnered with Jeronimo Nunes da Costa, agent of the Portuguese Crown in Amsterdam, to acquire Andalusian and Spanish American goods for Portuguese and Dutch markets.[50]

Álvares Nogueira also occasionally worked with Jeronimo Nunes da Costa, who was not only an agent of the Portuguese Crown but also the principal factor of the General Company for the Commerce of Brazil (Brazil Company) in Amsterdam. This was a joint-stock company modeled on the WIC that organized convoys to protect ships carrying goods from Brazil to Portugal and held certain trade monopolies itself.[51] With Nunes da Costa's aid alone Álvares Nogueira and Mendes de Brito would have been able to secure contacts in Lisbon to purchase Beni's grain and to sell him Brazilian tobacco.

Mendes de Brito (Jacques Alberto) was reportedly the one who sold the tobacco in Cádiz, most likely by securing bribes or false papers with the aid of relatives and associates there. This venture, after all, was not the first in which he and Álvares Nogueira partnered with his relative living in Andalusia, Fernando Dias de Brito, to execute joint Dutch-Portuguese trade deals in Cádiz and other Andalusian ports like Málaga.[52] He likely also received aid from Álvares Nogueira's associates or kinsmen, like the wealthy Rodrigues Isidro family that had returned to Cádiz from the Jewish community in Hamburg in the 1660s. The ruse apparently worked, and the profits were subsequently used to send the goods Beni loaded in La Rochelle to the Canaries. He acquired a new *registro* license in the island of La Palma after Francisco de Orejón again requested luxury Canary wine to be delivered to Havana under a royal license. The request, of course, was made so that a new round of voyages could be made along the route described above, from the Canary Islands to Venezuela, presumably with a stop at Curaçao, and from there to Havana, the Campeche coast, and then back to Europe.[53]

In this multicultural and transimperial network, Álvares Nogueira, under the alias of Alberto Dirksen, and Diego Mendes de Brito, under the alias of Jacques Alberto, exemplify how Portuguese Jews became integral to the private trade ventures that increasingly defined transatlantic commerce in the second half of the seventeenth century. The Portuguese war of independence and the Spanish financial crisis of the 1640s forced both the Spanish and Portuguese monarchies to liberalize their foreign trading policies. The provisions of the Peace of Münster in 1648 underscored this by requiring Philip IV of Spain to recognize the right of Jews living under Dutch rule to access Spanish ports.[54] The treaty, of course, did not mean that Jews (or Protestants) could trade freely in Spanish ports but rather that *all* merchants of the Dutch Republic were protected under its articles. As a result, after 1657 some Portuguese Jews began to present themselves as "Netherlanders" and to use Dutch aliases in official business transactions with Spain and Spanish America, whether as investors in Amsterdam or Curaçao or on the less frequent occasion that they themselves traveled to Spanish ports. In either case they became equal partners in commercial associations that cannot be definitively described as either Spanish or Dutch, but rather operated multinationally and globally.

Portuguese Jewish merchants increased their reliance on Iberian correspondents who were not family members or close associates throughout the Atlantic world. Francesca Trivellato has observed this among the Sephardic Jews of Livorno, emphasizing that successful business ventures required trust that was not automatically present among kin but that could be constructed among nonkin business associates to secure mutually beneficial interests.[55] Other scholars have corroborated the extent to which Portuguese Jewish merchants trading in Dutch Atlantic networks worked closely together with non-Jewish and non-Iberian business partners in the early modern period.[56] Nonkin business associates did not replace kin networks, which remained crucial to Portuguese Atlantic trade in the second half of the seventeenth century across religious and political boundaries. They did, however, help to expand Portuguese trade interests and reinforced already-existing Portuguese Jewish participation in European imperialist ventures.[57]

By observing economic patterns and commercial enterprises it becomes apparent that Jewish heritage did not prevent the formation of working relationships between (Jewish) Iberians in Dutch lands and (Catholic) Iberians in Spanish or Portuguese ones. All evidence suggests that aside from the Inquisition, which continued to forcefully prosecute people suspected of practicing Judaism, Islam, or any Protestant religion, there was a trend toward tolerating non-Catholics and non-Iberians in the early modern Iberian world for the sake of imperial expansion and commerce. Apart from the growing connections between Portuguese Jewish merchants and a broad stratum of Iberians, this can be especially observed in Spanish and Portuguese Atlantic trading centers, as is evident in the active Dutch trading community in the central imperial port of Cádiz or the English one in Lisbon.

Toward a Commercial Approach to Jewish Entanglement with the Atlantic World

The *navíos de registro* system offers a case study for the way in which imperial systems were manipulated by intercultural groups of traders to engage in widespread private trade. This was done with little regard for royal interests. However, in the case of the *navíos de registro*, the Spanish Crown found ways to profit off contraband by essentially "selling" pardons. Both the Portuguese and the Spanish Crowns saw the value of investing in foreign agents. They were already familiar with the Portuguese merchant diaspora, which had traditionally served as an intermediary for royal and private trade in the Low Countries. This included the Portuguese merchant nation that embraced Judaism in Amsterdam, which was well established in what remained Europe's entrepôt throughout the seventeenth century. Both Crowns were willing to overlook the fact that the community was Jewish and that many of its members were considered apostates by the Catholic Church.

Classic studies of how this community remained tied to the Iberian world have focused heavily on the cultural and religious ties of Portuguese Jews to their past as New Christians. Such studies have contributed much to our understanding of Portuguese Jewish religious thought and of the anxieties that leaders in Amsterdam felt for most of the seventeenth century with regard, on one hand, to their community—composed largely of recent migrants and converts from Iberian lands—and, on the other, to Dutch authorities whose hostility to anything Iberian influenced Portuguese Jewish attitudes when constructing their community at the start of the century.[58] Yet these studies leave many questions to be answered.

How can we explain the fact that communal leaders themselves maintained regular correspondence with partners or agents in Lisbon, Seville, and other Iberian trade centers? Jeronimo Nunes da Costa (Mosseh Curiel), for example, despite his role as agent of the Portuguese Crown and his extensive ties to Portuguese agents across the Atlantic world, held thirteen high-profile leadership positions within various communal institutions between 1655 and 1696, the year before his death.[59] Antonio Lopes Suasso (Ishac Israel Suasso) rivaled Nunes da Costa in wealth, contacts, and influence to the point of being ennobled as the Baron de Avernas-le-Gras by the regency council of Charles II in 1676 for his services provisioning the Spanish Army of Flanders.[60] Lopes Suasso, who was the highest taxpayer after Nunes da Costa in the 1660s, also held various influential leadership positions within the Jewish community between 1654 and 1672, including that of *gabay* in 1656–57.[61] Manuel Belmonte, whose wealth and ties to the Spanish monarchy eventually rivaled the wealth and influence of Nunes da Costa and Lopes Suasso, also held important communal positions, including that of *gabay*, between 1697 and 1703, two years before his death.[62] Furthermore, both Belmonte and Nunes da Costa were elected in 1681 by the *Mahamad* as "deputies of the nation" to represent the Jewish community in front of the Amsterdam City Council, the States General in The Hague, and elsewhere for "general cases of the nation."[63]

It is true that communal leaders maintained a rhetoric of orthodox religiosity and painted the community as a haven for victims of the Inquisition.[64] This was, however, also a community constructed by merchants and molded in their image of the world. In 1681 the community records were still being kept in Portuguese, and even the "deputies of the nation" were charged with acting as *procuradores* of the Jewish community, a term used by both Portuguese merchants and royal agents to refer to business correspondents abroad.[65] The records left to us by this Jewish community were written by individuals who saw their world through a mercantile lens. In order to understand the religious and social rhetoric that permeates these records (i.e., in order to understand this Jewish community) we must contextualize them within the commercial and economic world that influenced their authors. This was a thoroughly Atlantic Iberian diaspora community, albeit a unique one that embraced Judaism as its confessional framework.

The case of the Portuguese Jews problematizes any dichotomy of New Christian and Jewish, or Jewish or Christian categories of identification. It also problematizes the idea that Iberian royal restrictions or prerogatives were fully guided by religious considerations. This is demonstrated in the Jewish (or non-Catholic) activity prevalent within Iberian networks over the course of the seventeenth century, and the shifting attitudes that royal officials had toward the expansion of commerce. Studying Portuguese Jewish participation in Spanish imperial networks not only expands our understanding of how Jewish communities functioned in the early modern period, but also highlights the openness of Spanish and Spanish American merchants and others involved in Atlantic commerce to building working and long-term relationships with non-Iberians and non-Catholics.

CHAPTER 3

To Trade Is to Thrive

The Sephardic Moment in Amsterdam's Atlantic and Caribbean Sugar Trade in the Seventeenth Century

YDA SCHREUDER

In the seventeenth century, Sephardim in the Atlantic world were the Spanish and Portuguese Jews who acknowledged their converso or crypto-Jewish origins in the context of the Portuguese Nation. They had a shared history of persecution, conversion to Christianity, and/or forced exile from Spain and Portugal. This experience was deeply rooted and formed the basis of cultural traditions that had a lasting impact on Sephardic communities in the Caribbean. At the same time—as members of the Portuguese Nation—Sephardic merchants were often transient and readily shifted alliances when circumstances necessitated or when trading opportunities occurred.[1] The experience of many wealthy Amsterdam Sephardic merchants engaged in the Atlantic sugar trade illustrates the dynamics of the trading networks in the westward expansion of sugar cultivation in the seventeenth century.[2] For much of the century, the center of activity for most Sephardic sugar merchants was Amsterdam, which connected Jewish and converso or crypto-Jewish communities in Lisbon, Hamburg, London, Brazil, Barbados, and Jamaica as well as similar communities in the French colonies.[3]

I thank our editors for their insightful and very useful comments on earlier drafts of this chapter.

Historians have introduced the term "Port Jew" to denote Jewish merchants as members of trading communities, transmitting news and purveying goods and services along the Atlantic seaboard and in the Mediterranean and Caribbean world.[4] Wim Klooster describes the first stage in the establishment of Port Jews in the Americas in terms of cross-Atlantic trade that occurred between Portuguese converso merchants in Brazil and Portuguese merchants in Antwerp during the last few decades of the sixteenth century in what Jonathan Israel refers to as the first phase of Dutch Sephardi activity when Portuguese Brazil delivered an increasing amount of sugar to western Europe.[5] The second phase began after the unification of Portugal with Spain in 1580, when many converso merchants moved to Spain and set up business with Spanish American and Portuguese merchants, and their agents settled in Panama, Lima, Buenos Aires, and Cartagena. The third phase began with the blockades and embargoes on Antwerp imposed by the Dutch Republic at the end of the sixteenth century during the Eighty Years' War (1568–1648) with Spain, at which time many converso merchants from Portugal and Antwerp left and settled in Amsterdam, Hamburg, and other ports along Europe's Atlantic seaboard, where they began to profess Judaism openly. During all three phases, New Christian (converso or crypto-Jewish) and Sephardic merchants extended their networks and incorporated more trading partners.

The Dutch Republic emerged as a mercantile core of the Atlantic world and Amsterdam as the commercial center in the Atlantic sugar trade in the late sixteenth and early seventeenth century. It was at that time that Sephardic merchants began to establish themselves as part of the trading regime in the Caribbean region, transferring their trade networks from Brazil in the second quarter of the seventeenth century to the English sugar colony of Barbados, and to Jamaica and the French colony of Martinique in the second half of the century. Being in the vanguard of the emerging sugar production and trade in the Caribbean region and as merchants of the Portuguese Nation in the broader Atlantic world, Sephardic merchants established themselves by bridging the imperial divides of the seventeenth century. It is from this perspective that I will present the multifaceted trade relationships that developed along the Atlantic seaboard and in the Caribbean and discuss the imperial alignments and realignments in political-economic terms and in historical-spatial context. More often than not, being and becoming "entangled" played itself out against the rivalry and competition between the imperial powers that affected the development and expansion of sugar colonies in the Caribbean region, which in turn influenced the trade patterns of Sephardic merchant groups.

Sephardic merchants in Amsterdam in the early seventeenth century were an integral part of the merchant network referred to as the Portuguese Nation initially based in Lisbon, Oporto, and smaller port cities along Portugal's Atlantic coast.[6] Family and kin contacts with New Christian (converso or crypto-Jewish) merchants who had initially engaged in trade along the West Coast of Africa and the Atlantic islands of Madeira and São Tomé formed the core of the trade network as they engaged in the trade of slaves and sugar.[7] When sugar cultivation expanded to Portuguese Brazil, New Christian merchants extended their network of contacts across the Atlantic, and when the Dutch captured and then colonized Pernambuco in northeastern Brazil in 1630, Amsterdam's Sephardic merchants became an integral part of the Atlantic sugar trade network.[8] In the course of the seventeenth century these merchants became importers of Atlantic colonial staple goods, foremost sugar but also tobacco, cacao, ginger, indigo, brazilwood, and various other products that were warehoused and processed in Amsterdam and then distributed throughout northwestern Europe. The merchant network of the Portuguese Nation, including New Christian and Jewish merchants, extended by mid-century to Danzig in the Baltic, Hamburg in north Germany, and London, Bordeaux, and various other port cities in western Europe and the Mediterranean. Merchants engaged in trade via these networks often maintained contact with each other and were able, thereby, to take advantage of various trade opportunities as they presented themselves.[9]

As Amsterdam developed into a major sugar trade, processing, and distribution center and as sugar colonies developed and succeeded each other as leading production centers, the Portuguese merchant networks in the Atlantic trading world transformed repeatedly, and members of the community migrated and relocated frequently, each time reconnecting with other members of the trade network. Several new Jewish communities were established in the Greater Caribbean in the 1650s and 1660s, most of them offshoots of the Brazil-Amsterdam Sephardic merchant community.[10] Jane Gerber characterizes the "Western Sephardi Diaspora," also referred to as the "Portuguese Jewish Diaspora," as a highly mobile merchant community that showcased great flexibility and adaptability in a shifting imperial world.[11] Often, Sephardic merchants continued to trade within the orbit of the Portuguese Nation and kept their trading relationships with Portugal and Spain intact while at the same time freely interacting with the Dutch Republic and port cities along

Europe's Atlantic seaboard. Over time, the Atlantic-oriented Portuguese Jewish merchant communities in the Caribbean region developed their own communities through creolization and became more rooted and interconnected. They shared a common cause, but their cultural roots within the Atlantic world and Amsterdam in particular remained intact.[12]

Sephardic merchants in the Atlantic sugar trade were important, if not crucial, to Amsterdam's expanding sugar market and greatly contributed to Amsterdam's prosperity.[13] As source material for the study of Amsterdam's staple trade I used freight records and protocols in the Notarial Archives in the Amsterdam City Archives.[14] Since the sugar trade was conducted by private merchants either with Dutch Brazil (1630–54) under the auspices of the West India Company or with Barbados and other islands in the Caribbean under British or French colonial rule, freight contracts were drawn up with a notary public in Amsterdam. Merchants and shipping companies or ship masters usually drew up a contract in which they described freight cargo and terms of agreements. The contract might include routes to be sailed, goods to be delivered, and return cargo to be taken on board as well as instructions to deliver within a specified period of time. Loan and insurance arrangements were usually part of the contract. When disputes arose, specific protocols were filed to address the issue and call the guilty party to order. The freight records for the Atlantic and Caribbean sugar trade in the notary public records range in time from 1645 until 1699.[15]

As opposed to the French and the English, the Dutch did not actively pursue colonization in the Caribbean region after they lost control over Brazil by mid-century, but they were heavily engaged in Atlantic colonial commerce, trading, again, both autonomously and under the auspices of the West India Company.[16] Merchants based in the Dutch Republic, including Amsterdam's Sephardic merchants, often engaged in the supply and carrying trade between the French and English colonies and western Europe, delivering supplies to those Caribbean colonies and carrying colonial goods back to Amsterdam. When France and England introduced trade and navigation laws to protect their colonial interest, the relationship changed and became more hostile.[17] Meanwhile, in Amsterdam's staple and distribution market, sugar, coffee, tea, tobacco, and spices were among the most profitable trade goods, and sugar in particular created great wealth in which Sephardic merchants shared.[18]

The "Sephardic Moment" in the Atlantic sugar trade occurred, I contend, during the period of Dutch rule in Brazil from 1630 until 1654 and the sugar boom years in Barbados from the late 1640s until the early 1670s.[19] The economic prosperity of Sephardic merchants in Amsterdam grew significantly in the middle and the second half of the seventeenth century when they also engaged in sugar refining and in the sugar reexport trade.[20] Amsterdam's sugar-processing industry had expanded rapidly in the course of the seventeenth century as records show. Twenty refineries were in production in the Dutch Republic in 1620, forty in 1650, and sixty-six, of which fifty were located in Amsterdam, in 1660. In terms of production, the industry seems to have peaked by the mid-1660s.[21] During the last quarter of the century, when the French sugar colonies developed but retained and processed their own sugar, and Jamaica replaced Barbados as the major sugar supply source for the English market and the commission trade was introduced, the role of Sephardic merchants in the sugar trade was reduced and network merchants reoriented themselves toward intercolonial trade via transit ports such as Willemstad (Curaçao), Oranjestad (Saint Eustatius), and Port Royal (Jamaica). Meanwhile, Amsterdam's Sephardic merchants turned their attention to financing and marketing and became engaged in commodity brokerage and in the London sugar reexport trade.[22]

The Sephardic Moment in Brazil

From the late sixteenth century onward New Christian and Portuguese Jews alongside Dutch merchants were residing and conducting business in Portuguese Brazil. They served as traders and as refiners of sugar and other colonial products when Brazil was still firmly under Portuguese rule. From the records it is not clear if Amsterdam's Portuguese merchants engaged in the sugar trade with Brazil were Sephardim or New Christians, since New Christian merchants in Amsterdam (re)converted to Judaism during the first decades of the century. Jessica Roitman has concluded that the difference between ethnic and religious identification was flexible and that the boundaries blurred when members of the Portuguese Nation shifted alliances as business prospects and opportunities dictated.[23] What is clear from the records is that there were close ties between the emerging Sephardic merchant community in Amsterdam and Brazil's New Christian sugar merchant network.[24]

New Christian merchants had lived in Brazil from the early days of Portuguese colonization, when sugarcane was introduced from Madeira and São Tomé. Some of the most detailed source materials for research on New Christian and Sephardic sugar merchants in Brazil are the records of the earliest Jewish community in Brazil collected by Arnold

Wiznitzer.²⁵ He posited that soon after discovery in 1500, New Christians were listed among the settlers of Brazil and that crypto-Jews were in charge of customs collection.²⁶ Some New Christians suspected of practicing the Jewish faith were sent to Brazil from Portugal shortly after the colonial administration was established in the 1530s. With the unification of Portugal and Spain in 1580, some New Christians in Brazil were persecuted, and the Holy Office in Bahia reported that there were many "persons of the Nation" in the province who professed Catholicism but secretly observed Jewish rites and customs. A visitation by the Holy Office in Pernambuco between 1593 and 1595 uncovered that a synagogue on the plantation of one of the suspects was the center of activity among Judaizers in Pernambuco.²⁷

Suspicions about Judaizing among "Men of the Nation" and collaboration with Jewish merchants abroad threatened the position of New Christians, which led to a further harshening of conditions in Portugal, from where a new exodus of conversos occurred in the late sixteenth century. Many moved to Brazil, while others relocated to the periphery of the Habsburg realm in northwestern Europe where they settled in Rouen or Antwerp, or further afield in Amsterdam and Hamburg.²⁸ Close personal and family connections between Portuguese merchants meant that numerous Portuguese New Christians were either related to or had associations with members of the Portuguese merchant community abroad, some of whom lived openly as Jews. Thus, association with Jewish merchants abroad jeopardized the New Christian merchants' existence in Spain and Portugal but also offered opportunities to seek refuge and trade with members of the Portuguese Nation elsewhere, including Jewish communities.

Visitations of the Holy Office in Bahia in 1618 and 1619 led to an assortment of accusations and denunciations that revealed contacts between Brazil, Antwerp, and Amsterdam Portuguese merchant families. For about twenty-five years, New Christians and crypto-Jews of Brazil and Antwerp and openly professing Portuguese Jewish merchants from Amsterdam had been in contact with each other through trade. They played the leading role in organizing the export of sugar from Brazil, and through their family and business connections with New Christian merchants in Portugal, the Amsterdam Sephardic merchant families thrived.²⁹ By 1618, crypto-Jews were no longer called New Christians in the records of the Holy Office in Bahia but were referred to as members of the Hebrew Nation; the same term was used in Amsterdam to denote Sephardic immigrants of the Portuguese Nation.³⁰ As Wiznitzer noted, the denunciations of New Christians were replete with references to Flanders and Amsterdam and the people who lived there and emigrated to and from Brazil.[31]

The estimate is that Amsterdam imported more than half of Brazil's sugar by the end of the first decade of the seventeenth century and that most of the sugar exported to Europe was transported in Dutch ships. Trade with Antwerp and Hamburg was linked to Amsterdam through Portuguese merchant networks, and together the three ports likely absorbed at least 75 percent of Europe's Brazilian sugar imports during the relatively open trade era of 1609-21, when a truce was observed during the Eighty Years' War. In fact, the value of the Brazil trade (most of which was sugar) is estimated to have been one-half or perhaps three-quarters of the total annual commerce of the Dutch Republic at that time.[32]

After 1621, when the truce ended and Spanish and Portuguese trade embargoes were again imposed on Dutch shipping, the sugar trade was severely interrupted, but most of the sugar, legally or illegally, still ended up being transported to Amsterdam via the merchant networks that were now well established between Brazil, Portugal, and the Dutch Republic. Contraband trade thrived under the conditions of attacks at sea and port embargoes. Merchants exchanging goods via their trade networks changed shipping routes and chose to sail under a different flag as circumstances dictated or allowed.[33] Jonathan Israel maintains that it was with the advent of Brazilian sugar entering the European markets via Lisbon and Amsterdam that a significant Portuguese Atlantic merchant network was established. In fact, he argues that the sugar trade cemented the emerging Sephardic merchant community in Amsterdam.[34] The sugar trade with Brazil generated a large pool of crypto-Jewish and Sephardic merchants engaged in and orientated toward Atlantic commerce, and when the Dutch took control of Pernambuco in 1630, this merchant community was instrumental in generating the most profitable trade for Amsterdam and the Dutch Republic.[35]

To undermine the Habsburg Empire, but also to protect and expand its interest in the sugar trade when war resumed in 1621, the Dutch founded the West India Company (WIC) and shortly thereafter captured Salvador da Bahia (1624) in Brazil in order to more firmly secure the sugar trade, which was jeopardized by Spanish trade embargoes.[36] After the short-lived Dutch occupation of Salvador, the WIC captured Pernambuco in 1630.

The Dutch occupation of Pernambuco proved to be quite profitable for Sephardic merchants from Amsterdam and Portuguese merchants in Brazil during Dutch colonial rule (1630-54).[37] For a while the sugar industry and trade were disrupted as many *engenhos* and sugar mills were destroyed and abandoned by Portuguese planter-settlers at the start of Dutch occupation and the WIC confiscated many mills and other properties that were subsequently sold to Dutch investors. The situation stabilized when the WIC appointed Johan Maurits of Nassau as governor of the colony in 1637. During the years of his administration from 1637 until 1644, Jews were guaranteed religious freedom and private merchants were offered commercial opportunities, and in 1639, the Dutch authorities agreed to Johan Maurits's proposals to allow the supply and sugar trade with Brazil to be conducted by shareholders of the West India Company.[38] This encouraged Sephardic merchants from Amsterdam to exchange goods in Brazil for sugar. Combined with the promise of religious toleration, this measure set in motion a new wave of immigration to Dutch Brazil that included many Portuguese Jews.[39] In the next few years Sephardic merchants played an increasingly important role in the supply and sugar trade to and from Brazil, as money lenders for slave purchases, financiers for sugar mill owners, owners of *engenhos*, and tax farmers.

Estimates are that perhaps more than a thousand Sephardic merchants made the crossing to northeast Brazil from the Dutch Republic in the decade after 1635. Many of them were well-to-do, but there were poor immigrants among them as well.[40] During this period, private merchants—many of them Portuguese Jews—accounted for more than two-thirds of the value of trade, while the WIC accounted for the remainder.[41] The colony rapidly expanded its sugar cultivation, and the high point of sugar production and export from Dutch Brazil occurred during the decade of the mid-1630s to the mid-1640s.[42] In order to facilitate the expansion, the WIC extended credit and loans to planters and mill owners while conducting the slave trade with the Guinea Coast and Angola on its own account. This allowed the planters to acquire slaves and more land and make investments in sugar cultivation. We do not know the exact extent of Jewish participation in business activities under the auspices of the WIC as most of the archival records were destroyed, but incidental evidence suggests that the participation rate was significant.[43] It was in this climate of prosperity and mutual dependency between the Sephardic community and the WIC that the Dutch authorities allowed Jewish religious practices to be openly conducted in Dutch Brazil. The first synagogue in the Americas was established in Recife in Pernambuco, and the first rabbi appointed in 1639.[44]

The WIC lost some of its monopolies but retained those in the slave trade and the trade in arms, ammunition, and dyewood (brazilwood).

According to the best estimate a total of twenty-six thousand slaves from West Africa were traded by the WIC between 1631 and 1651.[45] Slaves were sold on credit in Brazil with payment due in sugar at the next harvest. To avoid incurring bad debts, the WIC's board of directors ruled in 1644 that slaves could only be traded for cash. This ruling made it more difficult for Portuguese planters to expand sugar cultivation but opened up opportunities for Jewish merchants who as middlemen bought slaves at greatly reduced prices in cash and then sold them on credit to plantation owners.

Most of the sugar plantations continued to be owned and operated by Portuguese planters, mill owners, and managers. In 1645, the planters revolted against Dutch rule. Consequently, both sugar exports and slave imports dropped precipitously in one year.[46] As the rebellion was the beginning of the end of Dutch rule in Brazil, Sephardic merchants began to leave the colony, either returning to Amsterdam or moving to ports in the Caribbean region where they established new network connections or reinforced those already in place.[47] By the early 1650s, the Sephardic population of Dutch Brazil had been reduced to around 650, and at the time of the Dutch surrender in 1654 it is estimated that only a few hundred were still residing in Brazil. That year the last group of Sephardic merchant families left Brazil on three voyages with different destinations, but most returned to Amsterdam. Later on, several Jews relocated to islands and coastal areas in the Caribbean region and found their way to newly established Dutch colonies including Nova Zeelandia in Western Guyana, the Dutch colony of Curaçao, and the island of Cayenne. In addition, Portuguese Jews migrated to the English colonies of Suriname (which later became a Dutch colony) and Barbados.

In summary, during the seven years of Johan Maurits's rule, Jewish immigration to Brazil had reached its peak and Amsterdam's Sephardic merchants had increased their economic power considerably.[48] Meanwhile, the Sephardic community in Brazil had established its own synagogues and had appointed rabbis from the Amsterdam congregation to serve their community. The community had also established important merchant networks connecting Amsterdam and Brazil, and Jewish merchants had become active participants in the WIC whereupon they were granted trade privileges. In addition, they held most of the tax farming licenses with the Dutch authorities and conducted a large share of the private supply and sugar trade. In other words, they were well established in Brazil and for that they were also envied.

Both the West India Company and Amsterdam's Sephardic merchant community continued to play a role in sugar cultivation and trade in the Caribbean and Atlantic world. Several Sephardic merchant families established themselves in the English colonies, including Barbados, Suriname, and later Jamaica, where many remained engaged in the sugar trade.[49] Some Sephardic families followed leaders like David Cohen Nassi who founded new colonies under Dutch rule in the 1650s and 1660s. These colonies were mostly short-lived or occupied by other European powers as in the case of Cayenne, which became a French colony in 1664. Dutch authorities supported the efforts to establish new colonies and aided Sephardic merchants in their recruitment efforts in whichever way they could. Meanwhile, some Amsterdam Sephardic merchants began to trade alongside other merchants from Amsterdam in the supply and carrying trade with Barbados and Jamaica in the 1650s and 1660s.

The Sephardic Moment in Barbados and Other English Colonies

In the mid-seventeenth century, Barbados's rather diverse small-scale plantation economy based on tobacco and cotton changed to a much larger-scale and more specialized sugar plantation economy based on slave labor.[50] Englishmen and Frenchmen had settled several small islands in the eastern Caribbean region in the 1620s, and by the late 1640s, they were making significant investments in developing plantation economies. Barbados, founded as an English colony in 1627, engaged not only merchants from England but also Dutch merchants who provided the island with supplies and carried colonial produce to market in Amsterdam. In fact, Dutch merchants conducted a good deal of the carrying trade for the island, including tobacco, during the early decades of settlement and, if Richard Ligon is to be believed, Dutch merchants were instrumental in introducing sugar cultivation to the island during the mid-century.[51] Although the "Myth of the Dutch" is now mostly discarded and actual active Dutch involvement in introducing sugar to Barbados is not evident, freight records in the Notarial Archives of Amsterdam's Stadsarchief show a pattern of trade with Barbados in the 1650s that illustrates the sugar trade conducted with the island that involved Sephardic merchants from Amsterdam.[52] The earliest written records referring to Jewish merchants resident in Barbados date from 1654, when a request was made to the Council of Barbados endorsed by the Dutch WIC to admit Jews from Brazil.[53] It is conceivable that some

Amsterdam Sephardic immigrants who had come from Brazil resided in Barbados before 1654.

Sugarcane had been introduced to Barbados in 1637, but until the mid-1640s, tobacco and cotton were still the primary export staple goods. During the 1640s these crops began to lose their appeal when a glut on the European market caused by the cultivation of tobacco and cotton grown in the English colonies in North America forced prices to drop. After 1645, when prices on the Amsterdam sugar market increased due to the downturn in production in Brazil, sugar as a plantation crop began to take hold in Barbados. Sugar production boomed in Barbados from the mid-1640s to mid-1650s, when the crop became the main source of wealth for English planters on the island.[54] At the same time, the Dutch West India Company sent slaves to market in Barbados. Slaves purchased at the West Coast of Africa, but undeliverable in Brazil due to the planters' uprising in 1645, were brought to the Lesser Antilles and Barbados, where they were sold on lenient credit terms.[55] From 1653 onward when the WIC was on the brink of bankruptcy, the company also allowed private merchants to sell slaves in the English and French Caribbean islands, and freight records indicate that Sephardic merchants on Barbados took part in the enterprise, but how many or how frequently slave deliveries were made by Dutch or Sephardic merchants remains unclear. As Barbados's planters experimented with sugar cultivation in the 1640s, it is likely that various elements of Brazil's sugar plantation complex were transferred to Barbados with the help of Dutch and Sephardic merchants.[56] The interests of Dutch and Sephardic merchants and Barbadian planters matched; planters depended on Dutch provisions, and Amsterdam's Dutch and Sephardic merchants needed new commodity supplies for the growing sugar market in Europe and new markets for slaves when Brazil was lost.

The success in the supply and carrying trade of the Dutch and Sephardic merchants led to an attempt to curtail Dutch trade by implementing the First Trade and Navigation Act in 1651. The act dictated that all colonial staple goods be shipped to England in vessels owned and manned by Englishmen or English colonial merchants and that European goods could only be transported by English ships or those of the country where the goods were produced. This greatly reduced commercial opportunities for Dutch merchants as Amsterdam was a staple port and warehoused more than just the goods originating from the Dutch Republic. For Sephardic merchants the situation was different as they stood prepared to transfer their residency and business to the English colonies and, in effect, change their orbit of operations to London or Bristol and other port cities in Europe. Initially, the Trade and Navigation Acts were ignored, and the Dutch supply and carrying trade continued as planters preferred to trade with Dutch merchants and extended their welcome to Sephardic merchants who had begun to arrive from Brazil and Amsterdam.[57] During the years 1653-58, merchants were able to circumvent the Trade and Navigation Act as the Cromwellian Protectorate tried to implement his Western Design for the development of English colonies in the Caribbean by engaging Amsterdam's Sephardic merchants. Subsequent acts imposed in 1660 and 1663 had more effect and eventually made merchants based in the Dutch Republic cut their close ties to Barbados.[58] Subsequently, Dutch merchants turned their attention to the French colonies in the Caribbean, but after the French imposed their trade ordinances in 1664 and 1673, much the same happened. All along and of increasing importance to the Amsterdam sugar market was the separate supply that emerged from Sephardic merchants engaged in the intercolonial trade and the reexport trade from London. Eventually, the Amsterdam sugar market succumbed to mercantilist pressures, and toward the end of the seventeenth century, the city's European sugar trade share had declined.[59]

Although the Dutch and Sephardic merchants linked to the Amsterdam staple market were disadvantaged by the passing of the 1651 Trade and Navigation Act, the impact was initially fairly limited as the English depended on the existing Atlantic trading network. But fairly soon, Oliver Cromwell realized that he had to tap into the Sephardic merchant network in order to carry out his plan for developing Barbados as a sugar colony as part of his Western Design. At the conclusion of the First Anglo-Dutch War (1652-54) a concerted effort between Cromwell, as Lord Protector, and Menasseh ben Israel, as leader of the Amsterdam Sephardic community, was undertaken to accommodate the Amsterdam Portuguese Jewish community's desire to establish residency in the English colonies. Amsterdam's Sephardic merchant population had increased in number after the return from Brazil and sought to expand commercial opportunities. In 1655, Cromwell invited Menasseh to address Whitehall (House of Parliament) with the request to allow Jews to be admitted as legal residents of England and by extension the English colonies.[60] Even though official admission by Parliament was denied after a special conference at Whitehall had been held, Cromwell proceeded with his own plan and assured London's crypto-Jewish merchants that they could conduct religious services in the privacy of their homes and that they would receive his personal protection as residents and merchants of London.[61] Over time, Sephardim who settled in London included merchants and commodity brokers engaged in trade with the Canary Islands, Barbados, and Jamaica, and some were involved in the sugar reexport trade with Amsterdam.[62]

Meanwhile, a growing number of Sephardic merchants from Brazil had relocated to Caribbean colonies, including Barbados.[63] Thus, over time, pressure mounted to extend English citizen rights or denizen rights to Jewish merchants in the colonies in order to allow them to conduct trade legally under the dictates of Trade and Navigation Acts. These merchants included Sephardim from Dutch Brazil who had first returned to Amsterdam and thereafter settled in the English and French colonies.[64] Amsterdam's Sephardic merchants remained actively involved in the Atlantic sugar business throughout the 1650s and 1660s, now also trading with both the French and English colonies. During Cromwell's reign in the 1650s, many English Royalist merchants had collaborated with the Dutch Republic in commercial enterprise and viewed the role of Amsterdam's Sephardic merchants as crucial in the Atlantic sugar trade.[65] In this relationship, the limitations and restrictions of the Trade and Navigation Acts were considered inconvenient but not an obstacle to trade as prominent merchants in London, among them crypto-Jewish merchants, requested denization papers for Amsterdam's Sephardic merchants in order to help develop the sugar trade with the English colonies and supply the London market. With the restoration of royal rule in England in 1660, this strategy continued, and most of the denization requests granted to Amsterdam and Barbados merchants were issued during the decade of the 1660s.[66] Of the 190 grants of endenization made to Jews in the English colonies between 1660 and 1700, seventy-two were issued to residents of Barbados or to Jews of London or Jamaica who had previously settled in Barbados.[67] The fee for applying for and obtaining endenization papers was substantial and thus likely not sought by poor immigrant merchants. Many of the well-to-do merchant families who obtained endenization letters lived or had contacts in London and other British colonies. From biographical information contained in the records it is evident that the Sephardic community comprised very few planters and that most Jewish freehold and leasehold properties were merchant properties in Bridgetown.[68]

The Sephardic Moment in the Atlantic Sugar Trade

In the discussion of Jewish trade in the Atlantic world in the seventeenth century, Pieter Emmer and Seymour Drescher have referred to the start of a second Atlantic system in which the Spanish and Portuguese were replaced by the English and the French as the major colonial powers.[69] In their opinion, the Sephardic Moment or Jewish Moment ended with the arrival and expansion of the second Atlantic system when the sheer volume of colonial trade demanded metropolitan trading companies to deliver the goods, and mercantilist policies dictated commercial relationships. In this transition, Pieter Emmer called the Sephardic merchants the "midwives" of the second European expansion system, spawning the transition but then being cast aside.[70] Drescher contends that in the Dutch realm the Sephardim played a more durable role in the slave trade. He calls the Jewish merchants the "pegs and nails," although not the "architects and master builders" in a world controlled by mercantilist principles.[71] In light of the discussion so far this would seem a reasonable assessment, but I contend that the Sephardic merchant network sustained the sugar trade centered on Amsterdam for an extended period of time in the second half of the seventeenth century. The city's fifty refineries in 1660 (and sixteen more in Rotterdam and Middelburg) processed more than half of all the refined sugar consumed in Europe at the time, and we know from the record that among the refiners were several converso and Sephardic merchants, some of whom had migrated to Amsterdam from Portugal or Spain or relocated to Amsterdam from Brazil.[72] This group included leading merchants and bankers with familiar names like de Pinto, Pereira, Suasso, da Costa, Teixeira, Henriques, and de Mezquita (among others), and many of these family names reappear in the records of Barbados and Jamaica. Many of the families had a financial interest in the sugar trade and processing industry and were well integrated into Amsterdam's financial establishment, which benefited the Atlantic sugar trade, including the sugar reexport trade from London to Amsterdam and the trade from Curaçao and Saint Eustatius. In fact, Amsterdam remained the main staple port for sugar and other commodities from the Caribbean region for distribution to the European market.[73]

After the fall of Dutch Brazil, Sephardic merchants formed new nodes and networks in the Atlantic by requesting and receiving denization papers and taking up residency in the English colonies and in London.[74] Meanwhile, Amsterdam's sugar trade and refining capacity increased significantly and experienced its boom years in the 1660s.[75] Obviously, the Dutch sugar trade continued after Dutch Brazil was lost, and Amsterdam remained the primary processing and distribution center for the European market for a good part of the seventeenth century.[76] As noted, among Amsterdam's sugar merchants and refiners in the mid-seventeenth century were several converso merchants who had migrated to Amsterdam in the 1640s and 1650s and had traded sugar with Lisbon and Oporto prior to transferring their business to Amsterdam. In Amsterdam they aligned themselves with the Sephardic merchant community. The new arrivals included immigrants from Castile, where the Inquisition had once again become active in pursuing New Christian Portuguese merchants. These men were drawn to Amsterdam as new business opportunities occurred after a peace settlement was signed in 1648 between the Dutch Republic and Spain, ending the Eighty Years' War. With the new impulse of capital, which was much needed after the collapse of Dutch Brazil, the Amsterdam Sephardic community experienced another economic boom that facilitated a reorientation. Although Dutch sugar refiners had tried to prevent members of the Portuguese or Hebrew Nation from entering the processing industry, at least four sugar refineries were operated by Sephardic merchants in the late 1650s. None stayed in the refining business for very long, and all but one of the Jewish sugar refiners had sold their business by the end of the 1660s.[77] We assume that they foresaw that the more stringent English Trade and Navigation Acts of the 1660s and the French Navigation Act of 1664 would lead to a decline in the supply trade of raw sugar to the Amsterdam market.

Still, the intriguing question remains why the Amsterdam sugar refining capacity increased after 1650 and peaked in the 1660s when import of sugar from Dutch Brazil had declined and halted and Suriname had not begun to produce for the Dutch market yet. Beyond the scope of this chapter but worthy to be studied in the future is the role French sugar colonies played in the sugar trade with Amsterdam. It is well known that the Dutch engaged in trade with the French colonies and that Sephardic merchants residing in Martinique, Guadeloupe, and Cayenne engaged in the sugar trade in the 1660s.[78] In the meantime, Barbados experienced its sugar boom years, and the first wave of Jewish immigration to the English colony occurred in the 1650s. Thus, the Sephardic Moment extended during the decade of transition and western expansion of the Atlantic sugar trade from Dutch Brazil to the English and French colonies. During the sugar boom years in Barbados from the late 1640s until the1670s and for some time thereafter, English merchant elites engaged in partnerships with members of the Portuguese Nation and leaders of Amsterdam's Sephardic congregation to transplant the sugar trade network centered on Sephardic merchants and facilitated their integration into the English sugar market by requesting and granting denization for Jewish residents. During the last quarter of the century, when the French sugar colonies developed but retained and processed their own sugar, and when Jamaica replaced Barbados as the major sugar supply source for the English market and implemented the commission trade system, the role of Sephardic merchants in the Caribbean sugar trade was reduced. Sephardic network merchants then began to reorient themselves toward Caribbean intercolonial trade conducted via transit ports. Meanwhile, Amsterdam's Sephardic merchants turned their attention to financing and marketing and became engaged in commodity brokerage and the London reexport trade. Their days in the sugar business were now behind them.

Chapter 4

Trading Violence
Four Jewish Soldiers between Atlantic Empires (ca. 1600–1655)

Victor Tiribás

On the morning of February 15, 1630, the fleet of the West India Company (WIC) emerged on the horizon off the coast of Pernambuco, in northern Brazil. The sixty-seven vessels, which had departed from Texel three months earlier, were carrying more than seven thousand troops, including some Jewish soldiers. According to friar Manoel Calado, the armada "started firing so many shells with the artillery that it look[ed] like they were raining from the sea to the land." Portuguese settlers escaped in an uproar, abandoning their properties and possessions. Parents were separated from their children, husbands lost their wives while escaping, "and so each one ended up where his strength had failed him, and where his fortune, or misfortune, took him." In the words of Calado himself, "the fear was great, the danger was certain, death was present."[1]

This essay follows the paths of four Jewish soldiers who fought among the WIC's troops and conquered, garrisoned, and eventually lost northern Brazil between 1630 and 1654: Moisés Cohen Henriques alias

---

I thank Wim Klooster and Aviva Ben-Ur for their invaluable comments, and also Lucia Furquim Xavier, who helped me decipher some notarial documents in Dutch. I thank Mallory Hope for her careful revision and suggestions. I am finally indebted to Ton Tielen and the anonymous peer reviewers. All translations of documents are mine, unless otherwise indicated.

Antônio Vaz Henriques; his brother, Lieutenant Jacob Cohen Henriques alias Jerônimo Vaz Henriques; Captain Moisés Cohen Peixoto alias Diogo Lourenço Peixoto; and his brother, Lieutenant Joshua Cohen Peixoto alias Antônio Mendes Peixoto.

With very few exceptions, the theme of Jews' military service in early modern armies has been neglected in scholarship.[2] Although Jews are featured in some studies as financiers of wars and army contractors, scholars rarely acknowledge that they did some of the fighting on the ground.[3] This choice, I believe, reflects a widespread tendency in Jewish studies to prefer "trading diaspora" as the model for how Jews participated in the early modern empires. Employing the softer vocabulary of "milder colonization" to describe Jewish participation in the Atlantic empires,[4] the narrative of "trading diaspora" detaches Jewish traders from the inherent violence (physical and symbolic) of imperial expansion. A further consequence of the "trading diaspora" model is to reduce the Americas to a place of mere economic exploitation and confine connectivity to trade.

By analyzing the lives of four soldiers, this essay reintroduces the theme of violence in the encounter between Judaism and the Americas. The period of Dutch control in northern Brazil marked a turning point in Jewish history, when Jews became more explicitly what some scholars called "colonized colonizers"—that is, they participated in colonial oppression as part of a local elite while still subjected to the religious prejudices of other groups.[5] In this sense, the trajectory of Jewish soldiers can be exemplary: at the same time that they killed and died in the name of Protestant empires and participated in the Atlantic slave trade, they were excluded from promotion to high rank because of their religious beliefs, commanding only other marginalized groups like Indigenous Americans and Africans. One of this essay's fundamental questions is this: Why did Jews choose military service when they experienced prejudice and limitations on their ascension in early modern armies, not to mention the possibility of death or disability?

Increasingly, there is a shared understanding among historians that behind the choices of conversos and Jews "was fundamentally a quest for social and material security."[6] For example, based on the inquisitorial trials of merchants who shifted between Catholicism and Judaism, David Graizbord argued that these renegades and returnees shared a "pragmatic religious mentality," that is, a willingness to accommodate the expression of their religious identities to economic opportunities.[7] According to Adam Sutcliffe, these conclusions may be extended to the Atlantic context, where traversing frontiers required "radical pragmatism."[8] In the hope of achieving commercial prosperity, Iberian Jews allegedly cultivated an ability to adapt to circumstances: "fluidity of identity" and "weak political loyalties" were hallmarks of the diaspora's economic strength.[9] Martyrs and soldiers, however, are not normally among the historical subjects of scholars who insist on the commercial pragmatism of Jews within the diaspora.

Parting ways with this historiography, I show that Jewish men joined the army out of a desire for status and religious zeal. The soldiers at the center of this essay received a solid education in Judaism and achieved social ascension within their communities through military service. None of the four soldiers treated in this essay ever oscillated in their faith once they started to serve. Public demonstrations of honor and courage lent soldiers prestige among their coreligionists and allowed them to assume religious and political leadership roles. As we shall see, their decision to fight Catholics and settle in the Americas was related to messianic prophecies about the dispersion of the Jews and the arrival of the fifth monarchy. Fighting for the Dutch WIC also presented an opportunity to seek vengeance for inquisitorial persecution. Poems written by two of this essay's subjects clearly drew parallels between the figure of the soldier and that of the martyr. In sum, though marginalized in scholarship, soldiers occupied a central role in the Jewish diaspora side by side with merchants and rabbis. Through military service they expressed their Jewishness, reinforcing, rather than weakening, their ties with Judaism.

The trajectories of the brothers Cohen Peixoto and the brothers Cohen Henriques connect Jewish hubs in the Atlantic, Europe, and the Mediterranean. They underline the need to reconsider the Jewish diaspora on a global scale, without losing sight of individuals, the close analysis of primary sources, or the concept of the Atlantic world as a unified, distinctive region.[10] The stories of these four soldiers will provide a medium for reflecting on entanglement between empires, religions, and ethnicities.

The first section centers on the roles of the soldiers Moisés Cohen Henriques and the brothers Moisés and Joshua Cohen Peixoto in the Dutch invasion of northern Brazil, probing the limits and obstacles to Jews' integration into the WIC's multiconfessional troops, and showing how early modern armies can be fruitful spaces for studying cultural history. The second and third sections focus respectively on the trajectories of the brothers Cohen Peixoto and Cohen Henriques to examine more closely their familial backgrounds and religious education, their strategic marriages and economic situations, and their first steps in their military careers. Such a reconstruction will allow us to better understand why these four soldiers joined the WIC's army. The fourth and last section continues with the soldiers' activities after the completion of their service in Dutch Brazil and their embodiment of what I have called the "colonial metamorphosis" of Judaism.[11] We will observe the soldiers acting as community leaders and informal rabbis. The theme of violence will reemerge with the participation of the Jews in the Atlantic slave trade, in their clashes with Christian authorities, and in the start of a new war between 1645 and 1654, when Portuguese settlers rebelled against the Dutch occupation.

A Babylonian Army

The WIC troops who landed on Pau Amarelo beach on February 15, 1630, constituted a Babylonian army. Dutch Calvinists, French Catholics, English Anglicans, German Lutherans, and Iberian Jews marched side by side. The company itself had encouraged such a multilinguistic and multiconfessional military configuration, publishing regulations in 1629 and 1634 that guaranteed freedom of religious conscience overseas to increase the number of enlistments.[12] It took only a few hours for WIC soldiers to subdue the capital Olinda, and in a matter of days the city of Recife and the island of Santo Antônio also fell. For years the Company's board of directors (*Heeren XIX*) had carefully planned the invasion of Pernambuco. They collected information about the captaincy through the reports of Indigenous Americans brought to the United Provinces, veterans of the attack on Bahia in 1624, as well as Jews and New Christians who had lived in the colony.[13]

Because some of the Jewish soldiers knew the region and Portuguese language well, they served as guides and translators during the invasion, and sometimes even represented the WIC as envoys to seal alliances with the Indigenous nations in Pernambuco's hinterlands.[14] One of these advisers aboard the invading squadron was Moisés Cohen Henriques. According to an inquisitorial denunciation, he "went with the said Hollanders and instructed them and gave them plans showing how to take the said place, for he had spent many days in the said Pernambuco and was well acquainted with the entrances and the exits."[15] Moisés then certainly participated in the violent sack of Recife described by Calado, perhaps even destroying the Catholic statues of saints alongside Protestant soldiers of the company.[16]

But if the *Heeren XIX* had carefully planned the invasion of Pernambuco, the occupation was not as well plotted. The commanders of the

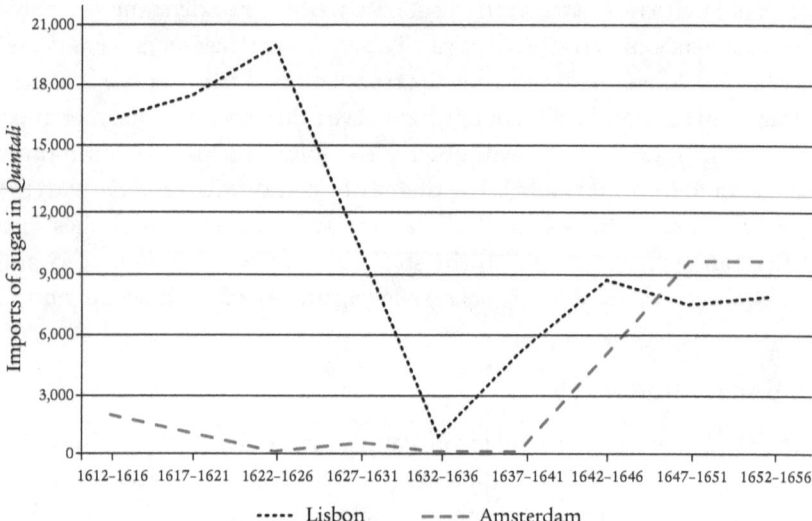

FIGURE 4.1. Import of sugar to Livorno from Lisbon and Amsterdam, five-year average. Source: Renato Ghezzi, *Livorno e l'Atlantico: I commerci olandesi nel Mediterraneo del Seicento* (Bari: Cacucci, 2011), 155–57.

WIC army soon realized that Olinda's location and the surrounding terrain would not allow for its fortification, leaving them no choice but to set the city on fire and transfer the capital to Recife. Moreover, Luso-Brazilian troops continually organized raids and guerrilla attacks in a style of fighting totally alien to the Dutch invaders that became known as "Brazilian war" (*guerra brasílica*).[17] As a result, the WIC's army reached an impasse, which disrupted the local sugar economy and impacted the transatlantic networks of Iberian Jews as far as Tuscany. In the most critical years of the war (1630–36), Livorno's importation of sugar from Lisbon abruptly decreased, while imports from Amsterdam increased immediately after the Dutch had consolidated their control of the colony.[18]

Though Moisés Cohen Henriques's deployment only lasted until 1631, it was long enough for him to share in the war's hardships. Without access to the sugar mills in the countryside, the WIC racked up debts on the order of millions of florins.[19] But the soldiers suffered the human costs of the stalemate. Unable to penetrate the territory, they were deprived of access to first-rate supplies. Little by little, reports of starvation among the soldiers began to arrive in Amsterdam through alternative channels, undermining the company's propaganda in the newspapers.[20]

The soldiers' basic diet was supposed to consist of bread, meat, vinegar, olive oil, and bacon and was to be distributed according to the portions indicated in the "charter" (*rantsoen-brieff*) of each officer. Soldiers stationed in Brazil, however, were forced to supplement meals by hunting wild doves and capybaras, collecting seaweed and fruit, or fishing. During expeditions in the countryside or during sieges, dogs, cats, horses, mice, and iguanas entered the menu.[21] Diseases such as scurvy, dysentery, and night blindness proliferated as a result of the shortage.[22] The historical literature on soldiers' experiences in the WIC army makes no mention of dietary accommodations for Jewish soldiers. It is also unclear how Jewish soldiers classified and related to local food sources, when many were seeing Brazilian fauna and flora for the first time. Under extreme conditions and the threat of starvation, they probably allowed themselves to violate the dietary law (kashrut).[23]

This Babylonian army of underpaid, underdressed, and malnourished men slowly and with great sacrifice gained headway in the war. New alliances with local Indigenous groups and the betrayals of crucial figures in the Luso-Brazilian resistance finally tipped the balance in favor of the Dutch.[24] In 1634, the WIC continued to invest heavily in breaking through the Luso-Brazilian siege, sending over 3,500 soldiers to consolidate its conquest.[25] It was during this influx of recruits that the brothers Captain Moisés Cohen Peixoto and Lieutenant Joshua Cohen Peixoto landed in Brazil.

According to an inquisitorial denunciation in Madrid, Moisés had recruited a "company of rebels" to go to Pernambuco and fight against "the Catholics that live there."[26] His troops comprised about a hundred Iberian Jews and Ashkenazim, including a physician, an apothecary, a barber, a preacher, and a Hebrew teacher. A second source confirmed that "two Dutch ships" arrived in Recife, "and they brought eighty or one hundred Jews as soldiers."[27] The presence of these medical and religious personnel alongside the combatants indicates both the kind of assistance that Jews may have needed in war and the regiment's intentions to settle in Dutch Brazil in the long term. Moisés also brought his younger brother Joshua along as his lieutenant. Most of the company crossed the Atlantic under Peixoto's command on the ship *Las Tres Torres*, which sailed with a mainly African-descended crew.[28]

Jewish soldiers usually traveled and fought in groups with their coreligionists, sometimes even with family members. The presence of a military installation called the "Sentinel of the Jews" in the outskirts of Olinda is one piece of evidence that there were distinctly Jewish companies in the WIC forces.²⁹ Jews served together for safety reasons. The religious stereotypes that permeated daily life in early modern Europe probably manifested themselves in their most aggressive forms within the army. Long Atlantic voyages, crowded camps during campaigns, and uncertain expeditions through the hinterlands created a powder keg for the tenuous alliances in the WIC's Babylonian army. Caspar Barlaeus did not hesitate to defame the Jewish soldiers of Dutch Brazil during the Portuguese insurrection of 1645, claiming that "the loyalty of the Jews, who were by nature inclined to underhanded practices, could not be trusted."³⁰ In this hostile context, it seems quite likely that any Jew traveling alone would be easy prey for every sort of abuse, such as WIC sailors' tradition of "baptizing" green recruits by submerging them in the sea on the way to the Americas.³¹

Captain Peixoto and his company of rebels certainly fought in the Paraíba campaign in November 1634. The offensive brought "a lot of bloodshed" for both sides and marked the beginning of the end of the Luso-Brazilian resistance.³² As we shall see, Moisés's younger brother, Lieutenant Joshua, died in one of these battles. After the bitter victory, Moisés remained in Paraíba. In January of the following year, Dutch authorities signed the "Capitulations of Paraíba" (1635), which enumerated the rights of residents throughout the occupied territory and extended liberty of conscience to Catholics. Once the invasion was over, colonial administrators were tasked with encouraging new settlement of the territory and with managing peaceful coexistence between the members of the Babylonian army, civilian immigrants, and local populations. Such religious and ethnic plurality was unprecedented in Europe. Dutch Brazil would become a true social laboratory, from which Judaism would emerge transformed.

Before moving on to the colonial metamorphosis to which our soldiers would be subjected, it is useful to understand who these characters were prior to their arrival in Pernambuco. What was their family background? What sort of Jewish education did they receive? Where did they acquire military experience? And why did they choose to fight for the Dutch?

Martial Honor and Prestige

Moisés Cohen Peixoto was probably born in Lamego, Portugal, between 1581 and 1593.³³ His brother and faithful comrade in battle, Joshua, came into the world a few years later, around 1597.³⁴ Aside from this scant information concerning their birth, little is known about either their family or their past in the Iberian Peninsula.[35] Around 1611 Moisés migrated to Livorno, a city that was gradually becoming a nodal port in the Mediterranean and a center of the Jewish diaspora.[36] In that period, however, he was still living publicly as a Catholic, known by his baptismal name, Diego Lorenzo Pisciotto, in the Italian style. His sojourn in Livorno was brief and tumultuous. A young man, Peixoto showed himself to be a trickster and a brawler who was jealous of his honor.

Behind the commercial success of Livorno lay a set of privileges known as *livornine* (1591–93), which assured Jewish merchants liberties that were unprecedented in Catholic territories. The *livornine* granted the community judicial autonomy, the cancellation of all previous debts, and exemption from inquisitorial examination for past apostasies. The charter also enabled Jews to acquire property, hire Christian servants, and live outside a ghetto.[37] Since Iberian Jews and New Christians spoke the same language, dressed similarly, and did business together, distinctions between the two groups became blurred, making room for many rumors and intrigues.[38] People in Livorno soon learned how to take advantage of this ambiguity, and through false denunciations sought to destroy the reputation of their enemies and commercial competitors, manipulating the Inquisition for personal ends.

On Christmas 1611, Peixoto requested an audience with the inquisitor of Pisa. He presented himself as a prosperous Portuguese merchant who wished to make a complaint to discharge his Catholic conscience.[39] Armed with an interpreter, Peixoto reported that a certain Dona Maria de Castro, a Portuguese resident of Livorno, had never attended church, always talked to Jews, and observed the Sabbath. He accused her of being a Judaizer, to which Dona Maria responded with the same counteraccusation. As investigations progressed, it was revealed that at the root of what appeared to be a disinterested accusation was a commercial dispute between Peixoto and Dona Maria. In this instance, the inquisitor suspended the trial without proclaiming a sentence, but it would not be long before the hot-headed Peixoto got into another mess.

In September 1612, a group of Jews was talking in front of the tailor Moisés Salama's shop when Peixoto passed by and greeted them, taking off his hat as a sign of courtesy. Everyone returned the gesture, with the exception of Salama, who had his back turned. Peixoto interpreted Salama's attitude as a deliberate insult:

PEIXOTO: "What does it mean that you don't take off your hat when I take off mine?"

SALAMA: "Forgive me, Sir, that I had not seen you."
PEIXOTO: "Don Bastard, you are very rude."[40]

Then Peixoto squared off with Salama, who roughly pushed him away. Angrily, Peixoto drew his dagger, but Salama instinctively disarmed him. Meanwhile, the colonel and sergeant of Livorno rushed in to separate both parties. Peixoto left the incident dishonored and disarmed. A few days later, he went after Salama, "gave him two blows and then put his hand to a half sword that he had underneath." Recovering in time once again, Salama took the first object that came to hand and hit Peixoto with a chair. Were it not for that, Peixoto "would have killed him or hurt him badly."

Members of the Jewish community who had witnessed the altercation wrote a public petition demolishing Peixoto's reputation: "He is not a gentleman, nor is he a merchant, but a weak and simple commissioner who survives through sending and receiving the goods of some Jews from Pisa."[41] Acceding to these pleas, the governor requested the grand duke to subject Peixoto to exemplary punishment for attempted murder. Peixoto was then forced to flee Livorno.

Moisés was not the only one of the Peixotos to have a run-in with justice around that time. In the same year of 1612, a scandal broke out in the island of Santiago, in Cabo Verde, involving his brother, Joshua (then living disguised under his baptismal name, Antônio Mendes Peixoto). He was seen among a group of "men of the Hebrew Nation" who gathered every Friday in the house of a certain Diogo Lopes Ferreira to celebrate the Sabbath.[42] When these rumors reached the governor of Cabo Verde, he dispatched a letter to the Inquisition in Lisbon. According to his report, a little boy had sneaked into the room where the worshipers used to meet and witnessed how "a calf which had golden horns was placed on a table and they were reading from a book." Because of its resemblance to the episode of the golden calf in Exodus, perhaps the story should be dismissed as nothing more than a child's fancy.[43] However, several testimonies confirmed the boy's story. A servant of the house even described in detail the calf as "very big, and compared it with the size of a chicken that she had in front of her, adding that the entire body of the calf was white, like the chicken's, and that it had golden horns."[44] Two years after the secret meetings were unveiled, the governor of Cabo Verde was still complaining to the inquisitors that they had done nothing to curb these misdeeds, and the inquiry apparently faded away without arrests. Afterwards, we lose track of Joshua for several years.

Meanwhile, Moisés reappeared in 1614 in Rome, working as a commercial agent.[45] From there he likely went to Antwerp, where he married Ester Peixoto and publicly assumed Judaism. Peixoto's brother-in-law, Vicente da Costa, also an inhabitant in that city, was a notorious *pasador* (a sort of early modern coyote) who smuggled crypto-Jews from Spain to Amsterdam.[46] Moisés himself soon immigrated to Amsterdam, arriving in 1615 or 1616. He became an active member in Neveh Salom, one of the two Jewish congregations in the city, donating to charity and paying the community tax (*imposta*). It is very probable that Peixoto also gained a more solid Jewish education in this period, since we find him officiating on the Sabbath in an informal synagogue years later in Paraíba.

Despite his integration into the Jewish community, Peixoto's first years in Amsterdam were characterized by personal and economic hardship. On September 1618 he suddenly lost his wife Ester.[47] The scant references to commercial transactions in his name are a strong indication that he never quite made a living as a merchant, though a notary defined him as such.[48] This is corroborated by the very small sums he contributed to charity, and also by the low amounts he paid in taxes, which were assessed as a percentage of his income.[49] In an episode from 1619 that is emblematic of Peixoto's financial struggles, his brother-in-law Abraham Serra refused to keep paying his rent, leaving Peixoto insolvent.[50]

As Peixoto never held a position in the Jewish community, nor does he seem to have been a successful merchant, it is plausible that after his wife's death he joined the army. By the time Moisés arrived in Pernambuco in 1634, he was a seasoned military officer with the rank of captain. He must have gained this experience between 1618 and 1634, fighting in either the Thirty Years' War (1618–48) or the Eighty Years' War (1568–1648).

Besides a regular stipend, a military career in the early modern period brought social prestige. Like other Jewish soldiers, Moisés did not hesitate to flaunt his military rank when the occasion arose.[51] It seems that it was precisely this prestige that allowed him to make an advantageous marriage in 1623 to Ester de la Faya, daughter of the prominent merchant Abraham de la Faya.[52] The alliances between the two families were strengthened by the simultaneous marriage of Moisés's younger brother, Joshua, to another daughter of Abraham, Rachel de la Faya.[53] While Moisés apparently remained at a distance from commercial affairs, Joshua formed a partnership with their father-in-law, importing sugar and fabrics from Porto and Madrid.[54] He also traded diamonds and became involved in the commerce of tobacco.[55]

But not everything was a bed of roses for the Peixoto brothers in those years. Between 1625 and 1628, they mourned together no less than five of their children, all buried in the Jewish cemetery of Ouderkerk.[56] Moisés began to struggle financially once again, for reasons that still remain obscure. While in 1631 he paid thirty-one guilders in taxes, in 1632 he paid only five guilders, and around seven guilders in 1634.[57] Moisés and his younger brother Joshua then had recourse to the biggest employer in the United Provinces at that time: the West India Company. They momentarily left the de la Faya daughters at home, recruited a "company of rebels," and headed toward northern Brazil to fight for the Dutch.

"Priests of the Law"

The path of the brothers Moisés Cohen Henriques and Jacob Cohen Henriques to the army in Pernambuco was distinct from the one taken by the Peixotos. Born in the first decade of the seventeenth century, likely in Andalusia, they came from a wealthy family of crypto-Jewish merchants and moved to Amsterdam with their father Abraham Cohen Henriques alias Francisco Vaz de Leão in 1617.[58] By that time, doctrinal divisions between the members of the Jewish community were increasing, and in 1618 a third congregation emerged in the city: the Bet Israel.[59] The newcomer Abraham and his sons affiliated with this third community.

In the following years, Abraham played a notable role in the congregation. Besides being periodically elected parnas, the most powerful position in the Jewish community, he also served as a director of the dowry society (*Dotar*) and made significant donations to the Jews in the Holy Land.[60] When in 1634 the Bet Israel was considering merging with Amsterdam's two other congregations, Abraham was chosen as one of seven representatives who would work out the terms of the agreement.[61] Meanwhile, his business in Amsterdam thrived, its branches extending to Antwerp, Bayonne, Livorno, and Saleh, where he traded tobacco, Moroccan almonds, and Brazilian sugar.[62]

As a diligent Jew, Abraham invested greatly in the education of his children, enrolling both Moisés and Jacob Cohen Henriques in a yeshiva. In 1621–22, Moisés was listed in the records of Bet Israel as a student (*talmid*), helping with the reading of the haftarot for Yom Kippur and giving to charity.⁶³ In this year he seems to have either finished or abandoned his studies. In any case, he left Amsterdam.

Between 1621 and 1627, Moisés probably launched his military career by fighting alongside Dutch forces in the Eighty Years' War against Spain, and he may have even taken part in the conquest of Bahia in 1624 by WIC troops under the command of Piet Heyn. When Moisés returned to Amsterdam, in 1627, he assumed his first institutional position as treasurer (*gabai*) of the brotherhood for ransoming Jewish captives in the Mediterranean.⁶⁴ After a one-year term as treasurer, he exchanged the comfort of his office in Amsterdam for a much more uncertain life as a privateer, participating in Heyn's capture of the Spanish treasure fleet off the coast of Cuba in 1628. Though only in his twenties by that time, Moisés was already an experienced fighter. Months before, he had journeyed to Spain under Catholic disguise to collect information in preparation for the assault on the flota.⁶⁵

While Moisés was invading Pernambuco with the Dutch in 1630, Jacob Cohen Henriques married and paid his annual membership fee (*finta*) in the Jewish community for the first time—two signs of entrance into adulthood.⁶⁶ His union with Judith Arari, daughter of Doctor David Arari alias Diego Lopes Telles, brought him an extraordinary dowry of sixteen thousand guilders.⁶⁷ Returning from Pernambuco in 1631, Moisés married Rachel Spinoza alias Rachel Figueroa and received a much smaller dowry of four hundred guilders.⁶⁸

The difference in the economic circumstances of the two brothers was considerable in the early 1630s, as their payments of taxes and charitable donations show.⁶⁹ Moisés followed in the footsteps of their father, investing in the sugar and almond trades in Morocco, the Canary Islands, and Livorno.⁷⁰ The activities of Jacob during this time are less well known. A balance sheet that offers a glimpse of his investments was prepared after the sudden death of his wife in 1633. Jacob owned shares in the WIC and Dutch East India Company and other assets including insurance contracts, bills of exchange, and promissory notes. Among his personal possessions were diamonds, jewels, and clothing made of linen and silk.⁷¹

After his adventures as a soldier, merchant, and privateer, Moisés finally gained entrance to the oligarchy of the *Mahamad*. He was elected parnas of Bet Israel for the first time in 1638.⁷² It seems that sometime between 1634 and 1639 Jacob followed the example of his brother and began a career in the army. In a denunciation to the Portuguese Inquisition from 1640, a person who claimed to have met Jacob in Amsterdam the previous year described him as "a man born in this Kingdom [of Portugal, and thus baptized] ... who used to say that he descended from the priests of the law." This informer also testified that Jacob earned his living as a soldier.[73]

The fact that Jacob was publicly boasting in Amsterdam that he descended from the "priests of the law" is revealing. By taking the surname "Cohen," which in Hebrew means "priest," his family was associating itself with the lineage of Aaron and the high priests.[74] Symptomatic of the genealogical strategy that certain clans employed to reinforce their Jewishness and detach themselves from their Catholic past in the Iberian Peninsula, the choice of that specific patronymic embodied the Cohen Henriqueses' aspirations for power within the Jewish community and preeminence in religious ceremonies.[75]

Like his brother, Jacob ascended the institutional hierarchy of the Jewish community of Amsterdam soon after his military service. In 1641, he was elected treasurer of the brotherhood for rescuing Jewish captives; a year later, Jacob was promoted to director.[76] But the overcrowded community and the union of the three congregations of Amsterdam in the Talmud Torah in 1639 may have imposed certain limits on institutional and social ascension. Moreover, people like Jacob Cohen Henriques and Moisés Cohen Henriques may have acquired a taste for war and expected to have more commercial opportunities in the Americas.

Trading Violence

The flow of civilians to Dutch Brazil increased significantly from 1635 onward, driven by military triumphs that swept away what remained of Luso-Brazilian resistance and the WIC's aggressive recruitment of new settlers.[77] Spanish and Portuguese Jews migrated en masse. It is estimated that in ten years the Jewish population of Dutch Brazil increased to between 1,000 and 1,450 people, almost equaling the Jewish population in Amsterdam or in Livorno during the same period.[78]

Among the first to request permission to embark for the colony were several of the Peixotos' relatives, including their father-in-law and the wife of Moisés Cohen Peixoto.[79] This woman, unnamed in the document, was not Ester, whom Moisés had married in 1623, but her sister Rachel. Moisés's younger brother, Joshua, had died in one of the bloody battles in the hinterlands of northern Brazil in 1634 or 1635, and thus Rachel was crossing the Atlantic to perform a levirate marriage.[80]

Even in peaceful times, founding a Jewish community in the New World was no easy task. In the Americas, Jews were required to put down roots in a setting that was very different from the Mediterranean region or northern Europe. Dutch Brazil stands out as a unique case in the history of the diaspora for several reasons, starting with the vastness of the occupied territory. The colony was much larger than Suriname, Cayenne, New Amsterdam, or the Caribbean islands. In addition, most residents of Brazil were Catholic and spoke Portuguese, like many Jews of Iberian origin. It was difficult to maintain a strict, normative Judaism in Dutch Brazil. The immense distances between rural settlements and close contact with Catholic residents made room for the proliferation of informal synagogues in the hinterlands, where the practice of a more flexible Judaism to attract New Christians was generally accepted.[81] One of these synagogues met in the home of Captain Moisés Cohen Peixoto.

Moisés settled with his family in Paraíba. Still serving in the army, Peixoto's stipend allowed him a more comfortable life than he had had in Livorno and Amsterdam. He lived in a house with "a big living room" and could permit himself to have books (rarities in those frontier lands).[82] Various testimonies confirm that since 1637 an improvised synagogue met in Peixoto's house. The group who attended Sabbath services included his comrades from the army, such as Moisés Navarro, who had participated in the Dutch invasion of Pernambuco in 1630. Intellectuals like the former priest Isaac Nunes, the poet Elias Machorro, and the polyglot and later martyr Isaac de Castro Tartas also attended.[83] Even New Christians considering conversion to Judaism came to the improvised Sabbaths at Peixoto's home.

Although it had no formal status, the Jewish community in Paraíba was numerous and reputable enough to call itself the Casa de David.[84] The choice of such a suggestive name reveals the congregants' messianic expectations about the New World. By calling their congregation the "House of David," Peixoto and his comrades indicated that they viewed their settlement in those remote lands as helping to disperse Jews across the globe, conditio sine qua non to the coming of the Messiah: a descendant from David's lineage destined to found the fifth monarchy, and whom the Iberian Jews meaningfully referred to as a "captain."[85]

Informally, Peixoto was considered the community's chief rabbi. Seeking to increase the number of congregants, he adapted the liturgy and admitted uncircumcised men to services. There was no Torah scroll, and the prayers took two hours, with "each person reading his own book of the said Law of Moses." The New Christians used "a book in Portuguese language since they did not know how to read Hebrew like the others." At the end Peixoto asked each congregant to contribute "alms for the poor Jews of Holland," which were sometimes offered in kind, in the form of sugar.[86]

The activities of the Paraíba Jewish community drew the attention of the Dutch authorities, who in 1638 sent the inspector Johannes Marischal to warn them that they were practicing their rites too publicly, offending the sensibility of Christians.[87] The Dutch guaranteed "freedom of conscience," which was quite different from "freedom of worship."[88] And yet, Peixoto and his group seem to have left the doors and windows open while they prayed and sang out loud. It is reported that they gathered in front of the house to speak about Judaism and entered in religious disputations with people on the streets, scandalizing the passersby.[89] Marischal, himself known as an "example of impiety," must have used excessive violence to suppress their meetings.[90] To the great shock of Protestant ministers, Peixoto's congregation attacked the inspector and shooed him out of the city.[91] The community eventually submitted a formal protest to the High Council against the uncivil treatment that they received.[92]

In many instances, the Paraíba congregation also defied Catholic authorities. In January 1637, the bishop of Bahia and former inquisitor in Lisbon, Dom Pedro da Silva e Sampaio, reported with horror the rumors that "in Paraíba [the Jews] publicly promise to take me in their hands and to drag me through the streets, and to tear me to pieces, out of hatred of the Holy Office."[93] On another occasion, Isaac de Castro Tartas quarreled with Catholic priests, agreeing with Protestant residents that they could not bear a cross in the city because that was "superstition."[94] It is hardly surprising, therefore, that during the General Assembly of August 27, 1640, the delegates of Paraíba petitioned the High Council—though without success—for the exile of the Jews from their province.[95] Four years later, the boldness of Peixoto and his comrades was still aggravating the local authorities, for they expressly ordered that the synagogue be removed to the city's outskirts, where worshipers could not disturb Christians.[96]

Meanwhile, a more institutionalized form of Jewish community was starting to develop in Pernambuco. Around 1636 the local Jewry had already established in Recife Sur Israel, the first official congregation in the Americas. Rapid demographic growth and the high cost of living in the city compelled many Jews to move to the island of Antônio Vaz, where by 1637 they founded a second congregation: Magen Abraham. In the following years, the community created all the administrative apparatus necessary for the consolidation of Judaism in Dutch Brazil: they elected a *Mahamad*, erected a synagogue, purchased land for the Jewish cemetery, and even instituted branches of the brotherhood for rescuing captives and of the dowry society, whose first president was the soldier Moisés Navarro, a friend of Captain Peixoto.[97]

Moisés and Jacob Cohen Henriques arrived in Pernambuco around 1642 or 1643, at the height of the slave trade in Dutch Brazil. For decades, the question of whether or not Calvinist settlements in the New World should be based on enslaved labor had been an object of fierce dispute among theologians, jurists, and directors of the WIC.[98] The opponents of these commercial practices were definitely defeated when the Dutch authorities realized both the profitability of the slave trade and the impossibility of keeping a plantation economy in full swing without recourse to forced labor.[99] In 1637, the Dutch first conquered Elmina, in Guinea, but it was only with the capture of Luanda a few years later that the traffic took off. The WIC soon developed its own guidelines for profiting from the trade. To avoid suffering shortfalls when planters who purchased slaves on credit defaulted on their obligations, after 1642 the company (which held a monopoly on the slave trade to Dutch Brazil) stopped extending credit and began to accept exclusively cash payments. Specie was a rarity in Dutch Brazil. The announcement of this new policy favored Moisés Cohen Peixoto, the brothers Cohen Henriques, and other merchants. In 1643, Peixoto and Moisés Cohen Henriques became tax farmers, purchasing the right to collect twenty-five thousand and twenty-four thousand guilders respectively.[100] Their friend, the soldier Moisés Navarro, became such a prosperous tax farmer, slave trader, and planter that he was able to purchase a large sugar mill. However, this level of wealth was exceptional.

The conquest of Luanda and the decision of the WIC to sell enslaved men and women exclusively for cash resulted in a precipitous drop in the price of one "piece" (*peça*).[101] If at the end of the 1630s the Jews were beginning to purchase slaves from the company, by the early 1640s they were heavily invested in this commerce. Benefitting from the WIC's cash-only policy, Jews' purchases of slaves rose to 63 percent of the company's total sales in 1643, or approximately 2,500 African men, women, and children.[102]

Peixoto purchased slaves in Pernambuco for the first time in February 1642: five Africans embarked in Guinea on the vessel *Nassau*, together valued at 2,640 guilders.[103] During 1644 he bid on a total of twenty-nine slaves, mostly from Angola, this time disbursing 3,802 guilders.[104] He participated in a massive auction in January of that year, in which in only two days the WIC sold no less than 1,152 Africans (a number roughly equivalent to half of Recife's free civilian population, or to the entire Jewish population in Dutch Brazil).

But Peixoto's investments look modest when compared to those of the Cohen Henriques family. Between 1643 and 1645, Moisés and Jacob purchased at least 114 slaves for 20,048 guilders.[105] In some cases it is possible to deduce from the very low price of each "piece" that they bought children or elderly and disabled people. Their youngest brother, David Cohen Henriques, who had arrived in the colony in 1637 to learn the family business, acquired 107 slaves for 20,277 guilders in the period 1644–45.[106] Like many other Jews, Peixoto and the Cohen Henriques probably resold their slaves on credit for a higher price and at interest to those planters who lacked the cash to participate in the WIC auctions.[107] Jewish slaveowners put their human property to work as domestic servants, or as porters and shop workers in urban contexts. It was also a common practice for Jews to lease their slaves to work for Catholic settlers in their sugar mills.[108]

By purchasing Africans and renting out their labor, the Jews of Dutch Brazil were underwriting a brutal branch of the Atlantic slave trade. When the WIC first began transporting slaves in earnest in the 1630s and 1640s, it lacked the practical knowledge of Portuguese captains. Dutch slave ships saw a much higher rate of mortality during the Middle Passage (around 20 percent and 30 percent), and many of these deaths, reportedly, were related to captains' ignorance and failure to ensure that enough potable water, food supplies, and space were allotted for captives during voyages.[109]

In spite of this incredible waste of human life, from the perspective of those who bought slaves in Brazil, the commerce was very profitable. Given the Jewish community's high level of involvement in the local traffic and demand for slaves, the *Mahamad* issued a special tax on these transactions: "Blacks that [Jews] buy from the Company [the owner] will pay five soldos for each piece."[110] On more than one occasion, the Dutch local authorities, recognizing the economic importance of the Jews to this business, suspended public auctions scheduled on Saturdays and Jewish holidays.[111] It was not a coincidence, therefore, that the slave market of Recife was located in the Jewish street (*Jodenstraat*), a scene captured by the brush of Zacharias Wagener.

FIGURE 4.2. "On the appointed day [of the auction], these poor people, half dead from hunger and thirst, are taken one by one, as if pigs or sheep leaving the pen, to be counted better." Zacharias Wagener, *Thierbuch*, plate 106 (ca. 1641) (Kupferstich-Kabinett, Ca 226a). Zacharias Wagener, *Thierbuch*, ed. Dante Martins Teixeira, trans. Álvaro Bragança Júnior (Rio de Janeiro: Editora Index, 1997), 195.

With the outbreak of an insurrection led by Luso-Brazilian residents of the colony in 1645, many Jews left Pernambuco, fearful that the defeat of the Dutch would bring back the old ghosts of the Inquisition. Those fit for military service who were unable or unwilling to leave were automatically enrolled in the militia. According to estimates, in Recife and on the island of Antônio Vaz alone there were 350 Jewish soldiers, who made up half of the local defensive force.[112]

Moisés Cohen Peixoto, Moisés Cohen Henriques, and Jacob Cohen Henriques remained until the final phase of the war, in 1654, but the sources do not mention the role they played in it. Given their previous experience, we can assume they were engaged in active combat and had relatively prominent positions. In November 1645, a soldier recorded in his diary that a ship departed from Recife "with forty Jews, commanded by a Jewish captain. They went North, and in Itamaracá they will be reinforced by some Indians."[113] It is possible that the anonymous captain was one of our characters. A more concrete trace of their service may be that a certain "Captain Cohen" complained to the governor of Bahia about the Portuguese rebels' treatment of Jewish prisoners.[114]

As a matter of fact, the Pernambuco insurrection followed the same pattern as the Dutch conquest, with both parties systematically breaking diplomatic agreements and descending into a vicious cycle of executions. The news was circulated that the Portuguese rebels were summarily executing and extraditing Jews to Lisbon, even though as subjects of the Dutch Republic since 1645 they were exempt from inquisitorial persecution and due proper treatment as prisoners of war.[115] One eyewitness, Johan Nieuhof, confirmed that this was why "the Jews, more than anyone else, were in a desperate situation and, therefore, preferred to die sword in hand than face their fate under the Portuguese yoke: the flames."[116]

Despite the war, Jewish institutional life in Dutch Brazil continued to develop. In 1648, the Sur Israel renewed its bylaws (*ascamot*) and mandated that all Jews living in Recife and the state of Brazil be automatically inscribed in the congregation and obliged to pay taxes, "whether they attended in Paraíba or in any other part."[117] Moreover, no other congregation was allow to exist, and whoever disobeyed the order would be "punished with all rigor and separated from the Nation as a disturber of peace and the general good."[118] The decision, motivated by doctrinal quarrels and economic hardship, dissolved what may have remained of Moisés Cohen Peixoto's authority as the informal rabbi of the disruptive Casa de David in Paraíba. The centralization of power, however, benefited Jacob Cohen Henriques, who finally reached the top of the Jewish oligarchy with his election to the *Mahamad* for the term 1651-52.[119]

But the relentless advance of the Portuguese rebels finally constrained the WIC's army to surrender on January 27, 1654, crushing the last hopes of the Jews to remain in Pernambuco. Moisés Cohen Henriques apparently fled to one of the Caribbean islands, while his brother Jacob returned to Amsterdam. Jacob then participated in the collection of money for resettling other refugees from Brazil who, having abandoned or lost everything, constantly arrived in Holland in conditions of extreme poverty.[120] One of them was Captain Moisés Cohen Peixoto, who would live thereafter on the community's alms.[121]

In 1655, both Jacob Cohen Henriques and Moisés Cohen Peixoto contributed sonnets to the *Elogios que zelozos dedicaron a la felice memoria de Abraham Nuñez Bernal*, a powerful celebration of two Judaizing martyrs burned alive by the Spanish Inquisition that year.[122] Cohen Henriques and Cohen Peixoto signed their poems using their respective military ranks of "lieutenant" and "captain," underlining the social prestige that such positions conferred within the Jewish community.[123]

The sonnets of Cohen Henriques and Cohen Peixoto each drew an analogy between the figures of the martyr and the soldier: both were distinguished by constancy in the face of the enemy and by the desire for an honorable death. While Peixoto praised the "boldness" and "heroic zeal" of the martyrs, Cohen Henriques devoted some lines to a moral reflection:

> Suffering and victory strengthen,
> he who dedicates his soul to the defense of serious matters.
> If triumphs are signs of valor,
> it is also a sign of valor to die.[124]

In this sense, the battle of the martyrs burned alive by the Spanish Inquisition and that of the Jewish soldiers who helped take control of Dutch Brazil were two fronts of the same war against Catholic tyranny. As Jacob Cohen Henriques wrote himself, it was better to burn alive challenging the Holy Office than to die "like a simple butterfly."[125]

This case study of the Cohen Peixoto and the Cohen Henriques brothers has shown the importance of reconsidering within Jewish studies the theme of colonial violence—both physical and symbolic—of which Jews in the early modern period were victims as well as agents. As we saw throughout this essay, the four soldiers risked their lives in the Atlantic as part of the Babylonian, multiconfessional army of the WIC, where they confronted prejudice and barriers to military promotion. To mitigate these challenges, Jewish soldiers traveled in groups and allied themselves with other marginalized fighters such as Indigenous Americans and Africans. In contrast to the European and Mediterranean centers of the diaspora, the Americas offered Jews an entirely new environment. Ongoing wars against the Iberian empires provided occasions to seek vengeance for Catholic persecution. Due to the immensity of the colonial territory, Jews could sometimes afford to disrespect and attack Dutch authorities or strive with Protestant theologians without fearing severe reprisals. Brazil, finally, opened to Jewish settlers unique economic opportunities based on the traffic and labor of enslaved Africans.

The discrimination, limited careers, and bloody battles in the corners of the Americas, heretofore examined, call into question the idea that the formation of religious identity in the early modern period was a pragmatic and circumstantial choice. From the close analysis of the four soldiers' lives it has emerged that economic gain was only one of the reasons why Jewish men joined the WIC army—when it was a factor at all. In general, what animated the Cohen Peixoto and the Cohen Henriques brothers in that dangerous enterprise was a deep sense of revenge against the tyranny of Catholics embodied in the Inquisition, their messianic expectations about the dispersion of the Jews across the globe, and the possibility of gaining prestige within the Jewish community itself. Willing to kill and die for Judaism, their religious commitment seems beyond doubt.

Still neglected by scholarship, soldiers—men who knew how to wield swords and guns as well as pens, books, and bills of exchange—were as important a category within the Jewish diaspora as merchants and rabbis. They brought a measure of security and stability to the burgeoning Jewish communities in the Americas, and coreligionists' public recognition of their courage elevated soldiers to positions of both institutional and religious leadership with the return of peace. The trajectories of the four soldiers in this essay ultimately show how military service was constitutive of Jewish identity in the early modern period, especially in the nascent communities in the Atlantic world.

CHAPTER 5

Imperial Enterprise
The Franks Family Network, Commerce, and British Expansion

TONI PITOCK

On December 7, 1763, a group of Philadelphia merchants and traders drafted a memorial to the Board of Trade, which, they hoped, would "represent [their] Misfortunes to the Crown."[1] The memorialists appealed for reparations for the losses they had suffered in Indian predations on the frontier six months earlier. They believed they were entitled to compensation because they were British subjects, licensed traders, and had taken considerable risks in the service of British imperial interests. As traders, their enterprises in the Ohio River Valley contributed to "the late peace and Friendship established with [the Indians]," and helped "conciliate [them] to the British Interest." In fact, they had resumed trade even before the end of the Seven Years' War as a "Consequence of repeated Solicitations from the Natives," and it had been "countenanced and encouraged by the several Generals and officers." In other words, their commercial endeavors contributed to British expansion and dominion. They noted that their trading enterprises also promoted metropolitan interests. The sale of British manufactured goods in the colonies enriched English merchants and manufacturers, who had no way of getting goods to the frontier without their American colleagues.[2] Their appeal was denied, and the group devised another strategy, one that likewise tied their personal economic interests to British imperial aspirations. They applied for royal approval on a land grant that they had negotiated with several Indian tribes. This scheme would enable them to recover the value of their losses—they planned to divide and sell to settlers—but it also purported to advance a solution to the problem of integrating the vast territory in the North American interior that had come under British dominion in the peace settlement following the Seven Years' War.

Throughout the process, the syndicate solicited the support of powerful allies. They consulted Superintendent of Indian Affairs William Johnson, and they appealed to several personages who might champion their cause, including the Earl of Halifax, former president of the Board of Trade; the chief justice of Pennsylvania, William Allen; the proprietors of Pennsylvania, the Penns; and "as great a Number of merchants, trading to [Philadelphia] & New York, As possible."[3] To represent them before the Board of Trade, they appointed the London merchant Moses Franks. Franks was a scion of a prominent mercantile family, and he held a contract to supply the British troops in America, which made him an influential representative. But Franks also had a personal interest in the outcome of the appeal. He was supplier, creditor, partner, and brother of Philadelphia merchant David Franks, whose losses in the attacks represented more than one quarter of the total, which was estimated at approximately £80,000.[4]

Moses and David Franks are well known to historians of early Jewish America. Their father, Jacob Franks, settled in New York in the first decade of the eighteenth century and built up a successful mercantile business conducting trade between New York and London, the Caribbean, and other North American colonies. When his sons came of age they migrated to various Atlantic ports, expanding the family enterprise. Historians present the family as exemplars of the paradox American Jews faced as they strove to parse their lives into two domains, the secular and the religious. The family observed the Sabbath, holidays, and dietary laws, and Jacob Franks was a long-standing official of the governing body of New York's Congregation Shearith Israel. But Franks's business interests brought him into close contact with non-Jewish colleagues, and the family mingled with their families. Indeed, Jacob's wife, Abigaill Levy Franks, derived great "pleasure to Observe the faire Character Our Familys has in the place by Jews and Christians." Their conviction that they could maintain a separation between the religious and secular domains was shattered when two of their children married Christians in the 1730s.[5] The family does exemplify the challenge that early American Jews faced. However, the economic enterprises of Jacob Franks and his sons place them within an Atlantic world framework and reveal the intricacies of their endeavors in the British imperial context.

For one thing, the Franks family brings to light the Ashkenazi presence in the Atlantic world. Sephardim and the crypto-Jews and New Christians associated with them had long been circulating in the Atlantic world, where they developed kinship and ethnic networks that enabled them to engage extensively in cross-cultural and interimperial trade.[6] The scholarly emphasis on the Iberian-origin diaspora, however, has obscured Ashkenazi migration to the Dutch Republic and England and their colonies, which began toward the end of the seventeenth century. Like Sephardim, they formed networks that tied them to colleagues in far-flung locations even if, as newcomers, it took years. And while most Ashkenazim were shopkeepers and petty traders, some, like the Frankses, were prosperous merchants.[7]

The Franks brothers' integral involvement in the appeals to the Crown also points to the ways in which private entrepreneurs' enterprises were central to British imperial projects. In the middle of the eighteenth century, the colonies were seen as an essential component of empire. Colonial commerce heightened the economic prosperity of the mother country, and it also encouraged migration and facilitated the spread of British values. In other words, private enterprise promoted expansion. They were "closely linked and mutually dependent."[8] Thus, David and Moses Franks, prominent merchants in Philadelphia and London, participated in the process of integrating the mother country and the colonies by conveying American resources to the metropole and manufactured goods to the colonies. And when tensions leading to the Seven Years' War and the war itself prompted the British government to reassess colonial policies and to assert tighter control, the Frankses' interests became further entangled.[9] David Franks's trade ventures and land speculation tapped into evolving ideas about British dominion in the far reaches of the empire. In his capacity as contractor to the Crown, Moses's entanglements were even more intimate, as he and his American agents—including his brother David—were integrally involved in supporting direct British interventions in the American interior. Jewishness was not an obstacle.

The Franks brothers' prominence, however, their apparent identification with the empire, and their proximity to power still raise questions about their status as Jews. The family can be seen within the framework of the "Court Jew," a category that historians use to denote the elite Jews who mobilized financial sources and family relationships to fulfill roles as provisioners and financiers in service of absolutist rulers in German principalities.[10] Like Court Jews of a slightly earlier period, Moses Franks, a Jew with considerable financial resources, mobilized far-flung family relationships to supply British troops in America. Like Court Jews, Moses and his London-based uncles' access to aristocracy and David's inclusion in elite circles in Philadelphia led them to embrace a style of living that set them apart from most Jewish contemporaries. Like Court Jews, the Frankses were outsiders, at least to a certain extent. After all, the empire was widely conceived of as *Protestant*, commercial, maritime, and free, which meant that Jews were outsiders. Yet, by the middle of the eighteenth century, the British imperial setting was an increasingly tolerant environment, shaped by Enlightenment thinking and growing diversity, and notions of subjecthood were more expansive, especially after the Seven Years' War when the empire incorporated more diverse populations that were not Protestant, British, or free, according to "British notions of freedom." The idea of the "British subject" implied "allegiance and obedience" to a distant monarch and a belief in inherent protections and privileges. According to one scholar, "by claiming allegiance, subjects of the empire might all identify as British subjects regardless of religion, place of origin, or race."[11] Thus, Court Jews, unequivocally outsiders, rarely showed a strong sense of commitment to one particular government, while for the Frankses, ideas of British subjecthood fostered a sense of inclusion and acceptance. Their commercial enterprises contributed to the imperial project, which helped them demonstrate allegiance.[12]

In eighteenth-century Britain, private enterprise was considered an important component of Britain's expansion. Merchants were seen as contributing to Britain's power.[13] The Franks family engaged in commerce from the time that David and Moses's grandfather migrated to England. Abraham Franks was one of twelve "Jew brokers" on London's Royal Exchange in 1697, one of only two Ashkenazim. His sons Aaron and Isaac were prominent gem merchants who made a fortune in trade in the East Indies. Isaac, winner of £20,000 in the notorious 1719 South Sea lottery, was a stockholder in the Hudson Bay Company and left an estate estimated at £300,000 when he died in 1736, the equivalent of approximately £49,840,000 today. Wealth and status gave the London Frankses access to the most prestigious circles, including members of the aristocracy. Aaron lent jewelry to the value of £40,000 to the Princess of Wales, King George I attended Isaac's wedding, and Aaron, together with his father-in-law, appealed to George II to intercede with Empress

Maria Theresa when she issued an edict expelling the Jews of Prague.[14] While Aaron and Isaac Franks made their fortune in the east, not yet officially part of Britain's empire but certainly within its informal domain, Jacob set his sights on the western edge of the empire. When he settled in New York at the beginning of the eighteenth century, settlers and metropolitan authorities alike recognized British America's potential. The Board of Trade envisioned a vast empire where, according to one historian, "overseas territories could be secured ... by settling British people on the land and giving them the means to develop it through transatlantic trade and ... by using the imperial state's control over the distribution of land to shape these territories into model colonial dependencies."[15] Jacob Franks's sons continued to cultivate the family's enterprises when they came of age. Naphtali and Moses went to London where they worked with their uncles Isaac and Aaron Franks and, at the same time, engaged in trade with colleagues in Atlantic ports, including their brother David who, like his father before him, sought out a developing market in America.[16]

Pennsylvania was on the brink of rapid growth when David Franks settled in Philadelphia in 1741. Abundant fertile land attracted a steady flow of immigrants who produced flour, pork, beef, and lumber, valuable export resources. Beyond the agricultural zone lay the frontier with its plentiful animal populations that could feed Europe's appetite for fur and deerskins. Philadelphia, the gateway, was rapidly becoming the largest British port in the Western Hemisphere.[17] Franks emerged as one of its leading merchants thanks to his family network. He imported manufactures from London to sell to urban and rural customers and exported local commodities, including furs and skins, which were in high demand in Europe.[18]

The same colonial conditions that facilitated Franks's success as a transatlantic merchant—the surge of settlers in the Pennsylvania backcountry and the European appetite for animal pelts, which drew frontier traders to the Ohio River Valley—exacerbated rivalry between the British and French and precipitated the Seven Years' War. The French were determined to preserve their dominance in the region and especially their access to the Mississippi River, the conduit that connected Canada and Louisiana. In 1754, almost ten years before the attack mentioned in the 1763 memorial, together with Indian allies, the French launched a military campaign against Anglo traders. As a major supplier of merchandise to frontier traders, David Franks suffered enormous losses.[19]

Hostilities on the frontier brought trade to a standstill and compromised the Frankses' commercial enterprises. But within a few years David and Moses Franks intertwined their interests even more intimately with those of the empire. The British dispatched troops to the colonies with the goal of ousting the French. In 1759, in partnership with James and George Colebrooke and Arnold Nesbitt, Moses Franks was awarded a contract to victual the British troops in North America. The Colebrookes were merchant bankers involved in the East India Company and members of Parliament. Their support for Prime Minister Thomas Pelham, the Duke of Newcastle, was rewarded with a baronetcy.[20] Arnold Nesbitt was likewise a member of a mercantile banking family with a parliamentary seat and links to a series of prime ministers—Robert Walpole, Henry Pelham, and Thomas Pelham. The Colebrooke and Nesbitt families had long conducted trade in Europe, but they only expanded their interests to include North America early in the Seven Years' War. They joined forces with one another and two other London houses in 1756. Their influence with Thomas Pelham earned them a contract to supply payment for the troops in Louisburg. At the time, Newcastle was first commissioner of the Treasury and had the authority to grant such contracts. Three years later, with Moses Franks as part of their consortium, they were awarded the contract to victual the troops further south.[21] The Colebrookes' and Nesbitt's access to power was no doubt key to securing the coveted contract, begging the question why Moses Franks was part of their consortium. He had much to offer. In addition to the fact that his uncle and associate Aaron Franks was a leading diamond importer and a major investor in the East India Company, Moses Franks's network in America was crucial. It included long-time colleagues Oliver DeLancey and John Watts, both members of prominent New York trading families, Franks's New York-based father Jacob Franks, who was made principal agent to the contractors in the colonies, and his brother David in Philadelphia, who, together with merchant and former Philadelphia mayor William Plumsted, was appointed agent in Pennsylvania and the western territories.[22] Moses Franks's American colleagues could tap their own networks to procure provisions and coordinate distribution, which must have been an essential selling point for the Colebrooke, Nesbitt, and Franks consortium since Colebrooke and Nesbitt's prior contracts did not include provisioning the army.

For David Franks, the enterprise was extremely complicated and involved significant sums. In the first year alone, Plumsted and Franks billed the Crown nearly £70,000 for carriage and £63,000 for provisions (in total, roughly the equivalent of £15,000,000 and £14,000,000 today). The contract to supply the troops promised profit, but the Frankses' enterprises enabled them to demonstrate that their interests were not merely personal. Rather, they symbolized fealty to Britain. Indeed, others registered the significance of their endeavors. Commander-in-chief of the British army Jeffery Amherst indicated the import of Franks and Plumsted's duties when he alerted Governor James Hamilton of Pennsylvania that their ventures were in service to the Crown. "I cannot in Duty to the King, and in Justice to His Troops," he wrote, "Refrain from Requesting You to Grant them, upon every such Occasion, all the Aid and Assistance they may stand in need of, for the better, and more Effectual performance of the said Contract."[23] Indeed, fulfilling the terms of their contract required a high level of organization and coordination. Enormous quantities of flour, salt, meat, and other supplies had to be delivered to British forts in the Ohio River Valley and as far away as Quebec. Transporting the provisions across the immense landscape was a complex undertaking. Wagons carried the goods to Port Pitt. From there the goods had to be carried by packhorse or boats on the Ohio River. Scores of people were needed to cooperate at each point along the way, including suppliers, wagon drivers, agents to whom Franks and Plumstead subcontracted, and British army personnel.[24]

Franks was adept in two worlds. He mobilized an extensive web of both Jewish and non-Jewish partners and agents. On the one hand, he was at the center of a Jewish network that was developing in and around Philadelphia. A few Ashkenazi immigrants began arriving in Philadelphia each year after Franks settled, and he gave many of them their start by employing them as clerks or setting them up in backcountry stores. Some of them earned his trust through hard work, competence, and honesty. He earned their loyalty by launching their careers. By the time Franks was supplying the British troops, he had come to rely heavily on a few key Jewish colleagues.[25] However, Franks's network was not exclusively Jewish. His business ties challenge the notion that Jews prioritized business relationships with other Jews.[26] Instead, Franks family collaborations show that by the second quarter of the eighteenth century, credit and reputation were the linchpin of all trade relationships. Their negotiations with Jews and non-Jews alike indicate that merchants and traders carefully considered whether colleagues—all colleagues—were trustworthy, that is, whether they had a record of honesty and accountability. Franks was one of only a handful of Jews in the region when he settled. Engaging in trade would have been impossible if he was limited to Jewish associates. A higher degree of toleration facilitated intercultural interactions in the British Empire and legal institutions that were at merchants' disposal to protect their interests. Commercial interactions with non-Jews promoted his inclusion in the dominant culture and gave him access to Philadelphia's elite circles, including to his partner in supplying the troops, William Plumsted, merchant and shipowner and former Philadelphia mayor.[27]

The war presented other opportunities for David Franks as well. As soon as the conflict began, British authorities recognized that Native American support would be critical in the contest with the French on the frontier. They appointed two superintendents to oversee Indian affairs.[28] Sir William Johnson, the superintendent for the northern department, then appointed George Croghan to be the Crown's primary representative to the Iroquois. He was a deft negotiator and trader familiar with the Delaware and Iroquois languages. When the Pennsylvania backcountry was brought under control and the Indian trade resumed, he was also responsible for monitoring the Indian trade in the Ohio River Valley, including setting prices and giving out licenses to traders.[29] David Franks was already acquainted with Croghan, and he set up a strategic partnership with Croghan and his long-time associate William Trent, an Indian trader who had spent time on the frontier as factor for the Ohio Company in the 1740s. Franks imported manufactures from his London colleagues and exported the furs and skins that he and his partners procured from the frontier. Other partners in their consortium, Barnard Gratz, Joseph Simon, and Levy Andrew Levy, all Ashkenazi immigrants, coordinated conveyance of goods between Philadelphia and Fort Pitt and managed the Fort Pitt warehouse.[30]

The partnership enabled Franks to dominate the Indian trade to such an extent that competitors believed that Franks and his partners' near-monopoly in the Indian trade was due to the fact that Croghan bent the rules to their benefit.[31] James Kenny, clerk at the provincial trading store in Pittsburgh, complained that the group's practice of offering Indians credit gave them an advantage.[32] Another critic maintained that Croghan claimed to have been given "Liberty by ye Generals Orders to direct ye selling of Rum to Indians," and there was now great demand "at Trent & Levys Store," which was owned by the partnership. He complained to Colonel Henry Bouquet, commander of the Royal American Regiment, that the partners dominated the Indian trade by exchanging alcohol for "the Choicest of their skins & furs."[33] Franks's partners Levy Andrew Levy and William Trent ventured well beyond Fort Pitt selling goods and liquor not only to Indians but to French settlers living in the region and British troops that were stationed in forts. The troops were an especially advantageous market because they paid traders in sterling, making it easier to pay British suppliers and build their reputation with distant creditors.[34] The western trade represented a significant source of profit for Franks and his partners. Between April 1760 and mid-1763, they sent almost £26,000 worth of trade goods to Ohio Country and the Great Lakes region.[35]

It turned out that the peace and, consequently, a robust trade with the Indians were only temporary. Only a few months after the Peace of Paris was signed, the western reaches of the empire erupted in renewed conflict. Alarmed by the news that France had ceded its territory to the British and concerned about continued Anglo encroachment, a confederation of Indians from the Great Lakes Region, Ohio Country, and Illinois Country coordinated a series of attacks on British forts, Anglo-American settlements, and traders. These attacks marked the beginning of what became known as Pontiac's War, named for the Ottawa leader who led the offensive.[36]

The new wave of violence simultaneously hurt and boosted David Franks's interests. First, Franks and his trading partners were among those whose pack trains fell victim to ambushes. Goods were plundered and destroyed, and Levy Andrew Levy, one of Franks's Jewish partners, was one of about forty traders taken prisoner at Detroit. Ten of his servants were killed.[37] Franks and his colleagues valued their losses at £24,780, more than one quarter of the losses collectively claimed by Philadelphia merchants in their memorial to the Board of Trade discussed at the beginning of this essay.[38] However, British troops arrived back in the Ohio River Valley, escalating the demand for supplies. In their capacity as agents to the contractors, Franks and his partner William Plumsted were called upon once again to supply the troops. Conditions were unpredictable and perilous. Colonel Henry Bouquet expressed concern that fears of Indian attacks "will put a Stop to all Carriages, as no Country men will be prevailed upon to go up for some time without an [armed] Escort." Amherst recognized the need for haste and made extra funds available to Franks and Plumsted.[39] Nevertheless, both Bouquet and Amherst were aware of Britain's mounting debts and the need to cut costs, and ongoing mistrust and frequent disagreements came to define their relationship with Franks and Plumsted. Authorities accused Franks and Plumsted of extracting more money from the Crown by oversupplying the forts. But when Franks and Plumsted requested clarification regarding the "number of Eaters" they would have to feed and expressed concern about losses on the road because of "the weakness of Your horses &c.," Bouquet was unaccommodating.[40] He told them "it must depend on the Number of Troops that will be ke[pt] in the Department, and which I cannot yet ascertain." On the other hand, he complained about a shortage of livestock and predicted that shortages would intensify because of "Excessive heat," which "ruins Men Horses & Cattle."[41] Plumsted and Franks griped that Bouquet was vague and that untimely orders drove up their expenses. Bouquet countered that they had been given sufficient notice and should have prepared better.[42]

There were also disputes over remuneration. Plumsted and Franks claimed that in addition to the troops, they provided rations "to poor People in distress" who sought refuge from marauding Indians in the forts. Bouquet asserted that "Indulgence" of these settlers was only for the "first days of the Alarm," and had subsequently been forbidden. He refused to authorize payment and suggested that Franks and Plumsted approach commanding officers at each post, who had their own budgets. Plumsted and Franks expressed concerns about costs when Bouquet ordered delivery of goods with little notice, such as when Bouquet ordered them to purchase fifty thousand live hogs and to deliver them to Fort Pitt. Using the trump card, Bouquet reminded them of their duty to the Crown. "I am convinced that your Principals as well as yourselves would never upon such an emergency consider their Interest alone Exclusive of the Public Service, but would be Satisfy'd not to be loosers."[43] As dutiful and humble subjects, Bouquet implied, Franks and Plumsted owed obedience and allegiance, the proof of which was their willingness to serve the Crown.[44]

Disputes and suspicions notwithstanding, the Franks family network appears to have been indispensable in keeping the supply chain moving. When the contract held by Colebrooke, Nesbitt, and Franks expired in November 1763, of the consortium, only Moses Franks was retained as a contractor. The government claimed to be seeking to lower costs but did not even attempt to renegotiate with the Colebrooke/Nesbitt/Franks consortium. Colebrooke and Nesbitt were likely shunned when political leadership shifted. George Colebrooke (James Colebrooke died in the interim) and Arnold Nesbitt had backed Thomas Pelham, the Duke of Newcastle, who was removed from his position by George III. John Watts, the contractors' New York agent and Moses Franks's longtime friend and colleague, noted antagonism between Colebrooke and the new prime minister.[45] Together with Sir Samuel Fludyer, a merchant, director of the Bank of England, member of Parliament, and mayor of London, and Adam Drummond, a Scottish merchant, banker, and member of Parliament, Franks negotiated new terms when Grenville stepped into office.[46] Since a Jew could not hold office, perhaps Moses Franks was spared having to align himself with a party, or perhaps he believed that it was safer to avoid siding with a party and simply to declare allegiance to the Crown.

A shake-up occurred in Philadelphia as well. When Thomas Gage replaced Jeffery Amherst as commander of the army, he scrutinized accounts for Bouquet's area of command and questioned Franks and Plumsted's charges.[47] Then, when word of the new Fludyer, Drummond, and Franks contract reached Gage in February 1765, he confirmed the appointment of David Franks as the contractors' agent, this time with John Inglis and Gilbert Barkley as his partners. Both were Scottish merchants who were members of Philadelphia's elite. If the contractors and their agents in America were integral to securing and maintaining Britain's new territories as more troops were stationed on the frontier, the Franks brothers seem to have been the critical component. The terms of the new contract were more clearly defined. Lower costs were to be paid for rations, and Franks and his partners were required to deliver them within three months without charging additional fees. The British were to pay transportation costs separately from the price of the rations and cover the cost of excess provisions still being stored after six months.[48] But Henry Bouquet complained about the new contract. Troops were being stationed further west—in Illinois Country—and he expected transportation costs to rise.[49] Antagonism between Franks and Bouquet and General Gage persisted, but Franks's position was fortified in 1766 when the Crown renewed its contract with Nesbitt, Drummond, and Franks—Arnold Nesbitt, Franks's former partner, replacing Fludyer.[50]

The British sought to integrate newly conquered territories in North America into the empire, but different groups of inhabitants posed different challenges. French settlers in the lands to the east of the Mississippi River were considered to be a potential threat, a corrupting influence. Left to their own devices, they would entice French traders back into the region. The British deemed it necessary to introduce a military presence in the Illinois Country. But the "Western Indians" resented the military presence and strongly opposed direct rule over them. The British sought other ways to conciliate the Indians. Some officials believed that trade would induce Indians to embrace Britain's "civilizing influence."[51] Thus, in the spring of 1765 Superintendent of Indian Affairs

Johnson dispatched George Croghan on a diplomatic mission to assure the Native inhabitants of Britain's amity. Croghan left Fort Pitt with soldiers and representatives from neighboring Indian tribes. They brought boatloads of goods to distribute to the Indians as gifts, meant as a gesture of goodwill on behalf of the British. The firm of Baynton, Wharton, and Morgan, Franks's competitors in the Indian trade, received the official order for £2,000 worth of goods.[52]

Even though Franks lost out on the consignment of goods, in contravention of Johnson's orders, Croghan secretly took trade goods belonging to Franks and his partners valued at a similar amount.[53] In addition, Franks's ties to his brother Moses gave him an advantage over other Philadelphia merchants who hoped to profit from British expansion. Negotiations were still underway with the contractors when troops arrived in Fort Chartres in Illinois Country at the end of 1765. Local authorities therefore had to make temporary arrangements, which aroused the hopes of Franks's competitors. Franks negotiated a short-term contract according to which he charged per ration delivered to Fort Pitt, and the British had to transport the supplies from there.[54] But Gage also purchased supplies from Baynton, Wharton, and Morgan, the Philadelphia group who provided the goods for Croghan's expedition. That group had already set up a store in Fort Chartres in hopes of cornering the local market, and then offered British authorities a more efficient and cheaper strategy for supplying the troops. By transporting supplies for the troops together with the trade goods they intended to convey to Illinois, they could defray some of the army's cost. They also proposed that they could cut costs by supplying the fort with "Flour, Pork, etc.," that they expected to acquire from French settlers who had been inhabiting the region since before the Seven Years' War. The settlers, they anticipated, would barter their produce in exchange for manufactures at the Baynton, Wharton, and Morgan store.[55] But the contractors in London and the government agreed to new terms for conveying supplies to Illinois commencing in January 1767 with Franks as their agent once again, this time under the auspices of his partnership with Levy, in cooperation with an uncle on his mother's side.[56] Franks's rivals' store survived until 1768, when Franks stationed an agent, William Murray, in Illinois to manage his affairs more closely. Baynton, Wharton, and Morgan sold the stock remaining in their store to Franks, enabling him and his partners to dominate trade in Illinois as well.[57]

Even while trying to woo Indians with goods, British authorities recognized that the Indian trade intensified other problems. Dependency on European goods had led to indebtedness and, consequently, forfeiture of land to settle debts. The merchants and traders who came into possession of land aimed to sell it to settlers—a focus of Indians' resentment. Already throngs of settlers had pushed beyond the Proclamation Line, the boundary enacted by Parliament in 1763, right after Pontiac's War erupted, prohibiting settlement west of the Appalachian Mountains.[58] The policy that was being shaped focused on preventing new transfers of land, controlling settlement, and regulating trade. To that end, Sir William Johnson limited trade to those holding licenses. From the point of view of merchants and traders, however, licenses implied protections. This explains why David Franks and his colleagues and competitors who lost goods in the Indian attacks in 1763 appealed to the Crown for compensation. When they submitted their memorial, they tasked Assistant Superintendent of Indian Affairs George Croghan (who was also Franks's trading partner) with assisting Moses Franks in London representing their appeal to the Board of Trade. Given the ongoing discussions taking place in London about managing the new territory, Franks and his colleagues recognized that they needed to be strategic.[59] They thus sought to show that they had been, and continued to be, useful allies in promoting British imperial interests.

This was not Croghan's primary mission in London. He was sent to present Superintendent Johnson's proposal for overcoming the thorny overlapping problems of settlers, Indians, and land—a conundrum that was central to imperial policy. Johnson suggested that the British delineate a new, more effectively enforceable frontier boundary, in other words, a new colony. In addition, a new colony would also resolve the problem of the French settlers. A new colony would "induce the French to embrace Britishness."[60] In short, a new colony was a way to impose stricter control over new regions, a way of subordinating those regions to British authority.[61]

Talk of a new colony encouraged land speculation and inspired investors in Virginia, Maryland, Pennsylvania, New York, and Connecticut to form land companies. In fact, scores of investors already held land titles to tracts lying west of the Proclamation Line. As early as 1749, Croghan himself negotiated with "Chiefs of the Six Nations" for three tracts in the heart of the Ohio Valley in exchange for "a Large & valuable Quantity of Goods."[62] In 1763, David Franks and his partner William Plumsted acquired a sixty-thousand-acre tract from Croghan on the Youghiogheny River southeast of Fort Pitt. In addition to Croghan's two other responsibilities in Parliament, he also addressed his own problem, the fact that the imposition of the Proclamation Line threatened the value of those assets. He requested that policy makers reimburse him for his tract at the forks of the Ohio. Instead of financial compensation, he indicated that he would accept two hundred thousand acres in the Mohawk Valley, another region that attracted settlers.[63]

Thus, when Franks and his comemorialists' request for compensation for their losses in the 1763 Indian attacks was declined, the group changed their strategy, adopting an approach similar to Croghan's, and once again tied their own fortunes to British plans for managing its empire. They decided to obtain a land grant directly from the Indians within the region earmarked for a colony and to apply to the Crown for approval. For this purpose, they formed the Indiana Company, issuing shares to claimants in proportion to their losses. The group's leading advocate, William Trent—Franks and Croghan's partner in the Indian trade—worked on garnering as much support for the plan as possible. He offered shares to powerbrokers whose influence might help their cause, including Governor William Franklin of New Jersey and Joseph Galloway, speaker of the Pennsylvania Assembly. At a conference held at Johnson's New York estate in 1765, the Six Nations and Delaware Indians agreed to cede a tract of land on the Ohio—the land that would become a new colony if Parliament approved Johnson's plan.[64]

Superintendent Johnson formalized peace with Pontiac and his allies at a formal meeting in 1766 where he emphasized Britain's commitment to coexistence and free trade with the Indians, and the parties agreed to negotiate a new frontier boundary. Two years later, in 1768, British authorities gave Johnson the go-ahead to confer with the Indians about the boundary lines for a cession of land to the Crown. The Indiana Company's land grant, if approved, would be situated within the designated territory. Johnson convened a conference with the chiefs of the Six Nations and their dependent tribes at Fort Stanwix, New York. The Indians at the conference granted the Indiana Company a large tract in what is now West Virginia. The grant was made in the form of a sale for £85,916 New York currency, the amount being the value of goods stolen and destroyed in 1763. Although the grant had not yet received royal approval, the Treaty of Fort Stanwix signaled to all concerned that the Crown would soon permit settlement west of the Proclamation Line.[65]

The Indiana Company dispatched William Trent, another one of David Franks and George Croghan's partners in the Indian trade and the individual tasked with garnering support for the Indiana Company, to London to secure confirmation on their grant. Optimistic that approval was forthcoming, members of the group asked Trent to present another similar case on behalf of the "Sufferers of 1754" who had lost goods in attacks at the beginning of the Seven Years' War. Once again David Franks was a member of the group, and once again they asked Moses Franks for assistance in the matter, offering him a share in a second land company as compensation.[66] The latter addressed "the Kings Most Excellent Majesty in Council," asserting that the sufferers had "made Application to the Administration at the Time setting forth their extreme Losses and praying for a Compensation." They had been "favorably heard and Hopes given them of Relief. But the general War which soon followed occasioned every lesser Consideration to be postponed."[67] The response was encouraging, but once again opposition from some members of the Board of Trade stalled resolution.

Support for the Indiana grant waxed and waned in London. More pressing colonial business always took precedence. In hopes of expediting the process the group revised their strategy to make their proposal more attractive to the Crown. With the support of former prime minister Thomas Walpole, they sought to establish a new land company financed by American and English investors who would purchase from the Crown land ceded in the Fort Stanwix treaty. The new company became known as the Grand Ohio Company or the Walpole Company in England, and as Vandalia in the colonies. David Franks, his London-based brothers Moses and Naphtali, and his son Jacob (John) Franks, who had by then settled in London and was closely associated with his uncle Moses, were all shareholders. The group recruited influential investors in America, including Benjamin Franklin and his son William, governor of New Jersey, and in Britain, including Lord Gower, president of the Privy Council; Lord Rocheford, secretary of state for the Northern Department; Thomas Pownall, member of Parliament who had served as governor of New Jersey, Massachusetts, and South Carolina; John Pownall, secretary of the Lords of Trade and Plantations; Thomas Pitt; and George Grenville. Should they succeed, the Indiana Company shareholders hoped to profit via land sales.

The tract that the company representatives offered to purchase was much larger than the tract previously sought by the Indiana Company and included the Indiana grant and George Croghan's own grant. The purchasers offered to pay the Crown £10,160 7s. 3d. sterling (approximately equivalent to £2,000,000 today)—effectively reimbursing the Crown for the cost of the entire Fort Stanwix cession—to be paid in five installments plus a quit rent on improved lands after twenty years.

The shareholders were confident that the plan would be approved, but their goals were frustrated when other American speculators came forward with similar schemes. The Ohio Company of Virginia also claimed half a million acres on the Ohio River. Another group of Virginians, with George Washington among its members, claimed two hundred thousand acres near Pittsburgh, and the Mississippi Company claims overlapped as well.[68] Caught in a knot of competing claims compounded by the objections of Indians who had no part in the negotiations and objected to being dispossessed of their land, the British deferred a resolution. The Revolutionary War halted negotiations.[69]

The onset of hostilities between Americans and British in 1775 put the Franks family, and David Franks in particular, in a difficult position. The Nesbitt, Drummond, and Franks partnership was awarded a new contract to supply British troops who, this time, were fighting to bring rebellious American subjects to heel and to preserve the empire. Given the complexities of finding suppliers willing to support what they saw as British tyranny, the contractors shipped most supplies from elsewhere. David Franks, still his brother's agent, was tasked with victualing troops who had been taken prisoner by the Americans, having received permission from American authorities to fulfill his contract. Between November 1776 and February 1779, the cost amounted to £51,793.[70]

Like central European Court Jews, the Frankses exposed themselves to considerable risk in the process of fulfilling contracts, and they found themselves facing huge losses. The Treasury refused to remit payment on some of the invoices the contractors submitted for provisions that David Franks supplied to the English prisoners. And the contractors—Moses Franks being one of them—refused to honor the bills of exchange that David Franks had drawn on them for payment.[71] Instead, Moses advised his brother to attempt to procure payment from British authorities in New York.[72] In the meantime, Franks's ties to the British aroused suspicion. He was accused of treason and banished. He lived out his last years in London, where he applied to the Treasury for support on the grounds that he was "thrown out of a lucrative Business . . . and also deprived of the Emoluments arising from his Agency to the Contractors." It is unclear whether he received any relief.[73] American independence disrupted the campaign for royal approval of land grants, which, of course, had emerged from efforts to recover losses in Indian attacks. Thus, the war, Franks's banishment, and Britain's subsequent refusal to engage in trade with the newly independent United States shattered his commercial enterprises. Britain's contraction, then, diminished David Franks's economic enterprises.

Moses Franks also suffered losses. The value of the land that the brothers owned in America and their shares in land companies had plummeted. Once the war was over, he assigned a lawyer the task of chasing his debtors and liquidating his holdings in America. His debtors, including his brother, were all insolvent. In 1789 Moses Franks "died very much involved." His executors were "obliged to sell all his Estates" to pay his debts.[74] From the heights of wealth and prominence both men lost everything.

Unlike central European Court Jews, the Frankses were willing to pledge allegiance to a single power. As it turned out, the brothers' commercial enterprises collapsed precisely because they had tied themselves so closely to Britain. The Franks brothers' business successes and failures offer insight into their entanglements with the British Empire. Through colonial trade, especially the Indian trade, army supply, and land speculation, the Frankses' business interests were bound up with British imperial expansion. There is no evidence the British authorities regarded the Frankses as expendable because they were Jewish. Like many of their non-Jewish colleagues, they took advantage of opportunities that presented themselves, but those opportunities carried risk, as they did for their non-Jewish colleagues. The fact that David Franks was Jewish had once mattered to the Jewish newcomers whom he helped get started. However, when it came to collecting debts after the war, ethnoreligious ties and the fact that they were David Franks's protégés and trusted partners did not cushion them. The Frankses offered no concessions, even though their debtors were barely solvent. For the Frankses themselves, the fact that they were Jewish mattered little. The tiny number of Jews in the colonies when they each began their careers forced them to cooperate with non-Jews.[75] Their collaborations with white Christian trading partners enabled them to prosper and to participate in economic sectors that were accessible only to the wealthiest merchants. It was their participation in those sectors that facilitated their entanglements in British imperial projects.

CHAPTER 6

Declarations of Interdependence
Understanding the Entanglement of Jewish Rights and Liberties in the Anglo-Atlantic, 1740–1830

HOLLY SNYDER

In April 1807, the town of Trois-Rivières elected a Jew as one of its two representatives to the Legislative Assembly of Lower Canada. However, when Ezekiel Hart arrived at Québec City the following January to take the required oaths of office and assume his seat, his right to serve was challenged on the grounds that two of the three required oaths of office, including the Oath of Abjuration, had not been taken by him and that the third was not executed in the form prescribed by law. In fact, Hart—who had sought legal advice on this point prior to his arrival in Québec City—had attempted to effect a compromise between the requirements of secular and Jewish law by placing his hand on his head (in lieu of retaining his hat) and replacing the word "Christian" with the word "Jewish" as he recited the oath specified under the 1791 Constitution Act. However well-meant, these careful adjustments to legal form were not sufficient to resolve the ambiguities surrounding his status as a Jew. After several weeks of debate, the assembly ultimately concluded that Hart, specifically because he professed the Jewish religion, "ne peut sieger ni voter dans cette chambre" (can neither be seated nor vote in this chamber).[1]

As fate would have it, the legislature was shortly thereafter dissolved by the governor, and new elections were called. Hart, determined to overcome the barriers that had been set before him, went home to Trois-Rivières to stand again and, in due course, won a majority for the second time. When he returned to Québec City in April 1809, however, he had resolved to take the oath without covering his head, this time using the Christian Bible, and without declining the requirement to swear on his honor "as a Christian," as specified for the Oath of Abjuration. Yet again, his colleagues in the assembly declined to seat him. When told that Hart had taken the oath "on the Evangelists," one legislator remarked that as a Jew, Hart was legally incapable of binding himself by means of this oath. Once again, Hart's right to serve the constituents by whom he had been duly elected—twice—was refused by the assembly.[2]

This oft-told tale—called "L'affaire Hart"—is well known to historians of Canadian suffrage and of Canadian and American Jewish history. Indeed, its very familiarity is due to the fact that it presents a quintessential conundrum to the liberal mindset. Was Hart the victim of an antisemitic campaign within the assembly, or merely a convenient pawn in the ongoing power struggle among forces contending for political control over the affairs of Lower Canada? Were his foes the Catholics at

FIGURE 6.1. Unveiling of bilingual plaque, Trois-Rivières Québec, 1959, commemorating Ezekiel Hart, whose unfulfilled elections to office are alleged to have inspired full civil rights for all citizens in 1832. Collection source: Canadian Jewish Congress photograph collection PC1-6-266. Repository source: Alex Dworkin Canadian Jewish Archives. Image courtesy of Canadian Jewish Archives, Montreal.

large? (It seems worth noting that Hart himself thought not, observing that three quarters of his constituents in Trois-Rivières were Catholics who had clearly not found his religion a barrier to his potential for representing their interests.) Or were Lower Canada's Anglo-Protestants to blame? In fact, those legislators who initially challenged Hart's right to sit in the assembly were of both French and English, Catholic and Protestant background—as, indeed, were Hart's supporters. And what had his opponents really intended? To deny place-holding to professing Jews, or to anyone of Jewish descent? At Hart's first appearance in 1808, it seemed only the former was at play. After all, one Samuel Hart had already been admitted to his place in the legislature of Nova Scotia after a formal conversion to Christianity in 1793.[3] But when Ezekiel Hart was refused for the second time in 1809, having eviscerated the palpable evidence of his Jewishness by removing his head covering and agreeing to take the Oath of Abjuration, it was no longer so clear whether it was his adherence to Judaism or his Jewish ethnic identity that formed the stumbling block. The case is indeed complex and mysterious, defying a prima facie interpretation.

Historical debate over the significance of L'affaire Hart in Canadian history has been hampered by the limited focus on the meaning of these events for Canada. What I propose to do here is to reconsider the events of 1807–9 through an alternate Atlantic lens so as to broaden its overall framing in time and geographical space. This is a tour with three parts: First, it will be necessary to examine the calculus of Jewish sociopolitical standing in English political thought, from the time of the Jewish readmission to the end of the eighteenth century. Second, we will take a closer look at Québec and its Jews in the general context of minority rights in British America during the eighteenth century. Third, I will provide a close reading of the political economy of Lower Canada at the moment of Hart's election to the assembly in the early nineteenth century. In so doing, I hope to expose some of the sinews that link Ezekiel Hart's experience to the political condition of Jews throughout British America—and the Atlantic world writ large—including both those in the thirteen former colonies that came to call themselves the "United States" after 1776 and those in the fourteen that remained in the British ambit after the American fracture.

Jews in British Political Thought, 1650–1791

Understanding the Canadian underpinnings of L'affaire Hart requires an overview of how Jews began to figure in British political thought from the time that Britain began to establish its transatlantic colonies in the seventeenth century to the turn of the nineteenth century. This, in some respects, required an entire rethinking of Jewish political status in Britain, as Jews had been expelled in 1290 by edict of Edward I, and it had been unlawful for Jews to live openly in England afterwards. Jews had thus been virtually absent from the British polity at the moment when Britain began to establish its colonies across the Atlantic, where it soon became necessary to decide whether Jews might assist in colonizing these new territories. While Jews occasionally filtered into parts of Britain in the intervening period, they were typically not able to openly identify themselves as professing Jews without risking punishment and deportation. Reconsideration of the status of Jews as potential subjects of the realm came only with the establishment of the Commonwealth government under Oliver Cromwell's leadership, following the execution of Charles I. Still, the Whitehall Conference of 1655, which brought open discussion of Jewish status to the fore, reached no consensus about whether Jews ought to be readmitted to England, and if so, what their legal status should be. The medieval English law which had deemed Jews to be the bondsmen, and thus the property, of the king—though it continued to play a significant role in legal lore—was no longer seen to be functional in the wake of the Commonwealth's repudiation of the monarchy and the establishment of a republic governed from Parliament. At any rate, the system of feudal villeinage in which the prior law had been grounded had long since been discarded.[4] Englishmen of the seventeenth and eighteenth centuries were thus pressed to create new arguments to justify the legal status they wished to ascribe to the Jews who began to reside in Britain and its colonies in increasing numbers.[5]

To fully comprehend the significance of arguments made about Jewish legal status, it is worth exploring the immediate seventeenth-century antecedents in England as well as their eighteenth-century application by British colonial jurisdictions in North America. In the European context, the key argument against Jewish political participation was the one leveraged by the Catholic Church at the Fourth Lateran Council (1215), and sustained until its Second Vatican Council of 1962–65, that "since it is absurd that a blasphemer of Christ exercise authority over Christians" Jews must be discredited from holding public offices in the governance of Christian nations.[6] This argument, which drew support to the segregation of Jewish populations into ghettos as well as the physical marking of Jewish difference (by means of required apparel in noted colors, or specified items added to apparel, such as badges or hats) across Europe, continued to hold sway in religious circles and was certainly espoused by many believers.[7] Nevertheless, its potency abated in the wake of the Reformation, a steep decline spurred both by the growth of mercantilism and by Protestant approaches to the conversion of nonbelievers that diverged sharply from those of the Catholic Church. By the seventeenth century, Protestant theologians were beginning to distinguish between Jews who were hostile to Christianity, who ought to be banished, and Jews who were more friendly and open to discussion. The latter, in this view, might be welcomed, in hopes of eventual conversion and assimilation, which might render them worthy of inclusion in a Christian society. A more trenchant argument against Jewish civil participation now emerged from the standpoint of political economy, building on the commonplace English understanding of Jewish self-governance under halachah, Jewish religious law. From this perspective, seventeenth-century English political theorists of all persuasions argued, as James Harrington put it, that Jews were unlikely to make good citizens, "for they of all nations never incorporate but, taking up the room of a limb, are of no use or office unto the body, while they suck the nourishment which would sustain a natural and useful member."[8] Even supporters of Jewish readmission, such as the theologian John Dury, observed that "the Jewes come into Christian Common-wealths, not as members thereof, but as strangers therein, and yet forme a societie, or kind of Commonwealth amongst themselves."[9] Though they held different positions on the question at hand, Harrington and Dury agreed that the admission of Jews into the English Commonwealth posed certain legal problems. They differed only in how the problems might be handled. Harrington argued that settling the Jews in the margins of the English empire was the only means by which to both obtain profit from their economic activities and also avoid the damage that Jewish distinctiveness would inevitably cause to the English commonwealth were they to be allowed equal access to the heart of the country. Dury, on the other hand, proposed that readmission of the Jews to England was possible, but that "Our state doth wisely to goe warily... [because Jews] have wayes beyond all other men, to undermine a State" and, accordingly, they "must be restrained in some things" in order for their admission to have a beneficial impact on the nation.[10]

While these tracts were purposefully speculative at the time they were originally published in the 1650s, they proved especially influential in subsequent decades as the English began to confront the growing presence of professing Jews both in their expanding overseas empire and in the home countries of the British Isles. It soon became evident that the existing legal precedents that had carried over from the medieval period of Jewish settlement were now politically outmoded, but in the wake of the Whitehall Conference of 1655 the underlying issues did not generate sufficient interest for either Parliament or the Privy Council to make new laws or dictate specific policy recommendations to govern how Jews fit or did not fit into British imperial aims. The ongoing lack of clarity from London left individual colonies to wrestle with the question at hand on their own, which happened only in the most peripatetic manner—when and if Jews happened to appear and claim the rights of British subjects. In this, they already faced stiff competition from the Dutch, who had determined several decades earlier that incorporating Jews into commerce brought significant benefit to the Dutch Republic, both in the Netherlands and in the growing Dutch colonization presence overseas.

An early case of Jews claiming rights under English law occurred in 1684, in Rhode Island (the only non-Puritan colony in colonial New England), when a group of Jewish traders residing in the town of Newport were challenged and disavowed as "aliens" by William Dyer, surveyor general of the colony. The merchants appealed to the Rhode Island General Assembly for legal protection, along with the return of property that had been seized. This case took place despite a much-vaunted guarantee for "Libertie of Conscience" written into the original colony patent that colony founder Roger Williams was able to obtain from Charles I in 1644 (later confirmed in the Rhode Island colony charter granted in 1663 by Charles II). Williams was a noted advocate for the separation of church and state who had himself been cast out of the Massachusetts Bay Colony for his advocacy of religious practice free from interference by the mechanisms of the state. He had written of his particular pride in having orchestrated this then-unique guarantee from the Crown for the infant colony. But though sincere in his advocacy of conscience, Roger Williams simply lacked the power within the colony to make it conform to the interpretation that he had intended when he originally drafted this provision. Upon hearing the petition of the Jews, the assembly echoed the more common understanding of Jews as a people apart, and granted only "as good protection as any strangers being not of our Nation, they [the Jews] being obedient to his Majesty's laws."[11]

In part, perceptions of Jewish separateness were strengthened by, if not derived from, the way in which Jews represented themselves in public discourse. A petition to the Crown of June 28, 1695, for example, claimed to support the interests of "severall of ye Hebrew Nation setled in Jamaica & Barbados."[12] While the petitioning merchants asserted their status as legal denizens under English law, their titular description of themselves as part of a "Hebrew Nation" that had "settled" in the Caribbean colonies did not challenge, and could only serve to reinforce, the prevailing English notion of Jews as outsiders and therefore marginal to the English polity. As David Katz has noted, this perspective began to change only in the wake of the Glorious Revolution in 1688, when the ascension of the Dutch prince William of Orange to the throne of England as William III altered English perspectives on the viability of Jews as English subjects, as well as Jewish perspectives on what residence in England and the prospect of becoming an English subject had to offer.[13]

The Toleration Act of 1688, enacted in the wake of the Glorious Revolution, tacitly extended the official right to worship to Jews, but excluded them (along with Protestant sects that dissented from the Church of England, Catholics, and Unitarians) from office-holding. Nevertheless, in the decades following its enactment, the social, intellectual, and cultural atmosphere in England became more accepting of a Jewish presence. The enlarged sense of tolerance eventually led to the 1714 publication of an unusual tract advocating for the naturalization of Jews in Britain and Ireland, written by the Irish rationalist and freethinker John Toland. Toland had previously advocated for a measure designed to naturalize Protestants from foreign places in 1709, and this new tract was in keeping with his interest in shifting British national policy toward an expanded notion of subjecthood for Hanoverian Britain. Although the 1709 measure was repealed a year after its passage, and his 1714 tract, *Reasons for Naturalizing the Jews*, remained something of a curiosity, Toland had nevertheless stimulated discussion among government officials of key issues surrounding naturalization. Decades later, and partly under the pressures of administering its varied overseas colonies in the Americas, some of which had persistent difficulties in attracting permanent settlers, Toland's ideas were incorporated into a new law, popularly known as the Plantation Act or the Naturalization Act—officially designated as the Act of 13 Geo. II (1740), c. 7—that authorized the naturalization of both Jews and foreign-born Protestants. But Crown policy continued to hold onto Harrington's notion that Jews and other foreigners should be kept at arm's length, insofar as the act applied only in Britain's American colonies and only to those Jews and foreign Protestants who had been resident there for a minimum of seven years. Although an attempt was made by Parliament to pass a modest bill for the naturalization of Jews in England in 1753, public outcry about the prospect of Jews taking on the mantle of Englishmen was so loud that it was forcibly repealed within a year. The effect thus remained that Jews had greater rights and better claim to the privileges of his majesty's subjects in the American colonies than they did in London.[14]

Lower Canada and the Context of Minority Rights, circa 1800

By way of setting L'affaire Hart into the larger context of British colonization in North America, it may be useful to examine how the general question of minority rights and privileges was handled in other British colonies. Much notoriety has been attached to the Puritan colonies in New England (Massachusetts Bay, Plymouth, Connecticut, New Haven, and New Hampshire) during their founding phase in the seventeenth century, for their harsh strictures against anyone who did not conform to Puritan beliefs and behaviors. As expressed by Rev. Nathaniel Ward, author of the *Massachusetts Body of Liberties*, "all Familists, Antinomians, Anabaptists and other Enthusiasts shall have free Liberty to keepe away from us, and such as will come to be gone as fast as they can, the sooner the better."[15] A litany of tract literature soon emerged to document the persecutory treatment meted out to nonconformists of all varieties by Puritan authorities, and in particular to a wide assortment of dissenting Protestant denominations—notably Quakers, Baptists, and Antinomians—who would ultimately join Roger Williams to found the new colony of Rhode Island. Quakers, Catholics, and Jews were all, at times, proscribed by law in the English Caribbean colonies, where the Church of England was designated as the established church. As Patricia Bonomi observes, toleration in the seventeenth and eighteenth centuries could be grudging at best, even where leaders declined to establish an official colony church, as in Maryland, so as to leave room for the toleration of Catholics and others whose faith might otherwise be readily proscribed; or, where the religious diversity of the colonists resulted in any proposed establishment of an official church having no practical effect, as happened organically in New York.[16]

In the wake of the Revolutionary War, minority rights and privileges took on special significance in the newly formed United States, as legislators attempted to work out ways to unify a disparate population within a singular political framework. Indeed, Congress amended the federal Constitution to, among other things, adopt a provision based on

Virginia's Statute of Religious Freedom, authored by Thomas Jefferson, to guarantee freedom of religion to citizens of the new nation. But guarantees at the federal level were not routinely adopted by the individual states. Indeed, some were roundly rejected. North Carolina provides a case contemporaneous to L'affaire Hart that both parallels and diverges from Ezekiel Hart's experience, though the two cases have never been compared. Like Ezekiel Hart, North Carolina's Jacob Henry was twice elected to a seat in the state assembly. In 1809, at the beginning of his second term, a fellow legislator rose to move that Henry's seat be vacated because Henry "denies the divine authority of the New Testament, and refused to take the oath prescribed by law for his qualification." The following day, the North Carolina assembly held a debate on the matter. But it is there that the similarities between the two cases end.

During Henry's first campaign to represent Carteret County in 1808, no one seems to have noticed that he was a Jew, although the North Carolina constitution of 1776 explicitly limited office-holding to Protestants. Unlike Ezekiel Hart, Henry served his first one-year term in the house without incident and was reelected to the seat for the following term. And as a sitting member, Henry also had access to the floor of the house. After having been challenged by fellow legislators, Henry (again, unlike Hart, who was limited to submitting a demure petition seeking the right to occupy his seat) made an impassioned plea for "the natural and unalienable right to worship Almighty God according to the dictates of . . . Conscience," pointing to the apparent conflict between the declaration of rights and the state constitution, which had been adopted just one day apart. The speech was long considered such a model of eloquence that in 1828 it was included in Samuel Clark's *The American Orator*, a textbook regarded as "the means of instilling into the minds of youth, the principles of civil and religious freedom." Henry's fellow legislators were evidently unimpressed by his arguments as to conscience as the religious test remained on the books until a new state constitution was written in 1868. Nevertheless, Henry kept his seat because the legislators fashioned a unique interpretation of the state constitution that construed the prohibition on non-Protestants serving in the "Civil Department" as having no application to the legislature. This allowed Jews and Catholics to serve as legislators, but continued their exclusion from office in the executive and judicial branches of state government.[17]

A later case that attempted to utilize and build on the example set by Ezekiel Hart's election to the Assembly of Lower Canada in 1808 took place in Jamaica, just over a decade after Hart was denied his seat for the second time. There, in July 1820, a group of liberal Jews in Kingston staged a test of the political waters for attaining the right to vote by sending one of their number to the polls to cast his ballot in the local election for assembly. The man in question, Levy Hyman, was possessed of more than enough real estate to satisfy the property qualifications established in the voting laws set by the Jamaica Assembly. Hyman's appearance at the polling booth on July 5 was orchestrated by the group, who preceded their "assault" on the polling station with a public campaign to elevate awareness of Jewish claims to the rights of English subjects. During the four months prior to the election, members of the group sent letters to the island's newspapers in which they argued, using the rhetoric of English liberty, that the denial of the vote to Jews was a violation of both Jamaican law and the English Constitution. In addition, they made personal visits to each Jewish freeholder to solicit his appearance at the polls.[18] When the events of July 5 culminated in the denial of Hyman's right to cast his ballot, the advocates sprang to work: they pressed the wardens of Kingston's Princess Street Synagogue to take action on behalf of their congregants, they formed a committee to assert the Jewish right to the franchise, they encouraged Jewish freeholders to attempt casting their ballots at subsequent elections, and, informed that Levy Hyman intended to prosecute his claim under the Jamaican election laws against the deputy marshal who had refused to accept his poll, they set up a subscription fund to help him cover the costs of legal proceedings.[19] These efforts were doomed to failure in the short term, having been successfully circumvented by actions undertaken by the ruling elites—not only in the assembly and the island's courts, but also in the synagogue vestry—to resolve the question against the Jewish vote. Yet they represented the commencement of a long-term strategy that would, eventually, culminate in the passage of a law extending the franchise to Jamaican Jews in 1826.[20]

From the Canadian perspective, what is interesting about this attempt of Jamaican Jews to gain ground with respect to the exercise of voting rights lies in where both the advocates and the opponents found their justifications. In many respects, the rhetoric of the Jamaican newspaper debate is remarkably similar to the one that had taken place in Lower Canada a decade before. As in Lower Canada, the opponents of Jewish voting in Jamaica were able to capitalize on the ambiguous status of the Jews, which had never been explicitly defined by law, to overcome established precedents and even legal code leaning toward their Emancipation.[21] Moreover, the issue of Ezekiel Hart's election to the Assembly of

Lower Canada served the Jamaican proponents as an icon of what was possible in a liberal British Atlantic world. The key exchange was elicited when the editor of the *St. Jago Gazette*, espousing the position of the dutiful colonial, declared

> no man is eligible to vote at an election, who is not equally so to be elected himself. We have great respect for many of the Jewish nation in this island . . . but they may rely that any attempt to encroach on long established custom in so important a matter as that of voting for representatives in Assembly, cannot succeed. Until the Mother Country shew the example, we cannot swerve from accustomed practice.

In response to this diatribe, a writer using the pen name *A JEW* gave chapter and verse in the pages of the *Kingston Chronicle*, pointing out that Catholics and small landholders might vote on the island, though they could not hold elective office. Moreover, he retorted that the situation in Britain and its remaining American colonies was not as the editor had presented it:

> With regard to the British Parliament recognising the right of Jews to vote, I can confidently assert, that at Westminster and Middlesex the right of those Jews who have voted have never yet been disputed. In Canada, they not only vote, but also sit in the Provincial Parliament; as in 1808, at the election for the town of Three Rivers, which was sharply contested, Mr. Ezekiel Hart, a Jew, was chosen to serve for the town by a large majority, (*vide* Mr. John Lambert's Travels in Canada, in 1806, 7, and 8, page 493). Here, nothing has as yet been produced against the eligibility of a Jew's voting, but . . . resolutions and *custom*.[22]

To bolster that broad claim, the anonymous author of the letters reporting these events to a friend off the island claimed to have knowledge that Jews were already voting in English elections in 1820, and during the trial of Levy Hyman's case in February 1821 an attempt was made by Hyman's counsel to introduce the testimony of an English Jew who said that he himself had voted several times. Whether out of ignorance or rhetorical convenience, the advocates appear to have overlooked the fact that Ezekiel Hart was neither admitted to the assembly nor allowed to serve his constituents.

A second theme that has been largely ignored by historians is the potential link between the civil Emancipation of Catholics and that of the Jews. From the perspective of historians of Canada and Britain, this link is easy to miss. After all, Lower Canada's Catholics had had their political rights confirmed twice by legislative enactment—first by the Québec Act of 1774, and secondly by the Constitution Act of 1791—while Catholics in England and Ireland continued to suffer substantial disabilities until 1829.[23] In the Jewish case, by contrast, developments in England and Canada with respect to office-holding, if not voting, appear to have followed parallel tracks.[24] The two cases might appear, at first blush, to have little to do with each other. But here, again, viewing the Canadian experience through the wider lens of the British Atlantic allows us to see that the situation of Catholics and Jews was indeed intertwined in the last decades of the eighteenth century and the early years of the nineteenth century. As Aaron Hart, Ezekiel's father, had discovered on settling himself in in Trois-Rivières in 1764, the preceding decade of war had both impoverished the francophone population and diminished the ability of religious communities to recruit new members and maintain their existing properties, which the British hoped to gain by escheat as the religious brethren died out. Moreover, Catholics were effectively barred from holding elective office in these years, as British law specified the swearing of prescribed oaths that were unacceptable to professing Catholics. In effect, les Canadiens—the francophone Catholic citizens of Québec—found themselves in much the same position as the Jews in British colonies, that is to say, hostage to policies created in London but not necessarily adhered to by English politicians who ran local affairs in Québec. By the early nineteenth century, the freedoms promised by the Quebec Act had come to constitute something of a golden cage.[25]

Two references to my Jamaican example serve to underscore this point. First, as previously noted, the newspaper polemicist who styled himself *A JEW* pointed to the fact that Jamaican Catholics were already able to vote in local elections, thus drawing a direct connection between their condition and his own. Second, our detailed knowledge of the effort to effect the Jewish franchise in Jamaica comes from the publication of a series of private letters written by one of the advocates to a non-Jamaican friend. This volume was in print only briefly and is now exceedingly rare. Published by one A. MacKay Jr. in Belfast, the circumstances of its place of imprint are odd for a story that is purportedly about Jamaican Jews. The Jewish population of Belfast was inconsiderable at the time of its publication, and Northern Irish economic interests in Jamaica were scarcely worthy of note. The pamphlet appeared in

1823, however, at the height of the debate over Catholic Emancipation in the British Isles.[26] This, I believe, is a piece of evidence that makes an important link between the advocates of Catholic Emancipation and those for Jewish Emancipation. And, in fact, evidence from England and the United States suggests that the fate of Catholics and Jews was frequently linked through the late 1820s, although civil Emancipation was not delivered to them as coequal after that point. Both British and British colonial laws that disfranchised non-Protestants acted equally to disbar Catholics and Jews. In England, there was the requirement to take the Anglican sacrament in order to obtain full naturalization as an English subject—which remained active until finally removed from English naturalization laws in 1826. Only when the seventeenth-century Test and Corporation Acts were finally repealed in 1828 did the political condition of Anglo-Catholics diverge from that of the Jews, when a last-minute amendment to the bill of repeal continued the requirement that public officeholders make oath "on the true faith of a Christian." The formal Emancipation of Roman Catholics the following year meant that Jews were still excluded from full political participation, a situation that would persist into the 1850s. As Lord Chancellor Broughton put it in 1833, "His Majesty's subjects professing the Jewish religion were born to all the rights, immunities and privileges of His Majesty's other subjects, *excepting so far as positive enactments of law deprive them of those rights, immunities and privileges.*"[27]

In Rhode Island, Jews and Catholics alike had been disenfranchised by a mysterious statute that made its first appearance in the Rhode Island Digest of Laws in 1719 and explicitly banned non-Protestants from voting or holding elective office in the colony.[28] This purported statute appears to have been the wholesale fabrication of one man, Richard Ward—then secretary and general recorder for the colony, and a confirmed Seventh Day Baptist—who compiled the Digest of Laws at the order of the General Assembly, and apparently did so without meaningful supervision.[29] In March 1762, it became the principle basis on which the Newport Superior Court of Judicature (with Samuel Ward—son of Richard—presiding as chief justice) denied the petition of merchants Aaron Lopez and Isaac Elizer for naturalization under the terms of Parliament's Naturalization Act of 1740.[30] The official repeal of this fictitious statute as to Catholics in 1783 is said to have been due to the state's gratitude for the participation of French forces in the liberation of Rhode Island from British occupation during the war. In the minds of members of the Rhode Island General Assembly, at least, no such thanks were owed to Rhode Island's Jews, who had to wait another fifteen years before a new statute was enacted to reassert and guarantee religious freedom statewide, finally allowing for the franchise to extend to them.[31]

Local Identities and the Politics of Lower Canada in the Nineteenth Century

Having set the dual contexts for the ambiguity surrounding the possible role for Jews in British political economy and the more tangled question of minority rights, we now return to the specific case of Ezekiel Hart's election to represent Trois-Rivières and the subsequent events of 1808-10 in Lower Canada. And here, it is important to unpack a set of facts surrounding these events, facts that are seldom considered as part of the telling of Hart's story.

The acquisition of Québec in September 1759 brought to Britain issues of governance that the British had not confronted in other American colonies that the British won by conquest. The most trenchant of these was a large population of Euro-American colonists who, being proudly francophone and Catholic instead of anglophilic and Protestant, did not conform to any of the existing models for British colonial subjects. By the early 1770s, it became clear to Parliament that certain expectations would need adjustment if the goal was to successfully absorb Québec's large Catholic population and its existing French administrative structures into Britain's transatlantic empire. The Québec Act of 1774 (14 Geo. III c. 83), the end result of these considerations, guaranteed the free exercise of Catholicism and the restoration of French civil law in Québec, resolving some of the pressing administrative tensions.[32] In the wake of the American Revolution, Britain made further adjustments to governance in Québec through the 1791 Constitution Act (31 Geo. III c. 31), dividing Québec into two separate entities, Lower Canada and Upper Canada. The primary purpose of these changes, however, was less to protect the unique identity of the francophone population of Québec than to accommodate the growth of an anglophone community in Canada. Thus, while both of the newly created provinces would have constituent assemblies on the British model, and both would have an intermixture of francophone and anglophone population, Lower Canada would remain primarily French, while Upper Canada, comprising the underdeveloped western side of the original colony, was designated for future anglophone population growth—not only for the newly arrived distressed loyalist refugees driven out of the United States in the course of the war, but also for new emigrants coming straight from Britain. Yet, as Fernand Ouellet notes, the Constitution Act left in place the existing French customs in commerce, despite demands from English merchants for the establishment of English commercial law in their stead. In Canada, if in no other colony, British administration aimed to respond in nimble fashion to the competing claims of British subjects.[33]

Even as these changes to the administrative infrastructure of Québec were being set in place, the colony also faced economic consequences from structural shifts in the underlying fundamentals on which growth and commerce had for so long relied. Ouellet points to a long period of fluctuation lasting from 1793 to 1815, characterized by rapid price inflation accompanied by productive peaks in both the fur trade and agricultural exports from Québec, followed by contraction in the fur trade and a steep decline in Québec's agricultural exports. The rise of the timber trade helped to ameliorate the economic pain, but overall the trajectory of Québec's economy after 1802, buffeted by poor harvests and public health epidemics, had the trappings of inherent instability leading to economic depression.[34] These economic stresses were mirrored in emerging political tensions among Britain, the United States, and Napoleon's France that arose from long-standing disputes over international trade and national sovereignty.

The political situation within Québec was equally fraught. In 1774, the Québec Act had secured certain linguistic, legal, and religious concessions for the francophone population, while at the same time supporting the growing class divide between the landholding seigneurs and the rising middle class comprised of elite professionals and the mercantile bourgeoisie. After the reforms of the Constitution Act, which left key elements of Québec culture intact, many francophone Canadians began to see distinct advantages to British constitutional forms and parliamentary institutions. Influenced by ideas fomented in France and the United States, as delivered through the pages of newly established francophone journals such as *La Gazette du commerce et littéraire de Montréal* (1778-79) and its successor *La Gazette de Montréal* (1785-94), the new Canadien elite began to follow Encyclopedist ideas about governance and to philosophize about the advantages of science and freedom of the press. Nevertheless, the excesses of the French Revolution also led them to appreciate the particular advantages of the parliamentary system that Britain had delivered via the Constitution Act and the avenues it offered that would permit them to advocate for francophone interests.[35]

This was the political context of Lower Canada at the time when Ezekiel Hart determined to seek a seat in the Assembly of Lower Canada, which he first attempted in 1804. In making this decision, however, Hart was not thinking of the big picture of local politics. Instead, Hart drew on his personal context, as a Jew who was also a natural-born subject of the British Crown, born and raised in the town of Trois-Rivières where his father was both a notable landholder possessed of several seigneuries and religiously observant. His decision also relied heavily on the tutelage of his older brother, Moses, in every possible way an obstreperous, uncontainable man with political ambitions he had no realistic hope of fulfilling on his own account. His father had even warned Moses against dabbling in politics, fearing that Moses "would be opposed as a Jew" and admonishing that Moses would find no support from either the courts or the politicians should he try. Ezekiel's first run for office did not succeed. But by 1807 an incumbent in one of the two seats for Trois-Rivières had died, leaving the seat open, and he decided to make a second run. This time, he obtained a majority by the thin margin of two votes.[36] Unsure exactly how to proceed to assume his seat from that point, Hart sought the advice of an anglophone lawyer. While he befriended and helped his francophone neighbors, Hart—like his father before him—cultivated contacts among the anglophone population for the administrative benefits this would bring. His father had, after all, arrived in Canada with the British Army, accepted their patronage for his trading enterprise, and soon found that his economic success relied on those contacts. As Ezekiel Hart sought support for his struggle to take the assembly seat he had fairly won, he found ready allies among Lower Canada's anglophone minority, among them James Henry Craig, the British governor of Lower Canada. Craig, though newly appointed to the post in 1807, had by then spent more than three decades as an officer in the British Army, serving throughout North America between 1773 and 1781, and thereafter deployed to Ireland, the Continent, Africa, and India prior to his appointment as governor. Observers remarked that as a soldier, he was reportedly hot tempered, demanding, and grandiloquent, while also generous, devoted to duty, and loyal to his friends. While these qualities had served him well in the army, his lack of tact and diplomatic skill, combined with chronic illness and an overreliance on self-serving advice from anglophone merchants, made his tour as governor disastrous. Craig's limited focus on what would best promote British colonization within Canada and his deep antipathy toward the French quickly alienated the Canadien elite and put a target on his back for the Parti Canadien.³⁷ But during Ezekiel Hart's struggle to assume his seat in the assembly, Craig, though initially reluctant to intercede, nevertheless proved himself a friend and supporter.

Viewed from this perspective, we can see that the case of Ezekiel Hart was hopelessly entangled from the outset in the fraught struggle of the French Catholic Canadiens for political authority and civil equality in Lower Canada, a tense encounter between a divisive and deeply unpopular British governor and an incipient francophone political party that represented a majority of the population but suffered from its own internal division over tactics, between Memorialists willing to accept fewer rights if doing so preserved an antiquated notion of their cultural identity and Constitutionalists, led by Pierre-Stanislas Bédard and his new young colleague Louis-Joseph Papineau, who sought to push the anglophone minority to acknowledge francophone equality, both politically and culturally, by the terms of the very Constitution Britain had imposed in dividing the original province in two in 1791. As respected as Hart may have been by his Canadien neighbors and constituents in Trois-Rivières, his local popularity meant nothing to his Canadien colleagues in the assembly, who viewed the world through a larger geopolitical lens in which the anglophone elite, with Craig at their helm, sought only to undermine the authority of francophone legislators and deny the francophone citizens of Lower Canada the promise of equality guaranteed under the Constitution Act. Hart, they perceived, was a baked-in ally of the very governor who had thwarted them at every turn and unabashedly made himself their enemy. They did not need to stretch far to find the evidence of Hart's complicity in Craig's agenda. It was amply evidenced by Hart, in 1809, not only having entertained the governor in his home but also having named his newborn son James Henry Craig, in the governor's honor. What more proof could the Canadiens possibly have needed that Hart was in the governor's pocket? In any case, Hart had already provided evidence of his lack of interest in francophone political interests when he declined to vote for the preferred candidate of the Parti Canadien on the occasion of choosing a speaker for the assembly in 1809.³⁸

It is tempting, with the hindsight of the twenty-first century, to look back on the struggle of Ezekiel Hart and other Jews in British America both to vote and to seek and serve in elective office as part of a larger revolutionary movement toward democratic republicanism. In fact, the path toward civil equality for Jews in the Anglo-American and francophone portions of the Old and New Worlds was tortuously twisted and could better be described as checkerboard or patchwork than linear in nature. We would do well to heed the cautions implicit in some of the texts discussed here. In the case of Jamaica, for example, the advocates seem to have felt sharply constrained from citing two examples of places where rights for Jews had already been enlarged: France and the United States. They could hardly have raised France as an example of enlightened politics. The disdain for the Terror among British intellectuals, coupled with deep-seated fear among Anglo-Jamaicans of a Jacobin slave uprising similar to that of the 1791 revolt in nearby Saint-Domingue, discredited any reference to the Declaration of the Rights of Man from the outset. Jamaican Jews were further discomfited with using the French as a model for civic humanism by the knowledge that they had already been implicated by negative association with French Jacobinism. Just twenty years earlier, a French Jew named Isaac Yeshurun Sasportas had been captured in Jamaica while attempting to foment a slave revolt and had been summarily hanged in a public spectacle on the Kingston parade.[39] The United States, though not as problematic an exemplar in Jamaica as France, was hardly a better one for advocating Jewish rights. While ratification of the federal Constitution meant that Jews could vote in federal elections in the United States by the 1790s, the individual states had been slow to follow suit. Thus, in 1820, Jews could vote and hold elective office in some states (New York, Pennsylvania, Virginia, Georgia, and South Carolina, for example) but not others (Maryland, Massachusetts, New Jersey, and New Hampshire).[40] The patchwork growth of Jewish rights in the United States, coupled with the unsavory fact of Britain's tense relationship with the former colonies—rendered into open warfare between 1812 and 1815—made the United States itself a less than compelling model of republican principle for their intended audience. Instead, the advocates of civil rights for Jamaica's Jews chose to invoke the sacred authority of Britain's ancient constitution, memorialized by popular English political writers at both ends of the political spectrum, from Coke to Locke and Burke, using it as a tool to expand on the general atmosphere of rights and liberties. In furtherance of their cause, they cited Canada and England itself as their exemplars, rather than France and the United States. In effect, they were highlighting not Jamaica's capacity to make its own political choices, but its very interdependence with Britain and the remaining British colonies in the Americas.

Nevertheless, the vignettes presented here do offer some clues as to the efficacy of strategic interventions. In North Carolina, Jacob Henry had a multipronged attack to serving in the assembly, succeeding as much because he sought common cause with the minority Catholics in the state, who had also suffered the sting of proscription by virtue of their religion, as well as because he was an accomplished orator whose eloquence impelled his Protestant colleagues in the assembly to bend the exclusionary rules just enough so as to craft an exception. And in Jamaica, although the advocates were not successful in achieving the right to vote by forwarding the claims of Levy Hyman in 1820, they nevertheless brought the issue to light by working as a group to foment public discussion in ways that just a few years later, resulted in a bill for Jewish voting that passed in the Jamaica Assembly in 1826, was approved by the Crown in 1831, and articulated arguments that perhaps aided the cause of Catholic Emancipation in Britain. In this regard, L'affaire Hart can be read as a strategic failure on the part of Ezekiel Hart. Even with a good heart, excellent connections, and the best of intentions, Hart's lack of experience in politics was his Achilles heel, and he proved himself inept where it mattered most. He relied overmuch on his francophone constituents in Trois-Rivières and his anglophone connections to carry the day for him in the assembly, and foolishly neglected to build bridges to other legislators representing majority francophone districts. But, most importantly, Hart failed to find common ground with the francophone majority in the assembly or to court the support of the Parti Canadien at the very moment when its members were articulating an agenda for the expansion of civil equality in Lower Canada. That his refusal by the Assembly of Lower Canada was partisan and not personal is attested by the fact that his own son, Samuel Bécancour Hart, successfully petitioned the Assembly of Lower Canada in 1831 to remove the legal bars to Jewish office-holding applied by the British colonial government, with the full support of Louis-Joseph Papineau, then speaker of the assembly, and the assembly's francophone majority.[41]

In discussing L'affaire Hart, it is therefore most important to point to the position of Canada as the only place in British America where a majority of the population were both francophone and Catholic, creating an identity of intersectional minority status. Since the 1960s, francophone historians of the "Two Canadas" school, led prominently by Jean-Pierre Wallot, have made valiant efforts to speak to the position of the Canadiens during the critical period that is our focus here (1791–1815) in navigating the shifting ground beneath their feet among the geopolitics of British, French, and American interventions in Lower Canada. But their message has long been buried within a historiography that put its principal efforts into building a master narrative for a unified Canada. In the 1970s, Canadian historiography took up the banner of "limited identities" in an attempt to encapsulate the complex ways in which nationalization affected, and was effected by, Canada's diverse ethnicities. This was done in the face of the rising Parti Québecois. With its end goal of national sovereignty for Québec and its strong advocacy of separatism, the PQ drove public fears that Canada itself might be cleaved into separate pieces. But as an approach to history writing, "limited identities" proved to be of limited utility, balkanizing Canadian historiography rather than contributing to an inclusive national narrative.[42] L'affaire Hart provides us with an opportunity to revisit this buried historiography of francophone Canada in its most politically transformative period, and restore its unique perspective on Canada as an emerging entity within the context of the broader British colonial world. Using L'affaire Hart as our lens gives us the opportunity to see the ways in which Jews were easily entangled in the tectonic movements of British adventures and countertensions in the Americas. In serving that role, it should also highlight for us the trajectory of a broader intersectional discourse about rights and liberties then taking place both within and across the British Atlantic.

Chapter 7

Jews and Free People of Color in Eighteenth-Century Jamaica

A Case Study in Experiential and Ethnic Entanglement

STANLEY MIRVIS

Abraham Henriques de Souza was a mid-eighteenth-century Jewish planter in Jamaica's Saint Catherine parish. In Jamaica he stood at a crossroads of the entangled strands of the supra-imperial Portuguese diaspora with familial connections to both Amsterdam and London. He associated with the Portuguese Jewish community of Saint Jago de la Vega, requested a Jewish burial and a memorial prayer, and supported the Jewish orphan society. Like many of his Jewish and non-Jewish male counterparts in Jamaica, he found an alternative to marriage through a long-term relationship with Phillis, a free black woman, "who has lived with me for many years."[1] Abraham and Phillis had two "mulatto" daughters, Sarah and Rebecca Souza, who inherited their mother's limited freedom. Abraham died in 1773, and a year later his daughter Rebecca, a baptized Christian, received a personal privileges bill.[2]

This privileges bill elevated Rebecca above other free people of color in Jamaica by empowering her to testify against white Christians in court and exempting her from "deficiency" fees that penalized planters with a greater ratio of African-descendent over white laborers on their estates. Ironically, exemption from these fees gave Rebecca a slight economic advantage over her Jewish father. This exemption may indeed have been Rebecca's principal motivation in petitioning for a privileges bill. By 1811, as debates over civil enfranchisement for people like her and her father raged in the Jamaican Assembly, she was in possession of a substantial enslaved labor force of her own.³ Like other free people of color, Rebecca participated in the slave regime perhaps in part to undermine it from within by acting as a patron to enslaved kin and associates. This possibility is supported by her conspicuous manumission of nearly half of her slaves in her will. Still, even with a privileges bill, Rebecca, like her Jewish father and her free black mother, was prohibited from voting in elections, sitting on juries, or holding public office.

Rebecca Souza is the literal embodiment of the experiential, ethnic, and legal entanglements of the Atlantic world. Not only did Jews and free people of color possess nearly identical civil rights in Jamaica, and not only did white Christians stereotypically homogenize the two groups, but in the person of Rebecca and others like her, Jews and free people of color were literally one and the same. Rebecca was baptized as a Christian, and she may very well have been sincere in that faith, but she was ethnically Jewish, and she bore a name marking her as such, indistinguishable from other Jewish women on the island.⁴

When Rebecca died in the early nineteenth century, mixed-ancestry lobbyists together with the Board of Trade in London and abolitionists at home and abroad were pressuring the Jamaican Assembly to pass greater legal privileges for free people of color. At the same time, the assembly worried about the stagnation of white population growth in comparison to free people of color as well as the potential influence of revolutionary ideals emanating from Haiti. These factors combined to force the assembly to confront the inevitability that free people of color must be incorporated into civil society with full voting rights.⁵ Jews, who were similarly disenfranchised, feared falling behind free people of color in the march toward suffrage and initiated their own civil rights campaign. So began two decades of acrimonious competition between Jews and free people of color. Despite the undermining obstructionism of this competitiveness there were also some short-lived bursts of unity.

Some historians have argued that Jews undermined free people of color at the moment of Emancipation because of the Jews' aspirational, and essentially racist, association with white Christian planters. Those same historians assert that free people of color undermined Jews as a result of their own aspirational acculturation in keeping with the expectations of white plantocracy.⁶ Contrary to this interpretation, this chapter argues that the competitive bid for civil liberties in the early nineteenth century represents a culmination of a century of experiential and legal entanglement between Jews and free people of color. Their competitiveness was the product of their existential commonality rather than their attempts to graft themselves onto white Christian society.

This chapter is a study of interethnic entanglement.[7] That is, rather that approaching the history of Jews and free people of color comparatively, or as parallel pasts, it rather identifies points of contact and overlapping experiences. It then assesses the ways those points of contact created the conditions for competitive Emancipation in the early nineteenth century. "Entanglement" as a mode of inquiry challenges ethnic history in isolation, moves beyond the study of *similarities* in order to appreciate *commonalities*, and is a methodological refraction of the ethnic and cultural hybridities of the early modern Atlantic world.

Commonality is a term central to this analysis. Did Jews have more *in common* with free people of color than with white Christian settlers? Did white Christian settlers perceive Jews to have more *in common* with free people of color? And did free people of color see themselves as sharing more *in common* with Jews than with other free blacks or the enslaved? Commonality is a matter of perspective or even ideology. Sometimes, when it suited one goal, white Christian writers and lawmakers homogenized Jews and free people of color, and at other times, when it suited another goal, they disentangled them.

This chapter identifies four points of contact shared by Jews and free people of color in eighteenth-century Jamaica: civil liberties, urbanization, militia service, and fetishization. It concludes by describing the entangled competitiveness between Jews and free people of color in their race for civil liberties. But first, this chapter examines the experiences of Jews and free people of color in isolation, as parallel but not overlapping histories, in order to provide a point of reference for their entanglement.

Parallel Paths: Jamaica's Free People of Color

The knotted chords of entanglement that tied Jews and free people of color together in Jamaica were not inevitable. Their respective paths of migration and experiences upon arrival in Jamaica were decidedly disconnected. It was Jamaica itself, and the hybridity of the Atlantic world more broadly, that intricately entangled their destinies. The most glaring experiential difference between Jews and free people of color is that Jews migrated by choice, had not been enslaved, and had not experienced the irregular process of transitioning from bondage to freedom.[8]

British Jamaica was a slave society, that is, the majority of the inhabitants of the island were owned. By 1740, as sugar production boomed, Jamaican factors imported over seven thousand slaves a year.[9] In 1755, the enslaved made up nearly 90 percent of the total Jamaican population. On the eve of Emancipation in 1834, as the free people of color population grew, that of the enslaved fell to 84 percent, still a staggering majority.[10] Unlike in Dutch and Spanish colonies, where there existed some legal gradations of unfreedom, no such distinctions existed in Jamaica.[11] However, owners grafted external structural hierarchies onto the enslaved. For example, enslaved domestic servants sometimes held different privileges than enslaved plantation workers, enslaved overseers held authority over enslaved laborers, and children of owners who inherited their mothers' enslavement often held different expectations of treatment and hopes for freedom.

The enslaved maintained their own internal status distinctions. Most Africans transplanted to Jamaica before the 1770s were ethnically Akan from the highly centralized societies of the Gold Coast in modern-day Ghana.[12] In some sites, the enslaved and the Maroons perpetuated conflicts from this war-torn region and entangled those struggles with local Jamaican politics.[13] Some among the enslaved looked toward Akan nobility for leadership, especially during Tacky's Revolt in 1760.[14]

Freedom, along with all of its contradictions and limitations, was the only legally binding social distinction among blacks and racially blended people in Jamaica. Slavery was governed by the terms of the relatively fixed 1664 Slave Code and its few amendments. An amendment in 1717 provided incentives for owners to indoctrinate the enslaved with Christianity but did nothing to incentivize the enslaved to accept Christianity beyond a vague promise of becoming more "civilized."[15] Indeed, the slave code allowed for only a single path to freedom, manumission, which was achieved either by act of assembly or through the use of the devise in a will.

Manumission was extremely rare in colonial Jamaica, as in other Atlantic slave societies.[16] During the 1770s, only around 165 individuals were freed each year from among an enslaved population of 192,787, that is, less than 0.1 percent.[17] In addition, most of those manumissions took place in towns even though most of the enslaved lived in rural parishes.[18] Despite the low frequency of manumission, Jamaica had the largest population of free people of color in the English Atlantic, by far. In the 1770s there were over 4,000 free people of color living in Jamaica, compared to fewer than 850 in Barbados.[19] In absolute numbers, Jamaica's population of free people of color was comparable to that in Curaçao, although its share of the total population was smaller than in the Dutch island, and surpassed Dutch Suriname, another plantation-oriented slave society, where there were less than 3,000 according to the 1811 census.[20] Free people of color were also Jamaica's fastest growing community. By 1788 the population had grown by over 137 percent to around 9,500.[21] Yet, despite Jamaica's overwhelming presence of free people of color, the population came nowhere close to that in Saint-Domingue, which was home to around 25,000 free people of color at the time of the Haitian Revolution.[22]

In Jamaica, unlike other parts of the English Atlantic, free people of color were permitted to reside in the colony indefinitely following their manumission.[23] Borrowing from similar legislation in New York, in 1774 the Jamaican Legislature required the use of a security bond paid out annually to free individuals, providing a potential path for them to participate in the economy by ensuring a stable, if inadequate, income. This lifetime annuity also served to discourage the frivolous use of manumission.[24]

Most manumitted people in Jamaica were the children of white owners and enslaved women of African ancestry, generally referred to as "mulattos."[25] Manumission was a rare reward, typically for the "faithful service" of a domestic laborer or compensation for public service, or was purchased by the enslaved individual out of the profits earned from leasing their labor. Manumission was sometimes a manipulative tool wielded by white owners to incentivize obedience and not a recognition of freedom as a natural right.[26] By the early nineteenth century, less than 20 percent of freed people were referred to as "negroes," meaning blacks without European ancestry.[27] It is for this reason that Jamaican legislators and writers often used the term "mulattos" synonymously with free people of color.

The rarity of free blacks contributed to a deeply colorist ethos within the freed community that was stratified along lines of wealth and complexion. Those with lighter skin or greater degree of separation from a black ancestor held considerably more social capital. Indeed, many lighter-skinned people and those with white fathers sometimes held an expectation of privileges apart from freedom from slavery as part of a patrilineal birthright.[28]

Atlantic slave ownership is not synonymous with whiteness. On the contrary, owning slaves was a concrete way for free people of color to actualize their economic agency. Some scholars have suggested that slave ownership among free people of color was used as a way to subvert the slave system and to support their relatives, as much as it was used as an instrument of their economic and social advancement.[29] In this way, free people of color exercised the paradoxical role of guardians by enslaving their relatives and associates thereby preventing their sale to white masters.[30] For many it was simpler, cheaper, and faster to informally offer haven to enslaved kin rather than negotiate the expensive bureaucracy of manumission.

Parallel Paths: Jamaica's Jews

Jews in Jamaica had very different origins than free people of color. All Jews in Jamaica came to the island willingly, and none had personal memories of bondage. But Jamaican slave society blurred the lines of their freedom. The blended children of Jewish men in Jamaica inherited the enslavement of their mothers. Jews of color in Jamaica, as in other similar colonies, challenge a binary distinction between Jews and enslaved people, or the association of Jewishness with whiteness. It was among this rather elusive population of Jews of color that experiential entanglement was literally embodied.

The vast majority of Jews in eighteenth-century Jamaica were Portuguese. They had all, at one point, been conversos or direct descendants of conversos, meaning Catholics with Jewish ancestry. They belonged to a transcendent global diaspora consisting of Portuguese-speaking re-Judaized "New Jews" and conversos interlinked throughout networks of trade, patronage, and marriage that extended from the Caribbean to western Europe, Livorno, India, West Africa, and beyond. As such, the Jews of Jamaica existed within a confluence of political entanglement, looking both toward the diasporic mother community of Amsterdam and the imperial metropole of London as sources of authority. Their strong ties to Bayonne in southern France entangled them further into the web of supraimperial politics: they *resided* in an English colony yet *existed* in the Atlantic world, transcending the imagined borders separating the Spanish, English, French, and Dutch Empires.

Like other Atlantic diasporas, Portuguese Jewish communities and families were bonded together through networks of patronage.[31] Jews, like Irish, Huguenots, Quakers, Moravians, and Mennonites, facilitated the migration of their kin through sponsorship such as offering inheritance, employment, communal membership, dowries, or financial investments. Portuguese Jews in English Jamaica, as in other parts of the diaspora, used these patronal tools to incentivize the migration of their converso kin to "lands of tolerance" and to encourage their adoption of rabbinic Judaism.³² These patterns of patronage represent a parallel, though not intersecting, point of comparison with those free people of color in Jamaica who used slave ownership as a form of familial patronage.

As early as the 1670s, the Crown-appointed governors of Jamaica promoted a policy of religious tolerance. This was a purely mercantile, rather than humanitarian or ecumenical, consideration in an effort to grow the trade economy. Jews in Jamaica without a personal Act of Naturalization from Parliament could purchase a certificate of denization granting them access to the court system and permitting landownership. But whereas children inherited their parents' naturalized status, denization was not effective in perpetuity nor did it exempt the beneficiary from expensive alien trade tariffs. In 1740, hundreds of Jamaican Jews took advantage of an unprecedented legislation granting them access to perpetual citizenship through residency rather than purchased legislation. Seemingly, the 1740 Naturalization Act should have fully enfranchised Jews, but they were still denied basic civil rights such as holding public office, voting in elections, practicing law, or serving on juries.

These were just some of the roadblocks to the civil integration of the Jews in Jamaica. Anti-Jewish hostilities intensified after a devastating earthquake in June 1692. White Christian merchants continued an aggressively Judeophobic pre-1692 campaign to curtail Jewish trade activity. The assembly extorted Jews with discriminatory taxation until 1740. Late eighteenth-century white Christian pseudo-ethnographers polemically ridiculed, fetishized, eroticized, and stereotyped Jews. And on at least one occasion a mob physically threatened Jews in Kingston's Portuguese synagogue.³³

Jamaica's Jewish population never grew far beyond a thousand individuals in the eighteenth century and was subject to significant fluctuations. They were never more than 6 to 8 percent of the free population, making them far less numerous than free people of color (keeping in mind that some free people of color also held Jewish identities). They were nevertheless a conspicuous minority and experienced their own growth patterns that proportionally made them one of the most successfully replicated populations on the island. They also significantly contributed to the urban growth of Jamaica through residency in towns and large-scale real estate ventures.³⁴

Like free people of color, Jews sustained their own internal ethnic and class hierarchies. Parallel to the colorist distinctions prevalent among free people of color who sometimes asserted a sense of social superiority over free blacks and the enslaved, the more numerous Portuguese Jews often marginalized German-descendent, Yiddish-speaking Ashkenazim, who comprised a minority of the broader Jewish population. Ashkenazim did not communally separate from their Portuguese coreligionists in Jamaica until the 1790s, much later than in Suriname, and were deferential and even dependent on them. Portuguese Jews embraced a posture of ethnic superiority—even contempt—over the Ashkenazim that strongly manifested in their marriage patterns.[35]

Four Points of Contact: Jews and Free People of Color

The foregoing survey demonstrates that Jews and free people of color in Jamaica provide numerous points of comparison. This comparative analysis is a point of reference from which to identify where parallel experiences connect, overlap, and entangle. While not an exhaustive list, I identify four points of contact: civil liberties and lobbies, urbanization, militia service and sedition, and alien stereotyping and fetishization.

Civil Liberties and Lobbies, 1692–1760

Jews and free people of color had nearly identical civil rights in Jamaica, with some few, but important, exceptions. Both groups also lobbied for the amelioration of their civil status through aggressively coordinated transatlantic diplomacy, far more so than any other outsider groups. Legally, Jews had far more in common with free people of color than with white Christians, and free people of color shared more in common with Jews than with the enslaved. This was a stark reality especially since other alien and dissenter groups including German Moravians, French Huguenots, Dutch Calvinists, and Quakers had no such legal disabilities, and in any case, intermarried with the white Anglican society within a few generations.[36] Historians of Jamaica have frequently commented on this enmeshment. Holly Snyder writes, "Jews occupied their own peculiar place in British America, one which, when seen by a certain light, was more akin to the position of the Indians and those freed people of African background."[37] Similarly, Daniel Livesay writes more bluntly that "Jamaica law effectively put Jews into the same legal category as free people of color."[38] More broadly, in the words of the art historian Nicholas Mirzoeff, "the hybridity generated by diaspora is not just an interaction with the 'host' nation, but among diasporas themselves."[39]

Successive crises, including the Port Royal earthquake in 1692, the French invasion in 1694, and the Port Royal warehouse fire of 1703, compelled Jews to agitate for greater civil equality in the first decade of the eighteenth century. At this time, Jews gained the support of the Board of Trade in London in their efforts to challenge the assembly's discriminatory Jewish tax. In 1708 Jews initiated an energetic lobby campaign on the floor of the assembly. Concomitantly, and perhaps motivated by many of the same factors, free people of color also began their own vigorous campaign for greater civil rights.[40] The 1708 lobbies succeeded in convincing the assembly to debate the efficacy of, but not to repeal, the Jewish tax and to grant free people of color the right to trial by jury—a right held by Jewish denizens.

After granting these few concessions, the assembly responded to the emboldened lobbies of 1708 by resolving to codify the disabilities of Jews and free people of color so as to formally deny suffrage to both groups.[41] This resolution resulted in a 1711 legislation that formally barred nonwhite and non-Christian groups from holding public office and, with the phrase "no Jew, Mulatto, Indian, or negro, shall be . . . empowered to write in," uncompromisingly prohibited them from casting votes for representatives to the assembly.[42] This law entangled the legal status of Jews and free people of color by including them under the same umbrella of disabilities. Such sweeping language was not unique to this act alone, or even to Jamaica, but its impact in Jamaica was staggering. With this law the assembly established a colonial legal precedent through which it could later resist meddlesome metropolitan legal standards regarding alien rights.

The discriminatory 1711 legislation did not diminish the resolve of the lobbyists or their supporters on the Board of Trade. Over the next four years, Jews with the support of the board aggressively lobbied the assembly to remove the Jewish tax. Simultaneously, the board pressured the colonial government to increase civil liberties for free people of color, which the assembly rejected with some limited concessions.[43] The Board consistently advocated on behalf of the disenfranchised with the goal of increasing tariff revenues and stimulating population growth. It furthermore supported both lobbies by submitting recommendations to the governor based on key informant interviews demonstrating the deleterious effects of civil disabilities on Jews and free people of color alike.⁴⁴ Inasmuch as the assembly's discrimination entangled the legal fortunes of Jews and free people of color, the board's support did much the same.

Military tensions between the Portland Maroons (autonomous black communities) and the Jamaican militia between 1730 and 1740 reignited debates over the civil liberties of resident aliens in Jamaica. Approaching Maroons as a domestic threat, the assembly feared their possible alliance with disaffected minorities. In 1730 the assembly passed, and later repealed, a highly discriminatory legislation imposing sumptuary restrictions on free people of color, including the requirement to wear a distinctive badge.⁴⁵ At the same time, the assembly debated imposing higher taxes on Jews.⁴⁶

In 1733, against the backdrop of the First Maroon War, the assembly voted to grant personal privileges bills to petitioners of color who could prove European ancestry, Christianity, and a certain amount of wealth, including slave ownership.⁴⁷ Privileges bills grew out of a pre-existing "blanching program" through which, theoretically, a person of color three times removed from a black ancestor might qualify to vote.⁴⁸ The assembly deemed privileges bills necessary during the war as a "civilizing" measure to placate the protests of free people of color, and to also create a bulwark against rebellious slaves and combative Maroons. Some historians argue that privilege bills were meant to reinforce the slave regime by providing former slaves, or their children, with upward social mobility and to encourage population growth through miscegenation.⁴⁹

These personal privileges bills granted to free people of color were, however, extremely rare and did not offer uniform rights to all recipients. Individuals with privileges generally could testify against white Christians in civil court and were exempted from deficiency requirements.⁵⁰ This exemption was especially coveted since free people of color, like Jews, were prohibited from holding white Christian indentured labor and therefore had a greater proportion of black labor on their estates. But privilege bills generally did not endow the petitioner with voting rights or the power to serve in elected office. They were also rare, granted to only 128 people throughout the eighteenth century out of around 700 applicants.⁵¹

Between 1740 and 1760, as Jamaica's plantation economy peaked, colonial and metropolitan authorities alike were more forthcoming with civil liberties in response to the growing wealth of Jews and free people of color, along with a greater dependency on these two groups to bolster Jamaica's trade economy.[52] In 1740, Parliament passed the Naturalization Act that seemingly appeared to promise full civil equality to Jews as a reward for residency. In effect, the colonial law of 1711 limited its application. Nevertheless, those who applied for naturalization after 1740 formed a privileged class among the Jews, similar to those few people of color who had succeeded in obtaining privileges bills. The possibility of transcending alien disabilities through applying for naturalization or a privileges bill further entangled the experiences of Jews and free people of color.

The possibility of transcending legal disabilities during this period emboldened a few privileged individuals to assert their civil rights in defiance of the law. In 1750, Abraham Sanches Morao, a Jew naturalized by the 1740 act, brazenly cast a vote for his member of assembly. This defiant performance of civil rights only reinforced the disdainful attitude of the assembly and also drew censure from London Jewish community leaders, who preferred a less confrontational approach.[53] Similarly, in 1759, Francis Williams, a celebrated London-educated free person of color, educational reformer, and civil rights activist, impudently wrote a highly circulated ode to the sitting governor of Jamaica calling for social and legal parity with whites.[54] This highly public plea was similarly met with aggressive disdain from the white planter class.[55]

Disenfranchisement is one of the most powerful symbols of entanglement between Jews and free people of color, who were both denied voting rights in the exact same legislation. Their lobbying activities overlapped in time and character. The assembly reacted identically to audacious civil rights activists, free people of color in 1733 and Jews in 1750, by reinforcing the denial of voting rights.[56] Furthermore, the association of Jews and free people of color in debates over suffrage fostered a popular perception that they were even racially linked. One anti-Jewish petitioner celebrated the assembly's denial of Jewish suffrage in 1750 on the grounds that Jews were not only infidels but also "mulatto[s] of the fourth degree," therefore doubly disqualified.[57] From the perspective of this petitioner, Jews and free people of color were more or less one and the same.

Urban Enclaves

Jamaican towns, especially Kingston, were crucibles of ethnic and experiential entanglement. In an island with a mostly rural population, especially among the enslaved, Jews and free people of color were conspicuously urban. In a pattern familiar throughout the Americas, persisting well into the twentieth century, Jews and people of color settled together in the same districts.[58] In Kingston, Jews and free people of color dwelled together in the southwestern part of the town near the wharf and the "negro" burial grounds.

Half of the island's free people of color lived in Kingston. By 1788, it is estimated that free people of color comprised 12 percent of the total—enslaved and free—population of Kingston.[59] Jamaican Jews were likewise highly centralized in Kingston. Even the Jews who dwelled on estates in rural parishes typically owned real estate in the town.[60] Similar patterns of urban concentration of Jews and free people of color were found in the Dutch Caribbean ports of Paramaribo and Willemstad, which in this regard closely resembled Kingston.[61] This clustering was apparent to white Christian observers such as Edward Long who lumped Jews and free people of color together in his descriptions of urban spaces. For instance, Long described the Village of the Cross in Clarendon Parish as an exclusively Jewish and "Mulatto" settlement.[62] Similarly, Long's robust characterization of Jews was folded into his thematic portrayals of Kingston and Spanish Town, as if Jews were fixtures of town life.[63]

Jews and free people of color in Jamaica had more in common than residency in the same neighborhoods. In the 1790s, hundreds of French-speaking migrants from Saint-Domingue fleeing the Haitian Revolution settled in the southwestern district of Kingston. Most of these transplants also had African ancestry and therefore joined with the town's free population of color.[64] The arrival of French speaking people of color in Kingston represents a further point of contact with the Jews who were also perceived to have been French by virtue of their strong transatlantic connections to the towns of Bayonne and Bordeaux.[65]

One illustrative manifestation of the entanglement of Jews, urban spaces, people of color, and French character is seen in Isaac Mendes Belisario's 1837 lithographic portrayal of Afro-creole Kingston street culture. In one of the scenes, the Jew Belisario—the grandson of the Bordeaux-born and iconically French Alexandre Lindo—complimentarily portrays the elegant and graceful "French Set-Girls," distinctly dressed French creole dancers who participated in Kingston's Christmas parade.[66] The accompanying description refers to the large-scale migration of people of color from Saint-Domingue to Kingston in 1794. This one scene represents a powerful confluence of the intertwined experiences of being Jewish, French, and of mixed ancestry within Kingston's urban street culture.

Militia Service and Sedition

Militia service provided Jews and free people of color with one of the few points of access to Jamaican public life beyond the markets. Although excluded from civil society, the colonial government expected Jews and free people of color to participate in the military defense of the island. As such, militia service was often a point of pride for alienated minorities and also a key way for them to leverage amelioration of their civil status.

In 1695, nearly every Jewish male between the ages of fifteen and sixty served in the militia, earning commendation from the governor.[67] Jewish lobbyists later leveraged their militia service to combat civil disabilities. Similar to Curaçao and other parts of the Caribbean, colonial administrators held strong expectations of military service for free people of color.[68] In 1730, the assembly voted to impress them into active duty guided by the belief that people of color were more fitting than whites as soldiers against Maroons.[69] This policy was later overturned. By 1813, free men of color made up as much as 46 percent of the Jamaican militia.[70] Jamaica's governors likewise extended commendations to free people of color for their energetic participation during both the First and Second Maroon Wars.[71] Free people of color, in turn, leveraged their military service for greater civil equality.

Militia service was paradoxically a point of both social inclusion and exclusion for Jews and free people of color. Despite earning praise for minority groups, compulsory militia service was one of the starkest markers of ethnic difference in Jamaica. Jewish protests over militia service on their Sabbath—coming from both Jamaica and London—provided fodder to Christian colonists to lampoon Jewish difference, lack of masculinity, and manipulativeness. These anti-Jewish sentiments were at the forefront during Tacky's Revolt when the sitting governor criticized Jews for supposedly paying their way out of militia service.[72] By the 1790s the Jamaican militia was segregated with exclusively "mulatto" and Jewish companies.[73]

For both Jews and free people of color no amount of faithful military service could diminish the preconceived assumption held by many white Christian observers that they were seditious by nature. The colonial government accused free people of color of supporting the Maroons in the 1730s, even though they also praised them for their service.[74] Interrogators similarly accused Jews of providing Maroons with gunpowder.[75] During the Seven Years' War and the American Revolution, many believed Jamaican Jews to be French collaborators.[76] During the Haitian Revolution, the white ruling class expressed anxiety that local free people of color might hold similar revolutionary ambitions. In one case, fears of Jewish-French collusion and free people of color's revolutionary potential were entangled in the actions of a single individual. In 1799, the colonial government executed the French Jew Isaac Yeshurun Sasportas of Saint-Domingue for attempting to foment revolution among the Portland Maroons.[77]

Utility, Fetishization, and Stereotyping

Accusations that Jews and free people of color treasonously joined forces with Maroons, despite their otherwise praiseworthy militia service, speaks to a general tendency in colonial Jamaica to essentialize alien minorities. Edward Long, for example, characterized most Jews as unscrupulous and most free people of color as amoral.[78] Sometimes Jews were even fetishized as "mulatto." Long commented that if miscegenation trends in Jamaica were to continue unchecked, "English blood will become so contaminated . . . till the whole nation resembles the Portuguese."[79] Another writer expressed concern over the contamination of English blood and complexion through the "mixing with Jews and negroes."[80] Whereas in metropolitan England Jews were often derogatorily conflated with religious dissenters such as Quakers, in Jamaican slave society they were most closely associated with free people of color.[81]

Historian Brooke Newman argues that the limited privileges granted to Jews and free people of color rested upon stereotypes about their innate nature.[82] Privileges were rewards for utility, not humanitarian benevolence. The colonial government suffered Jewish denization because of Jews' economic utility to the island and their alleged adoration of profit, believed to be fixed in their nature. Lawmakers extended limited rights to free people of color in recognition of their utility as laborers and because of their perceived natural ability to withstand harsh tropical climates. In other words, Jews were expected to pay for their rights whereas free blacks and people of color were expected to work for them.

White Christian colonists measured the utility of both Jews and free people of color according to their contribution to the slave system. In this, however, Jews and free people of color stood at opposite sides of the spectrum. Whereas policy makers saw free people of color as a necessary bulwark to slavery, they believed Jews undermined it. On the one hand, the assembly hoped that privileges for people of color would motivate the enslaved to work for advancement rather than to rebel.[83] On the other hand, white Christian lawmakers sometimes justified Jewish disabilities in light of the accusation that Jews colluded with the enslaved at Sunday markets. Some feared that disloyal Jews and the enslaved might join together if the Jews could be sufficiently enticed with profit.[84] Although not enslaved themselves, Jews and free people of color were entangled by and within slave society.

Stereotyped perceptions of Jews' and free people of color's slave-owning patterns provides a further point of contact between caricaturing, utility, and the slave regime. White Christian planters accused both Jews and free people of color of being excessively cruel slave owners.[85] This canard might be understood as absolution through projection. That is, white planters responded to abolitionist critics by blaming the cruelty of the slave regime on alien outsiders. Historian Gad Heuman, however, takes this lampoon at face value and argues that free people of color perpetrated excessive violence against the enslaved out of a compulsive drive to compensate for their low status.[86] Jews were likewise accused of being pathologically abusive slave owners in Jamaica as in other slave societies such as Suriname.[87] But for Jews it was their alleged addiction to maximizing profit, rather than a drive to acculturate, that supposedly motivated their violence.[88]

The 1813 Civil Rights Act: A Competitive Entanglement

A century of experiential and legal entanglement joining Jews and free people of color in Jamaica culminated with the debates over enfranchisement between 1812 and 1831. By lumping Jews and free people of color together, white Christian lawmakers effectively pitted them against each other, adding a competitive edge to the race for Emancipation. In this race, Jews and free people of color measured their successes and failures against one another.

As in other places, Emancipation was a process rather than a rupture. In Jamaica, Emancipation was also entangled in the abolition of slavery. Abolitionists first began to influence colonial policy in the early 1780s by proposing major revisions to Jamaica's slave code.[89] Empowered by this abolitionist support of the enslaved, and inspired by the revolutions in France and Haiti, free people of color throughout the Atlantic world energetically advocated for their own civil rights throughout the 1790s. In Jamaica these passionate efforts resulted in improved privileges for people of color in criminal proceedings.[90] This success was a doubled-edged sword. Having approved these modestly expanded civil liberties for all free people of color, the assembly voted in 1802 to abolish the practice of granting personal privileges bills.

In 1813, two decades of lobbying culminated in a partially successful petition to the assembly signed by two thousand free people of color calling for greater civil liberties. The assembly responded with the Civil Rights Edict that normalized free people of color's rights to testify in court, abolished inheritance caps (in place since 1761), and exempted all free people of color from deficiency penalties.[91] The act was interpreted by lawmakers as intended to put free people of color on "the same footing with a very respectable class of inhabitants, the Hebrews."[92] Indeed it did just that. These interpretations of the act made it clear that in terms of civil liberties Jews and free people of color would be considered in relation to each other.

Driven by the energy of free people of color, and their successes, Jews lobbied for greater civil equality around the same time. Their initial efforts, however, were articulated in terms of rivalry rather than solidarity. Both groups laid claim to priority in gaining civil rights, free people of color by virtue of their demographic significance and their Christianity, and Jews by virtue of their wealth and lighter complexion. In the most acute manifestation of this rivalry, in 1812, three Jews confrontationally objected to free people of color's attempt to seek legal parity with them.[93]

Historians have explained the 1812 Jewish objection as stemming from a Jewish ambition to be considered together with white Christians rather than free people of color.[94] In this reading, Jews were insulted by the assembly's wording to create legal parity between them and free people of color. The historians Isaac and Edith Hurwitz described the Jewish mentality in 1812 as one troubled by the prospect that "for the first time the possession of a white skin, if by a Jew, carried with it no more privileges than that of a colored citizen of Jamaica."[95] Gad Heuman argues that Jews objected because their wealth and their lighter skin naturally connected them more to the white plantocracy than to free people of color.[96] These interpretations ignore a century of interethnic entanglement between Jews and free people of color. They falsely associate Jews with wealth, when in reality most Jews in Jamaica, as in other parts of the Caribbean, were poor. They also falsely equate Jewishness with whiteness.

The historian Holly Snyder expressed discomfort with this polarized interpretation of Jewish opposition to free people of color and argued that such readings overemphasize differences rather than similarities.[97] Instead, she contextualized the competitiveness in terms of deep-rooted anxieties over social status and deemphasized the racialized aspects. Taking into account a century of entanglement between Jews and free people of color preceding these events is the next step toward nuancing and building upon this position.

Jews were always more connected to free people of color than they ever were to white Christians. After all, the assembly and other white Christian commentators clearly saw them as inhabiting the same tier of society. To fully understand the Jews' objection in 1812, emphasis should be placed on their desire to *disentangle* from free people of color rather than to *entangle* themselves with white Christians. In other words, 1813 did not mark the start of a trend to artificially homogenize Jews and free people of color to which the Jews objected, but rather it was a culmination of a preexisting legal and experiential parity between the two. Having shared the same social status, lived together in the same neighborhoods, been insultingly stereotyped by white Christian society, and created families together, the success of one group bruised the honor of the other.

The Race for Suffrage

Encouraged by the results of 1813, free people of color, with support from the Crown, renewed their suffrage lobby in 1816.[98] Jews followed suit. In July 1820, Levy Hyman, perhaps hoping to gain an edge over free people of color, attempted to vote for his representative to the assembly.[99] This was the second time in seventy years that Jews asserted voting rights. But this time was different. Even though Jews were again denied suffrage in 1820, Hyman pressed his claim in court, a bold demonstration of his conviction.[100] And free people of color responded to Jewish civil rights efforts by again pushing for their own suffrage in 1823.[101] The failures and successes of one lobby mutually reinforced the other—the perfect expression of entanglement.

In October 1826, the Jewish community leader Moses Delgado anonymously authored a "petition of merchants" to the assembly calling for

Jewish suffrage. The core of his argument spoke to the competitive character of Emancipation in Jamaica. Delgado suggested that it would be a "great anomaly" for darker skinned people to achieve voting rights before lighter skinned Jews, that is, it would be unnatural "were civil rights and immunities granted to certain persons, who may have been formerly the slaves of Jews."[102] Free people of color in turn countered with their own petition arguing that it would be equally anomalous to grant equality to unfaithful Jews before Christians of color, especially those with light complexions.[103]

Delgado's petition bore fruit. The assembly passed an act in December 1826 granting full civil equality to Jews, including the right to vote. Despite this apparent success, however, aggressive lobbying efforts hardened the assembly's antialien posture. It summarily rejected the earlier petition of free people of color. Jewish success seemed to have come at a cost to people of color. However, the act granting voting rights to Jews was only a symbolic gesture. The assembly obstructed the implementation of Jewish suffrage by first requiring approval from the Crown, effectively delaying its implementation for the next five years.

In February 1830, emboldened by a supportive Whig majority in Parliament, free people of color mounted an aggressive yearlong campaign to secure voting rights against strong local opposition.[104] The recalcitrant assembly finally conceded, perhaps hoping to prevent a full-scale revolution in Jamaica.[105] In December 1830, the assembly enfranchised free people of color. And this time, unlike in 1812, Jews supported free people of color, believing that the assembly would never extend suffrage to people of color before them.[106] But, to the surprise of the Jewish lobby, that is what happened, and the short-lived unity between Jews and free people of color quickly dissolved.

In 1830, with their earlier grant of enfranchisement delayed by colonial power politics, Jews fell behind in the race for civil equality. George IV's Privy Council argued that monarchical approval of the 1826 bill was unnecessary since voting rights were supposedly included in the 1740 Naturalization Act. The assembly countered that Parliament's law was nullified by the colonial act of 1711. Sympathetic members of assembly subsequently petitioned the governor of Jamaica pointing out that it was a "peculiar situation" that Jews were now the only free people without suffrage rights and hoped he might press the issue with the Crown.[107]

Finally, in July 1831, the Crown granted its consent, and the assembly approved the 1826 act along with supplementary legislation intended to prevent further obstruction.[108] Given the extensive layers of entanglement between disenfranchised groups and the slave system, it is perhaps no coincidence that five months later the Baptist preacher Sam Sharpe spearheaded an armed revolt calling for an end to slavery, beginning the long-drawn-out process of abolition.

The often-violent encounters of the Atlantic world facilitated ethnic and cultural blending, even among peoples and traditions with little preexisting contact. Such was the case with Jews and free people of color. In some ways their experiences were comparable—their mutual cultivation of diasporic identities and their patterns of patronage, for example—but rarely did those experiences overlap or become entangled. The racialized legal hierarchies of eighteenth-century Jamaica's slave regime, conceived of by white Christian planters, was one source of external fusion. White Christian lawmakers amalgamated Jews and free people of color into an essentially singular legal category. These same white Christians also stereotyped both groups in nearly identical ways, sometimes even by conflating their complexions and almost always in connection to their utility to the slave system.

Life in colonial Jamaica also engendered experiential, cultural, and ethnic hybridities among Jews and free people of color independent of white Christian pressure. Jews and free people of color inhabited the same urban neighborhoods and created families together, which led to an existential bonding. Urbanization generated commonality, especially by dislocating free people of color from the enslaved population of rural parishes. Most profoundly, sexual relations between Jews and disenfranchised women of African descent, both free and enslaved, gave rise to a significant population of people of color with ethnically or even religiously Jewish identities. Jews of color were a significant enough population in Jamaica for some white Christian polemicists to indiscreetly conflate Jews and "mulattos." For these individuals, Jewishness and African ancestry were literally and inseparably entangled categories.

During the debates over enfranchisement, lawmakers weighed the cases of Jews and free people of color against one another. Assemblymen and lobbyists alike spoke in terms of creating parity between the two groups in recognition of their shared legal heritage. It was this entanglement that fostered the competition between Jews and free people of color. Having been joined for a century, it was a detriment to the honor of one if the other received civil liberties first. Jews and free people of color undermined each other only because they measured their successes against each other's failures.

Each of these trends was embodied in the life of Rebecca Souza. She was ethnically Jewish, of mixed ancestry, and religiously identified as a Christian: a powerful symbol of Atlantic entanglement. At birth, Rebecca's legal status in Jamaica was identical to that of her Jewish father and free black mother. But when Rebecca received a personal privileges bill in 1774, she gained a slight economic advantage. Rebecca's Jewish father broke the cycle of inherited civil disabilities by producing a racially blended child who was baptized as a Christian. Rebecca's privileged status, limited though it was, paradoxically legally disentangled her from the Jewish experience even though she qualified for those same privileges by virtue of her father's European ancestry and lighter complexion. This was but a foreshadowing of the competition that would play out between the two groups for civil rights at the time of her death in 1811.

CHAPTER 8

Jewish Involvement in the Age of Atlantic Revolutions
The Threat of Equality to the Jewish Way of Life
WIM KLOOSTER

"We have celebrated the long-desired holiday that was established for the planting and erection of the Tree of Liberty: we have, with heartfelt joy, sung for and danced around that delightful Tree, whose sweet fruits we reap that will be our descendants' main sustenance."[1] Thus Herman Bromet (1724–1812) began a speech in March 1795 in which he pronounced himself to be an unambiguous partisan of the Batavian and French Revolutions.[2] The Tree of Liberty, he went on, has been erected to announce that human rights were no longer violated. Inequality of birth, slavery, and violent domination would soon be a thing of the past. Bromet was an Amsterdam resident who had lived in Suriname and was reinventing himself as a political activist. Two and a half years later he would become one of the two first Jewish members of parliament in European history. He tirelessly advocated for the rights of his coreligionists, whom he reminded in his speech of 1795 that in most of enlightened Europe they were equated with beasts, and in some parts even placed behind them. The current revolution, however, would change that, because they would retrieve their rights, which had been trampled on for so long. They would find their place again among humans.[3]

In this chapter, I will try to provide an overview of the Jewish political and ideological activism Bromet embodied in favor or against the many revolutions occurring on either side of the Atlantic in the half century that began with the American Revolution. How did Jews entangle themselves with the new ideas and practices? The historiography on Jews in this age of Atlantic revolutions has tended to focus on the revolutions' impact on Jewish communities. What has been understudied is how

Table 8.1. Largest urban Jewish populations in Western, Central, and Southern Europe, late eighteenth century

CITY	POPULATION	YEAR
Amsterdam	23,000	1795
London	11,000	1791
Prague	8,215	1792
Hamburg	6,300	1800
Livorno	4,327	1794
Rome	3,909	1799
Berlin	3,300	1800
Frankfurt	3,000	1800
Bayonne	2,500	late 18th century
Fürth	2,400	1800
Metz	2,223	1790
Mantua	1,908	1797
Venice	1,625	1797
Ancona	1,594	1795
Bordeaux	1,500	late 18th century
Modena	1,260	1795
Trieste	1,250	1802

Sources: Amsterdam: S. E. Bloemgarten, "De Amsterdamse joden gedurende de eerste jaren van de Bataafse Republiek (1795-1798) I," *Studia Rosenthaliana* 1, no. 1 (1967): 67; London: Frederick Augustus Wendeborn, *A View of England towards the Close of the Eighteenth Century*, 2 vols. (London: G. G. J. and J. Robinson, 1791), 2:468; Prague: Michael K. Silber, "The Making of Habsburg Jewry in the Long Eighteenth Century," in *The Cambridge History of Judaism*, vol. 7, *The Early Modern Period, 1500–1815*, ed. Jonathan Karp and Adam Sutcliffe (Cambridge: Cambridge University Press, 2017), 768; Hamburg: Stefi Jersch-Wenzl, "Population Shifts and Occupational Structure," in *German-Jewish History in Modern Times*, ed. Michael A. Meyer, 2 vols. (New York: Columbia University Press, 1997), 2:57; Livorno: Carlo Mangio, "La communauté juive de Livourne face à la Révolution française," in *Les juifs et la Révolution française: Problèmes et aspirations*, ed. Bernhard Blumenkranz and Albert Soboul (Toulouse: Edouard Privat, 1976), 191; Rome: Alan Charles Harris, "La Demografia del Ghetto in Italia," *La Rassegna Mensile di Israel*, 3rd series, 33, no. 4 (1967): 41; Berlin and Frankfurt: Jersch-Wenzl, "Population Shifts and Occupational Structure," 57; Bayonne: Frances Malino, *A Jew in the French Revolution: The Life of Zalkind Hourwitz* (Oxford: Blackwell, 1996), 222, n. 39; Fürth: Jersch-Wenzl, "Population Shifts and Occupational Structure," 57; Metz: Pierre-André Meyer, "Démographie des Juifs de Metz (1740-1789)," *Annales de démographie historique*, 1993, 131, n. 20; Mantua: Harris, "La Demografia del Ghetto," 39; Venice: Harris, "La Demografia del Ghetto," 43; Ancona: Marina Caffiero, "Tra Chiesa e Stato: Gli ebrei italiani dall'età di Lumi agli anni della Rivoluzione," in *Storia d'Italia*, vol. 11, pt. 2, ed. Corrado Vivanti (Turin: Giulio Einaudi, 1997), 1095; Bordeaux: Malino, *A Jew in the French Revolution*, 40; Modena: Harris, "La Demografia del Ghetto," 40; Trieste: Lois C. Dubin, *The Port Jews of Habsburg Trieste: Absolutist Politics and Enlightenment Culture* (Stanford: Stanford University Press, 1999), 21.

Table 8.2. Largest Jewish populations in the Americas, late eighteenth century

COLONY/STATE	POPULATION	YEAR
Suriname	1,330	1791
Curaçao	1,095	1789
Jamaica	800–900	1776
New York	350	1790
South Carolina	300	1790
Pennsylvania	250	1790
Virginia	200	1790
Saint Eustatius	170	1790

Sources: Suriname: Wim Klooster and Gert Oostindie, *Realm between Empires: The Second Dutch Atlantic, 1680–1815* (Ithaca, NY: Cornell University Press, 2018), 133; Curaçao: Wim Klooster, *Illicit Riches: Dutch Trade in the Caribbean, 1648–1795* (Leiden: KITLV Press, 1998), 61; Jamaica: Eli Faber, *Jews, Slaves, and the Slave Trade: Setting the Record Straight* (New York: New York University Press, 1998), 58. United States: Ira Rosenswaike, "An Estimate and Analysis of the Jewish Population of the United States in 1790," *Publications of the American Jewish Historical Society* 50, no. 1 (1960): 34; Saint Eustatius: Judah M. Cohen, *Through the Sands of Time: A History of the Jewish Community of St. Thomas, U.S. Virgin Islands* (Hanover, NH: Brandeis University Press, 2004), 11.

Note: All numbers for U.S. states are high estimates.

Jews themselves participated in these revolutions with words and deeds, and there is no pan-Atlantic study of this question.

Jewish support for revolutionary change was limited in both Europe and the Americas. In much of Europe, the Jewish response to the presumed liberation offered by revolution and/or French invasion was mixed. In North America, Jews could be found in the revolutionary and loyalist camps, and some remained neutral as long as that was possible. Others may have changed their allegiance for practical reasons.[4] While Jews in Charleston, Savannah, and Philadelphia almost unanimously chose the side of the rebels, those in New York were split, and those in Newport, Rhode Island, remained loyal to Britain.[5]

The main formal outcome for Jews residing in countries swept up in revolution was the acquisition of equal rights. If Jews had never asked for equal rights before the age of revolutions, they certainly came out to support equality once it had been introduced, and often to point out the gap between law and reality. In Europe, the first step in the direction of civil equality was the adoption by the French National Assembly of the Rights of Man and Citizen in August 1789, which enshrined the principle of equality. Just five days later, the Ashkenazi Jews from Alsace and Lorraine penned a request that asked the National Assembly for explicit civil rights. They realized that the Declaration did not have automatic emancipatory consequences for the country's Jews. It would, indeed, take another two years for a formal law to be adopted by the National Assembly that ended formal regulations against Jews in France once and for all.

The full enjoyment of civil rights was also desired by the Jews of Pennsylvania. After the revolutionary war with Britain ended in 1783, the *Mahamad* (council of elders) of the congregation Mikveh Israel in Philadelphia respectfully approached the Council of Censors—a committee that was tasked with defending the rights of the state's citizens—to raise an issue that must have irked them since 1776. In that year, the Commonwealth of Pennsylvania had adopted a constitution that required the members of the House of Representatives to declare that they acknowledge "the Scriptures of the Old and New Testament to be given by Divine Inspiration." Their petition did not limit itself to the observation that the obligation to read this declaration would infringe on their civil rights, adding the arguments that limiting civil rights would make foreign Jews move to other states than Pennsylvania, that local Jews were economically active, that their religion was in consonance with the safety and happiness of the people of Pennsylvania, and that Jews had supported the Revolution and suffered the consequences of their support.[6]

While the American and French Revolutions were homegrown revolutions, many European Jews received equal rights after French invasions that spawned domestic revolutions, as was the case in the Batavian Republic. It also applied to the various Jewish communities in Italy, which must have experienced the three years of French military involvement in the peninsula that began in 1796 as a whirlwind. Historian Geoffrey Symcox has written that the Jews of Rome were

> buffeted hither and thither by revolution and counter-revolution, invasion and counter-invasion. In February 1798, after the Jacobin Republic was established, the French dismantled the Roman ghetto, planted the customary liberty tree, gave the Jews tricolor cockades to wear in exchange for their yellow badges, and told them to enroll in the National Guard. Seven months later, in October, the Neapolitan army took Rome and closed them back into the ghetto. But after an interval of just over a month the French returned, declared the Jews free and equal, and opened the ghetto once more. Six months later, however, in the spring of 1799, the French garrison was forced out of Rome by the armies of the coalition, and the Jews were consigned to the ghetto for a third time.[7]

How to respond to such turmoil? During revolutions of which the outcome is uncertain, the Jewish intellectual David Nassy (1747–1806) wrote in Suriname around the same time, Jews must be peaceful bystanders in order not to become the victims of the triumphant party.[8] Even keeping a low profile could not save them in Rome during the same French invasion of 1798. Before the French victory was secure, local mobs of religious fanatics went around massacring Jews, Frenchmen, and radicals. Numerous Jews were thrown alive into the Tiber River.[9]

Equality, at least on paper, put an end to the policy of tolerance that secular governments had pursued toward groups of Jews in their midst.[10] A new stage in the relationship between European secular governments and their Jewish subjects had begun in the mid-eighteenth century when, both in countries where Jews already enjoyed some form of toleration and in those where they were persecuted, new laws were approved that were intended to improve their condition as well as that of other religious minorities. For the governments, Enlightenment values, fiscal exigencies, and the related goal of centralization all played a role in this process. Nowhere did it result in full-fledged civil equality, and rarely did amelioration amount to the recognition of political rights.[11]

The difference between tolerance and religious freedom was expressed by the "Jews, settled in France" (those from the northeast) in a petition to the National Assembly a few months after the Declaration of the Rights of Man and Citizen had been adopted. "The word tolerance," they wrote, "which after so many centuries and so many *intolerant acts* seemed to be a word of humanity and reason, no longer suits a country that wishes to establish its rights on the eternal basis of justice.... To tolerate, indeed, is to suffer what one would have the right to prohibit." Under the new conditions, they went on, the dominant religion has no right to prohibit another religion from humbly placing itself by its side.[12] At the same time, the granting of equal rights could be seen as an expression of the Enlightenment notion of tolerance. That is how the politically active Jewish silversmith Moisè Formiggini (1756–1810) of Modena saw it initially.[13] Eventually, however, he also based his insistence on Jewish equality on rights instead of privileges granted within the framework of tolerance.[14]

Economic Equality

Economic equality had already been obtained by France's Jews—albeit not explicitly—on the eve of the revolution. In November 1787, King

Louis XVI had issued the Edict of Tolerance, by virtue of which non-Catholics were allowed to enter all professions. In response to the measure, gentiles fearing rivalry from Jews consistently interpreted the edict to only have a bearing on Protestants.[15] The next year, the Spanish and Portuguese Jews of Bordeaux therefore asked to be allowed to engage in both wholesale and retail trade and to become apothecaries, surgeons, physicians, and obstetricians.[16]

Economic equality was also disputed by gentiles in the Batavian Republic because of the potential of Jewish competition with Christians. Such opposition did not deter two leading Jewish activists, who aimed to create professional opportunities in their fight against the grinding poverty of Amsterdam's Jews, from pleading for equal rights. A few months into the Batavian Republic, Mozes Asser (1754–1826) railed against the guilds, labeling them privileged bodies that formed a state within a state. Some of the guilds, he added, prevented people from earning a living in an honest way. It was not until three years later, in 1798, that the Dutch guilds were finally abolished, and even then, it remained difficult for Amsterdam's Jews to embark on a career as an artisan.[17] At the same time, the Amsterdam parnassim may not have been eager to allow Jews to be trained in professions such as carpenter or bricklayer—at least, that is what they were accused of in a Yiddish periodical.[18]

Military Equality

Equal rights also implied financial parity: the special taxes that Jews paid were bound to come to an end. There were other advantages of civil equality, such as the ability to show one's dedication to the revolution and its principles by taking up arms. The American Revolutionary War may have been the first in which Jews served on an equal basis, historian Samuel Reznick writes.[19] Whereas some Jewish males fought as volunteers in the Continental Army, others were incorporated in the militias irrespective of their preference. Few of these militiamen saw military action.[20]

In Europe, the Prussian bureaucrat Christian Wilhelm von Dohm had already advocated Jewish inclusion in armies and civil militias in his influential work *Über die bürgerliche Verbesserung der Juden* ("On the Civil Improvement of the Jews," 1781), written at the request of the Jews of Alsace. Such incorporation, he argued, would underline Jewish allegiance to their countries of residence. Dohm conceived of Jewish Emancipation,

David Sorkin notes, "as a reciprocal process in which the Jews were to refashion themselves in exchange for rights."[21]

More than a few gentiles loudly objected to this notion, presenting Jews as unreliable people who would make bad soldiers. The issue also divided the Jewish community, especially when it came to the question whether Jews should serve on the Sabbath and Jewish holidays.[22] In Amsterdam in 1795, the (predominantly Jewish) Felix Libertate Society advocated the inclusion of Jews in the newly formed National Guard, but in a meeting with a representative of Amsterdam's municipality, both the Ashkenazi and Portuguese chief rabbis stated that Mosaic law did not permit Jews to bear arms on the Sabbath. The members of Felix protested, pointing out that in other cities, the Jews were carrying out civil defense tasks. In a pamphlet, one member, the abovementioned Herman Bromet, supported the society's position by arguing on the basis of historic precedents, statements by rabbis, and texts from the Bible, the Talmud, and other Jewish writings that Jews were allowed to carry arms on the Sabbath. They were forbidden to carry tools, Bromet remarked, but that ban did not apply to guns.

Jews would indeed be admitted to the armed forces, although by no means everywhere. Where they were, the Jews were filled with pride, as in Rome, where Isacho Baraffael was appointed major of the National Guard, in spite of protests from citizens who opposed the inclusion of any Jews in that force. Baraffael appeared on horseback at the head of his troops, which comprised many Jews.[23] In Paris, an advocate for Jewish Emancipation asserted in 1790 that 150 of the 500 local Jews had enrolled in the National Guard.[24] One of these men made himself heard by protecting the monarchist deputy Abbé Maury at the risk of his own life from a crowd of violent "patriots." Ironically, Maury had not only consistently spoken out against Jewish equality in the National Assembly, he had also remarked that Jews would be of little use as soldiers: "I do not know of a single general in the world who would want to command an army of Jews on the day of the Sabbath."[25]

Political Equality

What would have been highly unlikely anywhere in Europe was the kind of position that Francis Salvador (1747–76) and Mordecai Sheftall (1735–97) attained at the beginning of the American Revolution. In 1773, Salvador had moved from London to South Carolina, where he set up a plantation. He was elected to the state's first and second Provincial

Congress, was involved in the preparation of the state's first constitution, and served in the state's first General Assembly. Salvador died of wounds sustained as a militiaman in an encounter with Cherokee.[26] Sheftall, a well-to-do merchant and landowner, served as chairman of Savannah's equivalent of the Committees of Safety that sprang up all over the eastern seaboard to enforce the ban on trade with Britain.[27] Unlike Salvador, Sheftall survived the revolution, although his allegiance to the patriot cause cost him dearly. He spent time in British captivity and lost all his property during the war.[28]

The tone was set in the Declaration of Independence, which spoke of the self-evident truth "that all men are created equal, that they are endowed by their Creator with certain unalienable Rights, that among these are Life, Liberty and the pursuit of Happiness." This was followed by the more concrete guarantee of political equality adopted in the Constitution of 1787 that "no religious test shall ever be required as a qualification to any office or public trust under the United States." On a state level, Jefferson's declaration of 1776 was initially only echoed in the constitution of New York, where in colonial times Jews had already enjoyed more rights than elsewhere. Other states were slow to follow. In the states where Salvador and Sheftall settled, provisions that barred Jews from holding public office were not annulled until 1789 (Georgia) and 1790 (South Carolina).[29] By 1840, Jews still waited to receive full Emancipation in Connecticut, New Hampshire, New Jersey, North Carolina, and Rhode Island.[30]

In a few parts of Europe, Jews had enjoyed political rights as a corporation, but it was not until the age of revolutions that they were granted individual political equality. If political self-abnegation had always been the rule, Jews could now manifest themselves on the political stage.[31] The usual consequence was that a few Jewish men were admitted to positions of authority. In Frankfurt, for example, Mayer Amschel Rothschild became a member of an electoral college (in 1811), while the physician Josef Oppenheimer was granted a seat on the city council.[32]

Although theoretically, it may have been the most significant advance Jews made during this era, the extension of political rights received mixed reactions from the Jewish populations. In Amsterdam, home to twenty-three thousand Jews in the 1790s, which made it the city with the largest urban Jewish population in the world after Constantinople (table 8.1), the initial response was lukewarm at best. Local Jews were allowed to cast their vote when in February 1796 elections took place for the very first democratically elected National Assembly of the Netherlands. The country was divided into electoral districts, which each chose one representative for the assembly in The Hague. In one electoral district in Amsterdam, Jews made up 80 percent of the population, while in another one, almost half of the population was Jewish. Voters were therefore in a position to elect a Jewish delegate, but in the election week, they did not show up at the ballot box. In one subdistrict, only one Jew voted, while in another one, not a single Jew bothered to vote. And still, one Jewish candidate for the National Assembly was almost voted into office. Mozes Asser fell short by two votes, having received half of his votes from Christians.[33] Eighteen months later, however, two Jews were installed as members of the Dutch National Assembly, the first Jewish members of any European parliament.

No Jews were represented at France's highest political stage during the revolutionary decade, although some did occupy senior political posts on a local level. But whether or not they used the newly available political venues, French Jews did express their hopes and fears, which almost invariably were related to their own status. Such was the case with the Ashkenazim of northeastern France, who were not granted the voting rights that the wealthier and more established Portuguese Jews of Bordeaux had been granted. Most of these Ashkenazim did not dwell in cities. The vast majority of the more than twenty thousand Jews in Alsace lived in small communities that comprised one to twenty-five families in rural areas, while in Lorraine only 180 families had been allowed to live in a total of fifty-two communities prior to the revolution.[34] What distinguished the Jews residing in Alsace and Lorraine from their coreligionists in Bordeaux was their goal to emancipate all Jews of France, while those from Bordeaux merely aimed to obtain citizenship for themselves, based on the privileges they had enjoyed during the ancien régime. Explicitly rejecting equality for the northeastern Jews, and actively lobbying for themselves at the National Assembly, the Bordeaux men succeeded in reaching their goal during the first months of the revolution, while their brethren had to wait until September 1791.

Autonomy

For a long time, Berr Isaac Berr (1744–1828), leader of the Jews of Nancy (Lorraine), was committed to the principle of toleration and the continuation of communal autonomy. In the course of the revolution, however, he changed direction, applauding and defending citizenship for Jews in his region. The consequence would be, he said in a speech given on July 2,

1791, when he swore a civic oath at the town hall of Nancy, that the only difference that remained between Christian and Jews was their religion. Jewish crimes were henceforth punished individually, as were those of other Frenchmen. "If a Jew should regrettably make himself reprehensible, the Jews in general should not be accused. May not a whole commune be accused if one of its members were to deviate from his duty."[35] Here Berr echoed what the Dutch-Jewish philosophe Isaac de Pinto had written in his *Apologie des Juifs* (1763): one should not condemn entire peoples. Are all Englishmen guilty of beheading King Charles I and all Frenchmen to be blamed for the St. Bartholomew's Day's massacre?

The logical corollary of the granting of individual civil rights was that Jewish self-government came to an end, which was precisely what Moses Mendelssohn had advocated only a few years before the outbreak of the French Revolution. Pleading for civil acceptance of Jews, the leader of the Haskalah broke ranks with Christian Wilhelm von Dohm. In his sketch of a possible future, Dohm had proposed not only to overturn the age-old prejudices of state and society against Jews, but to maintain existing Jewish institutions. Civil matters could be adjudicated in Jewish courts as before, and Jewish elders could continue to issue bans of excommunication. Mendelssohn disagreed. Jews should appear before state courts, and their leaders should have no authority over opinions held by fellow Jews.[36] Where the movement for Emancipation was presented as logically linked to the liberation from the power of religious leaders, a wedge was driven between Jewish activists like Mendelssohn and the traditionalists in their communities, who tended to form the majority. That was as much true in Berlin as it was in areas more directly affected by revolution such as Amsterdam, Italy, and Alsace.

French Jews came out on both sides. Those residing in Paris embraced the end of autonomy, but then again, they had never really been organized as a self-governing entity. Hassidic Jews, on the other hand, viewed the French Revolution, no doubt in part because of the implication of the extension of civil rights that the Jewish community lost their autonomy, as a threat to their very existence.[37] Many French Ashkenazim considered the abolition of community autonomy a new form of persecution. It was difficult for them to see a distinction between a Jewish life without community autonomy and assimilation to mainstream Christian society. In their address to the king in August 1789, the Jews from Alsace claimed that autonomy was "in the interest of morals, order, subordination and peace in the assemblies and even in the interior of each family."[38] On the other hand, some Jews assimilated to the point of apostasy, such as a rabbi in Paris and another one in Orange. In Carpentras, at the height of the antireligious campaign that marked the Terror, several Jews met with the authorities to present the keys to the synagogue. They told them: "The god in whom we believe . . . can be worshipped by all the earth. We will all meet together in the temple of reason, where all men are brothers, and we will pray to God together, longing for the prosperity of the Republic, one and indivisible."[39] How voluntary such acts were remains to be seen. Increasing pressure was exerted by gentile revolutionaries on Jewish men to shave their beards and women to take off their wigs.[40]

Ironically, the French authorities did not allow the Jewish communities of Alsace and Metz to dissolve. The reason was that both had debts that the state did not want to take on. In order to pay off the debts, the municipalities had to levy taxes, which required that their administrative structure remained intact, at least temporarily.[41] Outside France, Jews usually ignored the news about the civil rights that their coreligionists had received in the land of revolution. In some places, the news did not even arrive or register. An Italian writer noticed during his travels in the peninsula in 1794 that the Jews of Rome reacted with surprise, and even dismay, when he told them that one goal of the revolution in France was to give equal rights to all people, regardless of their origin and religious affiliation. They did not believe him.[42]

On the other hand, he noted, the Jews of Tuscany had been informed about the momentous events in France. Those events did not exactly provoke an enthusiastic response, although some Jewish members of the lower class in Livorno expressed their joy at a liberty tree planted in their ghetto. Both the lay leaders (in Italy known as *massari*) and the vast majority of the Jewish community preferred maintaining the status quo to a transformation that included equal political and economic rights. Just how much the *massari* wanted to keep the newfangled ideas outside the door was shown by their exile of coreligionists who entangled themselves in the French Revolution. One of them was Juda Leone, who had gone to France, where he became a member of the National Guard of Bordeaux. In March 1791 he returned to Livorno, where he publicly extolled the principles of 1789, appearing in the theater in a French uniform that was adorned with the tricolor cockade. For this he was exiled from the Grand Duchy. Another local Jew returned from France in the same year after having served in the French army.[43]

In a journal article in 1799, the Livornese Jew Salomone Michell, a descendant of Jewish-Polish immigrants and one of the foremost intellectuals of his community, questioned the oligarchic structure of the Jewish community. He called on the French authorities to apply the principle of equality to the governance of the community and to reform it according to the new principles. However, the French did not feel the need to do so because they worked closely with the Jewish leaders after the beginning of the occupation.[44] As in other occupied parts of Europe and in the so-called sister republics, practical considerations trumped principles.

In Amsterdam, the 1790s saw a more broadly based critique of their community's oligarchic governance by a vociferous group of Jews.[45] During the Patriot revolt of the previous decade—a slow-moving revolution based on some of the same principles guiding the American and later the French Revolution—the Jewish population of Amsterdam had overwhelmingly supported the Orangist regime of the stadholder, which represented the status quo. This loyalty angered the Patriots and led

FIGURE 8.1. Cartoon of a Patriot rider who jumped into a Jewish pancake booth. Anonymous print, 1787. Rijksmuseum, Amsterdam.

in October 1787 to the killing by a civil Patriot patrol of three Jews. Tensions between the two parties ran high that month because of an invasion by the Prussian army, which restored the stadholder's authority. The gratitude of the Jewish population was expressed when a large number of them treated the Prussian soldiers to delicacies from the Jewish cuisine.[46]

Although the Patriots' return to power after the French invasion of 1795 was not accompanied by anti-Jewish violence, it did lead to major upheaval in the Jewish community. Almost immediately after the foundation of the Batavian Republic—the Dutch revolutionary regime under French auspices that was installed after France's military victory—a group of educated Jews founded Felix Libertate, the abovementioned society that would manifest itself as a pressure group that aimed to give the Dutch Jews equal rights according to the French model. Basing themselves on the French Declaration of the Rights of Man and Citizen, they targeted the parnassim of the two congregations in Amsterdam, those of the Ashkenazi and Portuguese Jews. At their insistence, the revolutionary Committee of Vigilance, whose task it was to control the town council, summoned the parnassim of both municipalities to the town hall and ordered them to read and affix the Declaration of the Rights of Man to the synagogues. The Portuguese parnassim tacitly ignored this request, if only because the declaration was made in Yiddish, but they could also afford to do so because of the complete lack of revolutionary fervor among its members. The Ashkenazi leaders, however, defended themselves. Their chief rabbi stated that they could not agree to the declaration of rights since the religious freedom enshrined in it would mean that from now on everyone could do "as he pleased, and there would no longer be any priority for the God-fearing over the renegade."[47]

This resistance in turn led to a fierce protest on the part of Felix Libertate, whose members stuck a proclamation in Yiddish to the doors of the synagogues and in public places in the city, denouncing the parnassim's behavior. They were certain that the parnassim were averse to reading the declaration out loud because they feared that poverty in the community would decline—presumably because Jews were henceforth free to choose any profession—which would reduce the parnassim's authority. Poor relief had always been one of their chief tasks, and it was a formidable one. Among the Ashkenazi population, poverty was acute, with thirteen thousand of the more than twenty thousand receiving allowances. The men of Felix Libertate also criticized the regulations of the Ashkenazi congregation, which they called undemocratic, contrary to the principle of religious freedom, and ineffective with regard to the care of the poor.[48]

That they acted as advocates for the poor did not automatically endear the men of Felix to the Jewish proletariat. The Jewish poor had always benefited, for example, from the slaughter and certification of kosher meat in the community's meat hall, the proceeds of which constituted an important source for the community's poor relief. The poor realized that religious freedom would negatively impact them, because Jews could no longer be obliged to buy meat exclusively in the meat hall, and the proceeds would decline accordingly, leaving the alms' box empty—as would actually happen.[49]

Both camps in Jewish Amsterdam did not budge an inch, not even after the formal Emancipation of the Dutch Jews on September 2, 1796. With all middle ground gone, Felix took the momentous step to establish a new congregation in March 1797. That was, of course, unacceptable to the parnassim, who began to fine people who joined the new congregation, and forbid bakers, midwives, and newspaper deliverers to help the new congregation in any way. On their part, the leaders of the new congregation used their opponents' uncompromising stand to urge the provincial authorities to dissolve the parnassim. They got their wish in March 1798, but the joy on the side of the revolutionary Jews was short-lived. After a coup d'état, a new national government came to power that restored the authority of the parnassim.[50]

On a much smaller scale, the feud echoed in the Dutch colony of Curaçao, home to the second-largest Jewish community in the Americas (table 8.2). In 1796, some Jews who attended the Neveh Salom synagogue in the neighborhood called Otrabanda, which was separated from the island's capital of Willemstad by a canal, attempted to free themselves of the power of the parnassim (who resided in the city) and elect their own parnassim. After the city parnassim had informed him that the terms of Neveh Salom's foundation did not allow such independence, the island's governor decided to maintain the status quo.[51]

The Value of Legal Equality

Despite legal changes that took place in the wake of the revolutions, often little changed on the ground, which led to protests among the Jewish population. The Newport merchant Moses Michael Hays (1739–1805) refused to take the oath to assist in the defense of the rebellious colonies, not because he was, as he called it, "inimical to my country," but because he had not been allowed to vote, and "never had the Continental Congress or the legislatures taken any notice . . . respecting the society of Israelites to which I belong." Besides, unlike gentiles, he had been pressed to take the oath.[52]

Even in Pennsylvania, where only one Jewish loyalist has been identified and where the *Mahamad* had successfully protested the law that had required Jews to affirm their belief in the divine inspiration of the New Testament in 1783 (see above), actual equality remained out of reach. Ten years later, prominent merchant Jonas Phillips was fined for refusing to appear as a witness on a Saturday, while another year later, the state legislature prohibited work on Sundays, which obviously was detrimental to the Jewish residents.[53]

Discrimination also continued in Mantua, where the Jewish community complained in a 1799 memorandum addressed to the government of the Cisalpine Republic about forms of inequality that persisted three years after Napoleon had created the republic. The term "Jew," they maintained, was still inserted before the name of a Jewish citizen in public documents. Jews were also blocked from acting as witnesses in notarial deeds or in lawsuits involving Christians, and instead of swearing an oath, Jews had to pronounce a formula from the book of Leviticus, the use of which they saw as blasphemous. Finally, Jews were denied access to public offices, particularly in the legal field.[54] A decade after Jewish Emancipation in the Netherlands, six Dutch Jews claimed that the situation of the Jews was worse than before. Jews had been passed over in appointments to official posts, and although they paid municipal taxes, Jews were not among the beneficiaries, as the proceeds went to teachers of the Dutch Reformed Church, hospitals, orphanages, and almshouses. In addition, one Jew, who had completed his training, had been refused recognition as a master blacksmith.[55]

The hopes of activist Jews that the acquisition of citizenship and equal rights would end their discrimination forever thus proved vain. But that does not imply that the accomplishments of these years were small. Later Jews would, after all, reap the benefits of the achievement of formal equality. In hindsight, it was the Declaration of the Rights of Man that provided European Jews with an opening that their leaders were eager to exploit in order to bring about the desired Emancipation. Such an opportunity was lacking in a country like Prussia, despite the work of David Friedländer (1750–1834), who in petitions and writings broke ground for his fellow believers. Even though the end goal he had in mind was full civil equality and although the first period of his activities coincided with the early years of the French Revolution, he never invoked the French declaration. Such a reference would only have reduced his chances of succeeding in Prussia.[56] But no matter what he tried, Friedländer's pleas fell on deaf ears. His goal was reached only two decades later after Prussia had come under the influence of France, where the principle of equality had never been abandoned.

The French declaration failed to incite movements for Jewish Emancipation in the Americas, where no more than a faint echo can be detected in the two largest Jewish communities—those of Suriname and Curaçao. Nor did the French document influence the United States, where advocacy for Jewish Emancipation had developed independently. It triumphed when the First Amendment to the American Constitution was adopted, which read that "Congress shall make no law respecting an establishment of religion, or prohibiting the free exercise thereof." Congress approved the amendment on September 25, 1789, a mere five weeks after the French Assembly had adopted the Declaration of the Rights of Man and Citizen. These documents offered Jews on either side of the Atlantic the means to effectuate equality, although genuine parity would remain elusive for many years to come.

Beyond Jewish Advocacy

As a rule, Jewish entanglement with the age of revolutions was tied to the plight of fellow Jews and their communities. A small group of Jews in the Atlantic world, however, took up causes that transcended religious boundaries. A total of nine Jewish women from Amsterdam, for example, signed documents in 1799 with fellow female Batavian citizens, in which radical demands were formulated.[57]

Isaac Hourwitz (1751–1812) moved away from Jewish advocacy in the course of his life. Born in Poland, he had moved to France as a young adult, where he made a living hawking goods before he was hired as a librarian. Even before the revolution, Hourwitz was an outspoken opponent of tolerance and a champion of Jewish citizenship, and once the revolution broke out, he manifested himself as a tireless advocate of his coreligionists' rights. At the same time, he embraced causes and policies unconnected to the Jewish question, expressing his disdain, for example, for the Catholic clergy. During the last months of the Directory, Hourwitz penned a fascinating proposal for the transformation of Paris, which was published in one of the capital's newspapers.

The plan, which would be ignored by the authorities, involved renaming the streets of Paris, some of which still bore names of saints, while others were indecent, ridiculous, or unpronounceable. Aiming to lay the foundations for a rational and enlightened identity, Hourwitz considered it necessary to completely overhaul the naming pattern. Henceforth, main streets were to be named after European countries and side streets after capitals or celebrities, who would also be honored by statues.[58]

Hourwitz was not alone among Jews in throwing himself wholeheartedly into the revolution and into writings that outlined revolutionary vistas. Others joined him in applying the notion of equal rights as widely as possible. One man he befriended, Abraham Furtado (1756-1817), was elected in March 1789 as one of four representatives of Bordeaux's Portuguese Jews to the local assembly of the Third Estate, which was to choose its own representatives to the Estates General. Although he was not among those who were elected to go to Versailles, he and the other electors soon came to make up the local town council. Young and wealthy, Furtado and some fellow Portuguese Jews founded Bordeaux's Society of the Friends of the Constitution—later known as the Jacobin Club—and dedicated themselves to supporting the work of the National Assembly.[59] In a speech for this society in 1791, Furtado defended the Jacobins against the charge that they were subordinating liberty to the whims of the masses. On the contrary, the Jacobins, he asserted, did yeoman work cultivating respect for the new laws. "What is liberty?" he asked.

> Liberty is not the right to do all that one wishes, but rather to not do that which one should not; . . . to obey with impunity the wise laws that one has made; . . . to participate in legislation, so as to be more bound to submit to the laws; . . . to march proudly and without fear and under the standard and shield of the law. Liberty constituted by the law, compels a religious respect for it, both from the magistrate who orders and the Citizen who obeys.[60]

As so many other revolutionaries, Furtado rode the waves of the revolution while simultaneously helping to shape it. In his function as a municipal councilor, he did not hesitate to disarm suspects in 1793, and he declared war on traditional beliefs and institutions, especially the Catholic Church. But the Terror led him to a complete revision of his ideas and an appreciation of traditional institutions. Furtado also came to attach more importance to his own Jewish faith than he had during his radical years.[61]

Furtado's active years as a revolutionary partly coincided with those of Junius Frey (1753-94), a man with a very different background. Born in Brno (Moravia) as Moses Dobruška, he grew up as an adherent to the Jewish sect of the Frankists, founded by his mother's cousin who claimed to be the Jewish Messiah. At twenty-two, Dobruška converted to Catholicism and took the name Franz Thomas von Schönfeld, although he did not cut his ties with the Frankists. Originally an admirer of Joseph II's reforms in Austria, he left in 1792 for France, where he chose the name Frey and became a fiery revolutionary, siding with France against foreign monarchies. Frey started his political activities as the editor of *Le Courrier*, the newspaper of the Jacobins of Strasbourg, and president of the club of the Friends of the Constitution, but soon moved with his brother to Paris, where they distinguished themselves for their bravery in the August 10, 1792, assault on the Tuileries palace.[62] Living large, they frequently received members of the convention in their Parisian home, which was decorated with busts of Brutus and Cicero and engravings of Franklin, Rousseau, Voltaire, and others. In the summer of 1793, Frey published a book that presented a proposal for a new constitution, in which he discussed the theological foundations he deemed necessary for a democratic regime. Of the "constitutions" of Moses, Solon, and Christ, he clearly preferred those of the latter two, and he took Moses to task for his failure to reveal the truth and for effectively perpetuating superstition. Frey was eventually arrested and executed, along with his brother, during the Terror, suspected of carrying out a secret mission for the Austrian emperor.[63]

Unlike Frey, the prolific Jewish writer, bookseller, and translator Saul Ascher (1767-1822) was an early convert to the French Revolution. Even before the storming of the Bastille, he had turned against absolute rulers who used the Enlightenment for their own ends. Anticipating the Marxist idea that revolutions laid the foundation for thorough social change, Ascher theorized that the revolutionary human spirit advances in three stages: first it moves into the realm of the senses, then into that of reason, and finally into that of the will. The sensual needs aim at freedom of enjoyment, reason at freedom of opinion, while the will strives to anchor the feeling of human dignity in general consciousness and to achieve moral freedom of action. The first stage, according to Ascher, was identified with economic interests, which were motivated by greed and found their expression in revolutionary struggles of previous centuries, including the American Revolution. The activity of the revolutionary spirit in the second stage coincides with the French Revolution, which eliminated the remnants of feudalism and time-honored religious prejudices, and gave birth to freedom of thought. What the French Revolution could not achieve was the highest stage: the establishment of a moral, harmonious, and happy social order in which everyone's freedom of will and action was guaranteed. That stage was bound to arrive in the future after a major battle between progressive and conservative forces. When Napoleon took over as the sole French leader, Ascher came to see the emperor as the incarnation of the revolutionary spirit and the liberator of peoples.[64]

Ascher's idea of liberation was, however, more universal than that of Napoleon, who ordered the reestablishment of slavery in the French colonies and never championed the rights of Blacks. Ascher, by contrast, translated *De la littérature des Nègres*, a work by the Abbé Grégoire, the famous French parliamentarian who consistently pleaded for both Jewish and Black equality. The book argued that Blacks were capable of everything that whites achieved, including in intellectual matters.

David Nassy stands out in this group of Jewish thinkers, because he never blindly followed the leaders of the French Revolution. On the one hand, he hailed "the irresistible progress of time, the breath of freedom that animates everything, the splendid example set by France for the benefit of the Jews, this gentle philosophy, this equality, founded on the morals of the people."[65] On the other hand, he condemned the revolution in no uncertain terms when he evaluated it in 1799. Its fate had ended up in the hands of vain, obscure men with unlimited ambition, cannibals.[66] They pretended to inaugurate a regime of equality but had in fact accomplished the opposite. Perfect equality between the citizens of a state, Nassy wrote, is a democratic chimera. Men are unequal in their faculties, virtues, talents, honestly acquired wealth, education, and physical strength. As for freedom, it has always existed. "I don't know any country in Europe where the government has taken from individuals their property rights, personal safety, and the right to be judged by the laws. However, when my will is subordinated to the general law, I am no longer free."[67] Any attempts to introduce pure democracy were destined to lead to anarchy and despotism.[68] Nassy thus placed himself squarely in the camp of the conservatives.

In light of these observations, it may not surprise that Nassy also distinguished himself from the others by refusing to extend freedom to Blacks. In an unpublished memoir he sent to the directors of the Society of Suriname (which ruled that colony), the slave-owning intellectual wrote that "until they have arrived at a certain degree of civilization, the idea of liberty and equality catapults them into an intoxication, which passes only after they have destroyed everything."[69]

Nassy's opposite in this respect was Isaac Sasportas. A native of Saint-Domingue, where his father was a merchant, Sasportas was a well-traveled young man, who spent time in France around the time when the revolution broke out. Having lost his parents, he moved in with his uncle Aaron in Charleston. If he wasn't a revolutionary yet, he must have become one under the influence of this man, who had fought Britain during the American Revolution and was a member of the local Jacobin club. Striking out on his own in the mid-1790s as a smuggler, Isaac Sasportas made regular visits to Jamaica, the island where he would end his days. In 1799, he came up with a plan for the French to invade and conquer Jamaica in order to abolish slavery in that colony and strengthen France's position in the Caribbean. These goals had been discussed in previous years but had never led to a concrete plan. The French at Saint-Domingue added to Sasportas's proposal to involve both Black soldiers from that colony as well as enslaved Jamaicans and Blue Mountain Maroons by having French Adjutant-General Jean-Baptiste Urbain Devaux and Sasportas recruit privateers at the Dutch island of Curaçao, who were to provide aid in the invasion. Although the mission to Curaçao failed due to Devaux's attempt to overthrow the local governor, the invasion plans continued.

Ultimately, the invasion—projected to take place around Christmas 1799—never materialized, not because of any mistake or oversight on Sasportas's part but because the plan ran counter to the goals of Toussaint Louverture, at this point the most powerful figure in Saint-Domingue. Louverture had just signed a commercial treaty with Jamaica and could not afford to provide soldiers since he was fighting a civil war with the troops led by André Rigaud. Pretending to support the invasion plan, Louverture informed the British consul in Saint-Domingue about its menace. Shortly afterward, the authorities in Jamaica arrested Sasportas, who had arrived on the island to make preparations. A military court condemned him to death by hanging.[70]

Jewish agency in the age of revolutions was usually tied to the quest for equal rights. When a revolution led to the granting of legal equality to Jews, in keeping with revolutionary principles, often little changed in practice. It was usually at this point that Jewish activists came out of the woodwork to claim an equality that should have already been theirs. These advocates of equality, who embraced revolutionary ideology, were not necessarily representative of the outlooks of their communities. The reaction to the American Revolution in the tiny Jewish communities on the eastern seaboard was mixed, while in Europe a conservative attitude often prevailed, as the majority opposed equality, since it was incompatible with the cherished autonomy that they enjoyed. Equality assumed Jewish integration into mainstream society, which many saw as jeopardizing the Jewish way of life. Jewish proponents of equality railed against autonomy, presenting the movement for Emancipation as logically linked to the liberation from the power of their own religious leaders, although some believed that it was possible to combine Emancipation and autonomy.

Jews' entanglement with the age of revolutions did not exclusively occur in the context of their own ethnoreligious communities. Some Jewish activists looked beyond these communities when they joined revolutionary movements, planning for a future society for Jews and gentiles alike. The few cases featured here suggest that their ideological trajectories resembled those of non-Jews, with some soon abandoning their revolutionary pursuits, while others never gave up hope that a better, and radically different, world could be achieved.

CHAPTER 9

Sex with Slaves and the Business of Governance
The Case of Barbados
AVIVA BEN-UR

This chapter focuses on an extremely small Jewish community that numbered at its peak in the mid-eighteenth century a few hundred individuals. Yet, as I will argue, paradigmatic things happened there, and one mandate of Atlantic Jewish history is that one must consider both large and small communities. Moreover, the Jewish community of Barbados was very long-lived, dating from the 1650s through the early twentieth century, and left a variety of serial, narrative sources behind. Finally, as John Dixon suggests, it is perhaps at the microlevel that we are most likely to loosen what he calls the "stranglehold" of U.S.-oriented narratives.[1] His comment—which refers to the story of full citizenship attainment by Jews—can arguably be applied to the emerging field of Atlantic Jewish history more generally.

In September 1810, Moses Belasco, cantor of the Jewish community of Barbados, entered his home, which abutted the synagogue, and sat down

---

This chapter is an expanded version of a keynote address delivered at the "Atlantic Jewish Worlds, 1500-1900" conference, the McNeil Center for Early American Studies, in partnership with the Herbert D. Katz Center for Advanced Judaic Studies, University of Pennsylvania, April 7-8, 2021. I would like to thank Honorary Archivist Miriam Rodrigues-Pereira for permission to consult the Portuguese Jewish collection at the London Metropolitan Archives and, for their generous assistance, the staff of the archives cited in this chapter.

for his Sabbath evening meal. Religious services had just ended. It was Elul, the Hebrew month designated for the daily penitential prayers that lead up to the holiest days of the calendar, the Jewish New Year and the Day of Atonement. After he had dined for about twenty minutes, Belasco spotted two female laborers peering through one of the sanctuary's windows and laughing. Stepping outside, he overheard them discussing the scene transpiring within the synagogue. Belasco quickly adduced that Isaac Massiah, the beadle charged with the upkeep of the building, was "having improper connection" there with "a black woman."[2] The *Mahamad*, the lay body of Jews charged with overseeing Jewish community affairs, convened an emergency meeting the following Sunday and a congregational trial immediately ensued. Several Jewish witnesses appeared, including one who testified that some months previously Massiah had unsuccessfully solicited an enslaved woman, belonging to one Mrs. Brice, for paid sex within the house of worship. The congregation's leaders were horrified, citing Massiah for "unprecedented vileness" and characterizing his acts as "heinous in the extreme." They unanimously resolved to remove Massiah from his position and declared a general fast upon the entire community, to take place the following Monday.[3]

Barbados, whose enslaved population on the eve of abolition in 1833 peaked at eighty-two thousand individuals or almost 80 percent of the

FIGURE 9.1. The synagogue building of Congregation Nidhe Israel of Barbados, with its adjacent cemetery. Photo Credit: D. Ramsay, EPG Caribbean, Barbados (2017).

total inhabitants, was a slave society, numerically dominated by people of African heritage.[4] Centering race is unavoidable when writing about any hemispheric American slave society. Studies that do so remain essential to historical understanding and interpretation. Yet, in overlooking class as an essential category of analysis, a particular problem in Atlantic Jewish historiography, scholars have all too often neglected economically disadvantaged whites and their multimodal intersections with the majority population. In Barbados, the presence of working-class whites was sizeable and consistent over time, so much so that the society cannot be bifurcated into white authorities (planters, managers, overseers) and enslaved or free people of African ancestry. Moreover, as historical archaeologist Matthew Reilly observes, lower-class whites and slaves arguably "had more in common with each other than either group did with the plantocracy."[5] Racial hierarchies and disparities, he points out, in no way prohibited or inhibited "frequent interactions between poor whites and Afro-Barbadians."[6] These interactions were both commercial and sexual, despite narrative primary sources that largely overlook this reality in both arenas.[7] One important reason for this neglect is the dearth of diachronic records created by white ethnic groups with any meaningful longevity in the colony. For that reason, a focus on the Jewish communal documents of Barbados offers an important lens for exploring relations between destitute Jews and their African-descended counterparts. This chapter argues that even when race acted as the explicitly deciding factor in framing such relations, class consistently trumped race.

At first glance, the conduct of the misbehaving synagogue caretaker Isaac Massiah seems to have been exceptional in its extremism, and therefore not representative of either the island's Jewish community or of broader society. A diachronic examination of the communal minutes, however, suggests that the deed was far more mundane than communal authorities would admit. Indeed, the synagogue grounds constituted a focal point for a wide range of "connexions" extending from the Jewish community into the heart of slave society. Located in the hub of Bridgetown's commercial district, properties owned by the congregation constituted the work- and dwelling-places of some of the most impoverished residents of the island, from synagogue functionaries and their family members to enslaved caretakers.[8] Bound together by penury, these individuals periodically breached the mandated borderlines between Jew and non-Jew and slave and free. In doing so, they also inadvertently exposed the hypocrisy of the community's wealthy leaders, whose norm-defying sexual behavior did not typically come under public scrutiny.

Their European origin qualified Barbadian Jews as free persons, while their religious nonconformity circumscribed both their civic and political status. Jews were permitted to earn their living as planters and merchants and to enter the petty trades, but were subject to heavy, discriminatory taxes (sometimes five times as high as those of Christians) and were limited in the number of slaves they could own, a prohibition a few Jewish landowners were able to circumvent.[9] The white, Anglican-dominant government banned Jews from holding civic or political office, restrictions that generally remained in place until the 1800s. The Jewish community of Barbados was somewhat smaller than its Jamaican counterpart, ranging from 250 individuals in the seventeenth century to perhaps 800 by the mid-eighteenth century, and constituting some 3 percent of the white population.[10] By the close of the century, the Jewish population was on the downward curve, dropping to under one hundred members in the first decades of the nineteenth century, at which time leaders began to refer with angst to their dwindling congregation.[11]

Record keeping was an essential practice of the Barbadian Jewish lay leaders (parnassim), whose principal tasks included managing their poor, administering the synagogue and its officials, and serving as a political liaison between their community and the colonial authorities. These records include an unusually rich testament to sexual engagement between Jewish synagogue functionaries and women of African descent. Such "improper connections" were omnipresent in slave societies like Barbados, but were very rarely documented anywhere in writing. The surviving communal minutes, dating from 1791 through 1905 and heretofore never diachronically mined, are peppered with both oblique and explicit references to sex with enslaved and manumitted women of African descent. These records indicate that many such sexual encounters, some of them paid, took place on synagogue grounds in the few decades leading up to the abolition of slavery in 1833. Mortifying to Jewish communal leaders, these incidents reveal the division between expected public and private behavior of Jewish men, the effects of venereal disease on individuals and families, and the claims enslaved women made for material resources and privileges, including legal belonging in the Jewish community.

In the long eighteenth century, most Jews living westward of the Atlantic Ocean lived in slave societies where unfree laborers of African descent constituted the cornerstone of the economy and formed either significant minorities or overwhelming majorities. Insofar as it has focused on entanglement, the emerging field of Atlantic Jewish history tends to emphasize the conversion of select slaves to Judaism and the consequent ethnogenesis of Eurafrican Jews, individuals born as Jews and legally incorporated into the Jewish community, most notably in the Dutch colony of Suriname. Studies have affirmed the "race-blind" nature of Jewish religious law, Jewish secular regulations assigning Eurafrican Jews a second-class status, and the active religious and political participation of Eurafricans within the Jewish community.[12] By focusing on the progeny of slave–master encounters, however, scholars obfuscate the broader historical reality of the sexual use of enslaved women by Jewish men and the historical and economic contexts in which this behavior manifested.

The sources hereunder considered speak to the emotional reaction of servile non-Jewish women (the laborers who peered into the synagogue and laughed) and affective relations between the *samas* and the enslaved women who reportedly competed for his attention. These aspects suggest we are dealing with something more than just "sexual use," but the absence of sources from these women's perspective impedes meaningful analysis in that direction. We stand on firmer ground if we understand these relations in practical terms. Echoing the insights of historians Stephanie Jones-Rogers on the U.S. South and Jessica Marie Johnson on the Franco-Atlantic world, the cases herein discussed suggest that the "close body work" enslaved women performed for Jewish and other men in Barbados constituted income-producing labor that was just as much a part of the island's economy and commercial negotiation as the work carried out by slaves on plantations or by hired-out laborers.[13] Within the context of the Barbadian Jewish community, sexual interactions also reflected strategic alliances forged by females of African descent, rather than simply the forced provisioning of sexual services that masters and other free men generally expected of owned women. As such, enslaved women constituted a hidden labor force and potential conduits for their children to access the material and political advantages of the Jewish community, including group membership.

Secondary sources on the enslaved population of Barbados, including works that focus on the experiences of women, make little or no mention of the local Jewish population, much less Jews' interactions with the majority society. Nor are they concerned with the possible or ascertained membership of African-origin people in the Jewish community.[14] This is unsurprising, given that only 3 percent of the island's white population was Jewish. Moreover, scholars often regard Jewish communal minutes as the exclusive purview of Jewish studies scholars. Yet, in a colony with a relatively high ratio of whites to nonwhites, where the population of European origin ranged anywhere from 44 to 50 percent in the colony's first decades, Judaism and ethnic Jewishness were a distinct potentiality and in some cases a verified actuality for slaves and their free descendants.[15] As such, an investigation of the cases herein explored serves as a corrective to an imagined world order where variants of Christianity or African creolized spiritual traditions, and to some extent Islam, were the only "religious" options available to people of slave origin in the Americas.[16]

Sex in the Synagogue

The initiative of Isaac Massiah to engage enslaved women in sexual intercourse violated a number of communal norms. One level of Massiah's offense was carrying out a commercial transaction on the Jewish Sabbath, a deed strictly forbidden in rabbinical law. But this paled in comparison to the nature of the offense itself. Houses of worship were sacred spaces synonymous with upholding the public morality of the time, as well as the power of the planter class, as Katharine Gerbner has shown in the Christian context. The legislature of Barbados recognized taverns, ale-houses, victualling-houses, and other similar buildings as places where "lewd and debauched Company" frequented, but did not suspect sanctuaries as potential brothels.[17]

For Jews, a sanctuary additionally bore the burden of the community's reputation. Nidhe Israel, Hebrew for "The Scattered of Israel," was the island's only synagogue, and also among the oldest institutions of Barbados, having been founded in the 1650s. Its communal leaders played an important diplomatic role in regulating the political, economic, and social status of Jews vis-à-vis the colonial and metropolitan authorities and the local white Christian population. Keeping scandal out of the Jewish community was a foremost concern of the *Mahamad*. Massiah's key misstep was to bring what was arguably a very common activity into the most public spotlight of the local Jewish community.

As we shall see, lack of discretion was a manifestation of Massiah's class. Synagogue functionaries like Massiah were salaried employees who barely eked out a living. True, they benefited from a number of perquisites, namely no-cost lodging on the synagogue grounds and the possibility of receiving periodic freewill offerings from the congregation on Sabbaths and holidays. But these perks masked the low pay scale and heavy demand on their time that made holding a second job generally illegal, according to the bylaws, and also pragmatically impossible. Synagogue functionaries frequently shirked their duties to pursue additional income, left their positions, or departed the island because they could not make ends meet.[18]

Although their place of employ was the symbolic seat of the community's wealth, salaried employees merely subsisted, if at all. This stark reality was openly acknowledged by Jewish lay leaders themselves, who were unsalaried and whose wealth qualified them for their position. In a letter to the London Portuguese Jewish agents in 1805 requesting their aid in finding a cantor, the parnassim sought a candidate who could "be content to live well as a poor man in the West Indies." Three years later, when the office was once again vacant, the *Mahamad* described the position to their London agents as an opportunity for "a genteel living for a man who cannot better himself in England."[19] By the early 1800s, the community was so diminished in number that the position packed three duties in one. The successful candidate would serve not only as cantor (hazan), but would also substitute as ritual slaughterer (*sohet*) and ritual meat inspector (*bodek*) in the case of the delinquency of the former. The cantor was also expected, at no additional pay, to teach the Hebrew language to the "poor of our nation." Anticipating the temptation to seek a secondary income, the parnassim explicitly forbade the cantor from keeping a shop of merchandise there, which had been the "delusion" of the former cantor and had prevented him from fulfilling his duty.[20]

If the pay was commensurate with the economic class of potential office-holders, so was their behavior. As a result, the *Mahamad* spent much of its time reprimanding neglectful employees or recruiting reputable men, preferably single, to replace vacant offices. In 1798, the parnassim had advertised the position of synagogue caretaker after the previous employee had departed the island penniless. The two applicants were Isaac Massiah and Judah Massiah, perhaps siblings. The *Mahamad* selected the latter man for the job, but over the next dozen years or so, each was alternately hired and fired amid periodic outbursts against the congregation's leaders and the usual reprimands for the shirking of duties. At the time of his hire, Judah Massiah was a paying member of the congregation (a *yahid*), but his annual synagogue tax (*finta*) lingered at the very bottom of the lowest tax bracket at £1.10 per year.[21]

The synagogue caretaker was expected to sleep rent free in the house provided him in the synagogue yard, a policy designed to both facilitate his timely arrival for work and bind him to a dependent relationship with the congregation. Records hint at the presence of an extended Massiah family living in the synagogue yard, penurious and reliant on the congregation as a source of income. Sarah D. Massiah, likely a close relative, had been tending to the Jewish ritual bath for an unspecified time by 1809, when she asked for a "small pittance annually as Banyadeira" (supervisor of the mikveh, or Jewish ritual bath) and was allotted £15. She was still a pensioner in 1822.[22] Two other women, Sarah Massiah and Angel Massiah, no doubt also close relatives, evidently had no active source of income, both receiving an annual pension of £1.10 in 1810.[23] In the next decade, both women successfully petitioned for an increase to their allotment.[24] Abigail Massiah was also a longtime pensioner.[25]

These Massiah family members were all implicated in "improper" connections. Had the lay leaders of the *Mahamad* paid more attention (or had they wanted to), they would have noticed something amiss on the synagogue grounds years before Isaac Massiah's public dalliances. In 1804, some years before Sarah D. Massiah assumed directorship of the Jewish ritual bath, she accepted an unremunerated position to maintain the cleanliness of the "*banyadeira*'s house" adjoining the mikveh and was given the key on condition that she not allow "any improper person [to] make use of the bath or any men to lodge in the [adjoining] house."[26] At some point thereafter, the key came into possession of Isaac Massiah, who was then serving as synagogue caretaker. In 1806, a complaint was lodged with the *Mahamad* about "the impropriety of a man keeping the key of the bathing house," a possible indication that Sarah D. Massiah, in connivance with Isaac, was providing local slaves with access to the ritual building. The lay leaders ordered Isaac to return the keys.[27] However, he refused to comply, and an illness conveniently prevented him from appearing before the *Mahamad* to explain his recalcitrance.[28] The *Mahamad* solved the dilemma by striking two additional keys for the front door and bathing house and giving them to the cantor, directing him that that "no *improper* person be permitted to visit or bathe in the bathing house."[29] Like other similarly underscored words in the communal minutes, the word "improper" signaled an ineffable public secret, most likely that women of African descent were observing the Jewish laws of ritual immersion incumbent upon married women.[30] This interpretation is strongly supported by a description of public synagogue offices written in 1821 and stipulating that the "keeper of the bath . . . not permit any persons but those of the Hebrew nation to use the bath."[31]

But bathkeeper Sarah D. Massiah was not always supportive of Isaac Massiah's deviant sexual behavior. Under oath as a star witness in his trial in 1810, she testified that she, too, had spotted two hired laborers

SEX WITH SLAVES AND THE BUSINESS OF GOVERNANCE

FIGURE 9.2. The Jewish ritual bath (mikveh), located near the synagogue building of Congregation Nidhe Israel of Barbados. Photo Credit: D. Ramsay, EPG Caribbean, Barbados (2017).

peering into the synagogue and laughing at what was transpiring within. It was her deposition that revealed Isaac Massiah had solicited in the gallery of the synagogue the sexual services of a "black woman belonging to Mrs. Brice," going so far as to hand her money.[32] There are other suggestions, too, that the Massiah family was implicated in sex work among slaves. By the mid-nineteenth century, one Hannah Massiah, identified as a "mulatto," was a noted hotel proprietor on Cumberland Street in Bridgetown catering to "merchants and colonial gentlemen."[33] Tavern keepers of the eighteenth and nineteenth centuries were typically "black, or mulatto" women who had obtained their freedom through a sexual relationship with "some *backra* man." Proprietress Hannah Massiah was likely a *madame* and perhaps herself a former sex worker.[34] A slave census from the 1810s indicates that Hannah owned four slaves, Lubbah and Molly, both fifty years of age, and Statira and Kate, seventeen and twenty, respectively. They are all described as domestics and black, save for Molly who is listed as "coloured."[35] These women may have helped Hannah operate the tavern, their housekeeping duties perhaps overlapping with the provision of sexual services. By at least the early eighteenth century, taverns or inns, most of them located in Bridgetown, were places where locals and travelers alike could purchase food, lodging, and sex, as Marisa Fuentes's work illustrates.[36] One observer noted euphemistically in the 1790s, "A bed may be had for half a dollar per night . . . and, for an additional sum well understood, the choice of an attendant to draw curtains."[37]

Members of the Massiah family were also at the center of the community's next sexual scandal, in 1812, when the heat shifted to Rafael Abendana. Three years previously, Abendana had been selected by the congregation's Portuguese Jewish agents in London to serve the Barbadian congregation as cantor.[38] Though also indigents, cantors earned twice as much as synagogue caretakers. Abendana's impecunious status is apparent in a number of petitions he placed before the *Mahamad*. Shortly after his arrival, for example, he requested of his superiors a lying-in bed for his heavily pregnant wife, who then possessed only a mattress.[39] In 1811, he was granted a new cloak in which to preside during the upcoming High Holy Days.[40] A petition he submitted the following year for financial support was rejected.[41] But less than two months later, Abendana's application to assume the additional office of synagogue caretaker was granted.[42] Thus, as he approached the High Holy Days of 1812, Abendana had passed three levels of scrutiny: once when London's Portuguese Jewish agents recommended him for office, again when the Barbados parnassim hired him as hazan, and a third time when he was approved for the office of *samas*.

Abendana's world turned upside down three days before the Jewish New Year, in September 1812. At a special meeting of the *Mahamad*, the *presidente* announced that he had suspended the cantor following confirmation of a medical report that Abendana had contracted venereal disease. A private inquiry revealed that the cantor had approached one Dr. Richards, complaining of "stricture in the urethra," and had dispatched a young man to purchase medicine for the alleviation of his condition. The ensuing trial, organized by the *Mahamad*, confirmed that Abendana had "defiled himself by intercourse with others, besides his wife," possibly a "hired negress" who apparently left Abendana's service in a "state of pregnancy for him." By this time, Abendana had spent all of his salary on medication and perhaps also on sex workers and could not borrow additional funds. The *Mahamad* resolved to present his wife and their offspring with £40, one half to be proffered immediately, the other after the delivery of their fourth child, an implicit gesture of sympathy for her in her now complete destitution.[43] Perhaps, too, the funds were explicit recognition that Abendana might have transferred "cupid's disease" to both his wife and newborn.

Abendana's trial began the following week. The first witness was Sarah Massiah. She testified that she had observed a "negro woman constantly following" Abendana around the synagogue yard and had overhead conversations "among Negroes" that verified a "connection" had taken place between the cantor and the woman in question. The next to be deposed was Moses Belasco, who confirmed that he had "heard the same talk among Negroes of such an improper connection." Another witness was Judah Massiah, who two years earlier had been sworn in as the new *samas* after Isaac Massiah had been suspended for "improper connections" with enslaved women in the synagogue. He testified that he had eye-witnessed "such instances of familiarity" between the defendant and the enslaved woman and had no doubt "that a connection existed" between them. Judah Massiah further testified that he had overheard the woman in question engaged in a jealous dispute with another enslaved woman over Abendana's affections. The witness had learned from one Betty Massiah that this second enslaved woman had also fallen "pregnant by her master," none other than Abendana. Judah Massiah also mentioned that an unnamed white woman had confided to him that she had been compelled to leave Abendana's service after he attempted "to take improper liberties with her." Standing before the *Mahamad*, Abendana could offer nothing in his own defense.[44]

Together, the intelligence gathered from witnesses demonstrated that Raphael Abendana actively initiated sexual contact with a number of lower-class women, both enslaved African and white, at least two of them in his employ. At his trial, he very nearly admitted to the accusations, conceding that "such an act would be a great sin" and promising "in future to behave better & endeavor to give more general satisfaction." Later in October, with the High Holy Days behind them, the *Mahamad* resolved to grant Abendana $20 a month for the support of his family for one year in addition to £75 for his dispatch to London with his family of six.[45] The communal minutes do not mention Abendana again, an indication that he soon left the island. We next hear of Abendana in 1826, when he was hired as a watchman at the cemetery of London's Portuguese Jewish community.[46] His semicoerced departure from the island was conducted via the *despacho*, a Portuguese Jewish institution operative all over the Atlantic world to rid local communities of indigent and scandalous Jews.

During his term as cantor of the Barbados Jewish community, Abendana had evidently engaged in sex solicitation that ranged from patently predatorial (in the case of his white servant woman) to "consensual," or at least "transactional." Class- and race-based power dynamics, as well as the absence of extensive first-person testimony, make it difficult to properly assess either his behavior or the responses of the women in question. Jessica Marie Johnson, in her analysis of black women of the French Atlantic, uses the felicitous phrase "the spectrum of coercion and what passed for consent in a slaveholding society."[47] Still, the Jewish communal minutes suggest that those solicited could possess some degree of agency, whether the ability to flee sexual advances or the power to either refuse or negotiate a relationship that could bring material and social advantages. The reference to a jealous dispute between two enslaved women, one of them impregnated by Abendana and both vying for his attentions, again suggests the overlap between paid sex and family formation.

There is evidence that the power of negotiation was pivotal in the creation of Jewish families that straddled the boundary between free and enslaved, Jewish and African. In 1826, the Barbadian congregation hired yet another synagogue caretaker, a man named Jacob J. de Meza. Like his predecessor, Isaac Massiah, Meza also provoked the *Mahamad*'s ire for indecent behavior on synagogue property. The complaints came soon after the devastating hurricane of 1831, which leveled the synagogue, as well as many other buildings, and claimed two thousand lives. The greatest impact was felt by the impoverished masses. One year after the hurricane, the *Mahamad* realized that Meza was harboring a "coloured family" in the synagogue yard. Communal leaders demanded that Meza remove "the nuisance" immediately, or else be fired.[48] This "nuisance," as the Jewish leaders explicitly acknowledged in their minutes, was Jacob J. de Meza's "wife & family."[49]

Jacob J. de Meza had arrived in Barbados from Suriname, where he had been a member of an extended free Eurafrican Jewish clan, some of whom were laid to rest in the "mulatto" row of a cemetery located in the Jewish village of Jodensavanne.[50] One member of this family, also called Jacob de Meza, had been a signatory of the 1793 petition that Eurafrican Jews in Suriname presented to the local governor to protest their marginal status within the Jewish community.[51] The route synagogue caretaker Jacob J. de Meza had traveled from Suriname to Barbados reinforced a long-standing relationship between the two colonies, which continued to exchange populations long after Suriname transitioned to Dutch rule in 1667. An island-wide plantation census carried out in Barbados in 1817, for example, lists a number of slaves as originating in that Dutch colony, as does the local newspaper.[52]

Whether Jacob J. de Meza had brought his enslaved family with him to Barbados from Suriname or had formed a new one upon arrival, his insistence on harboring them in the synagogue yard asserted the belonging of unfree relatives within the Jewish community. The Jewish leaders of Nidhe Israel, however, were not sympathetic, and Meza's surly behavior did not help. Two of them cited Meza for "abusive language and ungentlemanly conduct," while another noted he was in arrears to the synagogue for two months' salary he had borrowed.[53] When another community member, E. R. Miranda, applied for the position of synagogue caretaker during the proceedings, the *Mahamad* seized upon the opportunity to expel Meza and company from the synagogue yard, making Miranda's hire contingent on the Eurafrican family's removal.[54] By November 1832, the leaders noted with satisfaction that "Mr. De Meza & his family" had left the synagogue yard.[55]

The Sexual Behavior of Wealthy Men

So far, we have considered the sexual behavior of lower-class Jewish men who served their community as salaried employees. Of course, wealthy Jewish men also carried out sexual relationships with enslaved women, impregnated and formed semi-official families with them, and were infected with and spread venereal diseases. But arguably, these relations were less openly acknowledged, at least in written sources, similar to the pattern observed for the Jewish community of Suriname. In keeping with the nature of public secrets, everyone knew about these relations, but it was considered indecent to speak about them openly.

What difference, then, did class make in the integration of mixed-status families in the Jewish community? Again, the communal minutes of Barbados suggest some answers. This chapter opened with the anecdote of cantor Moses Belasco witnessing the use of the synagogue as a house of ill repute by the caretaker Isaac Massiah. As it turns out, Belasco himself had once been accused of similar behavior. In 1806, while serving as ritual slaughterer, Belasco was reprimanded by the *Mahamad* for "living with a coloured woman, in the synagogue yard." The parnassim resolved to demand that Belasco "remove the nuisance from the yard" or be fired, and Belasco promised to comply with the resolution.[56]

Moses Belasco's life trajectory is a clear indication that upward mobility was possible in the Jewish community of Barbados. In 1801, the congregation's agent in London had recommended Belasco as "a lad of good character" and engaged him at a starting annual salary of £65 as both ritual slaughterer and ritual inspector of meat for the island's Jewish congregation. Acknowledging Belasco's "indigent state," and in accordance with synagogue policy, the leaders offered Belasco the use of one of the synagogue's houses so long as he remained unmarried. Belasco's recommender in London characterized him as having "no talents, or ingenuity for any other but his present profession" and projected that the young man's "savings will produce little[,] as living here as now in all other countries is rather expensive."[57] But over the years, Belasco strategically positioned himself for an ascent up the community ladder, offering himself for higher positions of authority and remuneration, including as cantor, as soon as they became vacant.[58] Over the years, he was reprimanded for neglecting his duties, a hint that he had undertaken commercial interests on the side, as did so many other synagogue functionaries before and after, out of sheer necessity.[59] But unlike those who left the island destitute, Belasco prevailed, coming into ownership of two domestic slaves and securing a salary of £220 (more than double that of the *samas*) by 1831.[60]

As this chapter has argued, discretion was the major factor that distinguished the extralegal sexual behavior of upper- from lower-class Jewish men. But a watershed is detectable in the 1810s. Whereas previously "sex with slaves" among wealthy Jewish men had been a public secret, now it was discussed more and more openly, both orally, in communal meetings, and also as recorded in the minutes themselves. In 1821, during a discussion about revising the communal bylaws, Benjamin Elkin, chief leader of the Jewish community, openly questioned the custom that accorded to married men the honor of opening the Torah ark during formal worship. Elkin could not discover any rationale for this practice, other than "a presumption that married persons led a more virtuous and moral life than unmarried ones." This rationale, he continued, was patently erroneous, given the fact that many married men and widowers in the community were "living in the 'hideousness of vice'" and leading a "more irregular life than . . . even single men!" A lively discussion ensued. No one opposed the proposal to extend the ritual honor to single men, but two leaders moved that the embarrassing discussion should not appear in the communal minutes as a motion. The motion for censorship did not carry, but the proposal to abolish differential treatment did, with only two dissenting votes. The "gentlemen" present agreed that theretofore the ritual honor during services would be "given indiscriminately" to all adult male members of the community, regardless of their marital status.[61]

The changing discourse was occurring during the waning years of the slave regime, when the collective consequences of sexual exploitation increasingly blurred the boundaries between white and black, free and enslaved. By the 1820s, people of color constituted almost one quarter of the free population of Barbados. I argue that the increasingly open acknowledgement of sexual relations between wealthy Jews and their social inferiors of African origin was due not only to the growth of a free population of slave origins, but also to their emboldened demand for equal rights in the 1810s and 1820s. Largely because of this demand, the legislature passed a law in 1817 allowing free people of color to provide evidence in court against whites. In accepting this new privilege, as Melanie Newton shows, activists of African origin expressed support for white supremacy, explicitly recognizing the superiority of whites over them and acknowledging that where slavery exists, there must necessarily be a distinction between white and free people of color.[62] This privilege, which culminated in 1831 in full civil rights on par with whites, may have given Jewish elites license to speak more openly about their ties with free people of color.

In communal governance, too, race became less of a dividing factor in the Jewish community of Barbados during the waning days of slavery. This idea is reinforced by the case of Isaac Lopez Brandon (1795-1855). Brandon, as the research of historian Karl Watson first showed, was the Barbadian son of a slave and an affluent Portuguese Jewish sugar planter, Abraham Rodrigues Brandon (1766-1831).[63] Isaac Lopez Brandon was the second child of the union between Abraham and an enslaved woman named Sarah.[64] In 1801, Isaac's father Abraham manumitted him along with his younger sister Sarah Brandon (1798-1828).[65]

Abraham Rodrigues Brandon is a dramatic example of a Barbadian Jew whose economic status improved over time. In 1796, five years before he manumitted two of his children, Abraham was made a *yahid* of the Barbadian Jewish community.[66] At that time, his income must have been modest, as he paid the nearly bare minimum of £1.10 as his annual *finta*.[67] The following year, when the synagogue opened a subscription for funds supporting the British king in his fight against revolutionary France, Abraham had sufficient means to contribute £7.10 to the cause, alongside twenty-nine other men and women from the congregation who donated £10 or less.[68] Abraham's leadership status in the community began to change in the early 1800s, when he was twice elected to serve as *hatan*, an honorific position enacted during synagogue services on the Simhat Torah holiday, and typically a pathway to communal leadership. He refused to accept both times, a common response among *yehidim* who wished to avoid the mandatory charitable donation associated with the role.[69] In 1805, he was considered for the trusted position of *gabay* (treasurer). He once again declined, but only because of his plans to temporarily leave the island.[70] By the following decade, Abraham Rodrigues Brandon showed himself much more committed, perhaps due to his rising fortunes. His annual *finta* climbed from £5 in 1810 to £30 in 1819, by which time he owned 168 slaves, making him one of the largest slave owners of the island.[71] Beginning in 1810, he was sequentially elected as parnas, parnas *presidente* (the highest leadership position in Nidhe Israel, synonymous with the Anglophone term "warden"), and a member of the *ajunta*, a body of Jewish communal elders composed of former parnassim.[72] His consecutive stints as parnas *presidente* coincided with the turbulent 1820s, when an internal schism nearly put an end to the organized Jewish community.[73]

Abraham's son, the Eurafrican Isaac Lopez Brandon, formally converted to Judaism on a trip to Suriname in 1812. When he returned to Barbados the following year, he was officially a Jew, eighteen years of age, and on the path to first-class membership in the local Jewish community. In April 1813, the Barbadian *Mahamad* added him to a list of *yehidim*, the paying members of the synagogue, and assessed him an annual synagogue tax of £30.[74]

The internal schism of the 1820s concerned the so-called Hebrew Vestry Bill, which the Jewish leaders presented before the Barbadian Assembly in 1819. The bill sought to accomplish two tasks. First, it aimed to legally transform the Jewish congregation into a vestry, on par with its Christian parallel. Second, it intended to empower Jewish communal leaders to assess taxes among their constituents, and to enlist the colonial government to enforce payment of those taxes on pain of excommunication and heavy fines. The Hebrew Vestry Bill was a feisty effort to reinforce the rather arbitrary power the *Mahamad* controversially executed over its constituents.[75] If passed, it would have compelled every Jew resident on the island to be a member of the Jewish community and, if they were sufficiently solvent, to pay their assessed taxes to the congregational coffers. In brief, the Hebrew Vestry Bill sought to achieve for the *Mahamad* the same authority the Christian vestries of Barbados's eleven parishes enjoyed.

The Hebrew Vestry Bill provoked a backlash in the form of a counterpetition presented to the Barbadian Assembly by seven Jews, at least three of them slave-owning.[76] This faction argued that the power of Jewish leaders to arbitrarily assess taxes and enforce payment, under pain of excommunication and fines, was contrary to Jewish law, unconstitutional, and historically unprecedented in the British metropole and its overseas possessions. Jews, they argued, did not possess a territory of their own, as did Anglican churches in their respective parishes, and metropolitan laws banned religious nonconformists, including explicitly Jews, from holding public office. Metropolitan law also barred any "foreign state or potentate" from possessing any ecclesiastical or spiritual authority in the English realm. In referring to this law, the counterpetitioners implicitly cast Jews as strangers in the land. The dissenters regarded mandatory taxation by the *Mahamad* as a form of oppression, since they were already saddled with paying parish and other colonial taxes. They requested the privilege of belonging to the synagogue only if they desired to do so.[77]

From the start, the controversy between the Jewish communal leaders on the one hand, and the small Jewish faction on the other, took on both racial and class overtones. The counterpetitioners claimed that the Hebrew Vestry Bill was signed by "a parcel of apprentices and shopboys," even as they accused the Jewish communal leaders of nepotism, "tyranny ... and persecution." They also accused one of those leaders, Abraham, father of the Eurafrican Jewish Isaac Lopez Brandon, of desiring to tax the "Hebrew nation" in order to "send money to America to build a synagogue" for his son's "colored connexions." This barb was a reference to a trip Brandon senior had recently undertaken to Philadelphia and his involvement in fundraising for the purchase of a new building there for the Portuguese Jewish congregation Mikveh Israel, which had been founded in the 1780s.[78]

Not to be outdone in the arena of racial innuendos, Jewish leaders also deployed racially derogatory puns, implying that the faction was besmirched by association with people of African descent. Communal leaders accused the faction of attempting to "blacken and defame" them "in the eyes of the Christian community." A "Jew's heart must be black to the very core," they continued, to "inspirit Christians with additional hatred and prejudice against his brethren." They also referred to the "black envenomed malignity of these men." Thus, it would seem that both proponents of the Hebrew Vestry Bill of 1819 and its schismatic detractors regarded Jews of slave origins as fair rhetorical targets. For this reason, Abraham's son Isaac Lopez Brandon was thrust into the spotlight. As the only Barbadian Jew explicitly acknowledged in communal records as having slave origins, Brandon is an important marker for how the local Jewish community reckoned with upper-class members of an ambiguous legal and ethnic status.[79]

Interestingly, the Eurafrican Brandon had also been a signatory of the Hebrew Vestry Bill. His support of this bill clearly positioned him alongside the most conservative of the congregation's members, yet another indication that class trumped race in the Barbadian Jewish community.[80] Unfortunately for Brandon, the General Assembly that considered the Hebrew Vestry Bill in 1820 added a clause "to prevent persons descended from Negroes participating in the privileges of the said Bill."[81] The bill passed, forcing the *Mahamad* to rewrite its communal bylaws, which now included a clause that banned Jews of "negro" origins from acquiring *yahid* status, voting, and being elected to office. In 1821, Jewish communal leaders voted to remove Isaac Lopez Brandon from the list of first-class members.[82] But the vote, which passed with a 3–2 margin, was extremely controversial. Many additional Jewish communal leaders publicly opposed the ejection of Brandon from the community. At this moment, in 1821 and 1822, race seemingly became central to the Jewish community's internal rupture. But it is not that simple.

The timing of the Hebrew Vestry Bill was likely not coincidental. The 1810s were a decade when a variety of marginalized groups in Barbados sought to challenge the existing order. Among them were a group of middling planters of more recent wealth than the old, landed aristocracy. They organized the first Barbadian political party, the "Salmagundis," a word denoting a "general mixture" or a "miscellaneous collection." The Salmagundis allied themselves with lower-class whites to protest the oppression of the planter elite and swept most of the big planters from the House of Assembly in bitterly fought elections in 1819. They ultimately won control over the House of Assembly in the 1820s.[83]

Another marginalized group clamoring for political empowerment were free people of African descent. As Melanie Newton notes, these individuals tended to be politically conservative. Like Isaac Lopez Brandon, who inherited dozens of slaves from his father's estate, these free people were not abolitionists. Only after Emancipation did many begin to publicly embrace former slaves as their brethren, in the face of white racism.[84] Newton convincingly argues that free people of African ancestry did not constitute a well-defined group, since they were fragmented by class, gender, competing claims to authority, and conflicting stances on slavery.⁸⁵ The same might be said of the Jews of Barbados, whether planters, merchants, pensioners, or unaffiliated Jews—white and Eurafrican alike—who lived on the margins of the community, appearing in the communal minutes only when in need of occasional financial assistance or burial. The Hebrew Vestry Bill and its fallout, therefore, highlighted no ideologically clear factions within the Jewish community. But it did reflect the broader political turmoil in Barbadian society. Despite the Eurafrican Brandon's ejection from the Jewish community, ultimately class triumphed over race, just as it did in broader society. By at least 1837, Brandon had rejoined communal governance, regularly attending meetings and even sitting in the same vestry room as a fellow Jew who had once voted to ban from the *Mahamad* all Jews of "Negro" origins.⁸⁶

Let us now review the findings of this chapter. First, the communal minutes offer us a rare glimpse of the sexual behavior of lower-class Jewish men in Barbados. It opens up a view to the underclass, reminding us that most Jews of the Atlantic world were not the wealthy businessmen at the center of Alexander Fortune's book *Merchants and Jews*.⁸⁷ Primary sources heretofore discussed by scholars indicate that poor whites never or rarely "intermixed" with "enslaved or free Afro-Barbadians." As Matthew Reilly notes, this idea has "seeped into recent scholarship."⁸⁸ Reilly's own archaeological studies are strongly suggestive of close trade relations and shared material culture among poor whites and free and enslaved people of African descent. The communal records of the Barbadian Jewish community offer more concrete evidence that these relations not only occurred, but were in fact central in many ways to the operation of the Jewish community and both the public and private lives of its constituents. Thus, the cases herein discussed offer a counterpoint to the dominant historiography that would minimize the "intermixture" of poor whites with "enslaved or free Afro-Barbadians."⁸⁹ The evidence we have considered in fact demonstrates that the synagogue, synagogue yard, and its abutting properties served as the dwelling places of mixed-status Jewish families (or, from another perspective, mixed-status African families), whose reach extended from the organized Jewish community into the heart of slave society. These anecdotes further suggest a continuum between sexual exploitation, the quest for patronage, and family formation.

Second, by the 1810s, with the free population of African descent expanding and clamoring for enfranchisement, it was increasingly challenging for the Jewish community to perpetuate the public secrets of its elites. Island politics forced even Jewish leaders to openly acknowledge that "improper connections" were widespread not only among the poor, but also among the rank of the privileged. Finally, let us consider how Jewish these stories are. In every hemispheric American slave society, widespread sexual exploitation of women of African descent was the norm. In our anecdotes, the context (that is, the Jewish community), the place (that is, the synagogue, synagogue yard, and the homes of Jewish religious functionaries), the sexual initiators, and the judges are all Jewish. But not much else in this story is Jewish. This affords an important lesson for the burgeoning field of Atlantic Jewish history, one that gives scholars permission to find significant patterns and insights that are not uniquely or even intrinsically Jewish. On the other hand, perhaps there is indeed something specifically Jewish about this story. As Salo Wittmayer Baron reminds us, the pattern of Jewish history is not lachrymosity—not a relentless litany of persecution and resistance to persecution. Rather the overall norm of the Jewish past is integration into broader society.[90] The cases explored above thus allow us to normalize Jewish history by considering the integration of Jews in their Caribbean abodes. This integration affirms that the presence of enslaved and free people of African descent was absolutely central to the Jewish community's governance, if not its existence.

Chapter 10

Connecting Jewish Community
An Anglophone Journal, Rev. Isaac Leeser, and a Jewish Atlantic World

Laura Newman Eckstein

"It will give me pleasure to serve you in any way either as Regular Correspondent for yr newly projected paper or as Agt here, or as a canvas-ser for Subscribers," wrote the Charlestonian merchant Thomas Jefferson Moïse to Reverend Isaac Leeser, a prominent Jewish religious leader in Philadelphia during the mid-nineteenth century.[1] Leeser's reply to Moïse has not survived, but subsequent correspondence between the two men reveals that Moïse did in fact become an agent ("Agt") and "canvas-ser for Subscribers" for Leeser's periodical *The Occident, and American Jewish Advocate* (hereafter *The Occident*). Moïse's correspondence with Leeser reveals one example of the many relationships cemented or forged anew through the business conducted over Leeser's long career as an author and editor.

In addition to his role as founder, publisher, editor, contributor, and occasional typesetter for *The Occident* (1843–69), Leeser was an author and translator of popular religious texts of the age, including what became known as the "Leeser Bible," the first Jewish translation

---

I gratefully acknowledge the help and advice of Professor Beth S. Wenger, Professor Ryan Cordell, Professor Sarah Gordon, Dr. Arthur Kiron, Arnold Kaplan, Deanne Kaplan, Jim Green, Lynne Farrington, Cornelia King, Wesley Davis, Dahlia El Zein, and William Angus McLeod IV.

of the Hebrew Bible into English, and a *Hebrew Spelling-Book* (1838), the first Hebrew primer for children in the United States. He also translated many other religious texts, including Sephardic and Ashkenazic prayer books, Moses Mendelssohn's *Jerusalem*, and Joseph Schwartz's *Descriptive Geography and Brief Historical Sketch of Palestine*. Born in Neuenkirchen, part of Prussian Westphalia, in 1806, by the age of fourteen Leeser was an orphan. In Münster, while attending gymnasium, he met Rabbi Abraham Sutro, "a strong opponent of the burgeoning movement for Jewish religious reform" who would continue to influence Leeser for the rest of his life.[2] From Münster, Leeser immigrated to Richmond, Virginia, where his uncle, Zalma Rehiné, was a successful storekeeper.[3] Rehiné's wife, Rachel Judah, was related to two of the most prominent Jewish leaders in the Western Hemisphere, Isaac Seixas and Reverend Gershom Mendes Seixas. While in Richmond, Isaac Seixas taught Leeser the Sephardic rite, how to lead prayers with the Sephardic customs and melodies. Leeser also studied with Jacob Mordecai, the noted Ashkenazi teacher of the Warrenton Female Academy. In 1828, Leeser gained national attention after he published a response in *The Richmond Whig* to antisemitic attacks that appeared in the *London Quarterly Review*. In 1829, Leeser applied for and accepted a job as hazan, leader of prayers at Philadelphia's Congregation Mikveh Israel.[4] Over the years, Leeser clashed with his congregation's board, ultimately resulting in his firing in 1851.[5] In 1857, he became hazan at Beth El-Emeth of Philadelphia. Throughout his time in Philadelphia, Leeser was an avid participant in Jewish culture, writing, publishing, and rallying against what would become Reform Judaism, and interacting with notable Jews of the day including Rebecca Gratz. Leeser died in 1868 at the age of sixty-one.

Compared to the twentieth-century Jewish press in the United States, there have been few studies of the Jewish press in nineteenth-century America. One notable exception is Rudolf Glanz, who offers statistics of subscribers, lists different "Jewish communities," and asserts that the Jewish press was the only organization connecting Jews in the United States prior to the Civil War.[6] Robert Singerman, in "The American Jewish Press, 1823–1983: A Bibliographic Survey of Research and Studies," created a comprehensive bibliography of the Jewish Press in the United States.[7] In 1989, Arthur Goren as part of his article "The Jewish Press in the U.S." spent little time on early Jewish newspapers like *The Occident* and remarked mostly on news coverage of foreign events by early newspapers.[8]

Jonathan Sarna's "The History of the Jewish Press in North America" argued that the Jewish press's trajectory, "at least until recently, [is] a story of marked decay."[9] More recently, Arthur Kiron examined three mid-nineteenth-century Jewish newspapers: *The Occident, The Voice of Jacob,* and *First Fruits of the West.* Kiron argues that these three newspapers formed a network of Jewish culture, "a Jewish Republic of Letters" or an "Atlantic *Haskalah.*"[10] Challenging Kiron, Adam Mendelsohn refutes Kiron's embrace of the Port Jew schema to understand these newspapers and a larger Jewish Atlantic culture. Instead, Mendelsohn sees the 1840s as a moment of an Anglo-Jewish diaspora. Mendelson asserts that by the 1840s "the period of the Port Jew had passed. In its place emerged a nascent Anglophone diaspora, a cultural and social sphere whose tentacular grasp stretched across the expanding British Empire and deep into the American frontier."[11] More recently the scholar of nineteenth-century mobility and migration Shari Rabin embraced a national model, demonstrating how the newspapers of Isaac Leeser and Isaac Mayer Wise, through their subscribers and agents, functioned as larger projects and visions of American Jewish communal life, even in the most remote towns with scant Jewish populations.[12]

This chapter argues that Rev. Isaac Leeser foregrounded the Atlantic Jewish world in his attempt to build a readership and a sense of Jewish community by examining the material text of *The Occident* including often overlooked wrappers, as well as other agent and subscription lists. Scholars have profiled Leeser in various biographies and have used *The Occident* to discuss Jewish life in the United States during the mid-nineteenth century. The historian Bertram Korn described Isaac Leeser as the cornerstone of American Jewish life, insisting that "practically every form of Jewish activity which supports American Jewish life today was either established or envisaged by this one man."[13] For Korn, *The Occident* represented Leeser's crowning achievement. If Leeser "could have done only one thing," he explained, "we would single out publication of his monthly journal."[14] Rabbi Lance J. Sussman built on Korn's profile of Leeser in his biography *Isaac Leeser and the Making of American Judaism.* While Sussman's biography contains details on Leeser's role as publisher of *The Occident,* it focuses on Leeser's contributions to American Judaism more generally.[15] Absent from this and other secondary sources are some of the material aspects of Leeser's journal that are crucial to understanding the periodical's reach and mission beyond just an American scope.

In the inaugural article of his monthly publication, *The Occident*, Leeser explained that the periodical's purpose was to "endeavor to give circulation to everything which can be interesting to the Jewish inhabitants in the western hemisphere."[16] *The Occident* served as an aggregator and collector of the news of these communities, and Leeser hoped that the newspaper would function as a "one-stop" news source for the Jews of the Atlantic world. Behind this purpose lay what he saw as a religious and cultural mission. *The Occident*, with its curated articles and news, allowed Leeser to have some cultural control over this community in a diasporic framework. He expressed this underlying mission in 1845 and urged those who remained faithful subscribers to help him increase his readership:

> May we in this place urge upon our friends, who are anxious for the success and continuance of a Jewish organ in America, the propriety of endeavouring to increase the circulation of the Occident? . . . Will our friends try to respond to this call? We hope for a favourable consideration.[17]

For Leeser, the success of *The Occident* and the length of its list of subscribers reflected the progress or lack thereof of the Jewish community in the Atlantic world. An increase in subscriptions signaled the health and growth of the Jewish Atlantic community. In 1845, when the number of subscribers decreased, Leeser ascribed the downturn to a withering of Atlantic Jewry on his watch. He responded to the decline by calling on the faithful to encourage other Jews to subscribe, in essence trying to reengage the community.

The wrappers, the paper covers that functioned as the beginning and ending pages for each monthly edition, contained subscription lists (beginning in 1846), lists of the periodical's agents, and advertisements, including information about Leeser's other publications. These wrappers also provided important announcements that demonstrate shifts in the periodical's business model over time. Readers at the time often considered *The Occident*'s wrappers ephemeral and discarded them, even when subscribers saved the remainder of *The Occident*. The wrappers that still exist today are piecemeal, spread over various archives, and with many months missing. Yet the contents of these wrappers, in combination with the rich text of *The Occident*, shed light on Leeser's business operation and cultural mission for his paper. Leeser fostered an economic and religious community, a readership that was a far-flung network that helps us to reenvision Jewish community in America and the Western Hemisphere between 1843 and 1868.

Leeser followed a modified subscription publishing for all of his publications. *The Oxford Companion of the Book* defines subscription publishing as "a system of obtaining orders (and sometimes payment) in advance to enable publication of a book."[18] Leeser issued prospectuses that announced his plan to publish a certain book, often requiring a certain number of subscribers to begin production. After accumulating sufficient financial means from these initial subscribers, Leeser printed extra copies for future sales.[19] Leeser's model always depended on three important categories of actors. One was the agent, who acted on Leeser's behalf, receiving a bundle of papers and distributing them, collecting subscriptions, and recruiting new subscribers. Agents also corresponded with Leeser and negotiated for compensation. Another was the subscriber, who either paid Leeser or paid the agent. Subscribers were often connected to one another through familial ties, business, or friendship. They too played a critical role in expanding Leeser's readership base. Third, and unique to the periodical, were the contributors who received some sort of compensation by Leeser for their articles.

Leeser's approach deviated from the traditional business practice of subscription publishers. *The Oxford Companion of the Book* notes that "subscription publishing flourished in England for about two hundred years from the mid-seventeenth century. Lists of subscribers were frequently set out in order of the social hierarchy."[20] Subscription publishers used their lists to publish prominent names, like those of nobility, to make their publications more desirable. Leeser, less concerned with social prestige or economic remuneration, instead focused on increasing his subscription list for a publication that, to him, symbolized the vitality of Judaism. The periodical's motto, printed on the front cover of every issue, also reflected Leeser's focus on promoting Judaism and Jewish life, declaring its mission to promote "the diffusion of knowledge on Jewish literature and religion." In April 1846, Leeser called on the "presidents and secretaries of congregations and societies in England, West Indies, British America, and the United States" to send in announcements and news of their respective communities: "The Occident being established to diffuse information on Jewish subjects, we request all having local information to communicate the same to us at our own expense."[21] By sharing news with one another through a mass media publication rather than through a single letter, Jews separated by rough terrain and seas could build community and, to Leeser's mind, keep their Judaism alive.

The Occident reflected a dual process. News came from Leeser's correspondents and subscribers, while Leeser selectively curated this information for *The Occident*'s readership. Correspondents, agents, and subscribers were necessary to supply the news of their Jewish communities that kept the periodical relevant. At the same time, those correspondents, agents, and subscribers saw the paper as an authoritative source of news. Presumably, the publication of accurate news from each community would lend authenticity to news published about other communities, reinforcing confidence. Leeser, who received the news reports, in turn functioned as the editorial hub for the paper, choosing which news items to include and which to withhold.[22] Without both those who submitted the reports and the editor who compiled them, the paper could not function. Book history scholar Ryan Cordell discusses a similar duality in contemporary newspapers. Focusing on the role of newspaper editors in the pre–Civil War United States, Cordell writes: "Through the process of selection and republication, editors appropriated the collective authority of the newspaper system, positioning their publication as one node within larger political, social, denominational, or national networks."[23] While Cordell's editor model cannot be transposed onto *The Occident* precisely, Leeser, "appropriated the collective authority" of the Jewish Anglo-Atlantic by selecting articles and functioning as the gatekeeper of the news.[24] Letters written to Leeser with news announcements reveal this process of selection. In an 1849 letter, Sophia Tobias, president of the Ladies Sewing Association of New York's Congregation Shearith Israel, wrote: "I enclose you a report of the Ladies Sewing Association, if you deem it a worthy place in your valuable periodical, it is at your service."[25] The next volume of *The Occident* included Tobias's detailed report.[26] Tobias's letter and Leeser's subsequent publication of her notice reflects the growth of Jewish benevolent associations in the United States throughout the nineteenth century, as well as increasing involvement of women in American religious spaces and organizations.[27] In a separate piece of correspondence, Nathaniel Levine, secretary of Congregation Kahal Kadosh Beth Elohim of Charleston, wrote to Leeser, "enclose[d] . . . the copy of the Resolutions unanimously adopted by the Board of Trustees at a regular meeting convened this day" on March 3, 5627 (1867).[28] The April 1867 edition of *The Occident* carried the "copy of the Resolutions," attributed to "Nathaniel Levin," publishing it verbatim.[29] Tobias and Levine informed Leeser and his readership of the affairs of their respective organizations. It was at Leeser's discretion whether or not to include these announcements. In the August 1863 wrapper, Leeser noted that "several articles are omitted this month for want of room."[30] Leeser curated the pages of the paper, exercising his power of selection. Leeser's decision to publish the report of the Ladies Sewing Association and the resolutions from Kahal Kadosh Beth Elohim reflects Leeser's attitude toward Jewish community. Leeser saw Jewish organizations and congregations as crucial infrastructure to the growth and longevity of Jewish life in the United States, and therefore in the inaugural issue of his paper he "offer[ed] pages to congregations and societies as a medium of giving publicity to their intended assemblings and of their transactions."[31] Jewish "congregations and societies" took Leeser up on this "offer," and *The Occident* was filled with Jewish communal reports, meeting minutes, and announcements. Leeser was the gatekeeper of a newspaper that functioned as a public record-keeping system and archive of Jewish communal life for a disparate diaspora.

If part of *The Occident*'s mission was to "endeavor to give circulation which can be interesting to the Jewish inhabitants in the western hemisphere," then Leeser needed access to Jews who would relay news of their far-flung communities, advertise and deliver papers, and collect subscriptions.[32] To do so, Leeser developed a diasporic model of subscription publishing that was transnational. He relied on his authority as a Jewish leader to foster networks of other communal leaders throughout the hemisphere to act as agents, such as Reverend M. N. Nathan of Kingston, Jamaica, Aaron Wolff of Saint Thomas, and Rabbi Abraham de Sola of Montreal. This diasporic model developed over time. The May 1846 wrapper of *The Occident* signaled two significant changes in publishing practice. One change was noted at the end of a list of subscribers for the month: "We mean in the future to acknowledge receipts of money in a similar manner, when we are prevented from writing especial letters." This signaled a change from yearly to monthly subscription lists.[33] It also meant that each monthly subscriber list was not comprehensive, but rather part of a system through which Leeser could account for and acknowledge subscription payments without "writing especial letters." In a time when post roads and steam packets were not always reliable and railroads were expanding but still inaccessible in many places, it proved useful for subscribers to know if their payments had indeed reached Leeser.[34]

M. B. Simmonds's correspondence illustrates the precarious nature of reliance on specific transportation networks that encompassed the island of Saint Thomas. An agent for *The Occident*, Simmonds wrote to Leeser in June 1843 that he was "disappointed in not being able to remit you the amount of the subscription list for the Occident." Simmonds explained, "the fault is not mine," and suggested that Leeser "try & send them [*The Occident*] regularly by way of New York as there are numerous opportunities from that City for this place."[35] We do not know if Leeser had in fact sent the papers through New York. We do know from Simmonds that the other agent on the island, Aaron Wolff, *did* receive his packet of *The Occident* to distribute. Simmonds complained of this discrepancy in his letter: "Mr Wolff has received his May Number, and I have received none."[36] Perhaps Leeser sent the two shipments separately, but based on the fact that Simmonds and Wolff appear on the earliest known agent lists for *The Occident* from April 1843, Leeser undoubtedly knew he would be sending his periodical to these two men. It seems unlikely that he would send the periodical at different times to the same place. For unknown reasons, but illustrating the precarity and unreliability of delivery, in the 1840s, Leeser could not be sure that his paper would arrive safely to his agents and subscribers. His published subscriber lists at least provided a record for himself, his agents, and his subscribers of who should have received a copy of the periodical.[37]

The 1846 announcement, "Occident Advertiser," in prominent blackletter typeface signaled a new era for the periodical. This announcement stated that Leeser would double the pages of the wrapper to create more space to publish advertisements: "we make this month the experiment of issuing a double cover, so as to enable us to give more room for our advertising friends, and for our own purposes."[38] It is unclear why Leeser decided to change the format of the periodical. Perhaps he had received inquiries regarding advertisements, or perhaps he wanted to see whether he could profit financially.[39] As with the newfound monthly subscriber lists, Leeser sought out the best methods to coordinate the various cogs of his subscription publishing enterprise.

How did Leeser's marketing and distribution techniques compare to his colleagues in the field of religious publishing? The historian Rosalind Remer discusses the testing of various marketing and distribution techniques, albeit for booksellers and publishers, who wished to spread their volumes to the American backcountry between 1800 and 1830. For example, "William Woodward, a prominent publisher of religious works, employed an ad hoc network of ministers to sell his books."

Another publishing firm took a different approach. As Remer details, "the firm of McCarty and Davis dispatched professional traveling salesmen and later established branch stores in likely backcountry entrepots" to facilitate distribution of their publications. Jacob Johnson and Benjamin Warner, Quaker publishers, "traveled extensively themselves, opening branch stores and establishing large wholesale accounts with country storekeepers, printers, and booksellers." According to Remer, the varying business practices of these publishers illustrate how booksellers devised techniques to sell and advertise their books, particularly in rural areas. Their "strategies were experimental but not sequential, and there seems to have been no 'learning curve,' of progress in terms of evaluating the efficacy of distribution methods," Remer writes.[40] In some ways, Leeser's approach resembled that of Remer's booksellers. Leeser too talked of "experimentation" when discussing new practices. And like the booksellers, Leeser also had to establish a network to transport papers to subscribers in faraway places. Unlike Remer's booksellers, Leeser's attempt to reach those who resided far from Philadelphia was not solely about the bottom line, but also about his belief that *The Occident* kept Judaism alive in the far-flung communities of the Atlantic world.

Leeser developed a remarkable geographic reach as part of an anglophone diaspora. The 1846 *Occident Advertiser* announced: "Our works circulate extensively, though not in large quantities, over nearly all the United States, Canada, Jamaica, St. Thomas, Barbadoes [sic], St. Lucia, Venezuela, St. Domingo [sic], Curaçoa [sic], New South Wales, Van Diemen's Land, New Zealand and England."[41] Despite a subscriber base that reached into the Spanish and Dutch Atlantic, notably the vast majority of the subscribers were part of an anglophone diaspora. *The Occident* functioned as a tool, as scholar Adam Mendelsohn writes, that "knitted the Jewish communities of English-speaking countries into a new cultural, religious, and social sphere."[42] *The Occident* was at once a unifying cultural force in the Jewish anglophone diaspora but also offered new perspectives for its readers. Arthur Kiron describes Victorian-era Jewish newspapers in the Atlantic world as "provid[ing] a kind of a town hall . . . in which Jews and non-Jews of all different backgrounds, ideological commitments, and geographical locations could metaphorically sit together and learn about each other's views and circumstances."[43] Within this anglophone world, with a disparate subscriber base, *The Occident* aimed to function as a cultural harbinger of Jewish culture and

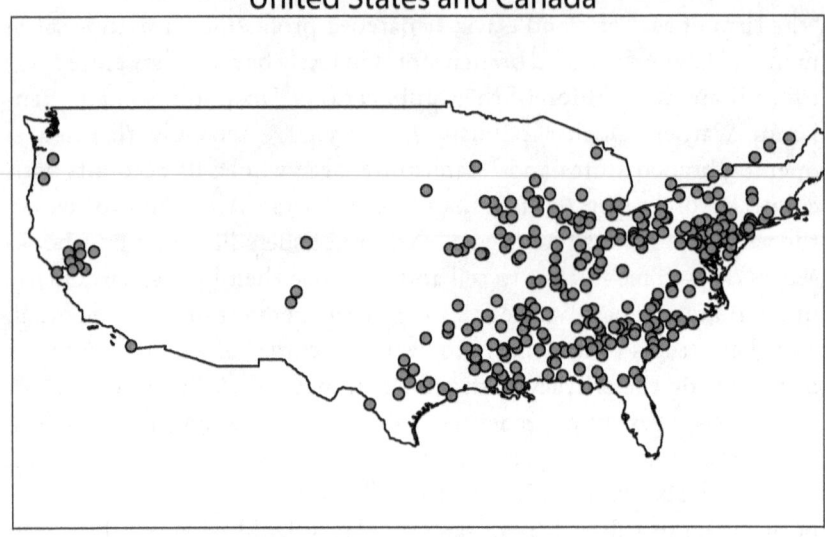
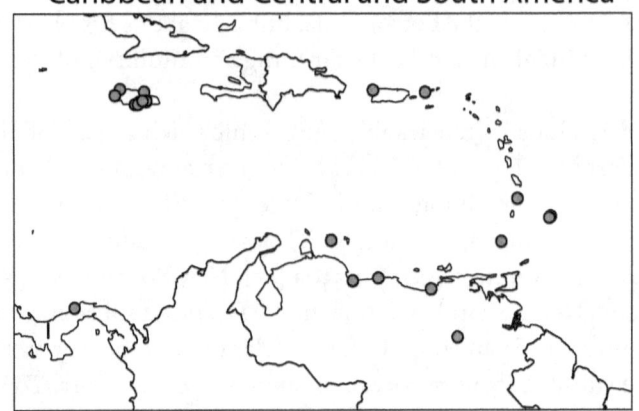
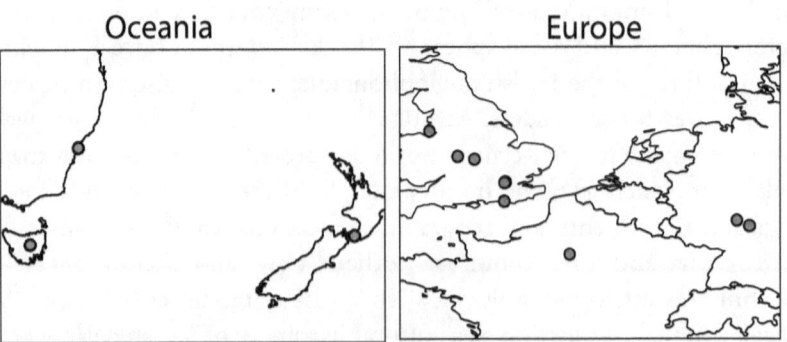

FIGURE 10.1. Subscribers to *The Occident*, 1843–69.

news. The map in figure 10.1 illustrates every person known to have subscribed to *The Occident* between 1843 and 1869, based on Leeser's subscription lists. From the subscribers in the Oceania region, to those in the Caribbean, to those throughout the United States, and scattered throughout Europe, the geographic diversity of Leeser's subscription base is clear.

As Leeser made a name for himself and his publications, he used personal travel to augment his system of agents and correspondents, and his networks of Jewish communities. In doing so, Leeser took on multiple roles: as editor, agent, contributor, and representative of the larger community he strived to serve. Through details from *The Occident* and other newspapers, we can trace Leeser's travels. In the news section of the October 1851 issue of *The Occident*, Leeser penned an article titled, "Consecration of the New Synagogue, Kenesseth Shalom, at Syracuse, New York." Reflecting back upon an earlier visit to the community, Leeser reminisced, "It is just seven years ago that we passed ... through the western part of the State of New York, on our return from Canada homeward. ... It was about the time when we passed through the city, that the Jewish community numbered seven members."[44] In 1851, Leeser returned to the growing community's newly built synagogue for its consecration, as part of a tour of congregations throughout the northern, western, and southern United States. It appears that the northern component of the trip (when he traveled to Syracuse for the second time) came during the fall of 1851. We find the only other reference to Leeser's northern journey in the wrapper of the November 1851 issue. Under the list of subscribers, Leeser wrote: "The EDITOR returns his thanks for the hospitable reception ... during his late northern journey. ... It is his intention, ... to visit, before long, the western and southern congregations, in order to urge in person, the necessity of sustaining his Magazine."[45] Leeser's northern journey served multiple purposes. His travel was a way to "urge in person, the necessity of sustaining his Magazine, the only strictly Jewish publication in the country," as well as his other publications. It gave him the opportunity to assess expanding communities, such as Syracuse; it gave him a literal and figurative pulpit in which to advertise and ascertain interest in *The Occident* as well as his other subscription publications (in this case the "Leeser Bible"); and it gave Leeser and subscribers the opportunity to connect personally.

Leeser traveled to various western and southern congregations in the late fall and winter of 1851–52.[46] "We set out on the 9th of

November, and returned on the 27th of February, after an absence of nearly sixteen weeks, during which we travelled upwards of five thousand two hundred miles, and visited at least twenty-five settlements or congregations of Israelites," Leeser described.[47] As with his northern trip, Leeser designed the trip to promote his many publications, including *The Occident*, to procure new subscribers, and to reconnect with long-time subscribers. Many of the Jews in each locale "had never seen us," Leeser wrote, and these prospective clients needed to "decide for themselves whether our claims to their kind support were well founded or not." Leeser continued, "we are happy to state here, that in a great degree our appeal to the public has not been in vain, as the number of our subscribers has increased at least one-third, and also for our other proposed publications we have received a fair portion of public support."[48]

In fact, looking at the population estimates provided by the *American Jewish Year Book*, the number of Jews in the United States had increased dramatically. In 1830 the publication reported that approximately six thousand Jews lived in the United States, by 1840, fifteen thousand, by 1850, one hundred thousand, and by 1860, two hundred thousand.[49] Like Christian mission societies, Leeser recognized that he had to forge connections to sustain his mission to connect the communities and disseminate the news of the Jewish communities of the expanding west. He used travel to connect personally with others and to act as his own agent, inserting himself into communities he visited. He admitted that seeing things firsthand gave him greater insight into Jewish life, noting that "it was well that we were thus enabled to judge for ourself [sic]."[50] Leeser's travels were not unusual for publishers. As Rosalind Remer explains, Christian "ministers succeeded at bookselling in part because they were influential figures in their communities, often taking charge of their congregants' moral and intellectual development."[51] While Leeser was not a bookseller who constantly traveled, his presence undoubtedly made a difference. In this sense, Leeser was a hybrid, wielding the influence of a religious leader, but also sometimes behaving like the bookseller that he was. Many publishers used travel to "evaluate the state of the market, the level of local competition, and status and financial standing of the tradesmen they met. They analyzed the local economies and calculated the best ways to demand and receive payment."[52] During his journeys, Leeser also procured subscribers for his Bible and for *The Occident*. Leeser's trips involved self-education and self-promotion, but also cemented and expanded his network of subscribers, agents, and correspondents in order to spark interest in *The Occident* and his other subscription publications.[53]

Leeser's lists of agents reveal the connection between the periodical and Leeser's other publications. Before he introduced *The Occident*, Leeser was already a prolific writer and published several books using a version of the subscription publishing model that he later employed with *The Occident* (see appendix to this chapter). Four publications, published prior to the first edition of *The Occident*, contained a list of Leeser's agents for each publication. The same names of agents appear repeatedly, and by the time Leeser began printing *The Occident*, he had a network of agents ready to help him sell and advertise his paper, as they had his books.

The Occident also became a forum for Leeser (and others) to advertise his publications, building a subscription network through *The Occident*. Through advertisements in *The Occident*, we can track the progress and eventual publication of Leeser's *The Law of God*, his first edition of the Pentateuch.[54] In August and September 1843, Leeser announced that he aimed to publish a translation of the Pentateuch. "We have not abandoned our plan of issuing, for Synagogue service, the Pentateuch, with a revised translation, together with the Haphtoroth, according to the custom of the various synagogues." Those who wished to receive a copy could hand their subscriptions to Leeser himself (on one of his trips or if they lived in Philadelphia) or to one of his agents. Further, Leeser continued, "the price for the five volumes will be twelve dollars and a half, payable on the completion of the third volume." Agents would be "allowed fifteen per cost for the trouble in getting subscribers and collecting the proceeds, and any person subscribing for seven copies w[ould] obtain an eighth gratis." Publication relied upon money from subscribers. Leeser already had one hundred, and "the work w[ould] be undertaken if [he] obtain[ed] three hundred."[55] "The ultimate success seems very probable," he reflected. Five months later, in April 1844, Leeser issued the same announcement. This time, he added that he "also intend[ed] to issue a cheap edition for Ten Dollars; subscribers will please to state whether they desire the finer or cheaper edition."[56] Eleven months later, in March 1845, the wrapper, titled "To Our Readers," reported that Leeser had enough subscribers: "We are about completing our arrangements for the speedy issue of the edition of the Pentateuch," though in the same paragraph he wrote "our subscription list is very small."[57] Whatever the number of subscribers, Leeser was on his way to publishing *The Law of God*. An important announcement, published in March 1845, declared that every agent for *The Occident* was now also an agent for the Pentateuch, titled *The Law of God*. The announcement appeared in the next two monthly editions of *The Occident* until a final proclamation in the June 1845 wrapper that promised that the book "will be issued about the fifth of June."[58] As it represented only the first of a multivolume set (the book of Genesis), Leeser continued, "the remaining volumes will be issued as fast as possible."[59] By September 1845, the headline in the same section of the wrapper proudly asserted that the first volume was "Now Ready."[60] The December 1845 issue contained notice regarding *The Law of God*. "The Pentateuch will probably be finished about the middle of January at farthest. The text of all the volumes is printed, and the appendixes are now in hand."[61] By March 1846 Leeser announced *The Law of God* was complete in its entirety, five volumes in total.[62]

These announcements illustrate that Leeser expressed his vision for bringing Jewish texts to readers through his roles as a publisher, translator, agent, and community liaison. He used *The Occident* as a communication device to spread not only news of Jewish life but also his ideas of Jewish culture. According to historian Lance Sussman, Leeser believed his Pentateuch provided Jews with the ability for correct interpretation of biblical texts. Leeser's Pentateuch was historic in that it was the first translation of the Hebrew Bible into English with a distinctly Jewish interpretation. Before its publication, Jews who were not multilingual had sole access to the King James version of the Bible.[63] Through the announcements and subsequent publication of *The Law of God*, Leeser acted not only as the publisher and purveyor of Jewish community news but as a shaper of transregional Jewish intellectual and religious thought and as an alternative to traditionally anti-Jewish theological interpretations of the Bible.[64]

Historical scholarship has painted *The Occident* as a cultural triumph that reflected Leeser's prowess as a leader across Jewish communities of the Western Hemisphere. Leeser *did* lead: his commitment to Jewish community was intertwined within and reflected through his publishing operations. To explain Leeser's success, however, historians must look to the subscription publishing operation that he created and maintained, which enabled *The Occident* and Leeser's other publications to succeed and be disseminated across a wide geographic space. Analysis of wrappers from *The Occident* provides a way in which to visualize this success. Leeser created a participatory network, which included agents, correspondents, and subscribers throughout

Jewish communities of the Atlantic world and beyond who were actively engaged in reading, spreading, creating, and collecting news. He enabled communication among far-flung communities and allowed them to remain in close touch despite distance. Leeser's agents acted as his surrogates, promoting subscriptions, collecting fees, and communicating more personally with subscribers. The correspondents wrote articles, contributing them to the paper for compensation, and the subscribers provided the financial means to keep the paper afloat and supplied the material at the heart of the periodical: news. He lived an influential and noteworthy life, made more remarkable by the structures he established to enhance a sense of Jewish community in Jewish outposts across the Atlantic world. Examining the wrappers of *The Occident*, with their lists of subscribers, agents, and advertisements offers us a new, decidedly transnational conception of the world of Jews in the Western Hemisphere during the middle of the nineteenth century. *The Occident* touched the lives of Jews throughout the Atlantic world and beyond, revealing the way in which Jewish communities lived in an interconnected world despite a diasporic geography.

Appendix to Chapter 10

List of agents for works by Rev. Isaac Leeser that were published prior to the publication of *The Occident, and American Jewish Advocate*. Agent names marked with an asterisk (*) indicate the person was later an agent for *The Occident*.

Instruction in the Mosaic Religion (1830)[65]

Moses Sarfaty*
Rev. Isaac B. Seixas*
J. B. Kursheedt
Jacob Mordecai
Editors of the Whig
Jacob I. Cohen
Eleazar Block
Nathan Hart
Dr. Jacob De La Motta
Moses Sarfaty*
Lewis Allen
J. L. Hackenburg

***The Jews and the Mosaic Law* (1834)**⁶⁶

Carey & Hart
J. L. Hackenburg
Rev. Isaac B. Seixas
Zalma Rehiné*
Jacob Mordecai
Dr. Jacob De La Motta
Nathan Hart
Jacob De La Motta Esq.*
Eleazar Block

***Discourses, Argumentative and Devotional on the Subject of the Jewish Religion, Second Series*, vol. 3 (1841)**⁶⁷

David Q. Henriques
Rev. Henry S. Samuel*
Rev. David Piza*
Aaron Wolff*
Rev. Moses N. Nathan*
Moses Sarfaty*
Moses M. Sollas*
S. Cohen
Jacob De La Motta Esq.*
Dr. Jacob De La Motta
S. N. Hart*
David Lopez
Isaac Lyons*
Phineas Moses
A. H. Cohen
Jacob Ezekiel*
Zalma Rehiné*
Mr. Judah
Eleazar Block
Rev. S. M. Isaacs*
M. H. Cardozo
Morland Micholl
Carey & Hart*

Advertisement (1842)⁶⁸

Carey & Hart*
Levine & Tavel*

Rev. S. M. Isaacs*
M. H. Cardozo
Z. Rehine*
Jacob Ezekiel*
Isaac Lyons*
Jacob De La Motta, Esq.*
Gershom Kursheedt*
Phineas Moses
M. M. Sollas*
M. Sarfaty*
Aaron Wolff*
Rev. David Piza*
David Q. Henriques
Henry S. Samuel*

Notes

Note on Terminology

1. This point has been made several times, beginning in 2015. See Aviva Ben-Ur, "Jewish Communities," in *The Princeton Companion to Atlantic History*, ed. Joseph C. Miller (Princeton, NJ: Princeton University Press, 2015), 263–67; "Een joods dorp in een slavenmaatschappij: Jodensavanne in de Nederlandse kolonie Suriname," in *Joden in de Cariben*, ed. Julie-Marthe Cohen (Amsterdam: Joods Historisch Museum, 2015), 131–54; "Atlantic Jewish History: A Conceptual Reorientation," in *Constellations of Atlantic Jewish History, 1555–1890: The Arnold and Deanne Kaplan Collection of Early American Judaica*, ed. Arthur Kiron (Philadelphia: University of Pennsylvania Press, 2014), 25–46; and *Jewish Autonomy in a Slave Society: Suriname in the Atlantic World, 1651–1825* (Philadelphia: University of Pennsylvania Press, 2020), 23–24. Some scholars who have recognized the ahistoricity of the term continue to employ it. See, for example, Sina Rauschenbach and Jonathan Schorsch, "Postcolonial Approaches to the Early Modern Sephardic Atlantic," in *The Sephardic Atlantic: Colonial Histories and Postcolonial Perspectives*, ed. Sina Rauschenbach and Jonathan Schorsch (Cham: Palgrave Macmillan, 2018), 2: they called themselves "mostly Spanish and Portuguese Jews, Portuguese Jews, Portuguese or simply A Nação (The Nation)." This ahistorical terminology has ramifications, as we discuss below.

2. Aviva Ben-Ur, "The Absorption of Outsiders in London's Portuguese Jewish Community," in *From Catalonia to the Caribbean: The Sephardic Orbit from Medieval to Modern Times. Essays in Honor of Jane S. Gerber*, ed. Federica Francesconi, Stanley Mirvis, and Brian Smollett (Leiden: Brill, 2018), 255–78.

Introduction

1. This comment pertains to almost all publications on American Jewish history published after the mid-twentieth century. See, for example, articles from the last half century or so published in *American Jewish History*, the field's leading journal; Hasia R. Diner, *A Time for Gathering: The Second Migration, 1820–1880* (Baltimore: Johns Hopkins University Press, 1992) and *A New Promised Land: A History of Jews in America* (Oxford: Oxford University Press, 2000); Gerald Sorin, *Tradition Transformed: The Jewish Experience in America* (Baltimore: Johns Hopkins University Press, 1997); William Pencak, *Jews and Gentiles in Early America, 1654–1800* (Ann Arbor: University of Michigan Press, 2005); and Jonathan D. Sarna, *American Judaism: A History* (New Haven: Yale University Press, 2004; 2nd ed., 2019). Neither the first nor second edition of

the latter title makes any mention of Atlantic history, nor its Jewish inflection, though the "Colonial Beginnings" chapter does pay attention to the metropole and the Caribbean.

2. For the treatment of Jews and crypto-Jews by scholars working outside the field of Jewish history, see, for example, Jonathan Israel, *Empires and Entrepôts: The Dutch, the Spanish Monarchy, and the Jews, 1585–1713* (London: Hambledon Press, 1990) and *Diasporas within a Diaspora: Jews, Crypto-Jews, and the World of Maritime Empires (1540–1740)* (Leiden: Brill, 2002); Stephen Alexander Fortune, *Merchants and Jews: The Struggle for British West Indian Commerce, 1650–1750* (Gainesville: University Press of Florida, 1984); and Daviken Studnicki-Gizbert, *A Nation upon the Ocean Sea: Portugal's Atlantic Diaspora and the Crisis of the Spanish Empire, 1492–1640* (Oxford: Oxford University Press, 2007).

3. See, among his many publications, Walter J. Fischel, *Ha-Yehudim be-Hodu* (Jerusalem: Machon Ben Zvi, 1960), "The Activities of a Jewish Merchant House in Bengal (1786-1798): A Contribution to the Economic History of London Jews in India," *Revue des études juives* 123, nos. 3-4 (1964): 433-98, and "The Indian Archives: A Source for the History of the Jews of Asia (from the Sixteenth Century On)," in "The Seventy-Fifth Anniversary Volume," *Jewish Quarterly Review* 57 (1967): 192-209; and Gedalia Yogev, *Diamonds and Coral: Anglo-Dutch Jews and Eighteenth-Century Trade* (Leicester: Leicester University Press, 1978).

4. Christopher Ebert, *Between Empires: Brazilian Sugar in the Early Atlantic Economy, 1550–1630* (Leiden: Brill, 2008).

5. See, for example, Pencak, *Jews and Gentiles in Early America*, 209-11; Mark Abbott Stern, *David Franks: Colonial Merchant* (University Park: Pennsylvania State University Press, 2010), x, xix-xx, chap. 2; and Allan M. Amanik, "Common Fortunes: Social and Financial Gains of Jewish and Christian Partnerships in Eighteenth-Century Transatlantic Trade," in *Doing Business in America: A Jewish History*, ed. Steve J. Ross, Hasia R. Diner, and Lisa Ansell (Ashland: Purdue University Press, 2018), 25–47.

6. Holly Snyder, "'Customs of an Unruly Race': The Political Context of Jamaican Jewry, 1670-1831," and Kay Dian Kriz, "Belisario's 'Kingston Cries' and the Refinement of Jewish Identity in the Late 1830s," both in *Art and Emancipation in Jamaica: Isaac Mendes Belisario and His Worlds*, ed. Tim Barringer, Gillian Forrester, and Barbaro Martinez-Ruiz (New Haven: Yale Center for British Art in association with Yale University Press, 2007), 151-62, 163-78.

7. Isaac Leeser, *Discourses on the Jewish Religion* (Philadelphia: Sherman & Co., 1867-68), 10:127, 271; Isaac Leeser, *Discourses, Argumentative and Devotional, on the Subject of the Jewish Religion* (Philadelphia: C. Sherman, 1840-41), 3:vii; Gershwind-Bennett Isaac Leeser Digital Repository, University of Pennsylvania Libraries, accessed September 1, 2021, http://leeser.library.upenn.edu/ilproject.php.

8. On central European immigration to the United States, see Sarna, *American Judaism*, 66.

9. Bernard Bailyn, "Introduction: Reflections on Some Major Themes," in *Soundings in Atlantic History: Latent Structures and Intellectual Currents, 1500–1830*, ed. Bernard Bailyn and Patricia L. Denault (Cambridge, MA: Harvard University Press, 2009), 1–43.

10. Harald E. Braun and Lisa Vollendorf, "Introduction. The Atlantic Turn: Rethinking the Ibero-American Atlantic," in *Theorising the Ibero-American Atlantic*, ed. Harald E. Braun and Lisa Vollendorf (Leiden: Brill, 2013), 7.

11. David M. Friedenreich, "Jews, Pagans, and Heretics in Early Medieval Canon Law," in *Jews in Early Christian Law: Byzantium and the Latin West, 6th–11th Centuries*, ed. John Tolan, Nicholas de Lange, Laurence Foschia, and Capucine Nemo-Pekelman (Turnhout: Brepols, 2014), 76 (Council of Elvira, ca. 306); epitaph of Salomonula, Adra, Spain, third century, in Emil Hübner, *Inscriptiones Hispaniæ Latinæ* (Berlin: Reimer, 1869), 268.

12. Jonathan Israel, "The Jews of Spanish North Africa, 1600–1669," *Transactions & Miscellanies (Jewish Historical Society of England)* 26 (1974–76): 86n106; Mohamed A. H. Ahmed, "A North African Judeo-Arabic Letter from the Prize Papers Collection," *Astarté: Estudios del Oriente Próximo y el Mediterráneo* 2 (2019): 121–30, and "18th-Century Judeo-Arabic Documents from the Prize Papers Collection," *Journal of Jewish Languages* 8 (2020): 1–23; Yigal S. Nizri, "Judeo-Moroccan Traditions and the Age of European Expansion in North Africa," in *The Sephardic Atlantic: Colonial Histories and Postcolonial Perspectives*, ed. Sina Rauschenbach and Jonathan Schorsch (Cham: Palgrave Macmillan, 2018), 333–60.

13. See for one approach to Atlantic Jewish history, Wim Klooster, "Jews in the Early Modern Caribbean and the Atlantic World," in *The Cambridge History of Judaism*, vol. 7, *The Early Modern Period, 1500–1815*, ed. Jonathan Karp and Adam Sutcliffe (Cambridge: Cambridge University Press, 2017), 972–96. The 1820s seem to make the most sense as the end point of Atlantic Jewish history, but sound arguments can be made for a later decade, depending on regional focus. Arthur Kiron argues for an Atlantic Jewish history that ends in 1890 because even after the expansion of U.S. Jewish communities toward the Pacific, the flow of goods, services, culture, institutions, and ideas continued to radiate from the east. Arthur Kiron, "Introduction: Constellations of Atlantic Jewish History, 1555–1890," in *Constellations of Atlantic Jewish History, 1555–1890: The Arnold and Deanne Kaplan Collection of Early American Judaica*, ed. Arthur Kiron (Philadelphia: University of Pennsylvania Press, 2014), 20–21.

14. Aviva Ben-Ur, "Atlantic Jewish History: A Conceptual Reorientation," in Kiron, *Constellations of Atlantic Jewish History*, 25–46; "Jewish Savannah in Atlantic Perspective: A Reconsideration of the First Intentional Jewish Community of North America," in Rauschenbach and Schorsch, *The Sephardic Atlantic*, 183–213; *Jewish Autonomy in a Slave Society: Suriname in the Atlantic World, 1651–1825* (Philadelphia: University of Pennsylvania Press, 2020), 12; and "The Atlantic World," in *Oxford Handbook of American Jewish History*, ed. Michael R. Cohen and Shari Rabin (forthcoming).

15. Paolo Bernardini and Norman Fiering, eds., *The Jews and the Expansion of Europe to the West, 1450–1800* (New York: Berghahn Books, 2001). For an assessment of the volume as Atlantic history, see Sina Rauschenbach and Jonathan Schorsch, "Postcolonial Approaches to the Early Modern Sephardic Atlantic," in Rauschenbach and Schorsch, *The Sephardic Atlantic*, 6. The "port Jew" concept as developed by Lois Dubin and David Sorkin attempts to transport the idea from the Mediterranean to the Americas and is therefore not Atlantic per se.

16. Richard L. Kagan and Philip D. Morgan, editors' preface, in *Atlantic Diasporas: Jews, Conversos, and Crypto-Jews in the Age of Mercantilism, 1500–1800*, ed. Richard L. Kagan and Philip D. Morgan (Baltimore: Johns Hopkins University Press, 2009), xvii.

17. Rauschenbach and Schorsch, *The Sephardic Atlantic*.

18. For "Vast Early America," see Karin Wulf, "Vast Early America: Three Simple Words for a Complex Reality," *Humanities* 40, no. 1 (Winter 2019): 26–31, 46–47, online at https://www.neh.gov/article/vast-early-america; Eliga Gould and Rosemarie Zagarri, "Situating the United States in Vast Early America: Introduction," *William and Mary Quarterly* 78, no. 2 (2021): 189–200. The field of Jewish studies adopts a regional understanding, preferring the terms "Americas," "early America," "Western Sephardi," and "Caribbean." See, for example, Katalin Franciska Rac and Lenny A. Ureña Valerio, eds., *Jewish Experiences across the Americas: Local Histories through Global Lenses* (Gainesville: University Press of Florida, 2022); Laura Arnold Leibman, *The Art of the Jewish Family: A History of Women in Early New York in Five Objects* (New York: Bard Graduate Center, 2020) and *Messianism, Secrecy and Mysticism: A New Interpretation of Early American Jewish Life* (Portland, OR: Vallentine Mitchell, 2012); Michael Hoberman, Laura Arnold Leibman, and Hilit Surowitz-Israel, eds., *Jews in the Americas, 1776–1826* (New York: Routledge, 2018); Jane S. Gerber, ed., *The Jews in the Caribbean* (Oxford: Littman Library of Jewish Civilization, 2014), and chap. 6 of her *Cities of Splendour in the Shaping of Sephardi History* (London: Littman Library of Jewish Civilization, 2020); Sarah Phillips Casteel, *Calypso Jews: Jewishness in the Caribbean Literary Imagination* (New York: Columbia University Press, [2016]); Julie-Marthe Cohen, ed., *Joden in de Cariben* (Amsterdam: Joods Historisch Museum, 2015); and the various works of Yosef Kaplan, including his edited volume *Religious Changes and Cultural Transformations in the Early Modern Western Sephardic Communities* (Leiden: Brill, 2019). The recently launched website AmericanJewishExperience.org, hosted by the Grant Center for the American Jewish Experience at Tulane University, describes itself as the "online home of scholarship addressing Jewishness in the U.S. and across the Americas." Laura Arnold Leibman's most recent book foregrounds race as an organizing principle but is implicitly Atlantic: *Once We Were Slaves: The Extraordinary Journey of a Multiracial Jewish Family* (Oxford: Oxford University Press, 2021). An important local study sensitive to transnationalism, but minimally concerned with people of African descent, is Judah M. Cohen, *Through the Sands of Time: A History of the Jewish Community of St. Thomas, U.S. Virgin Islands* (Hanover, NH: Brandeis University Press, 2004).

19. Peter Mark and José da Silva Horta, *The Forgotten Diaspora: Jewish Communities in West Africa and the Making of the Atlantic World* (Cambridge: Cambridge University Press, 2011); Ben-Ur, *Jewish Autonomy in a Slave Society*; Stanley Mirvis, *The Jews of Eighteenth-Century Jamaica: A Testamentary History of a Diaspora in Transition* (New Haven: Yale University Press, 2020).

20. Barry Stiefel, *Jewish Sanctuary in the Atlantic World: A Social and Architectural History* (Columbia: University of South Carolina Press, 2014). See also some of the titles in note 18 above.

21. Kate Freedman, "A Tangled Web: Quakers and the Atlantic Slave System 1625–1770" (PhD diss., University of Massachusetts Amherst, 2018); Katharine

Gerbner, *Christian Slavery: Conversion and Race in the Protestant Atlantic World* (Philadelphia: University of Pennsylvania Press, 2018); Ida Altman and David Wheat, eds., *The Spanish Caribbean and the Atlantic World in the Long Sixteenth Century* (Lincoln: University of Nebraska Press, 2019); D. L. Noorlander, *Heaven's Wrath: The Protestant Reformation and the Dutch West India Company in the Atlantic World* (Ithaca, NY: Cornell University Press, 2019); Robynne Rogers Healey, ed., *Quakerism in the Atlantic World, 1690–1830* (University Park: Pennsylvania State University Press, 2021).

22. Rauschenbach and Schorsch, "Postcolonial Approaches," 6; Caspar Battegay, "The Jewish Atlantic: Diaspora and Pop Music," in *Connected Jews: Expressions of Community in Analogue and Digital Culture*, ed. Simon J. Bonner and Caspar Battegay (Liverpool: Liverpool University Press, 2018), 109–30; Cecilia Enjuto-Rangel, Sebastiaan Faber, Pedro Garcia-Caro, and Robert Patrick Newcomb, eds., *Transatlantic Studies: Latin America, Iberia, and Africa* (Liverpool: Liverpool University Press, 2019).

23. The goal of these Nation of Islam publications has been "to name the enemy." Jonathan Schorsch, *Jews and Blacks in the Early Modern World* (Cambridge: Cambridge University Press, 2004), 1.

24. Rauschenbach and Schorsch, "Postcolonial Approaches," 7.

25. Eli Faber, *Jews, Slaves, and the Slave Trade: Setting the Record Straight* (New York: New York University Press, 1998), 6–8; Winthrop D. Jordan, "Slavery and the Jews: A Review of *The Secret Relationship between Blacks and Jews: Volume One*," *The Atlantic*, September 1995, 109–14; David Brion Davis, "Constructing Race: A Reflection," *William and Mary Quarterly*, 3rd series, 54, no. 1 (1997): 11 (critiquing Jordan for his "negative but legitimating review" of *The Secret Relationship*); Jonathan Schorsch, "American Jewish Historians, Colonial Jews and Blacks, and the Limits of *Wissenschaft*: A Critical Review," *Jewish Social Studies*, n.s., 6, no. 2 (2000): 121 ("the pseudo-academic work put out by the Historical Research Department of the Nation of Islam"), 121, 131 ("the Nation of Islam's pseudo-scholarly work"); Nathaniel Deutsch, "The Proximate Other: The Nation of Islam and Judaism," in *Black Zion: African American Religious Encounters with Judaism*, ed. Yvonne Chireau and Nathaniel Deutsch (New York: Oxford University Press, 2000), 109 ("a spurious history"); Robert Fitzgerald Reid-Pharr, "Speaking through Anti-Semitism: The Nation of Islam and the Poetics of Black (Counter) Modernity," *Social Text* 49 (Winter 1996): 141 ("limited as a piece of scholarship"); Harold Brackman, *Ministry of Lies: The Truth Behind the Nation of Islam's "The Secret Relationship between Blacks and Jews"* (New York: Four Walls Eight Windows, 1994); Marc Caplan, *Jew-Hatred as History: An Analysis of the Nation of Islam's "The Secret Relationship between Blacks and Jews"* (New York: Anti-Defamation League, 1993).

26. "Viewpoints: AHA Council Issues Policy Resolution about Jews and the Slave Trade," *Perspectives on History*, March 1, 1995, https://www.historians.org/publications-and-directories/perspectives-on-history/march-1995/aha-coun cil-issues-policy-resolution-about-jews-and-the-slave-trade; Davis, "Constructing Race," 11 (quote).

27. Caplan's book, *Jew-Hatred as History*, was indeed published by the ADL, but unfortunately engaged in historiographical analysis.

28. See, for example, Esther Webman, *The Global Impact of "The Protocols of the Elders of Zion": A Century-Old Myth* (London: Routledge, 2011).

29. Judeo-Arabic letters produced by Algerian Jewish merchants with business in Amsterdam, which may reveal the extent to which they were looped into the Atlantic world, have yet to be mined historically. Transcription, linguistic study, and translation of these sources has recently commenced. See Ahmed, "A North African Judeo-Arabic Letter from the Prize Papers Collection" and "18th-Century Judeo-Arabic Documents from the Prize Papers Collection." Innovative work relying on Hebrew, Arabic, and Judeo-Arabic (Nizri, "Judeo-Moroccan Traditions") suggests that the orientation of early modern Moroccan Jews was Maghrebi, rather than Atlantic. The mining of rabbinical literature for its potential relevance has been carried out by Schorsch, *Jews and Blacks in the Early Modern World*, 2, and Nathan Perl-Rosenthal, "Napoleon's Sanhedrin and the Colonization of Atlantic World Jewry," unpublished paper, "Atlantic Jewish Worlds, 1500–1900" conference, University of Pennsylvania, April 7–8, 2021.

30. The literature is vast. Leading this school of thought are Yosef Hayim Yerushalmi and Yosef Kaplan. For a recent historiographical assessment, see Anne Oravetz Albert, "Return by Any Other Name: Religious Change among Amsterdam's New Jews," in *Bastards and Believers: Jewish Converts and Conversion from the Bible to the Present*, ed. Theodor Dunkelgrün and Paweł Maciejko (Philadelphia: University of Pennsylvania Press, 2020), 134–55; and Juan Ignacio Pulido Serrano, "Plural Identities: The Portuguese New Christians," *Jewish History* 25, no. 2 (2011): 129–51.

31. Benzion Netanyahu, *The Origins of the Inquisition in Fifteenth Century Spain* (New York: Random House, 1995); Robert Rowland, "New Christian, Marrano, Jew," in Bernardini and Fiering, *Jews and the Expansion of Europe to the West*, 138 ("*fábrica de judeus*"); António José Saraiva, *Inquisição e Cristãos-novos* (Porto: Editorial Inova, 1969).

32. David L. Graizbord, *Souls in Dispute: Converso Identities in Iberia and the Jewish Diaspora, 1580–1700* (Philadelphia: University of Pennsylvania Press, 2004).

33. Rowland, "New Christian, Marrano, Jew," 133, 135–36.

34. Bruno Feitler, "Four Chapters in the History of Crypto-Judaism in Brazil: The Case of the Northeastern New Christians (17th–21st Centuries)," *Jewish History* 25, no. 2 (2011): 209; Pulido Serrano, "Plural Identities," 136–37.

35. Feitler, "Four Chapters," 209.

36. Pulido Serrano, "Plural Identities."

37. James Nelson Novoa, "A Family of the *Nação* from the Atlantic to the Mediterranean and Beyond (1497–1640)," in Kaplan, *Religious Changes and Cultural Transformations*, 38.

38. Norman Roth, *Conversos, Inquisition, and the Expulsion of the Jews from Spain* (Madison: University of Wisconsin Press, 2002), 375.

39. Richard Bulliet, *Conversion to Islam in the Medieval Period: An Essay in Quantitative History* (Cambridge, MA: Harvard University Press, 1979), 114–27; Thomas F. Glick, *From Muslim Fortress to Christian Castle: Social and Cultural Change in Medieval Spain* (Manchester: Manchester University Press, 1995), 52, and *Islamic and Christian Spain in the Early Middle Ages*, 23, 33–35. The dynamics of the

innovation-adoption curve Bulliet delineated, and hence his population estimates, remain persuasive. See Glick, *From Muslim Fortress to Christian Castle*, 60.

40. Robert I. Burns, "Muslims in the Thirteenth-Century Realms of Aragon: Interaction and Reaction," in *Muslims under Latin Rule, 1100–1300*, ed. James M. Powell (Princeton, NJ: Princeton University Press, 1990), 94.

41. Matthew Carr, *Blood and Faith: The Purging of Muslim Spain* (London: Hurst & Co., 2009), ix (quote); Bernard Vincent, "The Geography of the Morisco Expulsion: A Quantitative Study," in *The Expulsion of the Moriscos from Spain: A Mediterranean Diaspora*, ed. Mercedes García-Arenal and Gerard Wiegers (Leiden: Brill, 2014), 19. Carr indicates (35), without attribution, that 100,000–150,000 Jews chose exile over conversion to Christianity in 1492. For a discussion of estimates, which range from 150,000 to double that, see Peggy K. Liss, *Isabel the Queen: Life and Times* (1992; repr. Philadelphia: University of Pennsylvania Press, 2004), 309, 450n10, 451n23.

42. James B. Tueller, "The Moriscos Who Stayed Behind or Returned Post-1609," in García-Arenal and Wiegers, *The Expulsion of the Moriscos from Spain*, 197; Christine H. Lee, *The Anxiety of Sameness in Early Modern Spain* (Manchester: Manchester University Press, 2016), 165–77.

43. Kevin Ingram, "Diego Velázquez' Secret History: The Family Background the Painter was at Pains to Hide in His Application for Entry into the Military Order of Santiago," *Boletín del Museo del Prado* 17 (1999): 69–71.

44. Kevin Ingram, *Converso Non-Conformism in Early Modern Spain: Bad Blood and Faith from Alonso de Cartagena to Diego Velázquez* (Cham: Springer International, 2018), 183; Edgar Samuel, "The Jewish Ancestry of Velasquez," *Jewish Historical Studies* 35 (1996–98): 27–32.

45. Samuel, "The Jewish Ancestry of Velasquez," 32, 30 ("there is no reason to doubt that Velasquez and his father were of Jewish origin"); Kevin Ingram, "Secret Lives, Public Lies: The Conversos and Socio-Religious Non-Conformism in the Spanish Golden Age" (PhD diss., University of California, San Diego, 2006), 4n2 ("Diego Velázquez is, in my opinion, a converso"); Gilbert Stanley Marks, *Encyclopedia of Jewish Food* (Hoboken, NJ: John Wiley, 2010), 169. Julián Gállego, who is more concerned with Velázquez's nonnoble lineage, is inconclusive about any possible Jewish ancestry ("Yo no digo que Diego Rodríguez de Silva fuera 'marrano', pero tampoco puede asegurarse que no lo fuera"). Julián Gállego, *Velázquez en Sevilla* (Sevilla: Diputación Provincial de Sevilla, 1974; 2nd ed., 1994), 21.

46. Ingram, "Diego Velázquez' Secret History," 73.

47. Ingram, "Diego Velázquez' Secret History," 75.

48. Samuel, "The Jewish Ancestry of Velasquez," 28–29.

49. Ingram, *Converso Non-Conformism*, 180; Ingram, "Diego Velázquez' Secret History," 82; Samuel, "The Jewish Ancestry of Velasquez," 30.

50. Ingram, "Secret Lives, Public Lies," 4n2.

51. Jane S. Gerber, "Pride and Pedigree: The Development of the Myth of Sephardic Aristocratic Lineage," in *Reappraisals and New Studies of the Modern Jewish Experience: Essays in Honor of Robert M. Seltzer*, ed. Brian Smollett and Christian Wiese (Leiden: Brill, 2015), 85–103. Iberian society was "a crucible of many peoples, including Tartessians, Turdetans, Celts, Basques, Phoenicians,

Greeks, Romans, Jews, Suevi, Alans, Vandals, and Visigoths, while the Islamic conquest brought with it elements of Arab, Greco-Byzantine, Jewish, Persian, Kurdish, Egyptian, and Berber cultures.... In 711, Spaniard did not meet Arab; rather, two complex conglomerate civilizations came into contact." Dwight Reynolds, "The Music of Al-Andalus: Meeting Place of Three Cultures," in *A History of Jewish-Muslim Relations: From the Origins to the Present Day*, ed. Abdelwahab Meddeb and Benjamin Stora (Princeton, NJ: Princeton University Press, 2013), 973.

52. On this point see also Gállego, *Velázquez en Sevilla*, 18.

53. Gerber, "Pride and Pedigree."

54. Homero Serís, "Nueva genealogía de Santa Teresa," *Nueva revista de filología hispánica* 10 (1956): 366.

55. Serís, "Nueva genealogía," 365.

56. James H. Sweet, *Recreating Africa: Culture, Kinship, and Religion in the African-Portuguese World, 1441–1770* (Chapel Hill: University of North Carolina Press, 2003); Hannes Schroeder et al., "Origins and Genetic legacies of the Caribbean Taino," *Proceedings of the National Academic of Science* 15, no. 10 (March 6, 2018): 2341–46.

57. María Elena Martínez, *Genealogical Fictions: Limpieza de Sangre, Religion, and Gender in Colonial Mexico* (Stanford: Stanford University Press, 2008), 269–70.

58. Martínez, *Genealogical Fictions*, 6, 266. Similarly, members of the Armenta merchant family in Seville were able to "prove" their status as hidalgos by having another Armenta family (of Córdoba)—which had been ennobled in the Middle Ages—testify that they were related. Rafael M. Girón Pascual, "Capital comercial, capital simbólico: El patrimonio de los *cargadores de Indias judeoconversos* en la Sevilla de los siglos XVI y XVII," *Mediterranea* 16, no. 46 (2019): 340.

59. Tamar Herzog, *Defining Nations: Immigrants and Citizens in Early Modern Spain and Spanish America* (New Haven: Yale University Press, 2003).

60. The traditional paradigm also leaves its mark on scholarship about alleged Judaizers in Portuguese Asia. See, for example, Lucio de Sousa, "The Jewish Presence in China and Japan in the Early Modern Period: A Social Representation," in *Global History and New Polycentric Approaches: Europe, Asia and the Americas in a World Network System*, ed. Manuel Perez Garcia and Lucio de Sousa (Gateway East: Palgrave Macmillan, 2018), 183–218, where the author treats "Jew" as synonymous with "crypto-Jew," "New Christian," and "Sephardic," marginalizes or entirely ignores other accused groups, and takes accusations of Judaizing at face value. It is worthwhile to reflect that Portuguese New Christians comprised only 9 percent of the 3,800 individuals apprehended by the Goan Inquisition between 1561 and 1623. Moreover, after 1590, alleged Judaizers nearly disappear from the lists. Most of the accused were Indian converts to Catholicism and their descendants who allegedly engaged in crypto-Hinduism or, to a lesser extent, crypto-Islam. António José Saraiva, *The Marrano Factory: The Portuguese Inquisition and Its New Christians, 1536–1765* (Leiden: Brill, 2001), 346–47.

61. Arny Kaplan, "Prologue: The Path from a Collector to a Collection," in Kiron, *Constellations of Atlantic Jewish History*, xv ("an attempt to add to the understanding of the Jew in the New World both as Jew and as citizen"); Kiron,

"Constellations of Atlantic Jewish History," 2 ("to better understand the evolution of Jewish commercial, political social, and religious life in the transatlantic world"); Beth Wenger, "Preface," in Kiron, *Constellations of Atlantic Jewish History*, xii ("scholars will be able to ... uncover distinctive aspects of Jewish culture in the United States"); Sarna, *American Judaism*, xxvi ("In addition to being distinctive, the history of American Judaism is also far more complex and interesting than common wisdom would have us believe").

62. Albert, "Return by Any Other Name," 155.

63. Lila Corwin Berman, "Jewish History beyond the Jewish People," *AJS Review* 42, no. 2 (November 2018): 274, 279. The problem of categorization at the outset has also been identified by scholars of New Christians: see Pulido Serrano, "Plural Identities," 129.

1. The U.S. and the Rest

1. For more on Fischel, see Jonathan Waxman, "Arnold Fischel: 'Unsung Hero' in American Israel," *American Jewish Historical Quarterly* 60, no. 4 (1971): 325–43.

2. "The Death of Irving," *New York Times*, December 7, 1859, 4.

3. *The Historical Magazine, and Notes and Queries Concerning the Antiquities, History and Biography of America* 4, no. 1 (January 1860): 11–12.

4. Arnold Fischel, "Chronological Notes of the History of the Jews in America," *The Historical Magazine* 4, no. 2 (February 1860): 52–53.

5. Arthur Kiron, "Mythologizing 1654," *Jewish Quarterly Review* 94, no. 4 (2004): 583–94; Beth S. Wenger, "Rites of Citizenship: Jewish Celebrations of the Nation," in *The Columbia History of Jews and Judaism in America*, ed. Marc Lee Raphael (New York: Columbia University Press, 2008), 366–84; Aviva Ben-Ur and Julie-Marthe Cohen, "Unworthy of Their Ancestors: Representing Caribbean Jewry in 1954 and 2015," in *Caminos de leche y miel: Jubilee Volume in Honor of Michael Studemund-Halévy*, vol. 1, *History and Culture*, ed. Harm den Boer, Anna Menny, and Carsten L. Wilke (Barcelona: Tirocinio, 2018), 52–84.

6. Robert Liberles, "Postemancipation Historiography and the Jewish Historical Societies of America and England," in *Reshaping the Past: Jewish History and the Historians*, ed. Jonathan Frankel (New York: Oxford University Press, 1994), 45–65; Hasia R. Diner, "The Study of American Jewish History: In the Academy, in the Community," *Polish American Studies* 65, no. 1 (2008): 41–55; Howard B. Rock, "The Early Years of *American Jewish History*: Publications of the American Jewish Historical Society and the Minute Books of Congregation Shearith Israel," *American Jewish History* 99, no. 2 (2015): 119–44.

7. Stephen Massil, "The Foundation of the Jewish Historical Society of England, 1893," *Jewish Historical Studies* 33 (1992–94): 225–38; Mitchell B. Hart, "The Unbearable Lightness of Britain: Anglo-Jewish Historiography and the Anxiety of Success," *Journal of Modern Jewish Studies* 6, no. 2 (2007): 145–65.

8. See Charles P. Daly, *The Settlement of the Jews in North America*, ed. with introduction by Max J. Kohler (New York: Philip Cowen, 1893), xiv, 31n32, 80n85; Max J. Kohler, "Beginnings of New York Jewish History," *Publications of the American Jewish Historical Society* (hereafter *PAJHS*) 1 (1893): 41.

9. *Organization of the American Jewish Historical Society—Meeting Minutes,* June [6], 1892, 13–17, American Jewish Historical Society Records, I-1 (Box 109, Folder 30), Center for Jewish History, New York City; Cyrus Adler, "Address of Dr. Cyrus Adler, President of the American Jewish Historical Society," PAJHS 17 (1909): 2. For more on Gross, see Jeffrey S. Gurock, "Introduction," in "From *Publications* to *American Jewish History*: The Journal of the American Jewish Historical Society and the Writing of American Jewish History," special issue, *American Jewish History* 81, no. 2 (1993/94): 159.

10. American Jewish Historical Society, *Report of Organization: Abstract from the Minutes* (Baltimore: American Jewish Historical Society, 1892), 14. See also Gurock, "Introduction," 160.

11. Sebastian Conrad, *What Is Global History?* (Princeton, NJ: Princeton University Press, 2016), 3.

12. Meyer Kayserling, "The Colonization of America by the Jews," PAJHS 2 (1894): 73; Kayserling, *Christopher Columbus and the Participation of the Jews in the Spanish and Portuguese Discoveries* (New York: Longmans, Green, 1894).

13. Oscar S. Straus, "Address of the President," PAJHS 1 (1893): 1–4.

14. For instance, B. Felsenthal and Richard Gottheil, "Chronological Sketch of the History of the Jews in Surinam," PAJHS 4 (1896): 1–8; Samuel Oppenheim, "An Early Jewish Colony in Western Guiana, 1658–1666, and Its Relation to the Jews in Surinam, Cayenne and Tobago," PAJHS 16 (1907): 95–186; Abraham de Bediente, Ishak Gomez Henriquez, Abraham de Soza Mendez, and N. Darnell Davis, "Additional Notes on the History of the Jews of Barbados," PAJHS 19 (1910): 173–76. The *Jewish Quarterly Review* offered another outlet for research and included Meyer Kayserling, "The Jews in Jamaica and Daniel Israel Lopez Laguna," *Jewish Quarterly Review* 12, no. 4 (1900): 708–17.

15. P. A. Hilfman, "Some Further Notes on the History of the Jews in Surinam," PAJHS 16 (1907): 7–22. For an unknown reason, Hilfman did not publish this translation.

16. Cyrus Adler, "Address of the President," PAJHS 10 (1902): 3; Adler, "Trial of Jorge de Almeida by the Inquisition in Mexico," PAJHS 4 (1896): 29–79. George Alexander Kohut's sizeable article on the Inquisition in South America appeared in the same volume: George Alexander Kohut, "Jewish Martyrs of the Inquisition in South America," PAJHS 4 (1896): 101–87.

17. Cyrus Adler, ed., and David Fergusson, trans., "Trial of Gabriel De Granada by the Inquisition in Mexico, 1642–1645," PAJHS 7 (1899): 1–127.

18. Joseph Krauskopf, "The Jewish Pilgrim Fathers," PAJHS 14 (1906): 121–30.

19. Max J. Kohler, "Jewish Activity in American Colonial Commerce," PAJHS 10 (1902): 55, 56. See also Kohler, "Phases of Jewish Life in New York before 1800," PAJHS 2 (1894): 77–100 and PAJHS 3 (1895): 73–86.

20. Oscar S. Straus, "Address of the President," PAJHS 3 (1895): 4.

21. See Kayserling, "Colonization of America by the Jews."

22. Cyrus Adler, quoted in Liberles, "Postemancipation Historiography," 51.

23. See Adler's 1911 presidential address to the nineteenth annual AJHS meeting, quoted in PAJHS 20 (1911): ix–xi; Liberles, "Postemancipation Historiography," 52.

24. Peter Wiernik, *The History of the Jews in America: From the Period of the Discovery of the New World to the Present Time* (New York: Jewish Press Publishing Company, 1912).

25. Hasia R. Diner, *The Jews of the United States, 1654 to 2000* (Berkeley: University of California Press, 2004), 6, 74–75, 88.

26. Diner, "Study of American Jewish History," 43–45.

27. Lewis Abraham, "Correspondence between Washington and Jewish Citizens," *PAJHS* 3 (1895): 87–96; Wiernik, *History of the Jews in America*, 99–103.

28. Lee J. Levinger, *A History of the Jews in the United States* (Cincinnati: Department of Synagogue and School Extension of the Union of American Hebrew Congregations, 1931), 123–25; Morris A. Gutstein, *The Story of the Jews of Newport: Two and a Half Centuries of Judaism, 1658–1908* (New York: Bloch Publishing, 1936), 212–13.

29. Morris A. Gutstein, *To Bigotry No Sanction: A Jewish Shrine in America, 1658–1958* (New York: Bloch Publishing, 1958), 139–45.

30. Lee M. Friedman, *Jewish Pioneers and Patriots* (Philadelphia: Jewish Publication Society of America, 1942), 21.

31. *To Bigotry No Sanction: A Documented Analysis of Anti-Semitic Propaganda* (New York: American Jewish Committee, 1944).

32. On the recognition of Touro Synagogue as a National Historic Site, see Gutstein, *To Bigotry No Sanction*, 145–52. On the Freedom Train, see A. S. W. Rosenbach, "Address of the President," *PAJHS* 38, no. 1 (1948): 1–6; Stuart J. Little, "The Freedom Train: Citizenship and Postwar Political Culture 1946–1949," *American Studies* 34, no. 1 (1993): 35–67; Wenger, "Rites of Citizenship," 377.

33. Hyman B. Grinstein, review of S. Broches, *Jews in New England*, *William and Mary Quarterly* 4, no. 4 (1947): 534–35.

34. Diner, "Study of American Jewish History," 43–47.

35. Lee M. Friedman, "Know Thyself: A Program for American Jewish History," *PAJHS* 39, no. 4 (1950): 343, 340.

36. Lee M. Friedman, "E Pluribus Unum: Unity in Diversity," *PAJHS* 40, no. 3 (1951): 208. See also Friedman, "American History: The History of Immigrants," *PAJHS* 46, no. 3 (1957): 194–95.

37. Abram Vossen Goodman, *American Overture: Jewish Rights in Colonial Times* (Philadelphia: Jewish Publication Society of America, 1947), 11

38. Salo W. Baron, "American Jewish History: Problems and Methods," *PAJHS* 39, no. 3 (1950): 209.

39. Oscar Handlin, *Adventure in Freedom: Three Hundred Years of Jewish Life in America* (New York: McGraw-Hill, 1954), 21. See also Oscar Handlin and Mary F. Handlin, "The Acquisition of Political and Social Rights by the Jews in the United States," *American Jewish Year Book* 56 (1955): 43–98.

40. Henry L. Feingold, *Zion in America: The Jewish Experience from Colonial Times to the Present* (New York: Twayne Publishers, 1974), 20.

41. Jacob Rader Marcus, "The Periodization of American Jewish History," *PAJHS* 47, no. 3 (1958): 125–33.

42. Jacob Rader Marcus, *The Colonial American Jew, 1492–1776*, 3 vols. (Detroit: Wayne State University Press, 1970); Marcus, *United States Jewry, 1776–1985*,

4 vols. (Detroit: Wayne State University Press, 1989-93); Marcus, *The American Jew, 1585-1900: A History* (Brooklyn: Carlson Publishing, 1995). See Jacob Rader Marcus, ed., *The Jew in the American World: A Source Book* (Detroit: Wayne State University Press, 1996). Interestingly, Marcus broke with his standard formulation of American Jewish history in his volume *The American Jewish Woman, 1654-1980* (New York: KTAV Publishing House, 1981), which separated American Jewish history into a colonial period (1654-1775), early republic and age of expansion (1775-1865), and the new industrial society (1865-1980).

43. Marcus, *The Colonial American Jew*, 1:xxv.

44. Marcus, *The American Jew*, 17-40.

45. Jacob R. Marcus and Stanley F. Chyet, eds., Simon Cohen, trans., *Historical Essay on the Colony of Surinam, 1788* (Cincinnati: American Jewish Archives, 1974).

46. Jacob Rader Marcus, "The West India and South American Expedition of the American Jewish Archives," *American Jewish Archives* 5, no. 1 (1953): 6-7; Ben-Ur and Cohen, "Unworthy of Their Ancestors," 60-65.

47. Isaac S. Emmanuel and Suzanne A. Emmanuel, *History of the Jews of the Netherlands Antilles*, 2 vols. (Cincinnati: American Jewish Archives, 1970), 1:7.

48. Emmanuel and Emmanuel, *History of the Jews of the Netherlands Antilles*, 1:151-80, 509.

49. Marcus, *The Colonial American Jew*, 1:xxv.

50. Marcus, *The Colonial American Jew*, 1:209-11.

51. Diner, "Study of American Jewish History," 47-48.

52. Edmund S. Morgan, "Slavery and Freedom: The American Paradox," *Journal of American History* 59, no. 1 (1972): 6.

53. Moses Rischin, review of Jacob Rader Marcus, *The Colonial American Jew: 1492-1776, William and Mary Quarterly* 30, no. 2 (1973): 353-55. See also Rischin, "Review: Jacob Rader Marcus: Historian-Archivist of Jewish Middle America," *American Jewish History* 85, no. 2 (1997): 175-81.

54. Moses Rischin, *The Promised City: New York's Jews, 1870-1914* (Cambridge, MA: Harvard University Press, 1962).

55. Eli Faber, *A Time for Planting: The First Migration, 1654-1820* (Baltimore: Johns Hopkins University Press, 1992), 4.

56. On Atlantic history's emergence in this period, see David Armitage, "The Atlantic Ocean," in *Oceanic Histories*, ed. David Armitage, Alison Bashford, and Sujit Sivasundaram (Cambridge: Cambridge University Press, 2018), 85-110.

57. Paolo Bernardini and Norman Fiering, eds., *The Jews and the Expansion of Europe to the West, 1450-1800* (New York: Berghahn Books, 2001); Richard L. Kagan and Philip D. Morgan, eds., *Atlantic Diasporas: Jews, Conversos, and Crypto-Jews in the Age of Mercantilism, 1500-1800* (Baltimore: Johns Hopkins University Press, 2009).

58. Jane S. Gerber, ed., *The Jews in the Caribbean* (Oxford: Littman Library of Jewish Civilization, 2014).

59. Sina Rauschenbach and Jonathan Schorsch, eds., *The Sephardic Atlantic: Colonial Histories and Postcolonial Perspectives* (Cham: Palgrave Macmillan, 2018).

60. Jonathan I. Israel, *Diasporas within a Diaspora: Jews, Crypto-Jews, and the World Maritime Empires (1540-1740)* (Leiden: Brill, 2002).

61. Eli Faber, *Jews, Slaves, and the Slave Trade: Setting the Record Straight* (New York: New York University Press, 1998); Seymour Drescher, "Jews and New Christians in the Atlantic Slave Trade," in Bernardini and Fiering, *Jews and the Expansion of Europe to the West*, 439–70; Jonathan Schorsch, *Jews and Blacks in the Early Modern World* (Cambridge: Cambridge University Press, 2004); Laura Arnold Leibman, *Once We Were Slaves: The Extraordinary Journey of a Multiracial Jewish Family* (Oxford: Oxford University Press, 2021).

62. On the Port Jew concept, see Lois C. Dubin, "Port Jews Revisited: Commerce and Culture in the Age of European Expansion," in *The Cambridge History of Judaism*, vol. 7, *The Early Modern World, 1500–1815*, ed. Jonathan Karp and Adam Sutcliffe (Cambridge: Cambridge University Press, 2017), 556.

63. David Cesarani, ed., *Port Jews: Jewish Communities in Cosmopolitan Maritime Trading Centres, 1550–1950* (London: Frank Cass, 2002); David Cesarani and Gemma Romain, eds., *Jews and Port Cities, 1590–1990: Commerce, Community and Cosmopolitanism* (London: Vallentine Mitchell, 2006); David Cesarani, Tony Kushner, and Milton Shain, eds., *Place and Displacement in Jewish History and Memory: Zakov v'Makor* (London: Vallentine Mitchell, 2009).

64. "Port Jews of the Atlantic," special issue, *Jewish History* 20, no. 2 (2006).

65. For example, Matthias B. Lehmann, "A Livornese 'Port Jew' and the Sephardim of the Ottoman Empire," *Jewish Social Studies*, n.s., 11, no. 2 (2005): 51–76; C. S. Monaco, "Port Jews or a People of the Diaspora? A Critique of the Port Jew Concept," *Jewish Social Studies*, n.s., 15, no. 2 (2009): 137–66; Laura Leibman, "From Holy Land to New England Canaan: Rabbi Haim Carigal and Sephardic Itinerant Preaching in the Eighteenth Century," *Early American Literature* 44, no. 1 (2009): 71–93.

66. Armitage, "The Atlantic Ocean," 87, 88.

67. Armitage, "The Atlantic Ocean," 87.

68. Adam Sutcliffe, "Jewish History in an Age of Atlanticism," in Kagan and Morgan, *Atlantic Diasporas*, 20, 21, 22.

69. Holly Snyder, "Navigating the Jewish Atlantic: The State of the Field and Opportunities for New Research," in *The Atlantic World*, ed. D'Maris Coffman, Adrian Leonard, and William O'Reilly (New York: Routledge, 2014), 413.

70. Armitage, "The Atlantic Ocean," 88, which quotes Bernard Bailyn, "Hot Dreams of Liberty," *New York Review of Books* 62, no. 13 (August 13, 2015): 50.

71. In asserting the World War II and Cold War origins of Atlantic history, Sutcliffe followed Bernard Bailyn, *Atlantic History: Concept and Contours* (Cambridge, MA: Harvard University Press, 2005).

72. Conrad, *What Is Global History?*

73. Eli Faber, "The Borders of Early American Jewish History," in Gerber, *Jews in the Caribbean*, 281, 282.

74. Faber, "Borders of Early American Jewish History," 282.

75. Faber, "Borders of Early American Jewish History," 287.

76. Snyder, "Navigating the Jewish Atlantic," 413, 421.

77. Sanjay Subrahmanyam, "Connected Histories: Notes towards a Reconfiguration of Early Modern Eurasia," *Modern Asian Studies* 31, no. 3 (1997): 735–62; Jürgen Kocka, "Comparison and Beyond," *History and Theory* 42, no. 1

(2003): 39–44; Michael Werner and Bénédicte Zimmermann, "Beyond Comparison: *Histoire Croisée* and the Challenge of Reflexivity," *History and Theory* 45, no. 1 (2006): 30–50; Eliga H. Gould, "Entangled Histories, Entangled Worlds: The English-Speaking Atlantic as a Spanish Periphery," *American Historical Review* 112, no. 3 (2007): 764–86. For important differences between connected history, entangled history, and *histoire croisée*, see Sanjay Subrahmanyam, *Empires between Islam and Christianity, 1500–1800* (Albany: State University of New York Press, 2019), 19–23.

78. Aviva Ben-Ur, *Jewish Autonomy in a Slave Society: Suriname in the Atlantic World, 1651–1825* (Philadelphia: University of Pennsylvania Press, 2020), 12.

79. Bénédicte Zimmermann, "*Histoire Croisée*: A Relational Process-Based Approach," *Footprint* 14, no. 1 (2020): 7–14.

2. Atlantic Commerce and Pragmatic Tolerance

1. Jonathan Israel, *Empires and Entrepôts: The Dutch, the Spanish Monarchy, and the Jews, 1585–1713* (London: Hambledon Press, 1990) and *Diasporas within a Diaspora: Jews, Crypto-Jews, and the World Maritime Empires (1540–1740)* (Leiden: Brill, 2002).

2. Yosef Haim Yerushalmi, *From Spanish Court to Italian Ghetto: Isaac Cardoso* (New York: Columbia University Press, 1971); Yosef Kaplan, *From Christianity to Judaism: The Story of Isaac Orobio de Castro*, trans. Raphael Loewe (Oxford: Littman Library, 1989); Daniel Swetschinski, "The Portuguese Jewish Merchants of Seventeenth-Century Amsterdam: A Social Profile" (PhD diss., Brandeis University, 1980); Miriam Bodian, *Hebrews of the Portuguese Nation: Conversos and Community in Early Modern Amsterdam* (Bloomington: Indiana University Press, 1997).

3. David Graizbord argues that the Portuguese Jewish community contained such a variety of individuals that the categories of neither "Portuguese" nor "Jewish" are sufficient to describe them fully. However, he concludes that only a cultural and anthropological study of this community can answer questions of religious and ethnic identity, minimizing the centrality of commerce to the community's leadership: Graizbord, "Between Ethnicity, Commerce, Religion, and Race: The Elusive Definition of an Early Modern Jewish Atlantic," in *Theorising the Ibero-American Atlantic*, ed. Harald E. Braun and Lisa Vollendorf (Leiden: Brill, 2013), 125–28. For the diversity and precarious position of impoverished members of the community, see Tirtsah Levie Bernfeld, *Poverty and Welfare among the Portuguese Jews in Early Modern Amsterdam* (Oxford: Littman Library, 2012), 61–76.

4. This position complements studies on Portuguese Jewish concepts of race rooted in their participation in European colonial projects; see Jonathan Schorsch, *Jews and Blacks in the Early Modern World* (Cambridge: Cambridge University Press, 2004); Aviva Ben-Ur, *Jewish Autonomy in a Slave Society: Suriname in the Atlantic World, 1651–1825* (Philadelphia: University of Pennsylvania Press, 2020).

5. For Moriscos in Spanish America, see Karoline P. Cook, *Forbidden Passages: Muslims and Moriscos in Colonial Spanish America* (Philadelphia: University of Pennsylvania Press, 2016).

6. Recent scholarship has differentiated between "tolerance," as an ideological framework, and "toleration," as pragmatic policies or actions that grew in response to specific situations. The difference is important in considering how local actors made pragmatic decisions that did not always align with legal or ideological policies on the state or church level. Benjamin J. Kaplan, *Divided by Faith: Religious Conflict and the Practice of Toleration in Early Modern Europe* (Cambridge, MA: Belknap Press of Harvard University Press, 2007); Jesse Spohnholz, *The Tactics of Toleration: A Refugee Community in the Age of Religious Wars* (Newark: University of Delaware Press, 2011).

7. Henry Kamen, *The Spanish Inquisition: A Historical Revision* (New Haven: Yale University Press, 1997).

8. Stuart B. Schwartz, *All Can Be Saved: Religious Tolerance and Salvation in the Iberian Atlantic World* (New Haven: Yale University Press, 2008).

9. Jack P. Greene, "Negotiated Authorities: The Problem of Governance in the Extended Politics of the Early Modern Atlantic World," in Jack P. Greene, *Negotiated Authorities: Essays in Colonial Political and Constitutional History* (Charlottesville: University Press of Virginia, 1994), 1–24.

10. J. H. Elliott, "The Spanish Monarchy and the Kingdom of Portugal, 1580–1640," in *Conquest and Coalescence: The Shaping of the State in Early Modern Europe*, ed. Mark Greengrass (New York: E. Arnold, 1991), 50, 54.

11. Pedro Cardim, Tamar Herzog, José Javier Ruiz Ibáñez, and Gaetano Sabatini, eds., *Polycentric Monarchies: How Did Early Modern Spain and Portugal Achieve and Maintain a Global Hegemony?* (Brighton: Sussex Academic Press, 2012).

12. James C. Boyajian, *Portuguese Bankers at the Court of Spain, 1626–1650* (New Brunswick: Rutgers University Press, 1983), 18–41, and appendices A-1 to A-18.

13. His correspondence can be found in Biblioteca Nacional de España, MSS/899-900, *Correspondencia de D. Manuel de Belmonte com D. Juan José de Austria y D. Mateo Patiño sobre acontecimientos politicos y militares europeos observados desde Amsterdam [Manuscrito]*, años 1666–1667, 494 folios, años 1668–1679, 719 folios.

14. Swetschinski, "Portuguese Jewish Merchants," 243–72. I use the term "slave asiento" instead of *asiento de negros* or its direct English translation in order to convey to English readers that this royal contract pertained to the transatlantic slave trade.

15. Linda Rupert, *Creolization and Contraband: Curaçao in the Early Modern Atlantic World* (Athens: University of Georgia Press, 2012), 42, 74.

16. Wim Klooster, *Illicit Riches: Dutch Trade in the Caribbean, 1648–1795* (Leiden: KITLV Press, 1998).

17. Johannes M. Postma, *The Dutch in the Atlantic Slave Trade, 1600–1815* (New York: Cambridge University Press, 1990), 23–24, 111–13.

18. Rupert, *Creolization and Contraband*, 74.

19. Jonathan Israel, *The Dutch Republic: Its Rise, Greatness, and Fall, 1477–1806* (Oxford: Oxford University Press), 16.

20. Klooster surveys the avenues that Jews used for smuggling in the Caribbean in Wim Klooster, "Contraband Trade by Curaçao's Jews with Countries of Idolatry, 1660–1800," *Studia Rosenthaliana* 31, nos. 1/2 (1997): 58–73.

21. His original reports can be found in Archivo General de Simancas (henceforth AGS), Estado 8394, fol. 62; and AGS, E, EEH, legajo 838; copies exist in Archivo General de Indias (henceforth AGI), Indiferente General 1668, *Decretos, consultas y otros documentos relativo a fraudes cometidos en Indias por ingleses y holandeses, al comercio de negros y otras mercancías*, fols. 372r–829v.

22. Zacharias Moutoukias, "Power, Corruption, and Commerce: The Making of the Local Administrative Structure in Seventeenth-Century Buenos Aires," *Hispanic American Historical Review* 68, no. 4 (1988): 787–88.

23. Moutoukias, "Power, Corruption, and Commerce," 774–75.

24. Moutoukias, "Power, Corruption, and Commerce," 780–81, 787–88.

25. Moutoukias, "Power, Corruption, and Commerce," 780–82.

26. For the extensive business operations maintained between Portuguese Jews in Amsterdam and Portuguese New Christians in Portugal and Brazil in the period 1598–1627, see Daniel Strum, "Institutional Choice in the Governance of the Early Atlantic Sugar Trade: Diasporas, Markets, and Courts," *Economic History Review* 72, no. 4 (2019): 1202–28. For agents that Portuguese Jews retained in Madrid and Seville, and for the correspondents that New Christian bankers in Madrid kept in northern Europe after 1630, see Israel, *Empires and Entrepôts*, 396.

27. Israel, *Empires and Entrepôts*, 418–19.

28. For these correspondents, see the 1655 list gathered by Spanish intelligence efforts at the Spanish embassy in The Hague to trace Portuguese Jewish business networks between Amsterdam and Spain, AGS, Estado 8396 (*Libros de la Haya*), XXXVIII, fol. 143, reprinted by Israel in *Empires and Entrepôts*, appendix 1, 414.

29. A model for studying the presence of Protestants in Iberian ports can be found in Cacey Farnsworth, "Atlantic Lisbon: From Restoration to Baroque Splendor, 1668–1750" (PhD diss., University of Florida, 2019), 86–139.

30. Interestingly, several of the advisers who helped the Count-Duke of Olivares set up the *almirantazgo* were Germans and Dutch merchants and two Portuguese New Christians, one of whom had previously lived as a Jew in Amsterdam before settling in Madrid, Israel, *Empires and Entrepôts*, 211, 213–45.

31. María Cristina Navarrete Peláez, "De las 'malas entradas' y las estrategias del 'buen pasaje': El contrabando de esclavos en el Caribe neogranadino, 1550–1690," *Historia Crítica* 34 (2007): 160–83.

32. AGI, Contaduría 239, *Rs. Cedulas de Indultos y Perdones concedidos, a las personas que sin permiso han comerciado en las Indias, y de otros delitos cometidos, y de varias causas formadas. Desde 1601 a 1728*.

33. AGI, Contaduría, *Real Cedula de 12 Diciembre de 1650*.

34. AGI, Contaduría, *Reales. Cedulas desde 1601 a 1728*.

35. Moutoukias, "Power, Corruption, and Commerce," 782.

36. AGI, Contadina 239, *Real Cedula de 10 de Diciembre 1659*.

37. Wim Klooster, "Inter-Imperial Smuggling in the Americas, 1600–1800," in *Soundings in Atlantic History: Latent Structures and Intellectual Currents, 1500–1830*, ed. Bernard Bailyn and Patricia L. Denault (Cambridge, MA: Harvard University Press, 2009), 141–44.

38. Before being appointed governor, he had a long career serving the Crown, first as a soldier then as a field marshal, and ultimately as governor of Gibraltar from 1659 until 1662: AGI, Indiferente General 124, N.8, *Méritos: Francisco Dávila Orejón Gaston*, fols. 1r–2v. He was a *vecino* (permanent resident) of Sanlúcar: AGI, Contratacion 5433, R.21, N.3 *Francisco Davila Orejon Gaston*, fols. 1r–4v; AGI, Indiferente General 1668, fols. 143r–744v.

39. For this venture, see the intelligence reports compiled by Ambassador Gamarra at The Hague, AGI, Indiferente General 1668, fols. 700r–701v, 726r–727r, 743v–744r, 759r–760v.

40. For his correspondents in Spain, see Israel, *Empires and Entrepôts*, appendix 1, 414. His alias appears in notarial documents detailing his numerous business deals, such as the venture to ship goods from Lisbon he undertook with Abraam and Ishac Pereyra in 1654, Stadsarchief Amsterdam (henceforth SAA), NA 2197, fol. 439 (notary A. Lock). He should not be confused with Albert Dirksen den Ouden, an alias used by another Portuguese Jew, Manuel Toralta: Bloom, *Jews of Amsterdam*, 90n64; Israel, *Empires and Entrepôts*, 413, 413n264.

41. For trade with the Pereyras to Lisbon, SAA, NA 2197, fols. 439–40, act of October 20, 1654 (notary Adriaen Lock); SAA, NA 2269A, fol. 656, act of October 20, 1654 (notary Adriaen Lock). Lopes Suasso was listed among Álvares Nogueira's creditors in 1659, SAA, NA 2207, fols. 923–924, act of December 8, 1659 (notary Adriaen Lock). For partnerships with Nunes da Costa, SAA, NA 1538, fol. 250 (notary J. V. Oli).

42. He exported tobacco from Martinique. See his venture with Aaron Gabay and David Torres in the summer of 1654: SAA, NA 2201, fol. 153, act of September 1656; and his venture with Alexander Mogeres in the winter of 1657: SAA, NA 2202, fol. 152, act of February 5, 1657; SAA, NA 2272, fol. 67r–67v, act of February 5, 1657 (all notarized by Adriaen Lock).

43. Diogo Carlos apparently conducted payment exchanges for the two by remitting payments between Hamburg and Amsterdam, SAA, NA 2207, fol. 924 (notary Adriaen Lock); SAA, NA 2201, fol. 478, act of November 1656 (notary Adriaen Lock); SAA, NA 2271, fol. 783r–v, act of November 8, 1656 (notary Adriaen Lock). Rodrigues Isidro also used the alias Jacob Baruch in the synagogue and was a business partner of Jeronimo Nunes da Costa in the shipment of North Atlantic cod to Lisbon. In the 1660s, he and Jacob returned to Spain where they lived as Catholics, first in Madrid and then in Cádiz. Manuel died in 1666, but his son continued to maintain ties with his Jewish family: Israel, "An Amsterdam Jewish Merchant," 26–27; Weinstein, "Senior Stones," 129.

44. For his alias, see SAA, NA 2890, fol. 985, act of April 25, 1661 (notary Pieter Padthuijzen); SAA, NA 2213B, fol. 964, act of November 1662 (notary Adriaen Lock); Bloom, *Jews of Amsterdam*, 90n65. Mendes de Brito traded regularly with Bayonne where he first lived after leaving Portugal in the 1650s before relocating to Amsterdam. There he also traded across the nearby Spanish border with Pamplona in Navarre and with Bilbao and San Sebastián in the Basque Country. He appears to have been a relative of the Madrid *asentista* Francisco Dias Mendes de Brito and maintained contact with his family in Spain, who

acted as his correspondents in Andalusia. For his ties to Bayonne and Pamplona, see SAA, NA 2270, fols. 506r–509r, act of September 8, 1655; SAA, NA 2199, fols. 353, 368–71, act of September 1655 (all notarized by Adriaen Lock). For his correspondents in Bilbao and San Sebastián, and relationship to Francisco Dias, see Israel, *Empires and Entrepôts*, 414, 414n267; SAA, NA 2197, fol. 113, act of July 1654 (notary Adriaen Lock). For his correspondent in Málaga, Fernando Dias de Brito, see SAA, NA 2201, fols. 71–72, act of August 30, 1665 (notary Adriaen Lock).

45. AGI, Indiferente General 1668, fol. 787v.

46. AGI, Indiferente General 1668, fols. 700r–701v, 726r–727r, 743v–744r, 759r–760v.

47. AGI, Indiferente General 1668, fol. 787r.

48. AGI, Indiferente General 1668, fol. 787r–v.

49. This cargo was paid for by the company of Guillaume Belin de la Garde, the French partner resident in Amsterdam.

50. For Álvares Nogueira's debtors, see SAA, NA 2207, fols. 923–24 (notary Adriaen Lock). For the Rodrigo da Sousa brothers and Lopes de Azevedo, see Israel, "An Amsterdam Jewish Merchant," 24, 35.

51. C. R. Boxer, *The Portuguese Seaborne Empire, 1415–1825* (London: Knopf, 1969), 221–24.

52. Álvares Nogueira and Dias de Brito were part of a venture to trade with Seville and Cádiz undertaken in 1657 executed by a joint group of over a dozen Dutch and Portuguese merchants in Amsterdam, SAA, NA 2203, fols. 350–52, act of September 1657 (notary Adriaen Lock).

53. AGI, Indiferente General 1668, fol. 787v.

54. This clause was confirmed in an addendum that the Spanish Crown ratified in 1650. For a contemporaneous printed text of the Dutch-Spanish treaty, see Lieuwe van Aitzema, *Saken van Staet en Oorlog in ende omtrent de Vereenigte Nederlanden*, vol. 3 (Amsterdam: Veely, Tongerloo, ende Doll, 1669), accessed through the Huygens Institute for the History of the Netherlands digitized collection.

55. Francesca Trivellato, *The Familiarity of Strangers: The Sephardic Diaspora, Livorno, and Cross-Cultural Trade in the Early Modern Period* (New Haven: Yale University Press, 2009).

56. Jessica Roitman, *The Same but Different? Inter-cultural Trade and the Sephardim, 1595–1640* (Leiden: Brill, 2011), 93–120.

57. Strum, "Institutional Choice."

58. See note 2.

59. See the community's register book of elected officials from 1639–1795: SAA, 334, no. 155, fols. 10, 13, 25.

60. Swetschinski, "Portuguese Jewish Merchants," 263.

61. SAA, 334, no. 174, fols. 180–88, 201–12, 342–885.

62. SAA, 334, no. 158, fol. 17.

63. SAA, 334, no. 20, fol. 23, 26 Iyar 5441.

64. Bodian, *Hebrews of the Portuguese Nation*, 80.

65. SAA, 334, no. 20, fol. 23.

3. To Trade Is to Thrive

1. Daniel M. Swetschinski, "Conflict and Opportunity in Europe's Other Sea: The Adventure of Caribbean Jewish Settlement," *American Jewish History* 72, no. 2 (1982): 223. Miriam Bodian, *Hebrews of the Portuguese Nation: Conversos and Community in Early Modern Amsterdam* (Bloomington: Indiana University Press, 1997) refers to Spanish and Portuguese Jews in early seventeenth-century Amsterdam, recognizing that they were part of the Portuguese Nation, a term that denotes the trading network established by Portuguese converso merchants in the fifteenth and sixteenth centuries.

2. Yda Schreuder, *Amsterdam's Sephardic Merchants and the Atlantic Sugar Trade in the Seventeenth Century* (Cham: Palgrave Macmillan, 2019). Throughout this chapter I will refer to chapters and subsections in the book where the various topics are discussed.

3. In this study I use the term "converso" to refer to Portuguese New Christians without referring to Jewish identity or aspiration to be considered Jewish. The term "crypto-Jew" refers to New Christians who did adhere to Jewish traditions in secret and identified themselves as Jews. See David Gaizbord, "Religion and Ethnicity among 'Men of the Nation': Towards a Realistic Interpretation," *Jewish Social Studies*, n.s., 15, no. 1 (2008): 32–65.

4. David Sorkin, "The Port Jew: Notes towards a Social Type," *Journal of Jewish Studies* 50, no. 1 (1999): 87–97; and Lois C. Dubin, "'Wings on their feet... and wings on their head': Reflections on the Study of Port Jews," *Jewish Culture and History* 7 (2004): 16–30. See also David Cesarani and Gemma Romain, eds., *Jews and Port Cities, 1590–1990: Commerce, Community, and Cosmopolitanism* (London: Vallentine Mitchell, 2006).

5. Wim Klooster, "Communities of Port Jews and Their Contacts in the Dutch Atlantic World," *Jewish History* 20, no. 2 (2006): 129–45; and Jonathan I. Israel, "The Economic Contribution of Dutch Sephardic Jewry to Holland's Golden Age," in *Empires and Entrepôts: The Dutch, the Spanish Monarchy, and the Jews, 1585–1713* (London: Hambledon Press, 1990), 419–20.

6. Daviken Studnicki-Gizbert, *A Nation upon the Ocean Sea: Portugal's Atlantic Diaspora and the Crisis of the Spanish Empire, 1492–1640* (Oxford: Oxford University Press, 2007).

7. Daniel M. Swetschinski, *Reluctant Cosmopolitans: The Portuguese Jews of Seventeenth-Century Amsterdam* (London: Littman Library of Jewish Civilization, 2000); Jessica Vance Roitman, *The Same but Different? Inter-cultural Trade and the Sephardim, 1595–1640* (Leiden: Brill, 2011).

8. James C. Boyajian, "New Christians and Jews in the Sugar Trade, 1550–1750: Two Centuries of Development of the Atlantic Economy," in *The Jews and the Expansion of Europe to the West, 1450–1800*, ed. Paolo Bernardini and Norman Fiering (New York: Berghahn Books, 2001), 471–84. See Schreuder, *Amsterdam's Sephardic Merchants*, 31–76.

9. Roitman, *The Same but Different?*; and Francesca Trivellato, *The Familiarity of Strangers: The Sephardic Diaspora, Livorno, and Cross-Cultural Trade in the Early Modern Period* (New Haven: Yale University Press, 2009). See also

Jonathan I. Israel, *Diasporas within a Diaspora: Jews, Crypto-Jews, and the World of Maritime Empires (1540–1740)* (Leiden: Brill, 2002), and Swetschinski, "Conflict and Opportunity," 223.

10. Wim Klooster, "Networks of Colonial Entrepreneurs: The Founders of the Jewish Settlements in Dutch America, 1650s and 1660s," in *Atlantic Diasporas: Jews, Conversos, and Crypto-Jews in the Age of Mercantilism, 1500–1800*, ed. Richard L. Kagan and Philip D. Morgan (Baltimore: Johns Hopkins University Press, 2009), 33–49.

11. Jane S. Gerber, "Introduction," in *The Jews in the Caribbean*, ed. Jane S. Gerber (Oxford: Littman Library of Jewish Civilization, 2014), 1–14.

12. See, for instance, Karl Watson, "Shifting Identities: Religion, Race, and Creolization among the Sephardi Jews of Barbados, 1654–1900," in Gerber, *Jews of the Caribbean*, 195–222; and Adam Sutcliffe, "Jewish History in an Age of Atlanticism," in Kagan and Morgan, *Atlantic Diasporas*, 18–30.

13. See for instance, Jonathan Israel, *Dutch Primacy in World Trade, 1585–1740* (Oxford: Clarendon Press, 1989) and Israel, "Economic Contribution."

14. Officially the collection is called Archives of Notary Publics of Amsterdam: Access number 5075. For a description, see Schreuder, *Amsterdam's Sephardic Merchants*, appendix 1, 263–65.

15. There is a separate collection of records related to the Portuguese Jews in Amsterdam: "Notarial Records Relating to the Portuguese Jews in Amsterdam up to 1639," published in *Studia Rosenthaliana* intermittently between 1967 and 2001.

16. The most noteworthy Dutch colonial development concerned free port settlements, the best known of which is Curaçao. Wim Klooster, "Curaçao and the Caribbean Transit Trade," in *Riches from Atlantic Commerce: Dutch Trans-Atlantic Trade and Shipping, 1585–1817*, ed. Johannes Postma and Victor Enthoven (Leiden: Brill, 2003), 203–18. See also Jonathan Israel, "Curaçao, Amsterdam, and the rise of the Sephardic Trade System in the Caribbean, 1630–1700," in Gerber, *Jews in the Caribbean*, 29–43.

17. Wim Klooster, "An Overview of Dutch Trade with the Americas, 1600–1800," in Postma and Enthoven, *Riches from Atlantic Commerce*, 370–72.

18. Israel, "Economic Contribution"; Swetschinski, *Reluctant Cosmopolitans*; and Roitman, *The Same but Different?*

19. I use the term "Sephardic Moment" as discussed in my book *Amsterdam's Sephardic Merchants*, 105–18.

20. Schreuder, *Amsterdam's Sephardic Merchants*, 233–62.

21. J. J. Reesse, *De suikerhandel van Amsterdam van het begin der 17de eeuw tot 1813: Een bijdrage tot de handelsgeschiedenis des vaderlands, hoofdzakelijk uit de archieven* (Haarlem: Kleynenberg, 1908), 30–32, 107–10; György Nováky, "On Trade, Production and Relations of Production: The Sugar Refineries of Seventeenth-Century Amsterdam," *Tijdschrift voor Sociale Geschiedenis* 23, no. 4 (1997): 459–89.

22. Schreuder, *Amsterdam's Sephardic Merchants*, 256–57.

23. Roitman, *The Same but Different?*, 247–51.

24. Daniel Strum, *The Sugar Trade: Brazil, Portugal, and the Netherlands, 1595–1630* (Stanford: Stanford University Press, 2013); Bruno Feitler, "Jews and

New Christians in Dutch Brazil, 1630–1654," in Kagan and Morgan, *Atlantic Diasporas*, 123–52.

25. Arnold Wiznitzer, *The Records of the Earliest Jewish Community in the New World* (New York: American Jewish Historical Society, 1954). See also Arnold Wiznitzer, *Jews in Colonial Brazil* (New York: Columbia University Press, 1960).

26. Wiznitzer, *Jews in Colonial Brazil*, 5–10.

27. Wiznitzer, *Jews in Colonial Brazil*, 12–32.

28. Studnicki-Gizbert, *A Nation upon the Ocean Sea*, 157–58.

29. Swetschinski, *Reluctant Cosmopolitans*; Roitman, *The Same but Different?*; Schreuder, *Amsterdam's Sephardic Merchants*, chap. 2.

30. Wiznitzer, *Jews in Colonial Brazil*, 36–42; Bodian, *Hebrews of the Portuguese Nation*.

31. Wiznitzer, *Jews in Colonial Brazil*, 40.

32. Klooster, "Overview of Dutch Trade with the Americas," 368–70; Christopher Ebert, "Dutch Trade with Brazil," in Postma and Enthoven, *Riches from Atlantic Commerce*, 49–75.

33. Wim Klooster, *Illicit Riches: Dutch Trade in the Caribbean, 1648–1795* (Leiden: KITLV Press, 1998), 35. Christopher Ebert, *Between Empires: Brazilian Sugar in the Early Atlantic Economy, 1550–1630* (Leiden: Brill, 2008), 12–16.

34. Jonathan Israel, "Jews and Crypto-Jews in the Atlantic World Systems, 1500–1800," in Kagan and Morgan, *Atlantic Diasporas*, 3–17.

35. Odette Vlessing, "The Economic Influence of the Portuguese Jews on the Dutch Golden Age," in *Il ruolo economico delle minoranze in Europa, secc. XIII–XVIII: Atti della "trentunesima Settimana di studi," 19–23 aprile 1999*, ed. Simonetta Cavaciocchi ([Florence:] Le Monnier, 2000), 303–24; and Israel, "Economic Contribution."

36. Henk den Heijer, "The Dutch West India Company, 1621–1791," in Postma and Enthoven, *Riches from Atlantic Commerce*, 77–112.

37. Ernst Pijning, "New Christians as Sugar Cultivators and Traders," in Bernardini and Fiering, *Jews and the Expansion of Europe*, 491–92.

38. Herbert I. Bloom, *The Economic Activities of the Jews of Amsterdam* (Williamsport, PA: Bayard Press, 1937), 125–27. See also Wiznitzer, *Jews in Colonial Brazil*, 48. Likewise, the number of Jewish depositors with the Amsterdam Exchange Bank increased. See Israel, "Economic Contribution," 422, table 14.

39. Wiznitzer, *Jews in Colonial Brazil*, 73–81.

40. Klooster, "Networks of Colonial Entrepreneurs," 35–36. Establishing exact figures on resident populations of Dutch Brazil has proven difficult. See Miriam Bodian, "The Formation of the Portuguese Jewish Diaspora," in Gerber, *Jews in the Caribbean*, 25n29.

41. Charles R. Boxer, *The Dutch in Brazil, 1624–1654* (Oxford: Clarendon Press, 1957), 148–49.

42. See Stuart B. Schwartz, "A Commonwealth within Itself: The Early Brazilian Sugar Industry, 1550–1670," in *Tropical Babylons: Sugar and the Making of the Atlantic World, 1450–1680*, ed. Stuart B. Schwartz (Chapel Hill: University of North Carolina Press, 2004), 169, fig. 6.1.

43. Boxer, *The Dutch in Brazil*, 291–93.

44. Wiznitzer, *Jews in Colonial Brazil*, 81.
45. Schwartz, "A Commonwealth within Itself," 169.
46. See Schwartz, "A Commonwealth within Itself," 169, fig. 6.1.
47. Klooster, "Networks of Colonial Entrepreneurs."
48. Israel, "Economic Contribution," 417–47.
49. By connecting family names from Wiznitzer's membership lists of two Jewish congregations in Brazil from 1648–53 and burial records in Eustace M. Shilstone, *Jewish Monumental Inscriptions in the Jewish Synagogue at Bridgetown, Barbados with Historical Notes from 1630* (New York: Macmillan, 1988), I was able to trace several Sephardic family names in Barbados with roots in Brazil. The records from Wiznitzer's "Personalia," in *Jews in Colonial Brazil*, 169–77, and from Shilstone show that most of the Brazil Sephardic Jews considered their home base Amsterdam, but of the twenty-two detailed biographical entries, about half can be identified with some certainty as residents of Barbados in the 1660s and 1670s.
50. Schreuder, *Amsterdam's Sephardic Merchants*, 105–18. Richard Dunn, *Sugar and Slaves: The Rise of the Planter Class in the English West Indies, 1624–1713* (Chapel Hill: University of North Carolina Press, 1972); Richard Sheridan, *Sugar and Slavery: An Economic History of the British West Indies, 1623–1775* (Baltimore: Johns Hopkins University Press, 1974).
51. Richard Ligon, *A True and Exact History of the Island of Barbadoes* (London, 1657).
52. Schreuder, *Amsterdam's Sephardic Merchants*, chap. 4. See also Russell R. Menard, *Sweet Negotiations: Sugar, Slavery, and Plantation Agriculture in Early Barbados* (Charlottesville: University of Virginia Press, 2006), 50–51, and John J. McCusker and Russell R. Menard, "The Sugar Industry in the Seventeenth Century: A New Perspective on the Barbadian 'Sugar Revolution,'" in Schwartz, *Tropical Babylons*, 289–330, for the dispute about the "Myth of the Dutch."
53. Shilstone, *Jewish Monumental Inscriptions*. The request was made by "several Jews and Hebrews, inhabiting in and about this Island" to the Council of Barbados, November 8, 1654, to admit Jews from Brazil. The meeting of council in January 1655, as recorded in the Minutes of Council, states "that during their stay, they shall enjoy the privileges of Laws and Statutes of the Commonwealth of England and of this Island relating to foreigners and strangers."
54. Matthew Edel, "The Brazilian Sugar Cycle of the Seventeenth Century and the Rise of the West Indian Competition," *Caribbean Studies* 9, no. 1 (1969): 24–44. Robert C. Batie, "Why Sugar? Economic Cycles and the Changing of Staples on the English and French Antilles, 1624–1654," *Journal of Caribbean History* 8, no. 1 (1976): 3–41. William A. Green, "Supply versus Demand in the Barbadian Sugar Revolution," *Journal of Interdisciplinary History* 18, no. 3 (1988): 405; and Menard, *Sweet Negotiations*, 22, table 3.
55. Wim Klooster, *The Dutch Moment: War, Trade, and Settlement in the Seventeenth-Century Atlantic World* (Ithaca, NY: Cornell University Press, 2016), 167–69.
56. Batie, "Why Sugar?"; Ligon, *A True and Exact History*, 85.
57. Yda Schreuder, "A True Global Community: Sephardic Jews, the Sugar Trade and Barbados in the Seventeenth Century," *Journal of the Barbados Museum and Historical Society* 50 (2004): 166–94.

58. Klooster, *Dutch Moment*, 167–69.

59. Schreuder, *Amsterdam Sephardic Merchants*, 233–62.

60. Cromwell's plans for expansion in the Caribbean region are often referred to as the Western Design. See Carla G. Pestana, *The English Atlantic in an Age of Revolution, 1640–1661* (Cambridge, MA: Harvard University Press, 2004). For a discussion about the efforts undertaken to coordinate the readmission of Jews to England, see Yosef Kaplan, ed., *An Alternative Path to Modernity: The Sephardi Diaspora in Western Europe* (Leiden: Brill, 2000), 155–67. For an overview of Menasseh ben Israel's mission to Cromwell, see Yosef Kaplan, Henri Méchoulan, and Richard H. Popkin, eds., *Menasseh ben Israel and his World* (Leiden: Brill, 1989).

61. Among the merchants involved in Cromwell's Western Design promoting denization for Sephardic merchants in Amsterdam and the British colonies were several well-established crypto-Jewish merchants in London. Schreuder, *Amsterdam's Sephardic Merchants*, 178–79.

62. Schreuder, *Amsterdam's Sephardic Merchants*, chap. 7. For evidence, see W. S. Samuel, R. D. Barnett, and A. S. Diamond, "A List of Jewish Persons Endenizened and Naturalised 1609–1799," *Transactions & Miscellanies (Jewish Historical Society of England)* 22 (1968–69): 111–44.

63. For an overview of the role of Menasseh ben Israel in the migration and colonization efforts of Sephardic merchants, see Jonathan Israel, "Menasseh ben Israel and the Dutch Sephardic Colonization Movement," in Kaplan, Méchoulan, and Popkin, *Menasseh ben Israel and His World*, 139–63. See also Schreuder, *Amsterdam's Sephardic Merchants*, 176–216.

64. Schreuder, "A True Global Community," and Schreuder, *Amsterdam's Sephardic Merchants*, 77–118.

65. Wilfred S. Samuel, "Sir William Davidson, Royalist (1616–1689) and the Jews," *Transactions of the Jewish Historical Society of England* 14 (1935–39): 39–79.

66. Schreuder, *Amsterdam's Sephardic Merchants*, chap. 6.

67. Wilfred S. Samuel, "A Review of the Jewish Colonists in Barbados in the Year 1680," *Transactions of the Jewish Historical Society of England* 13 (1932–35): 94–96.

68. Samuel, "Review of the Jewish Colonists." See also Martyn J. Bowden, "Houses, Inhabitants and Levies: Place for the Sephardic Jews of Bridgetown, Barbados 1679–1729," *Journal of the Barbados Museum and Historical Society* 57 (2011): 1–53.

69. Schreuder, *Amsterdam's Sephardic Merchants*, 105–18. Pieter Emmer, "The Dutch and the Making of the Second Atlantic System," in *Slavery and the Rise of the Atlantic System*, ed. Barbara L. Solow (Cambridge: Cambridge University Press, 1991), 75–96. Seymour Drescher, "Jews and New Christians in the Atlantic Slave Trade," in Bernardini and Fiering, *Jews and the Expansion of Europe*, 439–70.

70. Pieter Emmer, "The Jewish Moment and the Two Expansion Systems in the Atlantic, 1580–1650," in Bernardini and Fiering, *Jews and the Expansion of Europe*, 512–14.

71. Drescher, "Jews and New Christians in the Atlantic Slave Trade."

72. Reesse, *Suikerhandel van Amsterdam*, 30–32, 107–10.

73. Schreuder, *Amsterdam's Sephardic Merchants*, 233-62.

74. In addition, there was a great deal of collaboration between English and Dutch merchants. See Wim Klooster, "Anglo-Dutch Trade in the Seventeenth Century: An Atlantic Partnership?," in *Shaping the Stuart World, 1603-1714: The Atlantic Connection*, ed. Allan I. Macinnes and Arthur H. Williamson (Leiden: Brill, 2006), 261-81.

75. Reesse, *Suikerhandel van Amsterdam*, 30-32, 107-10.

76. Eddy Stols, "The Expansion of the Sugar Market in Western Europe," in Schwartz, *Tropical Babylons*, 237-88.

77. Bloom, *Economic Activities of the Jews*, 36-40, and Swetschinski, *Reluctant Cosmopolitans*, 154-55.

78. Mordechai Arbell, "Jewish Settlements in the French Colonies in the Caribbean (Martinique, Guadeloupe, Haiti, Cayenne) and the 'Black Code,'" in Bernardini and Fiering, *Jews and the Expansion of Europe*, 287-313.

4. Trading Violence

1. Manuel Calado, *O Valeroso Lucideno e Triumpho da Liberdade* (Lisboa: Paulo Craesbeeck, 1648), 10-11.

2. Arnold Wiznitzer, "Jewish Soldiers in Dutch Brazil (1630-1654)," *Publications of the American Jewish Historical Society* 46, no. 1 (1956): 40-50; Hermann Kellenbenz, *A participação da Companhia de Judeus na conquista holandesa de Pernambuco* (Paraíba: Universidade Federal da Paraíba, 1966).

3. An exception is Derek Penslar, *Jews and the Military: A History* (Princeton, NJ: Princeton University Press, 2013).

4. Paolo Bernardini, "A Milder Colonization: Jewish Expansion to the New World, and the New World in the Jewish Consciousness of the Early Modern Era," in *The Jews and the Expansion of Europe to the West, 1450-1800*, ed. Paolo Bernardini and Norman Fiering (New York: Berghahn Books, 2001), 1-23.

5. Sina Rauschenbach and Jonathan Schorsch, "Postcolonial Approaches to the Early Modern Sephardic Atlantic," in *The Sephardic Atlantic: Colonial Histories and Postcolonial Perspectives*, ed. Sina Rauschenbach and Jonathan Schorsch (Cham: Palgrave Macmillan, 2018), 4.

6. David Graizbord, *Souls in Dispute: Converso Identities in Iberia and the Jewish Diaspora, 1580-1700* (Philadelphia: University of Pennsylvania Press, 2004), 174-75.

7. Graizbord, *Souls in Dispute*, 171.

8. Adam Sutcliffe, "Jewish History in an Age of Atlanticism," in *Atlantic Diasporas: Jews, Conversos, and Crypto-Jews in the Age of Mercantilism, 1500-1800*, ed. Richard L. Kagan and Philip D. Morgan (Baltimore: John Hopkins University Press, 2009), 28.

9. Sutcliffe, "Jewish History," 24, 27-28.

10. Aviva Ben-Ur, "Atlantic Jewish History: A Conceptual Reorientation," in *Constellations of Atlantic Jewish History, 1555-1890: The Arnold and Deanne Kaplan Collection of Early American Judaica*, ed. Arthur Kiron (Philadelphia: University of Pennsylvania Press, 2014), 25-46.

11. Victor Tiribás, "Mobility, Clandestine Literature, and Censorship: A Case-Study in the Transatlantic Diaspora of a Migrant Circle," *Rivista Storica Italiana* 131, no. 3 (2019): 1050-84.

12. José Antônio Gonsalves de Mello, *Gente da Nação: Cristãos-novos e judeus em Pernambuco, 1542-1654* (Recife: Editora Massangana, 1996), 213.

13. José Antônio Gonsalves de Mello, *Tempo dos flamengos: Influência da ocupação holandesa na vida e na cultura do norte do Brasil* (Rio de Janeiro: Topbooks, 2002), 39-42.

14. Wiznitzer, "Jewish Soldiers," 40-41; Mark Meuwese, "Samuel Cohen (c. 1600-1642): Jewish Translator in Brazil, Curaçao, and Angola," in *The Human Tradition in the Atlantic World, 1500-1800*, ed. Karen Racine and Beatriz Mamigonian (New York: Rowman & Littlefield, 2010), 27-41.

15. Cyrus Adler, "A Contemporary Memorial Relating to Damages to Spanish Interests in America Done by Jews of Holland (1634)," *Publications of the American Jewish Historical Society* 17 (1909): 48. Unlike his father and brothers, Moisés Cohen Henriques did not pay the annual membership fee (*finta*) to the Jewish community of Amsterdam in 1630. See Stadsarchief Amsterdam (henceforth SAA), 334, no. 17, fol. 33. This adds credibility to the inquisitorial denunciation claiming he participated in the invasion of Pernambuco that year. The record dated 1630 containing his promises (*promessas*) to donate money to charity states, "for the account of the last six months," and refers to the second semester of 1629—year in which he is in fact listed as a donor. See SAA, 334, no. 11, fols. 15, 33.

16. Calado, *O Valeroso Lucideno*, 11-12.

17. Evaldo Cabral de Mello, *Olinda restaurada: Guerra e açúcar no Nordeste, 1630-1654* (São Paulo: Editora 34, 2007), 257-315.

18. Renato Ghezzi, "Il porto di Livorno e il commercio mediterraneo nel Seicento," in *Livorno (1606-1806): Luogo di incontri tra popolo e culture*, ed. Adriano Prosperi (Turin: Umberto Allemandi, 2009), 329, attributed the sudden drop to "the shortage of slaves, aggravated by a smallpox epidemic," without mentioning the Dutch invasion of northern Brazil.

19. Wim Klooster, *The Dutch Moment: War, Trade, and Settlement in the Seventeenth-Century Atlantic World* (Ithaca, NY: Cornell University Press, 2016), 136-38.

20. Michiel van Groesen, *Amsterdam's Atlantic: Print Culture and the Making of Dutch Brazil* (Philadelphia: University of Pennsylvania Press, 2016), 72-73, 84, 90, 100.

21. Bruno Miranda, "Gente de Guerra: Origem, cotidiano e resistência dos soldados do exército da Companhia das Índias Ocidentais no Brasil (1630-1654)" (PhD diss., Leiden University, 2011), 125-30, 142-46.

22. Klooster, *Dutch Moment*, 128-32.

23. For the medieval controversy concerning this violation in times of war, see Maimonides, *Hilchot Melachim uMilchamot* 8:1; Moses ben Nahman (Nahmanides), *Perush ha-Ramban al ha-Torah*, Deut. 6:10. A few soldiers may have been aware of this debate, if they had received a solid religious education.

24. Ronaldo Vainfas, *Traição: Um jesuíta a serviço do Brasil holandês processado pela Inquisição* (São Paulo: Companhia das Letras, 2008), 86-91.

25. Miranda, "Gente de Guerra," 37.

26. Julio Caro Baroja, *Los Judíos en la España Moderna y Contemporánea*, vol. 3 (Madrid: Istmo, 1986), 362. See also Archivo Histórico Nacional (henceforth AHN), *Inquisición*, libro 1103, fol. 484r–84v.

27. Arquivo Nacional da Torre do Tombo (henceforth ANTT), *Inquisição de Lisboa*, livro 220, fol. 402r.

28. Adler, "A Contemporary Memorial," 49.

29. Caspar Barleus, *Rerum per octennium in Brasilia et alibi nuper gestarum* (Amsterdam: Johan Blaeu, 1647), plates 9 and 10. For the participation of Jews in civil militias in the Caribbean, see Jessica Roitman, "Creating Confusion in the Colonies: Jews, Citizenship, and the Dutch and British Atlantics," *Itinerario* 36, no. 2 (2012): 75–76.

30. Caspar Barlaeus, *The History of Brazil under the Governorship of Count Johan Maurits of Nassau, 1636–1644*, trans. Blanche Koning (Gainesville: University Press of Florida, 2011), 227.

31. Klooster, *Dutch Moment*, 118.

32. Calado, *O Valeroso Lucideno*, 14.

33. ANTT, *Inquisição de Lisboa*, processo 11562, fol. 46r; Archivio Arcivescovile di Pisa (henceforth AAPi), *Inquisizione*, filza 5, fol. 381r; SAA, 5075, no. 942, fols. 295–96.

34. SAA, 5001, no. 669, fol. 200.

35. For their brother Henrique Mendes Peixoto, a wealthy merchant who lived as a crypto-Jew in southwestern France, see AHN, *Inquisición*, libro 1103, fols. 292v–293r; Baroja, *Los Judíos en España*, 363.

36. Giuseppe Laras, "Diego Lorenzo Piccioto: Un delatore di marrani nella Livorno del seicento," in *Scritti in Memoria di Umberto Nahon: Saggi sull'Ebraismo Italiano*, ed. Roberto Bonfil et al. (Jerusalem: Fondazioni Sally Mayer, 1978), 65–104.

37. Lucia Frattarelli Fischer, *Vivere fuori dal ghetto: Ebrei a Pisa e a Livorno (secoli XVI–XVIII)* (Turin: Silvio Zamorani, 2008).

38. Giuseppe Marcocci, "Itinerari marrani: I portoghesi a Livorno nei secoli dell'età moderna," in Prosperi, *Livorno (1606–1806)*, 405–17.

39. AAPi, *Inquisizione*, filza 5, fols. 380r–381r. For what follows, see fols. 382r–400v.

40. Archivio di Stato di Livorno, *Governatore e Auditore*, filza 3168, no. 549.

41. Archivio di Stato di Livorno, *Governatore e Auditore*, filza 3168, no. 549.

42. ANTT, *Inquisição de Lisboa*, livro 205, fol. 229r.

43. For one of the most famous false accusations based on a child's testimony, see Juan Ignacio Pulido Serrano, *Injurias a Cristo: Religión, política y antijudaísmo en el siglo XVII* (Madrid: Universidad de Alcalá, 2002).

44. ANTT, *Inquisição de Lisboa*, livro 205, fol. 230r.

45. AAPi, *Inquisizione*, filza 5, fol. 586v.

46. Baroja, *Los Judíos en la España*, 363.

47. SAA, 334, no. 1, fols. 114, 163.

48. SAA, 5075, no. 380B, fol. 609; no. 484, fol. 372.

49. SAA, 334, no. 9, fols. 30, 38, 40, 41, 56, 74, 94, 102, 104, 118, 177; no. 3, fols. 64, 121.

50. SAA, 5075, no. 484, fol. 595.

51. Moisés Cohen Peixoto and Jacob Cohen Henriques included their military ranks when signing their poems for a printed book (see below).

52. SAA, 5001, no. 669, fol. 200. After his second marriage, Moisés's tax payments significantly increased. See SAA, 334, no. 9, fols. 56, 70, 77, 83, 91, 107, 122, 132, 143.

53. SAA, 5001, no. 669, fol. 200.

54. SAA, 5075, no. 631, fol. 313.

55. SAA, 5075, no. 941, fol. 157; no. 942, fols. 531-33.

56. SAA, 334, no. 1, fols. 128, 132, 134, 159, 160, 171.

57. SAA, 334, no. 9, fols. 152, 172.

58. SAA, 334, no. 1141, fol. 76. Jonathan Israel, "Piracy, Trade and Religion: The Jewish Role in the Rise of the Muslim Corsair Republic of Saleh (1624–1666)," in *Diasporas within a Diaspora: Jews, Crypto-Jews, and the World of Maritime Empires (1540–1740)* (Leiden: Brill, 2002), 293–307, claimed that the Jewish alias of Francisco Vaz de Leão was Moisés Cohen Henriques, confounding father and son. But their separate identities are unmistakable. See SAA, 5075, no. 942, fols. 565-66, 592; SAA, 5001, no. 671, fol. 285; SAA, 1555A, fols. 281-84. The birth date and alias of Moisés Cohen Henriques have been the subject of much confusion. Before the Inquisition, Isaac Cohen Henriques claimed that "Antônio Henriques" was his baptismal name, and not that of his brother Moisés, whom he said was called Rodrigo and was born in 1611 or 1612 (ANTT, *Inquisição de Lisboa*, processo 7820, fols. 6v-7r). The statement, however, is contradicted by the records of the Jewish community in Amsterdam, which indicate that Moisés held office as early as 1627 (see below). It seems that Isaac deliberately assumed his brother's alias, adopting the common tactic of using fake names or the names of relatives who were beyond the reach of the Inquisition.

59. Daniel Swetschinski, *Reluctant Cosmopolitans: The Portuguese Jews of Seventeenth-Century Amsterdam* (London: Littman Library of Jewish Civilization, 2000), 165–87.

60. SAA, 334, no. 10, fols. 105, 107, 113, 120, 130-32, 134, 156, 162; no. 1142, fols. 1, 33-34, 131.

61. SAA, 334, no. 10, fol. 160.

62. SAA, 5075, no. 941, fols. 146-55, 234-37, 248-49, 651-53; no. 942, fols. 449-50, 1338-39, 1375-77.

63. SAA, 334, no. 3, fol. 116; no. 1051, fol. 11r.

64. SAA, 334, no. 10, fol. 135.

65. Adler, "A Contemporary Memorial," 48.

66. SAA, 5001, no. 671, fol. 214; SAA, 334, no. 11, fols. 30, 33.

67. SAA, 5075, no. 942, fols. 1392-93.

68. SAA, 5001, no. 671, fol. 285.

69. SAA, 334, no. 11, fols. 33, 51.

70. SAA, 5075, no. 941, fols. 516-17; no. 942, fols. 565-66, 591-92.

71. SAA, 5075, no. 942, fols. 438-39, 465-66, 1392-93, 1568-69.

72. SAA, 334, no. 10, fol. 178.

73. ANTT, *Inquisição de Lisboa*, processo 11139, fols. 25v-26r.

74. Isaac Cohen Henriques, Jacob's brother, insisted on this very narrative to justify the change of the family name from *Israel* to *Cohen*: "they were descendants of the tribe of Levi and of the strain of Aaron by the male line, for which reason they were invested with the priesthood, and consequently with the title of Cohen." ANTT, *Inquisição de Lisboa*, processo 7820, fol. 12r.

75. On the meanings behind choices of Jewish names, see Aviva Ben-Ur, *Jewish Autonomy in a Slave Society: Suriname in the Atlantic World, 1651–1825* (Philadelphia: University of Pennsylvania Press, 2020), 36-37. For the role that genealogy played among Iberian Jews and conversos, see Jane Gerber, "Pride and Pedigree: The Development of the Myth of Sephardic Aristocratic Lineage," in *Reappraisals and New Studies of the Modern Jewish Experience: Essays in Honor of Robert M. Seltzer*, ed. Brian Smollett and Christian Wiese (Leiden: Brill, 2014), 85-103.

76. SAA, 334, no. 157, fols. 24-25.

77. Gonsalves de Mello, *Gente da Nação*, 218-23.

78. There is still no consensus in historiography about the size of the Jewish population in Dutch Brazil. See Tiribás, "Mobility, Clandestine Literature, and Censorship," 1055.

79. Nationaal Archief Nederland (henceforth NAN), OWIC [Oude West-Indische Compagnie] 14, fol. 68r.

80. ANTT, *Inquisição de Lisboa*, processo 11562, fol. 46r; SAA, 5001, no. 690, fol. 198. For the levirate marriage among Iberian Jews in Amsterdam, see Tirtsah Levie Bernfeld, "Religious Life among Portuguese Women in Amsterdam's Golden Age," in *The Religious Cultures of Dutch Jewry*, ed. Yosef Kaplan and Dan Michman (Leiden: Brill, 2017), 68.

81. Bruno Feitler, *Inquisition, juifs et nouveaux-chrétiens au Brésil: Le Nordeste XVIIe et XVIIIe siècles* (Leuven: Leuven University Press, 2003), 147-56.

82. ANTT, *Inquisição Lisboa*, livro 217, fol. 518v.

83. Feitler, *Inquisition, juifs et nouveaux-chrétiens*, 151-52. For Machorro, see Meyer Kayserling, "Une Histoire de la Littérature Juive de Daniel Lévi de Barrios," *Revue des études juives* 19 (1889): 287.

84. Elias Lipiner, *Izaque de Castro: O mancebo que veio preso do Brasil* (Recife: Massangana, 1992), 12.

85. The messianic meaning behind the name is evident in a passage of the *Siddur berakha: Orden de bendicion conforme el uso del K.K. de Sepharad* (Amsterdam: Menasseh ben Israel, 1634), unnumbered folio: "We shall not be ashamed in the world to come, and the kingdom of the House of David, Your anointed, shall soon return to its place in our days." Throughout his work, Menasseh ben Israel refers to the Messiah as both, a descendant from the "House of David" and a "captain." For just one earlier example, see Menasseh ben Israel, *De la resurrección de los muertos* (Amsterdam: Menasseh ben Israel, 1636), 151-52. In his inquisitorial trial, the martyr Isaac de Castro Tartas, a member of the congregation in Paraíba, continually insisted on the theme of the Messiah awaited by the Jews, calling him "a captain with a prophetic spirit": ANTT, *Inquisição de Lisboa*,

processo 11550, fols. 51r, 86v, and 93r–94r. For messianism in Jewish congregations in the Caribbean, see Wim Klooster, "Networks of Colonial Entrepreneurs: The Founders of the Jewish Settlements in Dutch America, 1650s and 1660s," in Kagan and Morgan, *Atlantic Diasporas*, 41–42, 48; Aviva Ben-Ur with Rachel Frankel, *Remnant Stones: The Jewish Cemeteries and Synagogues of Suriname. Essays* (Cincinnati: Hebrew Union College Press, 2012), 105–17.

86. ANTT, *Inquisição Lisboa*, livro 217, fols. 518v–520r. For another mention of Peixoto as a rabbi in Paraíba, see AHN, *Inquisición*, libro 1103, fol. 292v. A third witness claimed to have heard that he held an "office in the synagogue" of Amsterdam, but I found no trace of it: AHN, *Inquisición*, libro 1101, fol. 766v.

87. Gonsalves de Mello, *Gente da Nação*, 228–31.

88. Benjamin J. Kaplan, *Divided by Faith: Religious Conflict and the Practice of Toleration in Early Modern Europe* (Cambridge, MA: Belknap Press of Harvard University Press, 2007), 177–79.

89. NAN, OWIC 68, *Dagelijkse Notulen*, November 22, 1638.

90. Frans Leonard Schalkwijk, *Igreja e Estado no Brasil Holandês (1630 a 1654)* (São Paulo: Cultura Cristã, 2004), 315.

91. NAN, OWIC 68, *Dagelijkse Notulen*, November 22, 1638.

92. NAN, OWIC 68, *Dagelijkse Notulen*, September 28, 1638.

93. ANTT, *Inquisição de Lisboa*, livro 220, fol. 387r.

94. Lipiner, *Izaque de Castro*, 12.

95. "Actas da Assemblêa Geral," *Revista do Instituto Archeologico e Geographico Pernambucano* 30–31 (1886): 228.

96. NAN, OWIC 70, *Dagelijkse Notulen*, October 27 and November 12, 1644.

97. Klooster, "Networks of Colonial Entrepreneurs," 34–35.

98. Van Groesen, *Amsterdam's Atlantic*, 108–12.

99. Pedro Puntoni, *A Mísera sorte: A escravidão africana no Brasil holandês e as guerras do tráfico no Atlântico sul, 1621–1648* (São Paulo: Hucitec, 1999), 71–122.

100. Arnold Wiznitzer, *Jews in Colonial Brazil* (New York: Columbia University Press, 1960), 71.

101. Ronaldo Vainfas, *Jerusalém colonial: Judeus portugueses no Brasil holandês* (Rio de Janeiro: Civilização Brasileira, 2010), 123.

102. Gonsalves de Mello, *Gente da Nação*, 233–36.

103. NAN, OWIC 57, no. inv. 190.

104. NAN, OWIC 59, no. inv. 69–70; OWIC 60, no. inv. 14–15.

105. NAN, OWIC 58, no. inv. 6, 10, 183–84, 348–49; OWIC 59, no. inv. 55, 72; OWIC 60, no. inv. 14, 18, 52–53.

106. NAN, OWIC 59, no. inv. 55, 69, 72; OWIC 60, no. inv. 14, 17–18, 50–53.

107. Vainfas, *Jerusalém colonial*, 124. For examples of Jews reselling slaves as part of an intra-Caribbean trade, see Eli Faber, *Jews, Slaves, and the Slave Trade: Setting the Record Straight* (New York: New York University Press, 1998), 54–55.

108. Gonsalves de Mello, *Tempo dos flamengos*, 197. For a deconstruction of the myth that slaves preferred Jewish owners, see also Jonathan Schorsch, *Jews and Blacks in the Early Modern World* (Cambridge: Cambridge University Press, 2004), 296.

109. Johannes Postma, *The Dutch in the Atlantic Slave Trade, 1600–1815* (Cambridge: Cambridge University Press, 2008), 227–58.

110. SAA, 334, no. 1304, fol. 9.

111. Lucia Furquim Xavier, "Sociabilidade no Brasil Holandês (1630–1654)" (PhD diss., Leiden University, 2018), 155–56; Wiznitzer, *Jews in Colonial Brazil*, 72–73.

112. Wiznitzer, "Jewish Soldiers," 42–46.

113. Anonymous, "Diário ou Breve Discurso acerca da Rebellião e dos pérfidos Desígnios dos Portuguezes do Brasil," *Revista do Instituto Arqueológico, Histórico e Geográfico Pernambucano* 32 (1887): 159; see also 139, 167, 190, 195.

114. Herbert Bloom, "A Study of Brazilian Jewish History 1623–1654, Based Chiefly upon the Findings of the Late Samuel Oppenheim," *Publications of the American Jewish Historical Society* 33 (1934): 95.

115. Vainfas, *Jerusalém colonial*, 221–48; Schalkwijk, *Igreja e Estado*, 318–19; Bloom, "A Study of Brazilian Jewish History," 103–4. The Jews of Dutch Brazil received the status of subjects before their coreligionists in Amsterdam. See Jessica Roitman, "Economics, Empire, Eschatology: The Global Context of Jewish Settlement in the Americas, 1650–70," *Itinerario* 40, no. 2 (2016): 298.

116. Wiznitzer, "Jewish Soldiers," 46.

117. SAA, 334, no. 1304, fol. 3 (*Ascama* 10).

118. SAA, 334, no. 1304, fol. 3 (*Ascama* 9).

119. SAA, 334, no. 1304, fols. 25–29.

120. Tiribás, "Mobility, Clandestine Literature, and Censorship," 1062. For this refugee crisis in Amsterdam, see Steven Nadler, Ton Tielen, and Victor Tiribás, "Two New Documents on Spinoza's Biography," *Journal of the History of Philosophy* 58, no. 4 (2020): 805–10.

121. SAA, 334, no. 174, fols. 118, 136, 166, 172, 191.

122. Tiribás, "Mobility, Clandestine Literature, and Censorship."

123. The poet and captain Daniel Levi de Barrios did the same throughout his *Coro de las musas* (Amsterdam: Juan Luis de Pas, 1672). For a further example, see the translation that Captain Joseph Semah Arias made of Flavius Josephus, *Respuesta de Josepho contra Apion Alexandrino* (Amsterdam: David de Castro Tartas, 1687).

124. Daniel de Ribera et al., *Elogios que zelozos dedicaron a la felice memoria de Abraham Nuñez Bernal* (Amsterdam: David de Castro Tartas, 1656), 19, 116.

125. Ribera et al., *Elogios*, 138.

5. Imperial Enterprise

1. David Franks, Baynton & Wharton, et al., Philadelphia, to Moses Franks and George Croghan, December 12, 1763 in *Papers of Sir William Johnson*, vol. 4, ed. Alexander C. Flick (Albany: University of the State of New York, 1965), 267.

2. "Memorial of the Merchants of the Province of Pennsylvania concerned in the late Trade with the Indians" to the Lords Commissioner for Trade and Plantations, December 12, 1763, in *Papers of Sir William Johnson*, 4:267.

3. Franks, Baynton & Wharton et al, Philadelphia, to Franks and Croghan, December 12, 1763, 267.

4. £80,000 in 1763 was approximately equal to £17,000,000 in 2021.

5. Quote from Abigaill Levy Franks to Naphtali Franks, May 7, 1733, in *The Letters of Abigaill Levy Franks, 1733–1748*, ed. Edith B. Gelles (New Haven: Yale University Press, 2004), 3–6. See also Eli Faber, *A Time for Planting: The First Migration, 1654–1820* (Baltimore: Johns Hopkins University, 1992); Jacob Rader Marcus, *Early American Jewry*, vol. 1 (Philadelphia: Jewish Publication Society, 1953); William Pencak, *Jews and Gentiles in Early America, 1654–1800* (Ann Arbor: University of Michigan Press, 2005); Jonathan Sarna, *American Judaism: A History* (New Haven: Yale University Press, 2004).

6. Lois Dubin, "Introduction: Port Jews in the Atlantic World," *Jewish History* 20, no. 2 (2006): 117–27. See also Miriam Bodian, *Hebrews of the Portuguese Nation: Conversos and Community in Early Modern Amsterdam* (Bloomington: Indiana University Press, 1997); David Cesarini, ed., *Port Jews: Jewish Communities in Cosmopolitan Maritime Trading Centres, 1550–1950* (London: Frank Cass, 2002); David Cesarini and Gemma Romain, eds., *Jews and Port Cities, 1590–1990: Commerce, Community and Cosmopolitanism* (London: Vallentine Mitchell, 2006); David Sorkin, "The Port Jew: Notes toward a Social Type," *Journal of Jewish Studies* 50, no. 1 (1999): 87–97; Jonathan Israel, *Diasporas within a Diaspora: Jews, Crypto-Jews, and the World of Maritime Empires (1540–1740)* (Leiden: Brill, 2002); Paolo Bernardini and Norman Fiering, eds., *The Jews and the Expansion of Europe to the West, 1450–1800* (New York: Berghahn, 2001); Richard L. Kagan and Philip D. Morgan, eds., *Atlantic Diasporas: Jews, Conversos, and Crypto-Jews in the Age of Mercantilism, 1500–1800* (Baltimore: Johns Hopkins University Press, 2009); Jessica Vance Roitman, *The Same but Different? Inter-cultural Trade and the Sephardim, 1595–1640* (Leiden: Brill, 2011); Yda Schreuder, *Amsterdam's Sephardic Merchants and the Atlantic Sugar Trade in the Seventeenth Century* (Cham: Palgrave Macmillan, 2019); Daviken Studnicki-Gizbert, *A Nation upon the Ocean Sea: Portugal's Atlantic Diaspora and the Crisis of the Spanish Empire, 1492–1640* (New York: Oxford University Press, 2007); Daniel M. Swetschinski, *Reluctant Cosmopolitans: The Portuguese Jews of Seventeenth-Century Amsterdam* (Portland, OR: Littman Library of Jewish Civilization, 2000); Francesca Trivellato, *The Familiarity of Strangers: The Sephardic Diaspora, Livorno, and Cross-Cultural Trade in the Early Modern Period* (New Haven: Yale University Press, 2009).

7. Toni Pitock, "'Separated from Us as Far as West Is from East': Eighteenth-Century Ashkenazi Immigrants in the Atlantic World," *American Jewish History* 102, no. 2 (2018): 173–93. See also Natalie Zemon Davis, "Epilogue," in Kagan and Morgan, *Atlantic Diasporas*, 213–17.

8. Peggy Liss, *Atlantic Empires: The Network of Trade and Revolution, 1713–1826* (Baltimore: Johns Hopkins University Press, 1983), 2–5; P. J. Marshall, *The Making and Unmaking of Empires: Britain, India, and American, c. 1750–1783* (Oxford: Oxford University Press, 2007), 5–7, 13.

9. Liss, *Atlantic Empires*, 15–17; Marshall, *Making and Unmaking of Empires*, 7, 57–59, 113–18, 157–60.

10. Michael Graetz, "Court Jews in Economics and Politics," in *From Court Jews to the Rothschilds*, ed. Vivian B. Mann and Richard I. Cohen (Munich: Prestel,

1997), 27–43; Jonathan Israel, *European Jewry in the Age of Mercantilism, 1550–1750*, 3rd ed. (Portland, OR: Littman Library of Jewish Civilization, 1998).

11. Hannah Weiss Muller, *Subjects and Sovereign: Bonds of Belonging in the Eighteenth-Century British Empire* (New York: Oxford University Press, 2017), 2, 6–7, 9. See also Carla Pestana, *Protestant Empire: Religion and the Making of the British Atlantic World* (Philadelphia: University of Pennsylvania Press, 2009).

12. Graetz, "Court Jews," 39; Israel, *European Jewry*, 101.

13. Marshall, *Making and Unmaking of Empires*, 13.

14. W. Rubinstein and Michael A. Jolles, eds., *The Palgrave Dictionary of Anglo-Jewish History* (Hampshire: Palgrave, 2011), 293–96; Matt Goldish, "The Strange Adventures of Benjamin Franks, an Ashkenazi Pioneer in the Americas," in *The Jews in the Caribbean*, ed. Jane S. Gerber (Oxford: Littman Library of Jewish Civilization, 2014), 311–18; Walter J. Fischel, "The Jewish Merchant-Colony in Madras during the 17th and 18th Centuries: A Contribution to the Economic and Social History of the Jews in India (Concluded)," *Journal of the Economic and Social History of the Orient* 3, no. 2 (1960): 175–95; *Letters of Abigaill Levy Franks*, xix–xx; Jacob Rader Marcus, *The Colonial American Jew, 1492–1776*, 3 vols. (Detroit: Wayne State University Press, 1970), 1:379; Cecil Roth, *The Great Synagogue: London 1690–1940* (London: Edward Goldston & Son, 1950), 26, 62–63; Malcolm H. Stern, *Americans of Jewish Descent: A Compendium of Genealogy* (Cincinnati: Hebrew Union College Press, 1960); Gedalia Yogev, *Diamonds and Coral: Anglo-Dutch Jews and Eighteenth-Century Trade* (Leicester: Leicester University Press, 1978), 65, 113, 152–54; Rachel Daiches-Dubens, "Eighteenth Century Anglo-Jewry in and around Richmond, Surrey," *Transactions of the Jewish Historical Society of England* 18 (1953–55): 146, 150; Todd M. Endelman, *The Jews of Georgian England, 1714–1830* (Ann Arbor: University of Michigan Press, 1999), 132, 251.

15. S. Max Edelson, *The New Map of Empire: How Britain Imagined America before Independence* (Cambridge, MA: Harvard University Press, 2017), 2–3.

16. *Letters of Abigaill Levy Franks*, 133. See also Eli Faber, *Jews, Slaves, and the Slave Trade: Setting the Record Straight* (New York: New York University Press, 1998), 134, 179; Marcus, *The Colonial American Jew*, 2:580, 617, 712–23, 723–24.

17. Jerome H. Wood Jr., *Conestoga Crossroads: Lancaster, Pennsylvania, 1730–1790* (Harrisburg: Pennsylvania Historical And Museum Commission, 1979), 93–94; Thomas M. Doerflinger, *A Vigorous Spirit of Enterprise: Merchants and Economic Development in Revolutionary Philadelphia* (Chapel Hill: University of North Carolina Press, 1986), 15, 76; Marshall, *Making and Unmaking of Empires*, 15, 19, 20; Judith Ridner, "Relying of the 'Saucy' Men of the Backcountry: Middlemen and the Fur Trade in Pennsylvania," *Pennsylvania Magazine of History and Biography* 129, no. 2 (2005): 133–62; A. T. Volwiler, "George Croghan and the Westward Movement, 1741–1782," *Pennsylvania Magazine of History and Biography* 46, no. 4 (1922): 273–311.

18. Toni Pitock, "Commerce and Connection: Jewish Merchants, Philadelphia, and the Atlantic World, 1736–1822" (PhD diss., University of Delaware, 2016), 53–63, 60–69.

19. Franks was a member of a group of about two dozen traders, the "Sufferers of 1754," whose goods were destroyed in a series of attacks by the French

and their Indian allies. This group valued their combined losses at £48,000. See Mark Abbott Stern, *David Franks: Colonial Merchant* (University Park: Pennsylvania State University Press, 2010), 30; Volwiler, "George Croghan"; Sidney M. Fish, *Barnard and Michael Gratz: Their Lives and Times* (Lanham: University Press of America, 1994), 45, 81–84. See also Nicholas Wainwright, "An Indian Trade Failure: The Story of the Hockley, Trent and Croghan Company, 1748-1752," *Pennsylvania Magazine of History and Biography* 72, no. 4 (1948): 345; Edelson, *New Map of Empire*, 2–3.

20. Craig Bailey, "The Nesbitts of London and Their Networks," in *Irish and Scottish Mercantile Networks in Europe and Overseas in the Seventeenth and Eighteenth Centuries*, ed. David Dickson, Jan Parmentier, and Jane Ohlmeyer (Gent: Academia Press, 2007), 231; H. V. Bowen, "Colebrooke, Sir George, second baronet (1729–1809)," *Oxford Dictionary of National Biography*, online edition, September 2004, https://doi.org/10.1093/ref:odnb/37301.

21. Bailey, "The Nesbitts of London," 237–38.

22. Kings Warrant for payment to Sir James Colebrooke et al., contractors for supplying British forces in North America, signatures appearing include King George II, the Duke of Newcastle, and Moses Franks, 1760, Franks Family Papers, P-142, Box 1, Folder 12, American Jewish Historical Society, New York (hereafter AJHS); and in *The Papers of Henry Bouquet*, ed. Sylvester Kirby Steven et al., 19 vols. (Harrisburg: Pennsylvania Historical and Museum Commission, 1984), 4:468n; Account of Contractors for Victualing Troops, *Papers of Henry Bouquet*, 4:569; Stern, *David Franks*, 34–35.

23. Jeffery Amherst to Governor James Hamilton, March 21, 1760, SC 3651, American Jewish Archives, Cincinnati, Ohio (henceforth AJA).

24. Letter to David Franks, September 16, 1762; Letter to Messrs Thompson, Paris and Company, September 16, 1762; David Franks, Letters regarding Purchase of Supplies for British Garrisons, SC 3652, AJA (from Bouquet Papers, Public Archives of Canada); "The Crown in Account with William Plumsted and David Franks," for May 1760–May 1761, dated June 1761, Horatio Gates Papers, New-York Historical Society; David Franks to George Washington, June 27, 1758, SC 3656, AJA; Jeffery Amherst to Plumsted and Franks, June 19, 1763, *Papers of Henry Bouquet*, 6:243; see also Stern, *David Franks*, 33, 47.

25. Pitock, "'Separated from Us as Far as West Is from East.'"

26. Until recently, the scholarly focus on Jews' kinship and ethnoreligious networks emphasized the idea that a shared cultural heritage promoted trust, which was essential since trade was extremely risky. On Jewish networks, see Cornelia Aust, "Commercial Cosmopolitans: Networks of Jewish Merchants between Warsaw and Amsterdam, 1750–1820" (PhD diss., University of Pennsylvania, 2010); Noah Gelfand, "A People Within and Without: International Jewish Commerce and Community in the Seventeenth and Eighteenth Centuries Dutch Atlantic World" (PhD diss., New York University, 2008); Roitman, *The Same but Different?*; Sarah Abrevaya Stein, *Plumes: Ostrich Feathers, Jews, and a Lost World of Global Commerce* (New Haven: Yale University Press, 2008); Studnicki-Gizbert, *A Nation upon the Ocean Sea*; Francesca Trivellato, "Sephardic Merchants in the Early Modern Atlantic and Beyond: Toward a Comparative Historical Approach to Business Cooperation," in Kagan and Morgan, *Atlantic Diasporas*,

99-120, and Trivellato, *Familiarity of Strangers*; Tijl Vanneste, *Global Trade and Commercial Networks: Eighteenth-Century Diamond Merchants* (London: Pickering & Chatto, 2011).

27. Pitock, "Commerce and Connection," 116, 120-21.

28. Liss, *Atlantic Empires*, 15-16; Marshall, *Making and Unmaking of Empires*, 7, 15, 64.

29. Fred Anderson, *Crucible of War: The Seven Years' War and the Fate of Empire in British North America, 1754-1766* (New York: Alfred A. Knopf, 2000), 25-30; Walter S. Dunn Jr., *Frontier Profit and Loss: The British Army and the Fur Traders, 1760-1764* (Westport: Greenwood Press, 1998); Eric Hinderaker, *Elusive Empires: Constructing Colonialism in the Ohio Valley, 1673-1800* (New York: Cambridge University Press, 1997), 40-41; Volwiler, "George Croghan"; Nicholas Wainwright, *George Croghan: Wilderness Diplomat* (Chapel Hill: University of North Carolina Press, 1959).

30. David Franks Account Book, 1760-1767, (Phi) Am 0684 Franks, Historical Society of Pennsylvania, Philadelphia, PA (henceforth HSP); this account book pertains to Franks's joint venture with Simon, Levy, and Trent. Barnard Gratz account with David Franks, Gratz-Franks-Simon Papers (McA MSS 011), McAllister Collection, Box 2, Folder 64, Library Company of Philadelphia (henceforth LCP) [Barnard Gratz's Day Book]. David Franks Account Book, 1757-1762, Frank M. Etting Collection, Collection 0193, Box 1a, HSP; see also Joseph Simon to Barnard Gratz, August 17, 1762, August 29, 1762, May 30, 1763, Gratz-Franks-Simon Papers (McA MSS 011), McAllister Collection, Box 1, Folder 47, LCP.

31. George Croghan, Fort Pitt, to Trent and Lowery, February 5, 1761, *Papers of Henry Bouquet*, 5:282.

32. John W. Jordan, "James Kenny's 'Journal to Ye Westward,' 1758-1759," *Pennsylvania Magazine of History and Biography* 37, no. 1 (1913): 13.

33. John Langdale to Henry Bouquet, Pittsburgh, March 5, 1761, *Papers of Henry Bouquet*, 5:328-31.

34. Walter S. Dunn Jr., *Opening New Markets: The British Army and the Old Northwest* (Westport: Praeger, 2002), 2.

35. David Franks Account Book, 1760-1767, (Phi) Am 0684 Franks, HSP.

36. Anderson, *Crucible of War*, 453, 545, 558-59; Patrick Spero, *Frontier Rebels: The Fight for Independence in the American West, 1765-1776* (New York: W. W. Norton, 2018), xx.

37. David Franks to Michael Gratz, Philadelphia, June 12, 1763, Gratz-Franks-Simon Papers (McA MSS 011), McAllister Collection, Series 1, Box 1, Folder 17, LCP. It is unclear who Levy's servants were. "List of Indian Traders and Their Servants Killed or Capture by Indians": Henry Bouquet to Jeffery Amherst, September 30, 1763, *Papers of Henry Bouquet*, 6:412.

38. David Franks Account Book, 1760-1767, (Phi) Am 0684, HSP; List of Losses of Indian Traders, February 1765, in *Papers of Sir William Johnson*, vol. 11, ed. Milton W. Hamilton (Albany: University of the State of New York, 1953), 613.

39. Henry Bouquet to Jeffery Amherst, June 4, 1763, *Papers of Henry Bouquet*, 6:205-6.

40. Plumsted and Franks, Philadelphia to Henry Bouquet, July 18, 1763, *Papers of Henry Bouquet*, 6:319-20.

41. Plumsted and Franks to Henry Bouquet, July 18, 1763; Henry Bouquet, Fort Loudoun to Plumsted and Franks, July 19, 1763, *Papers of Henry Bouquet*, 6:319-21.

42. Henry Bouquet, Fort Pitt, to Plumsted and Franks, September 30, 1763, *Papers of Henry Bouquet*, 6:418-20.

43. Henry Bouquet, Fort Pitt, to Plumsted and Franks, October 26, 1763, *Papers of Henry Bouquet*, 6:440-42.

44. Weiss Muller, *Subjects and Sovereign*, 6-7.

45. John Watts, New York, to Moses Franks, April 14, 1764, in *Letter Book of John Watts, Merchant and Councillor of New York: January 1, 1762–December 22, 1765*, ed. Dorothy C. Barck (New York: New York Historical Society, 1928), 240.

46. Robert Harrison, "Fludyer, Sir Samuel, first baronet (1704/5-1768)," in *Oxford Dictionary of National Biography*, online edition, January 2008, http://www.oxforddnb.com/view/article/9777.

47. Plumsted and Franks to Thomas Gage, December 8, 1763, Gage Papers, American Series, vol. 10, William L. Clements Library, University of Michigan, Ann Arbor, MI; General Gage, New York, to Henry Bouquet, March 6, 1764, *Papers of Henry Bouquet*, 6:498-500.

48. Agreement between Franks, Inglis, and General Thomas Gage, February 4, 1765, Gage Papers, American Series, vol. 30, Clements Library (also in SC 3636, AJA); Thomas Gage, New York, to Henry Bouquet, February 6, 1765, Gage Papers, American Series, vol. 30, Clements Library.

49. Henry Bouquet, Philadelphia to Thomas Gage, June 21, 1764, *Papers of Henry Bouquet*, 6:575-76.

50. Franks and Inglis were retained as agents; Barclay had moved to Canada. Articles of Agreement between commissioners of his Majesty's Treasury and Nesbitt, Drummond, and Franks, July 14, 1766; Grey Cooper, Treasury Chambers, to Thomas Gage, August 20, 1766; and Nesbitt, Drummond, and Franks, London, to Thomas Gage, August 9, 1766, Gage Papers, English Series, vol. 7, Clements Library; Thomas Gage, New York, to Inglis and Franks, September 2, 1766; Thomas Gage to Inglis and Franks, September 29, 1766, Gage Papers, American Series, vol. 57; and Thomas Gage to Inglis, Franks, and Barclay, December 4, 1766, Gage Papers, American Series, vol. 60, Clements Library; Stern, *David Franks*, 86; Dunn, *Opening New Markets*, 161, notes the renewal of the contract with Fludyer, Drummond, and Franks.

51. Edelson, *New Map of Empire*, 2-3; Patrick Griffin, *American Leviathan: Empire, Nation, and Revolutionary Frontier* (New York: Hill and Wang, 2007), 25, 35-36; Spero, *Frontier Rebels*, 8-9, 119-24, 131-33; Marshall, *Making and Unmaking of Empires*, 115-18.

52. Charles Grant, Commander at Fort Loudoun, to Henry Bouquet, March 9, 1765, enclosure in Henry Bouquet to Thomas Gage, March 16, 1765, Gage Papers, American Series, vol. 32, Clements Library; Henry Bouquet, Philadelphia, to Thomas Gage, March 29, 1765, Thomas Gage, New York, to Governor Penn, March 30, 1765, Thomas Gage, New York, to George Croghan, April 4, 1765, Thomas Gage to Henry Bouquet, April 4, 1765, Gage Papers,

American Series, vol. 33, Clements Library; Dunn, *Opening New Markets*, 80–81, 99–100, 119.

53. George Croghan account with Simon, Levy and Company, March 23, 1765, in William Vincent Byars, *B. & M. Gratz: Merchants in Philadelphia, 1754–1798: Papers of Interest to Their Posterity and the Posterity of Their Associates* (Jefferson City: Hugh Stephens Printing, 1916), 69–71; Joseph Simon, Lancaster, to Barnard Gratz, February 17, 1767, Gratz Family Papers, Mss.Ms.Coll. 72, Series I, LCP; and Joseph Simon, Lancaster, to Barnard Gratz, May 10, 1767, Gratz-Franks-Simon Papers (McA MSS 011), McAllister Collection, Series 1, Box 1, Folder 47, LCP.

54. Inglis and Franks to Thomas Gage, September 4, 1766, Gage Papers, American Series, vol. 56, and Thomas Gage to Inglis, Franks, and Barclay, December 4, 1766, Gage Papers, American Series, vol. 60, Clements Library. According to Dunn, the rations cost £15,000 sterling in 1766 compared with £4,849 elsewhere. Dunn, *Opening New Markets*, 159.

55. Baynton, Wharton, and Morgan, Philadelphia, to Thomas Gage, December 26, 1765, and Thomas Gage, New York, to Baynton, Wharton, and Morgan, Gage Papers, American Series, vol. 46, Clements Library; Dunn, *Opening New Markets*, 161–63.

56. Marcus, *The Colonial American Jew*, 2:592; Stern, *David Franks*, 88.

57. William Murray, Fort Pitt, to Thomas Gage, August 24, 1767, Gage Papers, American Series, vol. 68, Clements Library; Proposal to Messrs Rumsey & Co for the purchase of Baynton and Co Goods, October 18, 1770, Rumsey and Murray account with David Franks, SC 3640, AJA; Dunn, *Opening New Markets*, 165.

58. Edelson, *New Map of Empire*, 9; Marshall, *Making and Unmaking of Empires*, 117–18, 162; Spero, *Frontier Rebels*, 8–9; Wainwright, *George Croghan*, 162–76.

59. The editors of *Papers of Sir William Johnson*, 4:199, note a September 1, 1763, entry in the Johnson calendar of the receipt of a letter from Franks and other merchants, asking for Johnson's support.

60. Griffin, *American Leviathan*, 35–39, 53–54; Dunn, *Opening New Markets*, 113.

61. Marshall, *Making and Unmaking of Empires*, 117.

62. *Papers of Henry Bouquet*, 5:439n; Barnard Gratz, Memorial to the House Representatives in the Pennsylvania General Assembly, n.d., Gratz-Sulzberger Papers, SC 4292, AJA (copies from AJHS).

63. Anderson, *Crucible of War*, 565–69; Griffin, *American Leviathan*, 55, 101.

64. Thomas Gage, New York, to George Croghan, May 22, 1765, and July 23, 1765, and Thomas Gage to Lieut. Gov. Penn, June 2, 1765, Gage Papers, American Series, vol. 7, Clements Library; Fish, *Barnard and Michael Gratz*, 84–85; Griffin, *American Leviathan*, 55–56.

65. Proceedings from Fort Stanwix, 1768, Grant from the Six Nations, Frank M. Etting Collection, Collection 0193, Ohio Company Papers, vol. 1, box 58, HSP; Spero, *Frontier Rebels*, 138–42; Fish, *Barnard and Michael Gratz*, 93–95; Griffin, *American Leviathan*, 84–85; Stern, *David Franks*, 62, 96–97. The actual size of the tract is unclear. According to Fish it was 3,500,000 acres.

66. Edward Shippen, Joseph Morris, Benjamin Levy, David Franks, Thomas Lawrence, Samuel Wharton to Moses Franks, January 4, 1769, Frank M. Etting Collection, Collection 0193, Ohio Company Papers, vol 1, box 58, HSP.

67. Memorial of Moses Franks to the King, Frank M. Etting Collection, Collection 0193, Ohio Company Papers, vol. 1, box 58, HSP.

68. See Fish, *Barnard and Michael Gratz*, 102–9; Griffin, *American Leviathan*, 88; Stern, *David Franks*, 97–98.

69. Barnard and Michael Gratz to George Croghan, April 27, 1772, Michael Gratz Letter Book 1769–1772, Frank M. Etting Collection, Collection 0193, Flat File 193, HSP; Toni Pitock, "Michael Gratz," in *Immigrant Entrepreneurship: German-American Business Biographies, 1720 to the Present*, ed. Marianne Wokeck, vol. 1, http://www.immigrantentrepreneurship.org/entry.php?rec=212; Griffin, *American Leviathan*, 72–94; Fish, *Barnard and Michael Gratz*, 100, 121.

70. A contract between the firm and King George III, dated April 2, 1776, survives stipulating that they were to furnish supplies to twelve thousand British troops from January 1776 to May 1777, SC 3684, AJA. But in his Loyalist claim, David Franks purported to have served as agent to the contractors from November 24, 1776, until February 25, 1779. See David Franks Loyalist Claims, SC 3653, AJA.

71. David Franks to Major John Andre, December 2, 1779, Clinton Papers, vol. 53:35, Clements Library; John Robinson, Whitehall, to Henry Clinton, April 30 and October 9, 1778, SC 10225, AJA; two sets of bills of exchange for £300 sterling each from David Franks to Nesbitt, Drummond, and Franks in favor of Tench Coxe, May 28, 1778, David Franks Legal Documents and Correspondence, 1744–1778, SC 3643, AJA. See also Pitock, "Commerce and Connection," 348.

72. Richard Rowland for Nesbitt, Drummond, and Franks, London, to David Franks, March 6, 1779, Clinton Papers, vol. 53:35, Clements Library; Moses Franks, London, to David Franks, April 4, 1779, Coxe Family Papers, Collection 2049, Series 2, box 8, folder 13, HSP.

73. David Franks Loyalist Claims, June 12, 1786, SC 3653, AJA.

74. Moses Franks, Jr., Isleworth, to Barnard Gratz, Richmond, [month illegible], 1789, Gratz Family Papers, Mss.Ms.Coll. 72, Series I, LCP.

75. When David and Moses Franks came of age, New York was home to the largest Jewish community in what would become the United States, approximately two hundred Jews. When David Franks moved to Philadelphia in 1741, he was one of a handful of Jews. During the course of the next decade, only ten to twenty Jewish families inhabited Philadelphia and the surrounding region. See Hasia R. Diner, *The Jews of the United States, 1654 to 2000* (Berkeley: University of California Press, 2004), 27; Faber, *A Time for Planting*, 34, 39; Pitock, "Commerce and Connection," 52–66, 71–82, 531.

6. Declarations of Interdependence

1. *Journal of the House of Assembly of Lower-Canada*, 4th Provincial Parliament, 3rd Sess. (1807): 602–4; 4th Provincial Parliament, 4th Sess. (1808): 22–23, 38–39, 60–61, 72–75, 106–9, 114–23, 128–31, 142–45; 5th Provincial Parliament, 1st Sess. (1809): 76–77, 106–13, 200–201, 218–19, 222–23, 242–51, 264–65.

2. Ezekiel Hart's story has been related in great detail, most recently by Sheldon and Judith Godfrey, Michael Brown, Gerald Tulchinsky, and Richard

Menkis, who provide complementary accounts. Sheldon J. Godfrey and Judith C. Godfrey, *Search Out the Land: The Jews and the Growth of Equality in British Colonial America, 1740–1867* (Montreal: McGill University Press, 1995), 171–85; Gerald Tulchinsky, *Taking Root: The Origins of the Canadian Jewish Community* (Hanover, NH: Brandeis University Press, 1993), 24–29; Michael Brown, *Jew or Juif? Jews, French Canadians, and Anglo-Canadians, 1759–1914* (Philadelphia: Jewish Publication Society of America, 1986), 196–98; Richard Menkis, "Antisemitism and Anti-Judaism in Pre-Confederation Canada," in *Antisemitism in Canada: History and Interpretation*, ed. Alan Davies (Québec: Wilfred Laurier University Press, 2006), 11–38. Attempts to analyze and understand L'affaire Hart go back to the nineteenth century, as Brown notes. Brown, *Jew or Juif?*, 308–9n100.

3. Godfrey and Godfrey, *Search Out the Land*, 146–52, 171–81, 238t–240t.

4. Henry Straus Quixano Henriques, *The Jews and the English Law* (London: Bibliophile Press, 1908), 177–78. Under the rule of the Plantagenet kings, from Henry I to John Lackland (roughly 1100–1201), Jewish trade and property had been specifically protected by the Crown on the theory that it was a resource that could be exploited at will through confiscation, taxation, or the imposition of special fees by the Crown. While this royal favor enabled Jews to engage freely in those activities that were specifically permitted to them (i.e., usury), English Jews were thereby made wholly dependent upon the intercession of the Crown to insulate them from the retribution of those to whom they lent money. On the condition of the Jews as serfs of the English Crown, see Salo Wittmayer Baron, *A Social and Religious History of the Jews*, 18 vols., 2nd ed., rev. and enl. (New York: Columbia University Press; Philadelphia: Jewish Publication Society of America, 1957), 4:75–86, 203–4.

5. See, e.g., David S. Katz, *Philo-Semitism and the Readmission of the Jews to England, 1603–1655* (Oxford: Clarendon Press, 1982), 158–231.

6. This dictum is laid out in canon 69 of the Fourth Lateran, which is one of four canons issued by the council that concern Jews. See H. J. Schroeder, trans., "Fourth Lateran Council, 'Canons Concerning Jews' (1215)," Council of Centers on Jewish-Christian Relations, December 20, 2008, https://ccjr.us/dialogika-resources/primary-texts-from-the-history-of-the-relationship/lateran4.

7. Distinctions in Jewish dress were laid out in canon 68 of the Fourth Lateran. Schroeder, "Fourth Lateran Council, 'Canons Concerning Jews' (1215)." For textual description and visual examples of clothing specifically mandated for Jews to wear in England as well as in various nations on the European continent between 1200 and 1600 CE, see Alfred Rubens, *A History of Jewish Costume* (New York: Funk & Wagnalls, 1967), 92–107.

8. James Harrington, *"The Commonwealth of Oceana" and "A System of Politics,"* ed. J. G. A. Pocock (Cambridge: Cambridge University Press, 1992), 6.

9. John Dury, *A Case of Conscience, Whether It Be Lawful to Admit Jews into a Christian Common-wealth?* (London: Richard Wodenothe, 1656), 4.

10. Dury, *A Case of Conscience*, 5, 9.

11. John Russell Bartlett, *Records of the Colony of Rhode Island*, 3:160. The case against the eight "fforeigne borne" Jews was brought to trial on March 13, 1685, and resulted in a jury verdict in favor of the eight merchants, with court costs

NOTES TO PAGES 122-127

charged to Dyer. The goods retained pursuant to the writ of attachment were subsequently returned to them. *Dyre v. Campanell et al.*, General Court of Trial, March Term 1685, Newport Record Book A, fol. 73, Collection of the Rhode Island Supreme Court Judicial Records Center.

12. The National Archives of the United Kingdom, CO 137/1, Petition of Anthony Gomez Serra, Nunes Fernandes Nunes, Andrew Lopez, and Manoel Lopez Pereyra of London, June 28, 1695, 230-31.

13. Holly Snyder, "A Sense of Place: Jews, Identity, and Social Status in Colonial British America, 1654-1831" (PhD diss., Brandeis University, 2000), 113-17. See also David S. Katz, *The Jews in the History of England, 1485-1850* (Oxford: Clarendon Press, 1996), 188-89.

14. Katz, *Jews in the History of England*, 234-36, 245-59; Dana Rabin, "The Jew Bill of 1753: Masculinity, Virility, and the Nation," *Eighteenth-Century Studies* 39, no. 2 (2006): 157-71.

15. Theodore de la Guard, *The Simple Cobbler of Aggavvam in America* (London: J. D. & R. I. for Stephen Bowtell, 1647), 3.

16. Patricia U. Bonomi, *Under the Cope of Heaven: Religion, Society and Politics in Colonial America* (New York: Oxford University Press, 1986), 17-29.

17. Jonathan D. Sarna and David G. Dalin, eds., *Religion and State in the American Jewish Experience* (South Bend: Notre Dame University Press, 1997), 4-5, 82-85; Leon Hühner, "The Struggle for Religious Liberty in North Carolina, with Special Reference to the Jews," *Publications of the American Jewish Historical Society* (1907): 46-52, 68-71; Samuel Clark, comp., *The American Orator, Selected Chiefly from American Authors; for the use of Schools and Private Families* (Gardiner: Intelligencer Office, 1828), 46-49.

18. *A Narrative of the Proceedings of the Jews, in Their Attempt to Establish Their Right to the Elective Franchise in Jamaica. To Which is Added, a Correct Report of the Action brought by Levy Hyman, Esq. Against Samuel Joseph Geoghegan, Esq. Returning Officer, for Refusing His Vote. In a Series of Letters, from a Gentleman of Kingston, to His Friend Off the Island* (Belfast: A. MacKay, Jun., 1823), 1-46. Letter writers who advocated Jewish voting rights included *Philanthropos, Vetus, Candidus, Justice, A JEW*, and *A Citizen of the World*; their letters appeared in the *Kingston Chronicle*, *The Royal Gazette* (Kingston), and the *Cornwall Chronicle* (Montego Bay). The anonymous author of the *Narrative* notes that some newspapers (notably the *Jamaica Courant* and the *St. Jago Gazette*) declined to print letters on this topic.

19. *A Narrative of the Proceedings of the Jews*, 53-70, 102-9.

20. The story of Levy Hyman's attempt to vote is recounted at greater length in Holly Snyder, "Rules, Rights and Redemption: The Negotiation of Jewish Status in British Atlantic Port Towns, 1740-1831," *Jewish History* 20, no. 2 (2006): 147-70.

21. Godfrey and Godfrey, *Search Out the Land*, 173-74; Snyder, "Rules, Rights and Redemption."

22. *A Narrative of the Proceedings of the Jews*, 20-23.

23. Helen Taft Manning, *The Revolt of French Canada: A Chapter in the History of the British Commonwealth* (New York: St. Martin's Press, 1962), 23-25.

24. Godfrey and Godfrey, *Search Out the Land*, table 6: 239-40. The Godfreys note that "exercise of the franchise [voting] without challenge" happened far

later in England (1867) than it did in Canada, where Nova Scotia and New Brunswick passed laws that enfranchised Jews in 1789 and 1810 respectively. The abolition of state oaths also occurred earlier in pre-Confederation Canada (1832 in Lower Canada and 1833 in Upper Canada) than it did in England (1858).

25. Denis Vaugeois, *The First Jews in North America: The Extraordinary Story of the Hart Family, 1760–1860*, trans. Kathe Roth (Montreal: Baraka Books, 2012), 73–74.

26. Ursula Henriques, *Religious Tolerance in England, 1787–1833* (Toronto: University of Toronto Press, 1961), 136–74. The publisher of the Jamaican volume, Alexander Mackay Jr., was of a Belfast Protestant family and inherited his printing and publishing business from his father of the same name. Embedded in the local Protestant publishing network in Belfast, MacKay's family associations leaned decidedly toward Protestant interests in Northern Ireland and lowland Scotland. Why he chose to publish a set of letters that could have been viewed as stimulative—or at least sympathetic—to the cause of Catholic Emancipation at this particular moment remains something of a mystery. For context, see Roger Dixon, "Belfast Publishing," in *The Irish Book in English, 1800–1891*, ed. James H. Murphy, The Oxford History of the Irish Book, 4 (Oxford University Press, 2011), 73; Frank Ferguson, "Ulster-Scots Literature," in Murphy, *The Irish Book in English*, 423–24. The history of the Mackay family as Belfast publishers is laid out in "Address and Presentation to Mrs. Henderson, Norwood Tower," *Belfast News-Letter*, November 16, 1887, 5.

27. As quoted in M. C. N. Salbstein, *The Emancipation of the Jews in Britain: The Question of Admission of Jews to Parliament, 1828–1860* (Rutherford, NJ: Fairleigh Dickinson University Press, 1982), 44 (emphasis added); David Feldman, *Englishmen and Jews: Social, Religious and Political Culture, 1840–1914* (New Haven: Yale University Press, 1994), 2–3; Katz, *Jews in the History of England*, 384–88. Salbstein observes that, after 1707, English law authorized the administration of the Oath of Abjuration ("upon the true faith of a Christian") to prospective voters. However, enforcement was contingent upon the request of a third party, and remarkably spotty. Consequently, as Katz notes, Jews did manage to vote in some areas prior to the removal of the oath-taking requirements in 1835. Salbstein, *Emancipation of the Jews in Britain*, 51; Katz, *Jews in the History of England*, 386; *A Narrative of the Proceedings of the Jews*, 3, 92. By this point, Jews had already been voting at the federal level without challenge in both the United States and Canada for at least three decades. See note 24, above.

28. *Acts and Laws of His Majesties Colony of Rhode-Island, and Providence Plantations in America* (Boston: John Allen, for Nicholas Boone, 1719).

29. Sidney S. Rider, *An Inquiry Concerning the Origin of the Clause in the Laws of Rhode Island (1719–1783) Disfranchising Roman Catholics*, Rhode Island Historical Tracts, Second Series, 1 (Providence: Sidney S. Rider, 1889), 1–9, citing Robert Walsh, *An Appeal from the Judgments of Great Britain Respecting the United States of America Part First Containing an Historical Outline of Their Merits and Wrongs as Colonies, and Strictures upon the Calumnies of the British Writers* (Philadelphia: Mitchell, Ames and White, 1819), 428–35; Bartlett, *Records of the Colony of Rhode Island and Providence Plantations* (1856), 1:504–19; 2:36–37. Close examination of Rhode

Island legislative history casts doubt on the validity of this law. Rider concluded that the purported "statute" as set out in the 1719 Digest of Laws was never officially enacted by the assembly, but rather was Ward's unauthorized invention. Examination of the assembly's 1663/64 proceedings by two subsequent Rhode Island secretaries of state, Samuel Eddy (in 1818) and John Russell Bartlett (in 1856), revealed no such enactment. Some years later, Ward was censured by the assembly after being caught red-handed "affixing the Colony's seal to false record" following an inconclusive assembly debate over the issuance of paper money. Bartlett, *Records of the Colony of Rhode Island* (1707–40), 4:456-63; William Wanton, *A True Representation of the Conduct of the Late Secretary Mr. Richard Ward, in Reference to Some Papers that Were Prepared to be Sent Home to England against this Colony* ([Newport], 1733). Despite its evident falsity, the 1719 "statute" appeared in each subsequent edition of the Rhode Island Digest of Laws, remained in common practice, and was actively used as a means of disfranchising Jews and Catholics to the end of the Revolution.

30. For the Petition of Lopez and Elizer for naturalization, see Record Book E of the Newport Superior Court of Judicature, fols. 171 (August 1761), 184 (March 1762), at the Rhode Island Supreme Court Judicial Records Center; Petition of Aaron Lopez, October 30, 1761, in Petitions to the Rhode Island General Assembly, Rhode Island State Archives.

31. Rider, *An Inquiry Concerning the Origin of the Clause*, 14-22, 24-26.

32. Philip Lawson, "'Sapped by Corruption': British Governance of Québec and the Breakdown of Anglo-American Relations on the Eve of Revolution," *Canadian Review of American Studies* 22, no. 3 (Winter 1991): 307-8. As Lawson notes, the shift was experienced by Anglo-Americans as so dramatically different from their expectations that it upended colonists' relations with the mother country.

33. Fernand Ouellet, *Economic and Social History of Québec, 1760–1850: Structures and Conjonctures* [sic], trans. Institute of Canadian Studies at Carleton University, The Carleton Library 120 (n.p.: Gage Publishing, for the Institute of Canadian Studies, 1980), 147-54.

34. Ouellet, *Economic and Social History of Québec*, 155-72, 175-203.

35. Jean-Pierre Wallot, "Revolution et Reformisme dans Le Bas-Canada (1773–1815)," *Annales historiques de la Révolution Française* 45, no. 213 (1973): 347, 352-62; Ouellet, *Economic and Social History of Québec*, 203-5, 209-11. On the impact of the French Revolution in Lower Canada, see Michel Tetu, "Québec and the French Revolution," *Canadian Parliamentary Review* 12, no. 3 (Autumn 1989): 2-6; Michel Brunet, "La Révolution Française sur les Rives du Saint-Laurent," *Revue d'Histoire de l'Amérique Française* 11, no. 2 (September 1957): 155-62; Gilles Chaussée, "Les effets de la révolution française sur la montée du nationalisme au Canada français dans la première moitié du 19e siècle," *History of European Ideas* 15, nos. 1–3 (1992): 297-303.

36. Vaugeois, *First Jews in North America*, 73-74, 85, 119-27. Vaugeois characterizes Aaron Hart's warning to Moses about seeking political office as bearing on Ezekiel as well, seemingly on circumstantial evidence of Ezekiel's doing so only after his father had died. Here, I present a different reading of this episode, suggesting that Aaron Hart aimed the warning only to Moses, while Ezekiel's

interest in politics evolved on a different timeline. As Vaugeois himself notes, Ezekiel's character was as sober, industrious, and gentlemanly as that of Moses was scandalous; it must have been obvious to both brothers that he made the better candidate.

37. Jean-Pierre Wallot, "Le Crise Sous Craig (1807–1811): Nature des Conflits et Historiographie," *Historical Papers / Communications historiques* 2, no. 1 (1967): 67. For general background on Craig's career as a soldier, see Chaim M. Rosenberg, "James Henry Craig: The Pocket Hercules," *Journal of the American Revolution*, October 30, 2017, https://allthingsliberty.com. For Craig's place in Canadian historiography, see Wallot, "Le Crise Sous Craig."

38. Vaugeois, *First Jews in North America*, 72, 135–36. The October 9, 1809, issue of *Le Canadien*, the primary organ of the Parti Canadien, included a chart that satirically ranked members of the late assembly, prorogued by Gov. Craig just the week before, as "Bon Sujet" ("vous avez vraiment manifesté votre attachement envers le Gouvernement de sa Majesté") or "Mauvais Sujet" (someone whose loyalty was questionable) according to their level of support for the governor's agenda. Hart, having been able to cast a few votes between his swearing in and his ultimate expulsion, was ranked as "Good Subject." Adherents of the Parti Canadien were ranked as "Bad Subjects." *Le Canadien*, Monday, October 9, 1809, 2 (enumerated as 191 on the printed page), https://numerique.banq.qc.ca/patrimoine/details/52327/3453406.

39. *Royal Gazette* (Kingston, Jamaica), December 21, 1799, 17, and December 28, 1799, 19; Zvi Loker, "An Eighteenth-Century Plan to Invade Jamaica: Isaac Yeshurun Sasportas—French Patriot or Jewish Radical Idealist," *Transactions & Miscellanies (Jewish Historical Society of England)* 28 (1981–82): 132–44. See also Wim Klooster's chapter in this volume for Sasportas.

40. Jacob Rader Marcus, *United States Jewry, 1776–1985*, 4 vols. (Detroit: Wayne State University Press, 1989), 1:84–87; Sarna and Dalin, *Religion and State*, 63, 94.

41. Godfrey and Godfrey, *Search Out the Land*, 199–203; Vaugeois, *First Jews in North America*, 154–58.

42. See H. J. Hanham, "Canadian History in the 1970s," *Canadian Historical Review* 58, no. 1 (March 1977): 2–3, 6; Phillip A. Buckner, "'Limited Identities' and Canadian Historical Scholarship: An Atlantic Provinces Perspective," *Journal of Canadian Studies* 23, nos. 1–2 (Spring/Summer 1988): 177–78; Ramsay Cook, "Identities Are Not Like Hats," *Canadian Historical Review* 81, no. 2 (June 2000): 262–63.

7. Jews and Free People of Color in Eighteenth-Century Jamaica

1. "Will of Abraham Henriques de Souza, 1773," Island Record Office, Twickenham, Jamaica Lib. 41, fol. 171.

2. "Privilege Bill of Rebecca Souza, 1774," The National Archives of the United Kingdom, Kew, United Kingdom, CO 139/31. I am deeply grateful to Professor Daniel Livesay for generously providing me with this reference.

3. "Will of Rebecca Souza, 1811," Island Record Office, Lib. 84, fol. 16.

4. For recent studies of Jews of color in the Atlantic world, see Aviva Ben-Ur, *Jewish Autonomy in a Slave Society: Suriname in the Atlantic World, 1651–1825*

(Philadelphia: University of Pennsylvania Press, 2020), 138-91, and her chapter in the present volume; Laura Arnold Leibman, *Once We Were Slaves: The Extraordinary Journey of a Multiracial Jewish Family* (Oxford: Oxford University Press, 2021).

5. On white Jamaican anxiety about the Haitian Revolution, see Daniel Livesay, *Children of Uncertain Fortune: Mixed-Race Jamaicans in Britain and the Atlantic Family, 1733–1833* (Chapel Hill: Omohundro Institute of Early American History and Culture; University of North Carolina Press, 2018), 238-39.

6. This view is most prominently expressed by Gad Heuman, *Between Black and White: Race, Politics, and the Free Coloreds in Jamaica, 1792–1865* (Westport: Greenwood Press, 1981), 15, 73.

7. My use of the terminology of entanglement draws from several influential studies, especially Jeffrey D. Burson, "Entangled History and the Scholarly Concept of Enlightenment," *Contributions to the History of Concepts* 8, no. 2 (2013): 3; other critical studies include Michael Werner and Bénédicte Zimmerman, "Beyond Comparison: *Histoire croisée* and the Challenge of Reflexivity," *History and Theory* 45, no. 1 (2006): 30-50; Eliga H. Gould, "Entangled Histories, Entangled Worlds: The English-Speaking Atlantic as a Spanish Periphery," *American Historical Review* 112, no. 3 (2007): 764-86; Jorge Cañizares-Esguerra, ed., *Entangled Empires: The Anglo-Iberian Atlantic, 1500–1830* (Philadelphia: University of Pennsylvania Press, 2018).

8. On the false binary between slavery and freedom in Jamaica, see Diana Paton, *No Bond but the Law: Punishment, Race, and Gender in Jamaican State Formation, 1780–1870* (Durham, NC: Duke University Press, 2004), esp. 5.

9. Edward B. Rugemer, *Slave Law and the Politics of Resistance in the Early Atlantic World* (Cambridge, MA: Harvard University Press, 2018), 128, 156. This represents a 60 percent increase from 1717 when 4,500 slaves were brought to Jamaica annually.

10. These figures are based on the population table in Brooke N. Newman, *A Dark Inheritance: Blood, Race, and Sex in Colonial Jamaica* (New Haven: Yale University Press, 2018), 17. For an extensive quantitative analysis of British West Indian slave society, see B. W. Higman, *Slave Populations of the British Caribbean, 1807–1834* (Baltimore: Johns Hopkins University Press, 1984).

11. For the Dutch context of "half-freedom," see A. Leon Higginbotham Jr., *In the Matter of Color: Race & the American Legal Process, the Colonial Period* (Oxford: Oxford University Press, 1978), 121-22; for the Spanish context, see Herman Lee Bennett, *Africans in Colonial Mexico: Absolutism, Christianity, and Afro-Creole Consciousness, 1570–1640* (Bloomington: Indiana University Press, 2005).

12. Laura M. Smalligan, "An Effigy for the Enslaved: Jonkonnu in Jamaica and Belisario's *Sketches of Character*," *Slavery & Abolition* 32, no. 4 (2011): 561-81.

13. Rugemer, *Slave Law*, 120-24.

14. Rugemer, *Slave Law*, 165. For a comprehensive study of Tacky's Revolt, see Vincent Brown, *Tacky's Revolt: The Story of an Atlantic Slave War* (Cambridge, MA: Belknap Press of Harvard University Press, 2020).

15. Newman, *A Dark Inheritance*, 31, 51-55; Rugemer, *Slave Law*, 129.

16. Robin Blackburn, "Introduction," in *Paths to Freedom: Manumission in the Atlantic World*, ed. Rosemary Brana-Shute and Randy J. Sparks (Columbia: University of South Carolina Press, 2009), 1-14.

17. David Beck Ryden, "Manumission in Late Eighteenth-Century Jamaica," *New West Indian Guide* 92 (2018): 232–33.

18. Ryden, "Manumission in Late Eighteenth-Century Jamaica," 232.

19. Marisa J. Fuentes, "Power and Historical Figuring: Rachael Pringle Polgreen's Troubled Archive," *Gender & History* 22, no. 3 (2010): 566n15.

20. Wieke Vink, *Creole Jews: Negotiating Community in Colonial Suriname* (Leiden: KITLV Press, 2010), 141n64. There were 3,714 free people of color in Curaçao in 1789. See Wim Klooster, "Manumission in an Entrepôt: The Case of Curaçao," in Brana-Shute and Sparks, *Paths to Freedom*, 168.

21. Newman, *A Dark Inheritance*, 113.

22. Stewart King, *Blue Coat or Powdered Wig: Free People of Color in Prerevolutionary Saint-Domingue* (Athens: University of Georgia Press, 2001), 108.

23. On residency prohibitions against free people of color in Virginia, see Higginbotham, *In the Matter of Color*, 48; for South Carolina, see 175.

24. On the use of a security bond in New York, see Higginbotham, *In the Matter of Color*, 129.

25. Ryden, "Manumission in Late Eighteenth-Century Jamaica," 212–14. For a nuanced recent discussion of sexual agency and coercion, see Jenny Shaw, "In the Name of the Mother: The Story of Susannah Mingo, a Woman of Color in the Early English Atlantic," *William and Mary Quarterly* 77, no. 2 (2020): 185–88.

26. See John F. Campbell, "How Free Is Free? The Limits of Manumission," in Brana-Shute and Sparks, *Paths to Freedom*, 143–59.

27. Heuman, *Between Black and White*, 4. Carol Barash, "The Character of Difference: The Creole Woman as Cultural Mediator in Narratives about Jamaica," *Eighteenth-Century Studies* 23, no. 4 (1990): 410.

28. Newman, *A Dark Inheritance*, 97; Heuman, *Between Black and White*, 15.

29. Erin Trahey, "Among Her Kinswomen: Legacies of Free Women of Color in Jamaica," *William and Mary Quarterly* 76, no. 2 (2019): 272, 282–83; Fuentes, "Power and Historical Figuring," 576, 580. Free people of color using slavery as a type of patronage for relatives is certainly not the case everywhere and in every instance. For an opposing perspective, see Susan M. Socolow, "Economic Roles of the Free Women of Color of Cap Français," in *More than Chattel: Black Women and Slavery in the Americas*, ed. David Barry Gaspar and Darlene Clark Hine (Bloomington: Indiana University Press, 1996), 285.

30. Trahey, "Among Her Kinswomen," 258–59, 282–83.

31. Daviken Studnicki-Gizbert, *A Nation upon the Ocean Sea: Portugal's Atlantic Diaspora and the Crisis of the Spanish Empire, 1492–1640* (Oxford: Oxford University Press, 2007), 58–59.

32. Stanley Mirvis, *The Jews of Eighteenth-Century Jamaica: A Testamentary History of a Diaspora in Transition* (New Haven: Yale University Press, 2020), 155–58.

33. Mirvis, *Jews of Eighteenth-Century Jamaica*, 99–100.

34. For discussions of Jewish population estimates in Jamaica, see Mirvis, *Jews of Eighteenth-Century Jamaica*, 10–11, 29, 31, 57, 70, 71, 100–101.

35. Mirvis, *Jews of Eighteenth-Century Jamaica*, chap. 6.

36. Natalie A. Zacek, "Great Tangled Cousinries? Jewish Intermarriage in the British West Indies," in *A Sefardic Pepper-Pot in the Caribbean*, ed. Michael Studemund-Halévy (Barcelona: Tirocinio, 2016), 136–55.

37. Holly Snyder, "A Sense of Place: Jews, Identity, and Social Status in Colonial British America, 1654–1831" (PhD diss., Brandeis University, 2000), 137.

38. Livesay, *Children of Uncertain Fortune*, 309. The correlation of Jews and free people of color is central to Newman's analysis; see Newman, *A Dark Inheritance*, 63, 105.

39. Nicholas Mirzoeff, "Introduction," in *Diaspora and Visual Culture: Representing Africans and Jews*, ed. Nicholas Mirzoeff (New York: Routledge, 2000), 3–4.

40. George Fortunatus Judah, "The Jews' Tribute in Jamaica: Extracted from the Journals of the House of Assembly of Jamaica," *Publication of the American Jewish Historical Society* 18 (1909): 21; Newman, *A Dark Inheritance*, 61–62.

41. Newman, *A Dark Inheritance*, 62.

42. *Acts of the Assembly of Jamaica Passed in the Island of Jamaica from 1681 to 1737, Inclusive* (London: Printed by John Baskett, 1738), 58. See the discussion of the 1711 law in Holly Snyder, "Rules, Rights and Redemption: The Negotiation of Jewish Status in British Atlantic Port Towns, 1740–1831," *Jewish History* 20, no. 2 (2006): 158.

43. Daniel Livesay, "Privileging Kinship: Family and Race in Eighteenth-Century Jamaica," *Early American Studies* 14, no. 4 (2016): 695.

44. For Jewish testimonials, see Stanley Mirvis, "Between Assembly and Crown: The Debate over Jewish Taxation in Jamaica (1692–1740)," *Journal of Early American History* 6 (2016): 215. For free people of color testimonials, see Newman, *A Dark Inheritance*, 64.

45. Heuman, *Between Black and White*, 5; Newman, *A Dark Inheritance*, 67.

46. Mirvis, "Between Assembly and Crown," 213.

47. Livesay, *Children of Uncertain Fortune*, 32–52.

48. Newman, *A Dark Inheritance*, 97.

49. Newman, *A Dark Inheritance*, 65; Livesay, *Children of Uncertain Fortune*, 41–43.

50. Livesay, "Privileging Kinship," esp. 692; Trahey, "Among Her Kinswomen," 268, 270n3.

51. Newman, *A Dark Inheritance*, 175–76.

52. Heuman, *Between Black and White*, 5.

53. Snyder, "Rules, Rights, and Redemption," 158. On Sanches Morao's censure by the London *Mahamad*, see "The Sexton of London to the Holy Community of Jamaica, 1751," London Metropolitan Archives, London, England, LMA/4521/A/01/03/002.

54. Brooke N. Newman, "Contesting 'Black' Liberty and Subjecthood in the Anglophone Caribbean, 1730s–1780s," *Slavery & Abolition* 32, no. 2 (2011): 178.

55. Newman, "Contesting 'Black' Liberty," 177.

56. Jews lagged behind free people of color in asserting voting rights. In 1733, seventeen years before the Sanches Morao controversy, John Golding—a well-known mixed-race planter and activist—illegally cast a vote for his member of assembly. This provocative gesture resulted in a formal reiteration of the voting ban on free people of color. See Livesay, "Privileging Kinship," 690–92.

57. Quoted from Snyder, "A Sense of Place," 111.

58. Newman, *A Dark Inheritance*, 123; Jack P. Greene, *Settler Jamaica in the 1750s: A Social Portrait* (Charlottesville: University of Virginia Press, 2016), 158–59.

59. Heuman, *Between Black and White*, 9.

60. Mirvis, *Jews of Eighteenth-Century Jamaica*, 71; Eli Faber, *Jews, Slaves, and the Slave Trade: Setting the Record Straight* (New York: New York University Press, 1998), 65.

61. For Paramaribo, see Rosemarijn Hoefte and Jean Jacques Vrij, "Free Black and Colored Women in Early-Nineteenth-Century Paramaribo, Suriname," in *Beyond Bondage: Free Women of Color in the Americas*, ed. David Barry Gaspar and Darlene Clark Hine (Urbana: University of Illinois Press, 2004), 145–68. For Curaçao, see Klooster, "Manumission in an Entrepôt," 162.

62. Edward Long, *The History of Jamaica: or General Survey of the Antient and Modern State of That Island*, 3 vols. (London: T. Lowndes, 1774), 2:62.

63. Long, *History of Jamaica*, 2:17–18 (Spanish Town), 2:28–29 (Kingston).

64. Heuman, *Between Black and White*, 10.

65. Mirvis, *Jews of Eighteenth-Century Jamaica*, 118–23.

66. Belisario's *Sketches of Character* are reproduced in full in Tim Barringer, Gillian Forrester, and Barbaro Martinez-Ruiz, eds., *Art and Emancipation in Jamaica: Isaac Mendes Belisario and His Worlds* (New Haven: Yale Center for British Art in association with Yale University Press, 2007), 231–34.

67. Mirvis, *Jews of Eighteenth-Century Jamaica*, 58.

68. For militia service in Curaçao, see Klooster, "Manumission in an Entrepôt," 168–69; Newman, *A Dark Inheritance*, 113.

69. Samuel J. Hurwitz and Edith F. Hurwitz, "A Token of Freedom: Private Bill Legislation for Free Negroes in Eighteenth-Century Jamaica," *William and Mary Quarterly* 24, no. 3 (1967): 428.

70. Heuman, *Between Black and White*, 27.

71. Newman, *A Dark Inheritance*, 258.

72. Mirvis, *Jews of Eighteenth-Century Jamaica*, 75.

73. Newman, *A Dark Inheritance*, 258.

74. Newman, *A Dark Inheritance*, 74.

75. James Robertson, "The 'Confession Made by Cyrus' Reconsidered: Maroons and Jews during Jamaica's First Maroon War, 1728–1738/9," in *The Jews in the Caribbean*, ed. Jane S. Gerber (Oxford: Littman Library of Jewish Civilization, 2014), 241–59.

76. Mirvis, *Jews of Eighteenth-Century Jamaica*, 74, 121.

77. Philippe Girard, "Isaac Sasportas, the 1799 Slave Conspiracy in Jamaica, and Sephardic Ties to the Haitian Revolution," *Jewish History* 33 (2020): 403–35; Zvi Loker, "An Eighteenth-Century Plan to Invade Jamaica: Isaac Yeshurun Sasportas—French Patriot or Jewish Radical Idealist?," *Transactions & Miscellanies (Jewish Historical Society of England)* 28 (1981–82): 132–44.

78. Long, *History of Jamaica*, 2:18 (Jews); 2:320 (free people of color).

79. Quoted in Livesay, *Children of Uncertain Fortune*, 125. "Portuguese" is often used synonymously with "Jew."

80. Livesay, *Children of Uncertain Fortune*, 126.

81. For the stereotyping of Jews and Quakers in England, see Erin Bell, "'Mrs. Weaver Being a Quaker, Would not Swear': Representations of Quakers and Crime in the Metropolis ca. 1696–1815," in *Quakerism in the Atlantic World*,

1690–1830, ed. Robynne Rogers Healey (University Park: Pennsylvania State University Press, 2021), 113–32.

82. Newman, *A Dark Inheritance*, 87.
83. Newman, *A Dark Inheritance*, 93.
84. Mirvis, *Jews of Eighteenth-Century Jamaica*, 75 (Sunday markets), 76 (collusion).
85. Fuentes, "Power and Historical Figuring," 576.
86. Heuman, *Between Black and White*, 14.
87. Vink, *Creole Jews*, 115–16.
88. Mirvis, *Jews of Eighteenth-Century Jamaica*, 87.
89. Newman, *A Dark Inheritance*, 55–59.
90. Heuman, *Between Black and White*, 25.
91. Livesay, "Privileging Kinship," 708–9; Trahey, "Among Her Kinswomen," 270.
92. Samuel J. Hurwitz and Edith Hurwitz, "The New World Sets an Example for the Old: The Jews of Jamaica and Political Rights, 1661–1831," *American Jewish Historical Quarterly* 55, no. 1 (1965): 46. The authors quote the Committee of Correspondences, an interpretive legal body found in all English colonies.
93. Hurwitz and Hurwitz, "The New World Sets and Example for the Old," 46; Snyder, "A Sense of Place," 320.
94. Hurwitz and Hurwitz, "The New World Sets an Example for the Old," 46. This position might find support in Jonathan Schorsch's argument that Jews in the Atlantic world asserted a white identity in response to industrialized and racialized slavery. Jonathan Schorsch, *Jews and Blacks in the Early Modern World* (Cambridge: Cambridge University Press, 2004), 166–216.
95. Hurwitz and Hurwitz, "The New World Sets an Example for the Old," 46.
96. Heuman, *Between Black and White*, 73.
97. Snyder, "A Sense of Place," 320–21n93.
98. Newman, *A Dark Inheritance*, 260; Heuman, *Between Black and White*, 29–37.
99. Snyder, "Rules, Rights, and Redemption," 147–48.
100. Newman, *A Dark Inheritance*, 262.
101. Heuman, *Between Black and White*, 49.
102. Quoted in Snyder, "A Sense of Place," 321; Hurwitz and Hurwitz, "The New World Sets an Example for the Old," 49.
103. Newman, *A Dark Inheritance*, 264.
104. Heuman, *Between Black and White*, 50.
105. Livesay, "Privileging Kinship," 710.
106. Heuman, *Between Black and White*, 73.
107. Hurwitz and Hurwitz, "The New World Sets an Example for the Old," 53.
108. Hurwitz and Hurwitz, "The New World Sets an Example for the Old," 53.

8. Jewish Involvement in the Age of Atlantic Revolutions

1. H. L. Bromet, *Aanspraak, gedaan in de sociëteit Felix Libertate, op den 7 maart 1795, het eerste jaar der Bataafse vrijheid* (Amsterdam: J. H. Van Laar Mahuët, de Erven Jac. Benedictus, 1795), 3 (quote), 7.

2. The Dutch Republic was renamed the Batavian Republic after the French invasion of 1794–95.

3. Bromet, *Aanspraak*, 21–22.

4. Jacob R. Marcus, *The Colonial American Jew, 1492–1776*, 3 vols. (Detroit: Wayne State University Press, 1970), 3:1278–1302.

5. William Pencak, "The Jews in Early North America: Agents of Empire, Champions of Liberty," in *The Cambridge History of Judaism*, vol. 7: *The Early Modern Period, 1500–1815*, ed. Jonathan Karp and Adam Sutcliffe (Cambridge: Cambridge University Press, 2017), 1009.

6. Jacob Marcus, "Jews and the American Revolution: A Bicentennial Documentary," *American Jewish Archives* 27, no. 2 (1975): 213–16.

7. Geoffrey Symcox, "The Jews of Italy in the *Triennio Giacobino*, 1796–1799," in *Acculturation and Its Discontents: The Italian Jewish Experience between Exclusion and Inclusion*, ed. David N. Myers et al. (Toronto: University of Toronto Press, 2008), 159.

8. David Nassy, *Lettre politico-theologico-morale sur les Juifs* (Paramaribo, [1799]), 70.

9. Renzo de Felice, "Gli ebrei nella repubblica romana del 1798-99," *Rassegna storica del Risorgimento* 40 (1953): 340.

10. David Sorkin, *Jewish Emancipation: A History across Five Centuries* (Princeton, NJ: Princeton University Press, 2019), 61. In addition to toleration and equality, a third status obtained in eighteenth-century Livorno and Trieste, where Jews found themselves in an intermediate position between the abovementioned extremes. As subject nations, these Jewish communities were privileged corporate entities that enjoyed what Lois Dubin calls "civil inclusion." Lois C. Dubin, "Subjects into Citizens: Jewish Autonomy and Inclusion in Early Modern Livorno and Trieste," *Jahrbuch des Simon Dubnow-Instituts* 5, no. 1 (2006): 55.

11. An exception to the withholding of political rights was the measure introduced by Peter Leopold, Grand Duke of Tuscany, in April 1789 that gave Jews along with other non-Catholics political equality and allowed them to hold municipal office. The Jews of Livorno were explicitly excluded from this measure. Francesca Bregoli, "The Port of Livorno and Its *Nazione Ebrea* in the Eighteenth Century: Economic Utility and Political Reforms," *Quest: Issues in Contemporary Jewish History*, no. 2 (October 2011): 65.

12. "Pétition des juifs établis en France, adressée à l'Assemblée Nationale," January 28, 1790, in *Adresses, mémoires et pétitions des juifs 1789–1794* (Paris: EDHIS, 1968), 17–18. While reflecting the demands and concerns of the northeastern Jews, this petition was actually written by Jacques Godard, a gentile lawyer from Lorraine.

13. A wealthy leader of the ghettoized local Jewish community, Formiggini was selected by Napoleon to serve in the parliament of the Cispadane Republic in October 1797. Federica Francesconi, "From Ghetto to Emancipation: The Role of Moisè Formiggini," *Jewish History* 24, no. 3/4 (2010): 332, 333.

14. Francesconi, "From Ghetto to Emancipation," 336, 345.

15. Lucien Simon and Anne-Marie Duport, *Les juifs du Pape à Nîmes et la Révolution* (Aix-en-Provence: Édisud, 1988), 35–37.

16. M. Liber, "Les Juifs et la convocation des États Généraux (suite)," *Revue des études juives* 65, no. 129 (1913): 93.

17. S. E. Bloemgarten, "De Amsterdamse joden gedurende de eerste jaren van de Bataafse Republiek (1795-1798) I," *Studia Rosenthaliana* 1, no. 1 (1967): 92. Salvador Bloemgarten, *Hartog de Hartog Lémon, 1755-1823: Joods revolutionair in Franse Tijd* (Amsterdam: Aksant, 2007), 41, 59.

18. Jozeph Michman and Marion Aptroot, *Storm in the Community: Yiddish Polemical Pamphlets of Amsterdam Jewry, 1797-1798* (Cincinnati: Hebrew Union College Press, 2002), 120, 122.

19. Samuel Rezneck, *Unrecognized Patriots: The Jews in the American Revolution* (Westport, CT: Greenwood Press, 1975), 10.

20. Marcus, *The Colonial American Jew*, 3:1303.

21. David Sorkin, *The Transformation of German Jewry, 1780-1840* (Oxford: Oxford University Press, 1987), 27.

22. Sina Rauschenbach, "Patriots at the Periphery: David Nassy, the French Revolution, and the Emancipation of the Dutch Jews," in *Religious Changes and Cultural Transformations in the Early Modern Western Sephardic Communities*, ed. Yosef Kaplan (Leiden: Brill, 2019), 592-93.

23. De Felice, "Gli ebrei nella repubblica romana," 341-42.

24. Christopher Tozzi, "Jews, Soldiering, and Citizenship in Revolutionary and Napoleonic France," *Journal of Modern History* 86, no. 2 (June 2014): 247.

25. Frances Malino, *A Jew in the French Revolution: The Life of Zalkind Hourwitz* (Oxford: Blackwell, 1996), 81, 98-99. Tozzi, "Jews, Soldiering, and Citizenship," 237.

26. Rezneck, *Unrecognized Patriots*, 24.

27. Mark I. Greenberg, "A 'Haven of Benignity': Conflict and Cooperation between Eighteenth-Century Savannah Jews," *Georgia Historical Quarterly* 86, no. 4 (Winter 2002): 561.

28. Marcus, "Jews and the American Revolution," 174-75.

29. Stanley F. Chyet, "The Political Rights of the Jews in the United States, 1776-1840," *American Jewish Archives* 10, no. 1 (1958): 45.

30. Chyet, "Political Rights of the Jews," 22-24, 31-32, 67.

31. David Vitale, *A People Apart: A Political History of the Jews in Europe, 1789-1939* (Oxford: Oxford University Press, 1999), 17.

32. Ralf Roth, "'. . . der blühende Handel macht uns alle glücklich. . . .': Frankfurt am Main in der Umbruchszeit 1780-1825," *Historische Zeitschrift*, Beihefte, n.s., 14 (1991): 393.

33. S. E. Bloemgarten, "De Amsterdamse joden gedurende de eerste jaren van de Bataafse Republiek (1795-1798) II," *Studia Rosenthaliana* 1, no. 2 (1967): 45-47.

34. Zosa Szajkowski, *Jews and the French Revolutions of 1789, 1830 and 1848* (New York: Ktav Publishing House, 1970), 45-46.

35. Jacques Godechot, "Les juifs de Nancy de 1789 à 1795," *Revue des études juives* 86, no. 128 (1929): 13.

36. David Sorkin, *The Religious Enlightenment: Protestants, Jews, and Catholics from London to Vienna* (Princeton, NJ: Princeton University Press, 2008), 197-98.

37. Roland Goetschel, "L'hostilité du monde hassidique à la Révolution française," in *Les juifs et la Révolution française: Histoire et mentalités. Actes du colloque tenu au Collège de France et à l'Ecole Normale Supérieure les 16, 17 et 18 mai 1989*, ed. Mireille Hadas-Lebel and Evelyne Oliel-Grausz (Louvain: E. Peeters, 1992), 273.

38. Quoted in Malino, *A Jew in the French Revolution*, 71.

39. Chobaut, "Les Juifs d'Avignon et du Comtat (suite et fin)," 32–33. Not until 1800 did the Jews have their synagogue back.

40. Éric Hartmann, *La Révolution française en Alsace et en Lorraine* (Paris: Perrin, 1990), 451–52. Nigel Aston, *Religion and Revolution in France, 1780–1804* (Washington, DC: Catholic Press of America, 2000), 256. Similarly, more than a few Catholic priests abjured the priesthood, usually under some form of pressure.

41. Aston, *Religion and Revolution in France*, 255.

42. Ulrich Wyrwa, *Juden in der Toskana und in Preussen im Vergleich: Aufklärung und Emanzipation in Florenz, Livorno, Berlin und Königsberg i. Pr.* (Tübingen: Mohr Siebeck, 2003), 153–54.

43. Carlo Mangio, *Politica toscana e rivoluzione: Momenti di storia livornese, 1790–1801* (Pisa: Pacini, 1974), 93–95; Carlo Mangio, "La communauté juive de Livourne face à la Révolution française," in *Les Juifs et la Révolution française: Problèmes et aspirations*, ed. Bernhard Blumenkranz and Albert Soboul (Toulouse: Edouard Privat, 1976), 196. Wyrwa, *Juden in der Toskana und in Preussen*, 159.

44. Wyrwa, *Juden in der Toskana und in Preussen*, 164–65.

45. Some Jews in the city of Groningen did the same: E. Schut, *De joodse gemeenschap in de stad Groningen 1689–1796* (Assen: Van Gorcum, 1995), 173.

46. Jozeph Michman, *The History of Dutch Jewry during the Emancipation Period, 1787–1815: Gothic Turrets on a Corinthian Building* (Amsterdam: Amsterdam University Press, 1995), 15–19. Bloemgarten, *Hartog de Hartog Lémon*, 25–26.

47. Bloemgarten, *Hartog de Hartog Lémon*, 48–49. Michman, *History of Dutch Jewry*, 55.

48. Bloemgarten, "Amsterdamse joden I," 83–84. Bloemgarten, "Amsterdamse joden II," 70.

49. Marco H. D. van Leeuwen, "Arme Amsterdamse joden en de strijd om hun integratie aan het begin van de negentiende eeuw," in *De Gelykstaat der Joden: Inburgering van een minderheid*, ed. Hetty Berg (Amsterdam: Joods Historisch Museum; Zwolle: Waanders Uitgevers, 1996), 61.

50. Bloemgarten, "Amsterdamse joden I," 69. S. E. Bloemgarten, "De Amsterdamse joden gedurende de eerste jaren van de Bataafse Republiek (1795–1798) III," *Studia Rosenthaliana* 2, no. 1 (1968): 44. Bloemgarten, *Hartog de Hartog Lémon*, 136–41, 144.

51. Isaac S. Emmanuel and Suzanne A. Emmanuel, *History of the Jews of the Netherlands Antilles*, 2 vols. (Cincinnati: American Jewish Archives, 1970), 1:281–82.

52. Rezneck, *Unrecognized Patriots*, 137. Hays later did take the oath.

53. William Pencak, *Jews and Gentiles in Early America, 1654–1800* (Ann Arbor: University of Michigan Press, 2005), 228.

54. Paolo Bernardini, *La sfida dell'uguaglianza: Gli ebrei a Mantova nell'età della rivoluzione francese* (Rome: Bulzoni, 1996), 234. One of the few exceptions was Mantua rabbi Abram Vita Cologna, who served on the legislative body of the Cisalpine Republic. The same man would later be the vice-president of the Grand Sanhedrin convened by Napoleon before serving as the chief rabbi of France.

55. Michman, *History of Dutch Jewry*, 30–33.

56. Steven M. Lowenstein, *The Berlin Jewish Community: Enlightenment, Family, and Crisis, 1770–1830* (New York: Oxford University Press, 1994), 82.

57. Their names were Roosi Arons, Lea Benjamin, Sara Benjamin, Judik Israel, Anna Levi, Sara S. de Vries, Sara Phlip, Rebekka Levie Rutje, and Judith Wolf. Nationaal Archief, The Netherlands, Archieven van de Wetgevende Colleges van de Bataafse Republiek en het Koninkrijk Holland, 358, address by mothers, citizenesses, and Batavian residents to the First Chamber of the Representative Body, July 8, 1799; 359, address by Johanna van Haren et al. to the Representative Body, August 28, 1799. I am grateful to Elisa Hendriks and Joris Oddens for unearthing these documents and to Oddens for making them available to me. See Elisa Hendriks and Joris Oddens, "Bataafse vrouwen, politieke rechten en het digitaliseringsproject Revolutionaire Petities: Twee onbekende verzoekschriften uit het jaar 1799," *Holland: Historisch tijdschrift* 52, no. 1 (2020): 11-19.

58. Malino, *A Jew in the French Revolution*, 149–50.

59. Frances Malino, *The Sephardic Jews of Bordeaux: Assimilation and Emancipation in Revolutionary and Napoleonic France* (Tuscaloosa: University of Alabama Press, 1978), 41–42.

60. Paul R. Hanson, *The Jacobin Republic under Fire: The Federalist Revolt in the French Revolution* (University Park: Pennsylvania State University Press, 2003), 162.

61. Malino, *Sephardic Jews of Bordeaux*, 60–61. See for the ties Furtado and other Jewish intellectuals maintained with the Abbé Grégoire: Alyssa Goldstein Sepinwall, "Strategic Friendships: Jewish Intellectuals, the Abbé Grégoire, and the French Revolution," in *Renewing the Past, Reconfiguring Jewish Culture: From Al-Andalus to the Haskalah*, ed. Ross Brann and Adam Sutcliffe (Philadelphia: University of Pennsylvania Press, 2004), 189–212.

62. Gershom Scholem, *Du frankisme au jacobinisme: La vie de Moses Dobruška alias Franz Thomas von Schönfeld alias Junius Frey* (Paris: Gallimard, Le Seuil, 1981), 43, 58, 64, 66–69. Susanne Wölfle-Fischer, *Junius Frey (1753–1794): Jude, Aristokrat und Revolutionär* (Frankfurt am Main: Peter Lang, 1997), 69, 81–85.

63. Scholem, *Du frankisme au jacobinisme*, 70–75, 84. Wölfle-Fischer, *Junius Frey*, 95–99.

64. Walter Grab, *Ein Volk muß seine Freiheit selbst erobern: Zur Geschichte der deutschen Jakobiner* (Frankfurt am Main: Büchergilde Gutenberg; Vienna: Olten, 1984), 476–77.

65. Nassy, *Lettre politico-theologico-morale*, 20.

66. Nassy, *Lettre politico-theologico-morale*, xxxiii–xxxiv.

67. Nassy, *Lettre politico-theologico-morale*, xx, xxiv.

68. Rauschenbach, "Patriots at the Periphery," 597-98.

69. Natalie Zemon Davis, "Judges, Masters, Diviners: Slaves' Experience of Criminal Justice in Colonial Suriname," *Law and History Review* 29, no. 4 (November 2011): 976.

70. Philippe Girard, "Isaac Sasportas, the 1799 Slave Conspiracy in Jamaica, and Sephardic Ties to the Haitian Revolution," *Jewish History* 33 (2020): 403-35.

9. Sex with Slaves and the Business of Governance

1. John Dixon, "Rethinking American Jewish Citizenship: George Washington's Newport Letter in Atlantic Perspective," paper presented at the "Atlantic Jewish Worlds, 1500-1900" conference, the McNeil Center for Early American Studies, in partnership with the Herbert D. Katz Center for Advanced Judaic Studies, University of Pennsylvania, April 7-8, 2021 (cited with his permission).

2. London Metropolitan Archives (henceforth LMA), LMA/4521/D/01/01/003, September 23, 1810 (24 Elul 5570). The laborers are alternatively denoted as "girls" and "women employed ... as labourers ... hired the preceding week." It is unclear whether they were enslaved.

3. LMA, LMA/4521/D/01/01/003, September 23, 1810 (24 Elul 5570).

4. Melanie J. Newton, *The Children of Africa in the Colonies: Free People of Color in Barbados in the Age of Emancipation* (Baton Rouge: Louisiana State University Press, 2008), 41.

5. Matthew C. Reilly, "'Poor Whites' on the Peripheries: 'Poor White' and Afro-Barbadian Interaction on the Plantation," in *Archaeologies of Slavery and Freedom in the Caribbean*, ed. Lynsey A. Bates, John M. Chenoweth, and James A. Delle (Gainesville: University Press of Florida, 2016), 51; Karl Stewart Watson, "'Walk and Nyam Buckras': Poor-White Emigration from Barbados, 1834-1900," *Journal of Caribbean History* 34, nos. 1-2 (2000): 130-56.

6. Reilly, "'Poor Whites' on the Peripheries," 52.

7. Reilly, "'Poor Whites' on the Peripheries," 64.

8. E. M. Shilstone, "The Jewish Synagogue," in *Chapters in Barbados History, First Series*, ed. P. F. Campbell (St. Anne's Garrison: Barbados Museum and Historical Society, 1986), 146, 148.

9. Pedro L. V. Welch, *Slave Society in the City: Bridgetown, Barbados, 1680-1834* (Kingston: Ian Randle, 2003), 122.

10. Shilstone, "The Jewish Synagogue," 144; Eric R. Seeman, "Jews in the Early Modern Atlantic: Crossing Boundaries, Keeping Faith," in *The Atlantic in Global History, 1599-1800*, ed. Jorge Cañizares-Esguerra and Erik R. Seeman (New York: Routledge, 2007), 43.

11. LMA, LMA 4521/D/01/01/002, Joseph Barrow to the Nidhe Israel *Mahamad*, February 3, 1803 ("few remaining members"; "small community"); Mr. Mendes Da Costa (*presidente*) to Joseph Barrow, Isaac Baruh Lousada, and Isaac DePiza Massiah (London), August 30, 1805 ("decayed & almost annihilated congregation of Jews in this island"; "small community"); LMA,

LMA/4521/D/01/01/003, Abraham Brandon to Raphael Brandon and J. S. Brandon, February 7, 1809 ("paucity of our members"); July 2, 1815 ("community . . . reduced in number"); Abraham Lindo (*presidente*) to Messrs. Barrow & Lousadas (the congregation's Portuguese Jewish agents in London), June 22, 1817 ("paucity of our members"). By 1820, the community had dwindled to thirty-five individuals. LMA, LMA 4521/D/01/01/08, July 3, 1820, 22.

12. Eli Faber, *Jews, Slaves, and the Slave Trade: Setting the Record Straight* (New York: New York University Press, 1998); Jonathan Schorsch, *Jews and Blacks in the Early Modern World* (New York: Cambridge University Press, 2004); Wieke Vink, *Creole Jews: Negotiating Community in Colonial Suriname* (Leiden: KITLV, 2010); Stanley Mirvis, *The Jews of Eighteenth-Century Jamaica: A Testamentary History of a Diaspora in Transition* (New Haven: Yale University Press, 2020) and his chapter in the present volume; Aviva Ben-Ur, *Jewish Autonomy in a Slave Society: Suriname in the Atlantic World, 1651–1825* (Philadelphia: University of Pennsylvania Press, 2020).

13. Stephanie Jones-Rogers, "'[S]he could . . . spare one ample breast for the profit of her owner': White Mothers and Enslaved Wet Nurses' Invisible Labor in American Slave Markets," *Slavery & Abolition* 38, no. 2 (2017): 337–55; Jessica Marie Johnson, *Wicked Flesh: Black Women, Intimacy, and Freedom in the Atlantic World* (Philadelphia: University of Pennsylvania Press, 2020). I thank Ellen Hartigan-O'Connor for her suggestion of the term "close body work."

14. Larry Gragg, *The Quaker Community of Barbados: Challenging the Culture of the Planter Class* (Columbia: University of Missouri Press, 2009), 37, 59, 76, 92; Marisa J. Fuentes, *Dispossessed Lives: Enslaved Women, Violence, and the Archive* (Philadelphia: University of Pennsylvania Press, 2016), 28; Newton, *Children of Africa in the Colonies*; Hilary McD. Beckles, *A History of Barbados: From Amerindian Settlement to Nation-State* (Cambridge: Cambridge University Press, 1990) and *A History of Barbados: From Amerindian Settlement to Caribbean Single Market*, 2nd ed. (Cambridge: Cambridge University Press, 2006).

15. For statistics, see Alfred D. Chandler, "The Expansion of Barbados," in Campbell, *Chapters in Barbados History*, 61, 65; Richard S. Dunn, "The Barbados Census of 1680: Profile of the Richest Colony in English America," *William and Mary Quarterly* 26, no. 1 (1969): 7–9; Jerome Handler and F. Lange, *Plantation Slavery in Barbados: An Archaeological and Historical Investigation* (Cambridge, MA: Harvard University Press, 1978), 16–17.

16. Michael Gomez, *Black Crescent: The Experience and Legacy of African Muslims in the Americas* (Cambridge: Cambridge University Press, 2005), 59; Judith Ann Carney and Richard Nicholas Rosomoff, *In the Shadow of Slavery: Africa's Botanical Legacy in the Atlantic World* (Berkeley: University of California Press, 2009), 174; Hishaam Aidi and Manning Marable, "The Early Muslim Presence and Its Significance," in *Black Routes to Islam*, ed. Manning Marable and Hishaam Aidi (New York: Palgrave-Macmillan, 2009), 6.

17. Richard Hall, *Acts Passed in the Island of Barbados, from 1643, to 1762, inclusive* (London: Printed for Richard Hall, 1764), 5; Katharine Gerbner, *Christian Slavery: Conversion and Race in the Protestant Atlantic World* (Philadelphia: University of Pennsylvania Press, 2018).

18. LMA, LMA/4521/D/01/01/002, April 15, 1808.

19. LMA, LMA/4521/D/01/01/002, Joseph Barrow, Isaac Baruh Lousada, and Isaac DePiza Massiah, August 30, 1805; Mr. Mendes Da Costa (*presidente*) to Joseph Barrow, Isaac Baruh Lousada, and Isaac DePiza Massiah (London), April 15, 1808.

20. LMA, LMA/4521/D/01/01/002, April 15, 1808; July 3, 1808 ("to teach the poor children *gratis*").

21. LMA, LMA/4521/D/01/01/002, March 18, 1798 (1 Nisan 5558).

22. LMA, LMA/4521/D/01/01/003, August 20, 1809, and LMA/4521/D/01/01/004, September 18, 1822.

23. LMA, LMA/4521/D/01/01/003, March 29, 1810. See also April 26, 1818.

24. LMA, LMA/4521/D/01/01/003, April 11, 1811 (Angel Massiah's request for an addition to her pension granted at 12 shillings 6 pence per month); LMA/4521/D/01/01/004, September 12, 1822.

25. LMA, LMA/4521/D/01/01/003, October 11, 1812, August 20, 1820; LMA/4521/D/01/01/004, July 15, 1821.

26. LMA, LMA/4521/D/01/01/002, August 16, 1804. The word *banyadeiras* is underscored and appears without the apostrophe.

27. LMA, LMA/4521/D/01/01/002, February 25 and August 14, 1806.

28. LMA, LMA/4521/D/01/01/002, July 31, 1806.

29. LMA, LMA/4521/D/01/01/002, August 14, 1806. In the original, the words appear as "bath." and "bathg." and "improper" is underscored.

30. LMA, LMA/4521/D/01/01/002.

31. LMA, LMA/4521/D/01/01/09, Duties of the Public Officers of Kaal Kadosh Nidhe Israel, "Keeper of the Bath," 6 (unpaginated).

32. LMA, LMA/4521/D/01/01/003, September 23, 1810.

33. Charles William Day, *Five Years' Residence in the Indies*, 2 vols. (London: Colburn and Co., 1852), 1:62.

34. Neville Connell, "Hotel Keepers and Hotels," in Campbell, *Chapters in Barbados History*, 106.

35. The National Archives of the United Kingdom (henceforth TNAUK), T 71.520, 1817, 193.

36. Fuentes, *Dispossessed Lives*.

37. Connell, "Hotel Keepers and Hotels," 107.

38. LMA, LMA/4521/D/01/01/003, January 22, 1809. For a different treatment of the Abendana case, see Laura Arnold Leibman, *Once We Were Slaves: The Extraordinary Journey of a Multiracial Jewish Family* (New York: Oxford University Press, 2021), 46-49.

39. LMA, LMA/4521/D/01/01/003, October 8, 1809.

40. LMA, LMA/4521/D/01/01/003, August 25, 1811.

41. LMA, LMA/4521/D/01/01/003, April 27, 1812.

42. LMA, LMA/4521/D/01/01/003, June 7, 1812.

43. LMA, LMA/4521/D/01/01/003, September 4, 1812; October 11, 1812 (three children).

44. LMA, LMA/4521/D/01/01/003, October 11, 1812. Albert Montefiore Hyamson, *The Sephardim of England: A History of the Spanish and Portuguese Jewish*

Community, 1492–1951 (London: Methuen, 1951), notes that "no reason" for Abendana's dismissal was recorded.

45. LMA, LMA/4521/D/01/01/003, October 18, 1812.

46. LMA, LMA/4521/A/01/03/009, Minutes of the Meeting of the *Mahamad* [London], June 2, 1826.

47. Johnson, *Wicked Flesh*, 39. For additional treatments of this topic, see Gerbner, *Christian Slavery*, 78 (enslaved women had "little choice or say"); Kirsten Fischer and Jennifer Morgan, "Sex, Race, and the Colonial Project," *William and Mary Quarterly* 60, no. 1 (2003): 197; Sharon Block, *Rape and Sexual Power in Early America* (Chapel Hill: University of North Carolina Press, 2006); Wendy Anne Warren, "'The Cause of Her Grief': The Rape of a Slave in Early New England," *Journal of American History* 93, no. 4 (2007): 1031–49; Saidiya V. Hartman, "Venus in Two Acts," *Small Axe* 26 (2008): 1–14; Fuentes, *Dispossessed Lives*; and Marisa J. Fuentes, "Power and Historical Figuring: Rachael Pringle Polgreen's Troubled Archive," *Gender & History* 22, no. 3 (2010): 564–84.

48. LMA, LMA/4521/D/01/01/004, September 12, 1832.

49. LMA, LMA/4521/D/01/01/005, October 23, 1832.

50. National Archief Nederland, Nederlands Portugees-Israëlitische Gemeente, Suriname, inv. no. 423, pp. 14, 19, 37 (Abigail, daughter of the "Mustiça/molata" Simha de Meza).

51. National Archief Nederland, Gouvernement Secretaris, inv. no. 538.

52. TNAUK, T 71.520, 1817, 143, 161, 343; *The Barbados Mercury and Bridge-Town Gazette*, passim.

53. LMA, LMA/4521/D/01/01/005, October 21 and October 23, 1832 (for the quote).

54. LMA, LMA/4521/D/01/01/005, October 23, 1832.

55. LMA, LMA/4521/D/01/01/005, November 12, 1832.

56. LMA, LMA/4521/D/01/01/002, April 28, 1806. The word "coloured" appears as "cold."

57. LMA, LMA/4521/D/01/01/002, February 15, 1801; April 15, 1801; Eliezer Montefiore (*presidente*) and Jos. Barrow (treasurer) to Messrs. Barrow Lousada and Co. (London); August 21, 1801.

58. LMA, LMA/4521/D/01/01/002, January 30 and April 19, 1803.

59. LMA, LMA/4521/D/01/01/002, 3 Elul 5565 [August 28, 1805]; March 28 and December 14, 1806. Hazanim were permitted to speculate in real estate.

60. TNAUK, T 71.520, 1817, 49; LMA, LMA/4521/D/01/01/004, September 2, 1832. His salary was reduced to £150 in 1832 as part of the retrenchment measures following the 1831 hurricane.

61. LMA, LMA/4521/D/01/01/004, April 19, 1821.

62. Newton, *Children of Africa in the Colonies*, 68.

63. Karl Watson, "Shifting Identities: Religion, Race, and Creolization among the Sephardi Jews of Barbados, 1654–1900," in *The Jews in the Caribbean*, ed. Jane S. Gerber (Oxford: Littman Library of Jewish Civilization, 2014), 220.

64. Watson, "Shifting Identities." See also Leibman, *Once We Were Slaves*; Laura Arnold Leibman, *The Art of the Jewish Family: A History of Women in Early*

New York in Five Objects (New York: Bard Graduate Center, 2020), chap. 3; Hannah Ruth London, *Miniatures of Early American Jews* (Rutland, VT: C. E. Tuttle, [1953]), 34.

65. Watson, "Shifting Identities," 220.
66. LMA, LMA/4521/D/01/01/002, May 15, 1796.
67. LMA, LMA/4521/D/01/01/002, September 4, 1796.
68. LMA, LMA/4521/D/01/01/002, April 3, 1798. An additional nine men contributed £50 and above.
69. LMA, LMA/4521/D/01/01/002, September 11 and 27, 1803; LMA, LMA/4521/D/01/01/003, September 13 and 17, 1809.
70. LMA, LMA/4521/D/01/01/002, 15 Iyar 5565 [May 14, 1805].
71. LMA, LMA/4521/D/01/01/003, March 29, 1810; March 10, 1819; TNAUK, T 71.520, 1817, 52–56.
72. He served actively in one or more offices, as documented in the communal minutes, from 1810 to 1826.
73. The fear that the schism would destroy "our religious establishment" is expressed by Benjamin Elkin in LMA, LMA/4521/D/01/01/004, September 13, 1820.
74. LMA, LMA/4521/D/01/01/003, April 18, 1813; Ben-Ur, *Jewish Autonomy in a Slave Society*, 158.
75. LMA, LMA/4521/D/01/01/09, passim; *The Barbados Mercury and Bridge-Town Gazette*, August 19, 1820, 2–3.
76. TNAUK, T 71.520, 1817, 360, 348, 429.
77. LMA, LMA/4521/D/01/01/004, July 3, 1820, 16–17.
78. Leibman, *Once We Were Slaves*, 95; Jonathan Sarna, *American Judaism: A History* (New Haven: Yale University Press, 2004), 48.
79. Another Eurafrican Jew was Benjamin Massiah who, along with one Henry Aaron, signed "the former counter-petition," which was perhaps an earlier version of it, as they were not included among the final signatories. LMA, LMA/4521/D/01/01/004, July 3, 1820, 30.
80. LMA, LMA/4521/D/01/01/004, April 30, 1820.
81. *The Barbados Mercury and Bridge-Town Gazette*, August 19, 1820, 2–3.
82. LMA, LMA/4531/D/01/01/004, February 18, 1821.
83. Melanie J. Newton, "The King v. Robert James, a Slave, for Rape: Inequality, Gender, and British Slave Amelioration, 1823–1834," *Comparative Studies in Society and History* 47, no. 3 (July 2005): 601–2.
84. Newton, *Children of Africa in the Colonies*, iv, 2.
85. Newton, *Children of Africa in the Colonies*, 8.
86. LMA, LMA/4521/D/01/01/004, December 10, 1820, 65 (for quote), and LMA/4521/D/01/01/06, January 30, 1837; April 12 and May 8, 1838.
87. Stephen Alexander Fortune, *Merchants and Jews: The Struggle for British West Indian Commerce, 1650–1750* (Gainesville: University Presses of Florida, 1984), 96.
88. Reilly, "'Poor Whites' on the Peripheries," 56.
89. Reilly, "'Poor Whites' on the Peripheries," 56.
90. Salo Wittmayer Baron, "The Jewish Factor in Medieval Civilization," *Proceedings of the American Academy for Jewish Research* 12 (1942): 1–48. See also

Joseph Shatzmiller, *Jews, Christians, and Art in the Medieval Marketplace* (Princeton, NJ: Princeton University Press, 2013); Lena Roos, *'God wants it!': The Ideology of Martyrdom in the Hebrew Crusade Chronicles and Its Jewish and Christian Background* (Turnhout: Brepols, 2006), chap. 2; Elka Klein, *Jews, Christian Society, and Royal Power in Medieval Barcelona* (Ann Arbor: University of Michigan Press, 2006), 195. By citing sources from the medieval era, I make an a fortiori argument for early modernity.

10. Connecting Jewish Community

1. Thomas Jefferson Moïse, "Letter from Thomas Jefferson Moïse to Isaac Leeser," October 19, 1850, Jesselson-Kaplan American Genizah Project. For Thomas Jefferson Moïse, see Frederick A. Ford, *Census of the City of Charleston, South Carolina, for the Year 1861* (Charleston: Evans & Cogswell, 1861), 99 and 167. Thomas Jefferson Moïse is listed at 27 Pickney Street and 6 Hayne Street under the name T. J. & C. H. Moise & Co.

2. Arthur Kiron, "Biographical Sketch of Isaac Leeser," Gershwind-Bennett Isaac Leeser Digital Repository, 2012, https://library.upenn.edu, 1-6.

3. "The Late Rev. Isaac Leeser," *The Occident and American Jewish Advocate*, March 1868, Historical Jewish Press, 594.

4. Leeser's duties as hazan were a subject of contention between Leeser himself and the board of the congregation. See this important article on the work of hazanim: Shari Rabin, "Working Jews: Hazanim and the Labor of Religion in Nineteenth-Century America," *Religion and American Culture: A Journal of Interpretation* 25, no. 2 (2015): 178-217.

5. "Leeser's tenure at Mikveh Israel was marked by constant bickering with the Board of the synagogue over the extent of the Hazan's authority, his status and independence, as well as over Leeser's on-going demands for a life-time contract and salary increase. The Board also resisted several innovations by Leeser, such as his introduction into the weekly service of a regular English language sermon." Kiron, "Biographical Sketch of Isaac Leeser," 1-2. See also Lance J. Sussman, *Isaac Leeser and the Making of American Judaism* (Detroit: Wayne State University Press, 1996), 56-59, 71, 118-20, 175.

6. Rudolf Glanz, "Where the Jewish Press Was Distributed in Pre-Civil War America," *Western States Jewish Historical Quarterly* 5 (1972): 1-14. Glanz's sole focus on subscribers in the United States is problematic. However, Glanz was mainly interested in understanding and tracking Jewish communities in America, part of a cohort of American Jewish historians who did not consider the Caribbean or the larger Atlantic world as part of their study.

7. Robert Singerman, "The American Jewish Press, 1823-1983: A Bibliographic Survey of Research and Studies," *American Jewish History* 73, no. 4 (1984): 422-44.

8. Arthur A. Goren, "The Jewish Press in the U.S." *Kesher*, no. 6 (1989): 4e-22e. Goren's other focus was the use of the English language. He devotes most of the article to the Yiddish press.

9. Jonathan D. Sarna, "The History of the Jewish Press in North America," *Alexander Brinn Forum*, 1994, 2.

10. Arthur Kiron, "An Atlantic Jewish Republic of Letters?," *Jewish History* 20, no. 2 (2006): 171–211.

11. Adam Mendelsohn, "Tongue Ties: The Emergence of the Anglophone Jewish Diaspora in the Mid-Nineteenth Century," *American Jewish History* 93, no. 2 (2007): 181.

12. Shari Rabin, *Jews on the Frontier: Religion and Mobility in Nineteenth-Century America* (New York: New York University Press, 2017). Shari Rabin, "The 'American Israelite' and American Israelites in the Era of Citizenship," in *Yearning to Breathe Free*, ed. Adam Mendelsohn and Jonathan D. Sarna (Princeton, NJ: Princeton University Press, 2022), 275–305.

13. Bertram Wallace Korn, "Isaac Leeser: Centennial Reflections," *American Jewish Archives* 19, no. 2 (1967): 133.

14. Korn, "Isaac Leeser: Centennial Reflections," 136.

15. Sussman, *Isaac Leeser and the Making of American Judaism*.

16. Rev. Isaac Leeser, "Introductory Remarks," *The Occident, and American Jewish Advocate*, April 1843, Historical Jewish Press, National Library of Israel, https://www.nli.org.il/en/newspapers/occ/1843/04/01/01/article/1.

17. Rev. Isaac Leeser, "Third List of Subscribers to the Occident," *The Occident, and American Jewish Advocate*, March 1845, Historical Jewish Press, National Library of Israel, https://www.nli.org.il/en/newspapers/occ/1845/03/01/01/article/10.

18. Brian Findlay, "Subscription Publishing," in *The Oxford Companion to the Book*, ed. Michael Suarez, S. J. Woudhuysen, and H. R. Woudhuysen (Oxford: Oxford University Press, 2010), https://www.oxfordreference.com/display/10.1093/acref/9780198606536.001.0001/acref-9780198606536-e-4727.

19. We know that Leeser issued a prospectus for *The Occident* in 1842, and he wrote to his uncle, Zalma Rehiné, in 1842 discussing how many subscribers he had procured. See Isaac Leeser, "Letter from Isaac Leeser to Zalma Rehine," October 19, 1842, Jesselson-Kaplan American Genizah Project. In later wrappers for *The Occident*, Leeser issued prospectuses, but they are reflections on the paper's publication for the previous year, rather than a call for subscriptions. See Isaac Leeser, "Prospectus for the Occident, Vol. IV," *The Occident, and American Jewish Advocate*, March 1846, sec. Advertising Wrapper, Library Company of Philadelphia. It is important to note that Leeser did not seem to depend on *The Occident* for income. Leeser wrote that *The Occident* barely broke even, and Leeser's will indicates that numerous subscribers owed him money.

20. Brian Findlay, "Subscription List," in Suarez, Woudhuysen, and Woudhuysen, *The Oxford Companion to the Book*, https://www.oxfordreference.com/display/10.1093/acref/9780198606536.001.0001/acref-9780198606536-e-4726. See also Francis J. G. Robinson and Peter J. Wallis, *Book Subscription Lists: A Revised Guide* (Newcastle upon Tyne: Harold Hill & Son, 1975).

21. Rev. Isaac Leeser, *The Occident, and American Jewish Advocate*, April 1846, sec. Wrapper, Library Company of Philadelphia. "At our own expense" indicates that *The Occident* would pay for the publication of the announcement rather than the congregation or society.

22. Mayer Sulzberger functioned in this authoritative role for a year after Leeser's death. Jonah Bondi did as well when he helped Leeser during the 1860s, but Leeser was the primary authority figure.

23. Ryan Cordell, "Reprinting, Circulation, and the Network Author in Antebellum Newspapers," *American Literary History* 27, no. 3 (September 1, 2015): 418.

24. When Cordell references republication he means an article's virality. He wrote, "Like some viral content online today, which can become noteworthy *because* of its virality, the system of newspaper exchanges produced a kind of feedback loop, in which texts circulated because of their perceived value to readers while that perceived value was often tied to a given piece's wide circulation." Cordell, "Reprinting, Circulation," 417–18.

25. Sophia Tobias, "Letter from Sophia Tobias to Rev. Isaac Leeser," November 7, 1849, Jesselson-Kaplan American Genizah Project, http://leeser.library.upenn.edu/documentDisplay.php?id=LSKAP0257.

26. "Ladies Sewing Association in New York, of the Congregation Shearith Israel," *The Occident, and American Jewish Advocate*, December 1849, Historical Jewish Press, https://www.nli.org.il/en/newspapers/occ/1849/12/01/01/article/9.

27. An important article that connects American Jewish women and their involvement in Jewish religious pursuits during the nineteenth century to other religious developments in the United States is Jonathan D. Sarna, "'God Loves an Infant's Praise': Cultural Borrowing and Cultural Resistance in Two Nineteenth-Century American Jewish Sunday-School Texts," *Jewish History* 27, no. 1 (2013): 73–89.

28. Nathaniel Levine, "Letter from Nathaniel Levine to Rev. Isaac Leeser," March 3, 1867, Jesselson-Kaplan American Genizah Project, http://leeser.library.upenn.edu/documentDisplay.php?id=LSTCAT_item26.

29. "Charleston, S.C.," *The Occident, and American Jewish Advocate*, April 1867, sec. News Items, Historical Jewish Press, National Library of Israel, https://www.nli.org.il/en/newspapers/occ/1867/04/01/01/article/10.

30. Rev. Isaac Leeser, *The Occident, and American Jewish Advocate*, August 1863, sec. Advertising Wrapper, Historical Jewish Press, National Library of Israel, https://www.nli.org.il/en/newspapers/occ/1863/08/02/01/article/3.1.

31. Leeser, "Introductory Remarks."

32. Leeser, "Introductory Remarks."

33. Rev. Isaac Leeser, *The Occident, and American Jewish Advocate*, May 1846, sec. Advertising Wrapper, The Library Company of Philadelphia, 6.

34. For more, see Joseph M. Adelman, *Revolutionary Networks: The Business and Politics of Printing the News, 1763–1789* (Baltimore: Johns Hopkins University Press, 2019).

35. M. B. Simmons, "Letter from M.B. Simmons to Rev. Isaac Leeser," June 22, 1843, Jesselson-Kaplan American Genizah Project, http://leeser.library.upenn.edu/documentDisplay.php?id=LSKAP0029.

36. Simmons, "Letter from M.B. Simmons to Rev. Isaac Leeser."

37. In addition, if payments were going through an agent intermediary (subscriber ◊ agent ◊ Leeser), this would assure both agent and subscriber that payment was reaching the editor in Philadelphia and no foul play was at hand.

38. Rev. Isaac Leeser, "Occident Advertiser," *The Occident, and American Jewish Advocate*, May 1846, sec. Advertising Wrapper, The Library Company of Philadelphia, 3. To be clear, double cover meant that instead of the original two pages (four usable sides) used for the wrapper (1r, 1v, 2r, 2v), now four pages (eight useable sides) would be used (1r, 1v, 2r, 2v, 3r, 3v, 4r, 4v), in effect doubling the advertising space. A wrapper is defined by *The Oxford Companion to the Book* as "a cover for a book or pamphlet without boards—typically paper." See "Wrapper," in Suarez, Woudhuysen, and Woudhuysen, *The Oxford Companion to the Book*. https://www.oxfordreference.com/display/10.1093/acref/9780198606536.001.0001/acref-9780198606536-e-5304.

39. The notes following *The Occident*'s third subscription list indicate that Leeser felt the demands of the precarious newspaper business in 1845. The loss of subscribers meant lost revenue. Therefore, as Leeser explains, he could not hire anyone to help with the work of publishing *The Occident*: "the labour of which falls to our lot is heavy indeed, as the receipts will not permit us to obtain any but voluntary assistance, without running the risk of a loss which we cannot afford." Leeser, "Third List of Subscribers," 616.

40. Rosalind Remer, "Preachers, Peddlers, and Publishers: Philadelphia's Backcountry Book Trade, 1800–1830," *Journal of the Early Republic* 14, no. 4 (1994): 499.

41. Isaac Leeser, "Occident Advertiser," *The Occident, and American Jewish Advocate*, May 1846, sec. Wrapper, Library Company of Philadelphia.

42. Mendelsohn, "Tongue Ties," 180.

43. Kiron, "An Atlantic Jewish Republic of Letters?," 181.

44. Isaac Leeser, "Consecration of the New Synagogue, Kenesseth Shalom, at Syracuse, New York," *The Occident, and American Jewish Advocate*, October 1851, sec. News Items, Historical Jewish Press.

45. Isaac Leeser, *The Occident, and American Jewish Advocate*, November 1851, sec. Wrapper, University of Pennsylvania.

46. Leeser never traveled to the Caribbean or to California. He made it as far west as Saint Louis, Missouri, and as far south as New Orleans, Louisiana.

47. Isaac Leeser, "To Our Readers," *The Occident, and American Jewish Advocate*, April 1852, Historical Jewish Press, 2.

48. Leeser, "To Our Readers" (April 1852), 1.

49. "United States Jewish Population," Current Jewish Population Reports (Jewish Federations of North America, Berman Jewish Data Bank), 2017, https://www.jewishdatabank.org/content/upload/bjdb/US_Jewish_Population_2017_AJYB_DataBank_Final.pdf, 9.

50. Leeser, "To Our Readers" (April 1852), 1.

51. Remer, "Preachers, Peddlers, and Publishers," 499.

52. Remer, "Preachers, Peddlers, and Publishers," 499.

53. While Leeser reflects in *The Occident* on his travels, more work needs to be done to assess what exactly he did during these trips.

54. It is important to note that Leeser edited two different prayer books for different rites (*nusach*): *Sidur Siphthei Tzaddikim / The Form of Prayers According to the Custom of the Spanish and Portuguese Jews* (1st edition, 1837), and *Siddur Divrei Tsadikim / The Book of Daily Prayers for Every Day in the Year According to the Custom of the German and Polish Jews* (1st edition, 1848).

55. Rev. Isaac Leeser, *The Occident, and American Jewish Advocate*, August 1843, sec. Wrapper, Library Company of Philadelphia; Isaac Leeser, *The Occident, and American Jewish Advocate*, September 1843, sec. Wrapper, Library Company of Philadelphia, 3.

56. Rev. Isaac Leeser, *The Occident, and American Jewish Advocate*, April 1844, sec. Wrapper, Library Company of Philadelphia.

57. Rev. Isaac Leeser, "To Our Readers," *The Occident, and American Jewish Advocate*, March 1845, sec. Wrapper, Library Company of Philadelphia, 3. Leeser did not make a profit from *The Occident* nor his other publications, at least initially. The hazan led a modest life and for many years lived as a border with the Cozens family of Philadelphia. Leeser's amended will shows a long list of debtors that still owed him money.

58. Rev. Isaac Leeser, "Will Be Issued about the Fifth of June, The Law of God, Volume One. Containing The Book of Genesis, Hebrew and English," *The Occident, and American Jewish Advocate*, June 1845, sec. Wrapper, Library Company of Philadelphia, 3.

59. Leeser, "Will Be Issued about the Fifth of June."

60. Rev. Isaac Leeser, "Now Ready, The Law of God, Volume One. Containing The Book of Genesis, Hebrew and English," *The Occident, and American Jewish Advocate*, September 1845, sec. Wrapper, Library Company of Philadelphia, 3.

61. Rev. Isaac Leeser, untitled notice, *The Occident, and American Jewish Advocate*, December 1845, sec. Wrapper, Library Company of Philadelphia, 2.

62. Rev. Isaac Leeser, "Completion of The Law of God, in Five Volumes," *The Occident, and American Jewish Advocate*, March 1846, sec. Wrapper, Library Company of Philadelphia, 3.

63. Rabbi Lance J. Sussman, "Another Look at Isaac Leeser and the First Jewish Translation of the Bible in the United States," *Modern Judaism* 5, no. 2 (1985): 172.

64. See Gavin I. Langmuir, *History, Religion, and Antisemitism* (Berkeley: University of California Press, 1990) and Gavin I. Langmuir, *Toward a Definition of Antisemitism* (Berkeley: University of California Press, 1996).

65. Rev. Isaac Leeser, *Instruction in the Mosaic Religion* (Philadelphia: A. Waldie, 1830), viii.

66. Rev. Isaac Leeser, *The Jews and the Mosaic Law* (Printed for the author, and sold by E. L. Carey and A. Hart, 1834).

67. Rev. Isaac Leeser, *Discourses, Argumentative and Devotional, on the Subject of the Jewish Religion: Delivered at the Synagogue Mikveh Israel, in Philadelphia, in the Years 5590–5593* (Philadelphia: Haswell and Fleu, 1842), 295–96.

68. Rev. Isaac Leeser, "Advertisement" (1842), Jesselson-Kaplan American Genizah Project, http://leeser.library.upenn.edu/documentDisplay.php?id=LSTCAT_item205.

Contributors

Aviva Ben-Ur is professor in the Department of Judaic and Near Eastern Studies at the University of Massachusetts Amherst. Her books include *Jewish Autonomy in a Slave Society: Suriname in the Atlantic World, 1651–1825* (2020) and *Sephardic Jews in America: A Diasporic History* (2009).

John M. Dixon is associate professor at the College of Staten Island and in the PhD Program in history at the Graduate Center, City University of New York. He currently explores the history of the early modern Atlantic world through the experiences of Jews, crypto-Jews, and conversos. He is the author of *The Enlightenment of Cadwallader Colden* (2016).

Laura Newman Eckstein is a PhD student in the Department of History at the University of Pennsylvania. Her studies focus on Jews in the early Atlantic world (seventeenth to nineteenth centuries), with a specific focus on trade networks, material culture, and digital humanities methodologies.

Wim Klooster is professor and Robert H. and Virginia N. Scotland Endowed Chair in History and International Relations at Clark University. His many books include *Revolutions in the Atlantic World: A Comparative History* (new edition, 2018) and *The Dutch Moment: War, Trade, and Settlement in the Seventeenth-Century Atlantic World* (2016).

Stanley Mirvis is associate professor of history in the School of Historical, Philosophical, and Religious Studies and the Harold and Jean Grossman Chair in Jewish Studies at Arizona State University. He is the author of *The Jews of Eighteenth-Century Jamaica: A Testamentary History of a Diaspora in Transition* (2020).

Oren Okhovat earned his PhD at the University of Florida. His dissertation focused on Portuguese merchants (Jews and Christians) and their activities across imperial boundaries in the seventeenth-century Atlantic world. He is currently a Fulbright postdoctoral fellow in Spain.

Toni Pitock is an assistant teaching professor in the Department of History at Drexel University. She is currently transforming her dissertation, titled "Commerce and Connection: Jewish Merchants, Philadelphia, and the Atlantic World, 1736–1822," into a monograph.

Yda Schreuder is professor emerita in the Department of Geography at the University of Delaware and research associate at the Hagley Museum and Library. She is the author of *Amsterdam's Sephardic Merchants and the Atlantic Sugar Trade in the Seventeenth Century* (2019).

Holly Snyder recently retired as curator of American Historical Collections and the History of Science at the John Hay Library in Providence, Rhode Island. Her dissertation was titled "A Sense of Place: Jews, Identity, and Social Status in Colonial British America, 1654–1831."

Victor Tiribás earned his PhD in history at Scuola Normale Superiore. He held a postdoctoral fellowship at Università degli Studi Roma Tre and a Harry Starr Fellowship at Harvard University and is currently a fellow at the Center for Netherlandish Art in the Museum of Fine Arts.

INDEX

Page numbers in italics refer to figures and tables.

Aaron, Henry, 270n79
Abendana, Rafael, 186–88
abolition of slavery, 6, 137, 150–51, 154, 178, 180
Adler, Cyrus, 27–29, 33
Africa, 7–8, 139, 141; Dutch colonies in, 48; West Coast, 64, 72. *See also* enslaved Africans; Eurafrican Jews
Albert, Anne Oravetz, 21
Algerian Jewish merchants, 220n29
Allen, William, 100
almirantazgo tax, 51, 230n30
Alsace, 158, 164–66
Álvares Nogueira, Balthasar, 55–58, 232n52
American exceptionalism, 1–2, 23, 31, 40
American Jew, 1585–1990 (Marcus), 33
American Jewish Archives, 29, 32–33
American Jewish Committee, 30
American Jewish Historical Society (AJHS), 23–28, 30–32, 40–41
American Jewish history, 8; goals of, 20; nationalistic metanarrative, 2, 7, 22–36, 39–41; periodization of, 28, 32–34, 226n42. *See also* United States
American Jewish Woman, 1654–1980 (Marcus), 226n42
American Revolution, 114, 129, 149, 157, 159, 161, 173, 175–76. *See also* United States
Amherst, Jeffery, 105, 107
Amsterdam: Ashkenazim, 168–69; autonomy, 165, 167–68; economic equality, 161; as haven from Inquisition, 61; Jamaica and, 141; Jewish community, 87–90, *157*, 239n15, 244n115; National Guard, 162; political rights, 163–64;
Portuguese Jewish merchants, 3, 14, 45–46, *47*, 60–61, 65, 67, 233n1; Sephardic merchants, 62–65, 75–77; sugar trade, 62–64, 66, 74–77, 82
Amsterdam Exchange Bank, 235n38
Ancona, *157*
Anglicans. *See* Church of England
Angola, 48, 69, 94
Anti-Defamation League (ADL), 11, 219n27
Antinomians, 123
antisemitism, 11–12, 29–30, 117, 198. *See also* prejudice
Antônio Vaz, 92–93
Antwerp, 63, 67–68
Arari, Judith, 89
archival documents, 12, 20
Armenta family, 222n58
Armitage, David, 37
Ascher, Saul, 173–74
Ashkenazim, 32, 101, 105–6, 143, 164, 168–69
Asser, Mozes, 161, 164
assimilation, 29, 165–66. *See also* integration
Atlantic Diasporas (2009), 9, 12, 37–38
Atlantic history, 7, 24, 37–38, 227n71
Atlantic Jewish history, 1–7; emergence of field, 24–25, 36–37; entanglement and, 1–7, 21, 39–41, 63–64, 80, 115, 135–37, 171, 180–81; overview of, 13–21; principles of, 8–13, 40; revisionism of, 13; temporal parameters, 1, 7, 11, 217n13
Atlantic Jewish studies, 11
Atlantic Jewry, use of term, 9
Atlantic system, second, 75
autonomy, Jewish, 164–69, 176

Baer, Yitzhak, 20
Bahia, 67, 81, 89, 92, 95
Bailyn, Bernard, 227n71
Baptists, 123
Baraffael, Isacho, 162
Barbados: enslaved population, 178–79; free people of color, 139; Jewish community, 70–74, 177, 236n49, 236n53; political rights, 180; Sephardic moment in, 71–74; sexual liaisons in, 6, 177–96; sugar trade, 3, 62–66, 71–74, 76–77
Barkley, Gilbert, 109
Barlaeus, Caspar, 84
Baron, Salo Wittmayer, 31, 196
Bartlett, John Russell, 255n29
Batavian Republic, 156, 159, 161, 168, 262n2
Bayonne, 141, 147, *157*
Bédard, Pierre-Stanislas, 132
Belaronda, Godefrois de, 57
Belasco, Moses, 177–78, 187, 189–90
Belin de la Garde, Guillaume, 55, 57, 232n49
Belisario, Isaac Mendes, 147
Belmonte, Manuel, 46–47, *47*, 60–61
Beni, Jacobus Alexander, 54–58
Ben-Ur, Aviva, 6, 40
Berlin, *157*, 165
Berman, Lila Corwin, 21
Bernardini, Paolo, 9
Berr, Berr Isaac, 164
Besalaar, Balthasar, 54, 56
Beth El-Emeth (congregation), 198
Bet Israel (congregation), 88–89
Bible, 162; Christian, 117; Hebrew, 197–98, 207–8, 210
Black people: rights of, 174–75; use of term, ix. *See also* enslaved Africans; Eurafrican Jews; Jews of color
Bondi, Jonah, 273n22
Bonomi, Patricia, 123
Bordeaux, 64, 147, *157*, 161, 164, 172
borderland history, 40
Bouquet, Henry, 106–9
Braganza dynasty (Portugal), 46
Brandon, Abraham Rodrigues, 191–92
Brandon, Isaac Lopez, 191–92, 194–95
Brandon, Sarah, 191–92
Brazil: Catholics in, 84, 91; Dutch rule, 48, 65, 68–70, 74–75, 78–98, 235n40, 242n78, 244n115; Inquisition, 13; Jewish community, 22–23, 90–97, 236n49, 242n78, 244n115; Portuguese rule, 50, 63–64, 66; religious freedom, 69; Sephardic population, 66–71, 74; sugar trade, 3, 62–71; trade goods, 57–58; trade with Spain, 50. *See also* Pernambuco

British maritime empire, 3–6; Board of Trade, 99–100, 103, 107, 111, 113, 137, 144; Catholic Emancipation, 134; commerce and colonial expansion, 4, 99–115; expulsion of Jews, 119; free people of color, 139–40; Parliament, 121–22, 153; political rights, 5, 102, 116–35, 253n24, 254n27; political thought, 118–23, 133; Privy Council, 121, 153; Royal Exchange, 102; subjecthood, 102, 122–23; supply contracts for North American troops, 102–15, 247n22, 251n70; toleration in, 28, 31, 106, 123; trade, 3, 62, 72–75, 238n74, 252n4; Western Design, 73, 237nn60–61. *See also* American Revolution; Barbados; Jamaica; Lower Canada
Bromet, Herman, 156, 162
Broughton, Lord Chancellor, 128
Buenos Aires, 49–50, 52, 63
Bulliet, Richard, 220n39

Cádiz, 44, 51, 54–57, 232n52
Calado, Manoel, 78
Calvinists, 143
Canada: voting rights, 253n24, 254n27. *See also* Lower Canada; Upper Canada
Canary Islands, 74
Cañete, Francisco, 55
Caplan, Marc, 219n27
Caribbean region, 123; Jewish communities, 6, 8, 11, 22–27, 33–35, 37, 64; sugar trade, 62–77; transimperial trade networks, 43–44. *See also* Barbados; Curaçao; Jamaica; Saint-Domingue; Suriname
Carr, Matthew, 221n41
Carrera de Indias, 50
Cartagena de Indias, 13, 50, 53, 63
Casa de David (congregation), 91, 96, 242n85
Castile, 26, 46, 53, 76
Castro Tartas, Isaac de, 91–92, 242n85
Catholic Church, 119, 264n40. *See also* Inquisition

INDEX

Catholics, 3; in Brazil, 84, 91; disenfranchisement in Rhode Island, 255n29; political rights, 5, 117–18, 126–28, 132, 134
Cayenne, 70–71, 76
Central American Jewry, 27
Cesarani, David, 37
Charles I of England, 119, 121
Charles II of England, 121
Charles II of Spain, 46, 60
Charleston, 158, 202–3
Chile, 48, 52
Christians, 4; of Iberian Jewish origin, 7 (*see also* conversion to Christianity; New Christians). *See also* Catholics; Church of England; Protestants; *specific denominations*
Church of England, 81, 123, 128, 143, 180, 193
Cisalpine Republic, 170, 265n54
Cispadane Republic, 262n13
citizenship, 19, 32, 36, 142, 164, 170–71, 177. *See also* political rights
Civil Rights Edict (1813), 151
Clark, Samuel, 124
class: as category of analysis, 179; sexual behavior and, 179, 182–95
Cohen Henriques, Abraham, 88, 241n58
Cohen Henriques, David, 94
Cohen Henriques, Isaac, 241n58, 242n74
Cohen Henriques, Jacob, 79–81, 88–90, 93–98, 241n51
Cohen Henriques, Moisés, 78–81, 88–90, 93–98, 239n15, 241n58
Cohen Peixoto, Joshua, 79–81, 83–84, 86–88, 97–98
Cohen Peixoto, Moisés, 79–81, 83–88, 90–98, 241n51, 243n86
Colebrooke, George, 104, 108
Colebrooke, James, 104, 108, 247n22
Cologna, Abram Vita, 265n54
Colombia, 13
Colonial American Jew, 1492–1776 (Marcus), 32–35
colonial era, 1, 25–26, 44
colorism, 140
Columbian quadricentennial, 25–26
commerce. *See* trade
commonality, 138, 154
congregations, 203; in Amsterdam, 87–89, 169; in Barbados, *178*, 182–89, *185*, 189, 192; in Brazil, 91–93, 96, 242n85; in Charleston, 202–3; Jewish press and, 207–8; in New York, 100, 202; in Philadelphia, 159, 193, 198, 271n5; in Syracuse, New York, 207; in United States, 203. *See also* synagogues
Connecticut, 111, 123, 163
Constitution Act (1791), 116, 127, 129–30, 132
contraband, 45, 49–61, 68
conversion to Christianity, 3, 221n41; forced, 7, 13–21, 26, 36, 43, 62; material considerations, 3; office-holding and, 118; political rights and, 118; Protestant approaches to, 120; religious pluralism and, 43. *See also* New Christians
conversion to Judaism, 91
conversos, 17–20, 28; adoption of rabbinic Judaism, 142; in Jamaica, 141; merchants in sugar trade, 62–63; migration from Portugal, 67, 75–76; pragmatism, 79; use of term, 233n3
Cordell, Ryan, 202, 273n24
Costa, Vicente da, 87
"Court Jew," 101–2, 114–15
Craig, James Henry, 131–32, 256n38
Croghan, George, 106, 111–13
Cromwell, Oliver, 73–74, 119, 237n60, 237nn60–61
crypto-Hinduism, 222n60
crypto-Islam, 222n60
crypto-Jews, 20, 62; use of term, 233n3. *See also* New Christians
cultural pluralism, 31
Curaçao: France and, 175; free people of color, 140, 258n20; free port settlement, 234n16; Jewish autonomy, 169; Jewish community, 34, 70, *158*, 169, 171; legal rights, 171; militia service, 148; trade, 48, 56, 58–59, 66, 75

da Costa family, 75
Danzig, 64
Declaration of Independence (US), 163
Declaration of the Rights of Man and Citizen (France), 133, 158–59, 168, 170–71
de la Faya family, 87–88
DeLancey, Oliver, 104
Delaware Indians, 106, 112
Delgado, Moses, 152–53
de Mezquita family, 75
democratic republicanism, 132

INDEX

denization, 3, 74–75, 77, 122, 142, 144, 149, 149, 237n61
de Pinto family, 75
Devaux, Jean-Baptiste Urbain, 175
Dias de Brito, Fernando, 58, 232n52
diasporas, 9, 154; Jewish press and, 199, 203, 205, 211; Portuguese Jewish, 60; "trading diaspora" model, 79
Diasporas within a Diaspora (Israel), 37
disabilities, legal, 8, 19, 30, 40, 142, 144–45
disenfranchisement, 4–5; in Jamaica, 142–46; in Rhode Island, 128–29, 254n29. *See also* office-holding; political rights; voting rights
Dixon, John M., 2, 7, 177
Dohm, Christian Wilhelm von, 161, 165
Drescher, Seymour, 75
Drummond, Adam, 109, 114
Dubin, Lois, 217n15, 262n10
Dury, John, 120
Dutch maritime empire, 28, 31, 34–35, 47–48, 238n74; freedom of conscience, 92; free port settlements, 234n16; Jewish political rights, 121; merchants in Barbados, 71; Portuguese Jewish merchants and, 42, 45–61; wars, 46, 56. *See also* Batavian Republic; Brazil; Curaçao; Suriname; West India Company
Dyer, William, 121

East India Company (British), 104
East India Company (Dutch), 89
Eckstein, Laura Newman, 6
economic equality, 160–61. *See also* poverty
economic pragmatism, 43–49
Eddy, Samuel, 255n29
Edict of Tolerance, 161
education, Jewish, 87–89
Edward I of England, 119
Eighty Years' War, 63, 68, 76, 87, 89
Elizer, Isaac, 128
Elkin, Benjamin, 190, 270n73
Elliott, J. H., 44
Emmanuel, Isaac, 34
Emmanuel, Suzanne, 34
Emmer, Pieter, 75
empiricism, 27
endenization papers, 74
English colonies. *See* British maritime empire

Enlightenment, 27, 29, 102, 160, 173
enslaved Africans, 18, 97; sexual exploitation of, 177–96; uprisings by, 133, 139, 148; use of term, ix. *See also* manumission; slavery
entanglement, 1–7, 21, 39–41, 63–64, 80, 115, 135–37, 171, 180–81
equality. *See* political rights
ethnic groups, 1, 7, 17–18, 31, 118, 179
Eurafrican Jews, 181, 188–89, 192–95, 270n79; use of term, ix
exile, 14, 62, 92, 166, 221n41

Faber, Eli, 36, 38–39
Faro, 57
Feingold, Henry, 31
Feitler, Bruno, 15
Felix Libertate Society, 162, 168–69
Ferdinand II of Spain, 26
fetishization, 149–50
Fiering, Norman, 9
fines. *See* pardons and fines
Fischel, Arnold, 22–26, 29–30, 34, 36
Flanders, 68
Fludyer, Samuel, 108–9
Formiggini, Moisè, 160, 262n13
Fort Pitt, 106, 111
Fort Stanwix, Treaty of, 112–13
Fortune, Alexander, 195
France. *See* French maritime empire; French Revolution
Frankfurt, 157
Franklin, Benjamin, 113
Franklin, William, 112–13
Franks, Aaron, 102–4
Franks, Abigaill Levy, 100
Franks, Abraham, 102
Franks, David, 100–115, 246n19, 251n70, 251n75
Franks, Isaac, 102–3
Franks, Jacob, 100–101, 103
Franks, Jacob (John), 113
Franks, Moses, 100–104, 108–9, 111, 113–15, 247n22
Franks, Naphtali, 103, 113
Franks family, 4
Freedom Train (exhibit), 30
free people of color: in Barbados, 191, 195–96; in Jamaica, 5, 136–55; political rights, 194–95; as slave owners, 140–41, 150, 258n29; use of term, ix. *See also* manumission
free trade, 48, 51

INDEX 283

French maritime empire: economic equality, 160-61; invasion of Dutch Republic, 262n2; Jewish autonomy, 164-66; Jewish community, 7, 164; in North America, 103; political rights, 133; settlers in British North America, 110-11; slavery, 174-75; sugar trade, 62, 66, 76-77; trade ordinances, 73. *See also* Haitian Revolution; Saint-Domingue
French Revolution, 130, 151, 156, 159, 165-67, 171-75
Frey, Junius, 173
Friedländer, David, 170-71
Friedman, Lee, 30-31
Fuentes, Marisa, 186
Furtado, Abraham, 172-73
Fürth, *157*

Gage, Thomas, 109-10
Gállego, Julián, 221n45
Galloway, Joseph, 112
Gamarra, Don Esteban de, 49, 55
genealogies, 16-19, 90, 222n58
General Company for the Commerce of Brazil, 58
George I of England, 102
George II of England, 102, 247n22
George III of England, 108, 251n70
George IV of England, 153
Georgia, 133, 163
Gerber, Jane, 17, 64
Gerbner, Katharine, 182
ghettos, 85, 119, 159, 166, 262n13
Glanz, Rudolf, 198, 271n6
global history, 37-39
Glorious Revolution (1688), 122
Goan Inquisition, 222n60
Godard, Jacques, 262n12
Gold Coast, 48, 139
Golding, John, 259n56
Goodman, Abram, 31
Goren, Arthur, 198
Gower, Lord, 113
Graizbord, David L., 13-14, 79, 228n3
Grand Ohio Company, 113
Gratz, Barnard, 106
Gratz, Rebecca, 198
Greene, Jack P., 44
Grégoire, Abbé, 174
Grenville, George, 109, 113
Grinstein, Hyman, 30
Gross, Charles, 25-27

Guadeloupe, 76
Guinea, 50, 93
Guinea Coast, 69
Gutstein, Morris, 30

Habsburg Crown (in Spain), 44-47
Habsburg Empire, 68
Haitian Revolution, 137, 140, 147, 149, 151
Halifax, Earl of, 100
Hamburg, 3, 46, 55, 58, 62-64, 67-68, *157,* 231n43
Hamilton, James, 105
Handlin, Oscar, 31
Harrington, James, 120
Hart, Aaron, 127, 255n36
Hart, Ezekiel, 4-5, 116-18, 124-26, 129, 131-32, 134-35, 251n2, 255n36, 256n38
Hart, Moses, 131, 255n36
Hart, Samuel, 118
Hart, Samuel, Bécancour, 134
Hassidic Jews, 165
Hays, Moses Michael, 169-70, 264n52
hazanim, 198, 269n59, 271nn4-5, 275n57
Hebrew Bible, 197-98, 207-8, 210
Hebrew Nation, 67, 76, 122
Hebrew Spelling-Book (1838), 198
Hebrew Union College, 29
Hebrew Vestry Bill (Barbados), 192-95
Henriques family, 75
Henry, Jacob, 124, 133-34
Henry I of England, 252n4
Herzog, Tamar, 19
Heuman, Gad, 150-51
Heyn, Piet, 89
Hilfman, Pinkus, 27
historicism, 10
historiography, 9; categorization in, 21; early American Jewish, 23-24
History of the Jews in America (Wiernik), 29-30
Hourwitz, Isaac, 171-72
Huguenots, 141, 143
Hurwitz, Isaac and Edith, 151
hybrid societies, 7
Hyman, Levy, 125-26, 134, 152

Iberian Peninsula, 7, 15, 19, 26, 28, 221n51
Iberian Union, 46, 50
Illinois Country, 109-10

INDEX

immigration: to Amsterdam, 67, 72, 76, 87; to Barbados, 74, 76; to Brazil, 69–70, 84; to North America, 6, 13, 25, 29, 32, 103, 105–6, 198
Immigration Act (US), 29
India, 2, 131, 141
Indiana Company, 112–13
Indians: alliance with French, 103; attacks by, 99–100, 103, 114; trade with British, 106–7, 109–10, 115; use of term, ix. *See also* Native Americans
Indigenous Americans, 18, 81, 97; use of term, ix
Inglis, John, 109
Ingram, Kevin, 16–17
Inquisition, 13–19, 28, 43, 45, 59, 61, 76, 79, 85–92, 96–98, 222n60, 239n15, 241n58
integration, 6, 19, 38–39, 43, 80, 87, 142, 176, 189, 196. *See also* assimilation
intersectionality, 21, 40, 134–35, 179
Iroquois Indians, 106
Isabella I, Queen of Spain, 26
Israel, Jonathan, 37, 63, 68, 241n58
Italy, 159–60, 165

Jacobins, 172–73, 175
Jamaica: economy, 145–46; free people of color, 136–38, 141, 143–55; Jewish community, 136–38, 141–55, *158*; militia service, 148–49; political rights, 5, 124–27, 133–34, 136–38, 143–46, 150–54, 259n56; revolutionaries and, 175; Sephardic merchants in, 71; sugar trade, 62–63, 66, 71, 74, 77; urban enclaves, 146–48
Jefferson, Thomas, 124, 163
Jewish Emancipation, 8; autonomy and, 176; in Europe, 161–62; in Jamaica, 150–51; in North America, 32, 126–28. *See also* disabilities, legal; disenfranchisement; political rights
Jewish History (journal), 37
Jewish history, goals of, 20
Jewishness: American Jewish history and, 29–31; clothing and, 145, 252n7; as difference, 119–22, 166; ethnic, 118; as indestructible and indivisible, 18, 20; military service and, 79–80, 97–98. *See also* religious identities
Jewish press, 197–211
Jewish self-rule, 5, 120; autonomy, 164–69, 176

Jewish studies, 10–11
Jews and the Expansion of Europe to the West (2001), 9, 12
Jews in the Caribbean (2014), 38
Jews of color, 5, 136–38, 141–42, 154
John Lackland of England, 252n4
Johnson, Jessica Marie, 181, 188
Johnson, William, 100, 106, 110–12
Johnson-Reed Act (1924), 29
Jones-Rogers, Stephanie, 181
Joseph II of Austria, 173
Juan José de Austria, 46
Judah, Rachel, 198
Judaizers, 14–15, 17, 27, 67, 85, 96, 141, 222n60

Kagan, Richard L., 9
Kahal Kadosh Beth Elohim (congregation), 202–3
Kaplan, Yosef, 3, 220n30
Katz, David, 122
Kayserling, Meyer, 26, 28
Kenesseth Shalom (congregation), 207
Kenny, James, 106
Kingston (Jamaica), 125–26, 133, 146–48, 203
kin networks, 64, 67, 247n26; trade and, 59, 105, 247n26
Kiron, Arthur, 199, 205, 217n13
Klooster, Wim, 5, 40, 53–54, 63
Kohler, Max J., 25, 27–28, 33
Korn, Bertram, 199

land speculation, 111–12, 115
Lateran Council, Fourth, 119, 252nn6–7
Latin American Jewish history, 8. *See also* Brazil
Law of God (Leeser), 209–10
leaders, Jewish: in Barbados, 178–84, 188–96; citizenship rights and, 164–70, 176; lay leaders, 166, 180, 183–84; in London, 146; military service and, 80–81, 98; Portuguese, in Dutch Atlantic, 42–43, 60–61, 71, 73, 77; on voting rights, 152–53; in Western Hemisphere, 25, 29, 197–98, 203. *See also* rabbis
Leeser, Isaac, 6, 197–211, 271nn4–5, 272n19, 274n46, 275nn53–54
legal equality, 8, 169–71, 175–76. *See also* political rights
Leone, Juda, 166
Leopold, Peter, 262n11

Lesser Antilles, 72
Levi de Barrios, Daniel, 244n123
Levine, Nathaniel, 202–3
Levinger, Lee, 30
Levy, Levy Andrew, 106–7
Ligon, Richard, 71
Lindo, Alexandre, 147
Lisbon, 62, 64, 76, 82
Livesay, Daniel, 143
livornine, 85
Livorno, 59, 82, 85, 141, *157,* 166, 262nn10–11
Lodeño, Antonio Rodriguez, 54–56
London, 64, 74–75, 141, *157,* 237n61
Long, Edward, 147, 149
Lopes de Azevedo, Francisco, 57
Lopes Suasso, Antonio, 55, 60
Lopez, Aaron, 128
Lorraine, 158, 164–65
Louis XVI of France, 161
Louverture, Toussaint, 175
Low Countries, 7, 60. See also *specific countries*
Lower Canada: L'affaire Hart, 116–18, 129–35; Legislative Assembly, 4, 116–18, 134; local identities and politics, 129–35; minority rights, 123–29; political economy, 118
Luso-Brazilians, 48, 82–84, 90, 95

Machorro, Elias, 91, 186
Mackay, Alexander, Jr., 127, 254n26
Maderia, 64, 66
Magen Abraham (congregation), 93
Maleo, Ignacio, 52
Mantua, *157,* 170
manumission, 137, 139–41, 180, 191. See also *free people of color*
Marcus, Jacob Rader, 29, 32–35, 226n42
Maria Theresa, 103
Marischal, Johannes, 92
Maroons, 145, 148–49
Martínez, María Elena, 19
Martinique, 63, 76
martyrs, 80, 96–97
Maryland, 111, 123, 133
Massachusetts Bay Colony, 121, 123, 133
Massiah, Benjamin, 270n79
Massiah, Isaac, 178–79, 182, 184–85, 189
Massiah family, 183–87
Maurits, Johan, 69–70

Maury, Abbé, 162
Menasseh ben Israel, 73, 242n85
Mendelsohn, Adam, 199, 205
Mendelssohn, Moses, 165, 198
Mendes de Brito, Diego, 55–56, 58, 231n44
mercantilism, 75, 120
messianism, 4, 80, 91, 98, 242n85
Metz, *157,* 166
Mexico, 19, 27
Mexico City, 13
Meza, Jacob J. de, 188–89
Michell, Salomone, 166–67
Middle Passage, 94
Mikveh Israel (congregation), 159, 193, 198, 271n5
military service: equality in, 161–62; in Jamaica, 148–49; Jewish soldiers in WIC, 4, 78–98
Miranda, E. R., 189
Mirvis, Stanley, 5
Mirzoeff, Nicholas, 144
miscegenation, 145, 149
Mississippi Company, 114
mixed ancestry, 14, 136–37, 148–49, 154–55, 189, 195, 259n56
mobility, 7, 9–10
Modena, *157*
modernity, ix, 8, 29, 32
Moïse, Thomas Jefferson, 197
morals, 10–12, 97, 149, 165, 173–74, 182, 190, 208
Moravians, 141, 143
Mordecai, Jacob, 198
Morgan, Edmund, 35
Morgan, Philip D., 9
Moriscos, 15–16, 43
Morocco, 7–8, 51, 88–89, 220n29
Moutoukias, Zacharias, 49–50, 52–53
"mulattos," 140, 149. See also *free people of color; manumission*
Muslim Iberia, 15, 26
Muslims, 13, 15–16

Napoleon, 174, 262n13, 265n54
Nassy, David, 160, 174–75
Nathan, M. N., 203
National Assembly (France), 158–59, 172
National Assembly (Netherlands), 163–64
Nation of Islam publications, 11, 219n23
Native Americans, 106; use of term, ix. See also *Indians*

Naturalization Act (1740), 5, 122, 128, 142, 146, 153
Navarro, Moisés, 91, 93
Navigation Act (French), 76
navíos de registro (registry ships), 44–45, 49–61
Nesbitt, Arnold, 104, 108–9, 114
Netanyahu, Benzion, 13
Netherlands: political rights, 170. *See also* Dutch maritime empire
Neveh Salom (congregation), 87
Neve Salom (congregation), 169
New Amsterdam, 48; Jewish settlement in, 22–23, 34, 36
Newcastle, Duke of (Thomas Pelham), 104, 108, 247n22
New Christians, 13–21; in Amsterdam, 3, 60; categorization of, 223n63; in Dutch Brazil, 91; in Livorno, 85; merchants, 3, 43, 45–46, 60, 62–77; Portuguese, 222n60, 230n30, 233n3; in Spanish commercial networks, 43, 45–46; sugar trade, 62–77
New England, 123
New Hampshire, 123, 133, 163
New Haven, 123
New Jersey, 133, 163
Newman, Brooke, 149
New Netherland, 48
Newport, Rhode Island, 29–30, 158
newspapers, 202, 273n24. *See also* Jewish press
Newton, Melanie, 191, 194
New York: American Revolution and, 158; Jewish community, *158*, 207, 251n75; Jewish press, 204; land speculation, 111; manumission, 140; political rights, 133, 163; religious diversity, 123
Nidhe Israel (congregation), *178*, 182–89, *185*, 189, 192
Nieuhof, Johan, 96
North American colonies: commerce and British colonial expansion, 4, 99–115. *See also* American Revolution; British maritime empire; Lower Canada; United States
North Carolina, 124, 133–34, 163
Nova Zeelandia, 70
Nunes, Isaac, 91
Nunes da Costa, Duarte, 46
Nunes da Costa, Jeronimo, 46, 51, 55, 57–58, 60–61, 231n43

Oath of Abjuration, 116–18, 254n27
The Occident (periodical), 6, 197–211; agents, 209; finances, 274n39, 275n57; prospectuses, 272n19; subscription publishing, 201–11, *206*, 274n39; wrappers, 199–200, 203–4, 207, 209–11, 274n38
oceanic history, 37
office-holding, 116–19, 122, 124, 127–29, 144, 156, 163, 170, 180
Ohio Company of Virginia, 114
Ohio River Valley, 99, 103, 105–7, 111
Okhovat, Oren, 3
Old Christians, 14, 16, 45
Olinda, 81–83
Olivares, Count-Duke of, 45, 230n30
Oporto, 64, 76
Oppenheimer, Josef, 163
Oranjestad, 66
Orejón, Francisco de, 54–56, 58
orthodox religiosity, 61
Ouellet, Fernand, 130

Pantaleón, Juan de, 53
Papineau, Louis-Joseph, 132, 134
Paraíba, 84, 91–92
Paramaribo, 147
pardons and fines, 51–53, 60
Paris, 172
Parti Canadien, 132, 134, 256n38
Parti Québécois, 135
Patriot revolt, *167*, 167–68
patronage, 46, 131, 141–42, 154, 195, 258n29
Peace of Münster, 58
Peixoto, Ester, 87
Pelham, Henry, 104
Pelham, Thomas. *See* Newcastle, Duke of
Pennsylvania, 103, 111, 133, *158*, 159
Pentateuch, 209–10
Pereira family, 75
Pereyra, Abraam, 55
Pernambuco: Dutch invasion and occupation of, 64, 68, 78, 81–84, 89, 91, 239n15; Jewish community, 92–96; persecution of New Christians, 67
Peru, 13, 48
Philadelphia, 99–100, 103, 106–7, 158, 197–98, 251n75
Philip III of Spain, 15
Philip IV of Spain, 16, 43–49, 58
Phillips, Jonas, 170
Pinto, Isaac de, 165

INDEX

Pitock, Toni, 4
Pitt, Thomas, 113
Plantagenet kings, 252n4
Plantation Act. *See* Naturalization Act (1740)
Plumsted, William, 104–8, 111
political economy, 63, 118, 120–29, 182
political rights: in Barbados, 180, 191, 194–95; in Jamaica, 5, 124–27, 133–34, 136–38, 143–46, 150–54, 259n56; in Livorno, 262nn10–11; in Lower Canada, 116–35; revolutions and, 158–76; in United States, 32. *See also* citizenship; office-holding; voting rights
political thought, British, 118–23, 133
Pontiac, 112
Pontiac's War, 107, 111
"Port Jew," 9, 12, 37, 63, 199, 217n15
Port Royal, 66, 144
Portugal: colonization of Brazil, 50, 63–64, 66; markets in, 51; war of independence, 57–58
Portuguese Jewish merchants: in Caribbean region, 64–65; as culturally European, 42–43, 58–59; diaspora of, 60; Spanish imperial *navíos de registro* trade, 42–45, 49–61; sugar trade, 62–77
Portuguese Jews: in early Spanish Empire, 3; hegemony among Atlantic Jewries, 8, 13; in Jamaica, 136, 141–42; as New Christians, 60–61; in Portugal, 13–19; use of term, ix, 228n3
Portuguese Nation, 3, 62–64, 66–67, 76–77; defined, 233n1
Portuguese New Christians, 222n60, 230n30, 233n3
postcolonial studies, 10–11
poverty, 168–69, 182–84
Pownall, John, 113
Pownall, Thomas, 113
pragmatism: commercial, 79–80; toleration, 43–49, 59–61, 229n6
Prague, 103, *157*
prejudice, 79, 94, 97, 165, 174, 193. *See also* antisemitism
prestige (within Jewish community), 4, 80, 87, 96, 98, 201
Princess Street Synagogue, 125
privileges, 8, 19; personal privileges bills in Jamaica, 136–37, 145–46, 151, 155
Proclamation Line, 111–12

Promised City (Rischin), 35–36
Protestants, 3, 43, 45, 51, 58–59, 79, 81, 92, 97, 103, 118, 120, 122–24, 129, 134, 161, 254n26
Publications (AJHS), 30
public office. *See* office-holding
publishing, religious, 204–5, 208. *See also* Jewish press
Pulido Serrano, Juan Ignacio, 15
Puritan colonies, 123

Quakers, 123, 141, 143, 205
Québec Act (1774), 127, 129–30
Québec City, 116–17

rabbinical culture, 5, 142
rabbinical law, 162, 182
rabbis, 6, 22, 30, 91–92, 198–99, 203, 265n54; in Brazil, 69–70; informal, 81, 91–92, 96, 98; on military service, 162. *See also* leaders, Jewish
Rabin, Shari, 199
racial hierarchies, 137, 179, 191, 261n94
Rauschenbach, Sina, ix, 9, 11
Recife, 81–82, 92–96
Reconquista, 15, 26
Rehiné, Zalma, 198, 272n19
Reilly, Matthew, 179, 195
religious identities, 15, 40, 61, 66. *See also* Jewishness
religious pluralism, 43
religious tolerance. *See* tolerance
Remer, Rosalind, 204–5, 208
Revolutionary War, 114, 161. *See also* American Revolution
revolutions, 5–6, 156–76; autonomy, 164–69, 176; economic equality, 160–61; Jewish involvement in, 158, 171–76; legal equality, 169–71, 175–76; military equality, 161–62; political equality, 162–64. *See also* American Revolution; French Revolution; Haitian Revolution
Rhode Island, 121, 123, 128–29, 163, 254n29; Newport, 29–30, 158
Rider, Sidney S., 254n29
Rigaud, André, 175
Río de la Plata, 49–51
Rischin, Moses, 35–36
Rocheford, Lord, 113
Rodrigues da Sousa, Simão and Luis, 57
Rodrigues Isidro, Jacob, 55, 231n43
Rodrigues Isidro, Manuel, 55

INDEX

Rodrigues Isidro family, 58
Roitman, Jessica, 66
Rome, *157,* 159–60, 162, 166
Roth, Cecil, 20
Rothschild, Mayer Amschel, 163
Rowland, Robert, 14

Saint-Domingue, 133, 140, 147, 149, 175
Saint Eustatius, 66, 75, *158*
Saint Thomas, 204
Salmagundis, 194
Salvador, Francis, 162–63
Salvador da Bahia, 68
Samuel, Edgar, 17
Sanches Morao, Abraham, 146, 259n56
Sanlúcar, 54
Santa Teresa de Ávila, 18
São Tomé, 64, 66
Saraiva, Antonio, 13
Sarna, Jonathan, 199
Sasportas, Isaac Yeshurun, 133, 149, 175
Savannah, 158
Schorsch, Jonathan, ix, 9, 11, 261n94
Schreuder, Yda, 3
Schwartz, Joseph, 198
Schwartz, Stuart, 43
secret Judaism, 3, 7, 13–15, 67, 87, 233n3
sedition, 148–49
Seixas, Gershom Mendes, 198
Seixas, Isaac, 198
Sephardic Atlantic (2018), 9, 12, 37
Sephardim: merchants in Atlantic sugar trade, 62–77; in North America, 32; use of term, ix
Serra, Abraham, 87
Seven Years' War, 99–107, 113, 149
Seville, 51, 54, 232n52
sexual liaisons: of lower-class Jewish men, 177–89, 195–96; of wealthy Jewish men, 189–95
sex workers, 178, 182, 185–88
Sharpe, Sam, 154
Shearith Israel (congregation), 100, 202
Sheftall, Mordecai, 162–63
Shilstone, Eustace M., 236n49
Silva e Sampaio, Dom Pedro da, 92
silver trade, 49–50
Simmonds, M. B., 203–4
Simon, Joseph, 106
Singerman, Robert, 198

Six Nations, 112
slavery and slave trade, 8; in Barbados, 6, 71–72; civil liberties and, 145; development of, 35; Dutch West India Company, 48, 69–70, 93–94, *95,* 97; free people of color as slave owners, 140–41, 150, 258n29; French Revolution and, 174–75; in Jamaica, 138–39, 257n9; Jews as slave owners, 150, 180, 193; New Christian merchants, 64; transatlantic slave trade, 46, 229n14; use of terms, ix; violence of, 94. *See also* abolition of slavery; enslaved Africans; manumission; Maroons
smuggling. *See* contraband
Snyder, Holly, 4–5, 38–39, 143, 152
social justice, 11
social mobility, 145, 190
Sola, Abraham de, 203
soldiers. *See* military service
Sorkin, David, 162, 217n15
South American Jewry, 22–27, 33–35. *See also* Brazil
South Carolina, 133, *158,* 162–63
Souza, Abraham Henriques de, 136
Souza, Rebecca, 136–37, 155
Souza, Sarah, 136
Spain: Jewish expulsion from (1492), 15, 26; Jews in, 13–19; markets in, 51. *See also* Inquisition
Spanish maritime empire, 22–23; financial crisis (1640s), 58; immigration restrictions, 13; *navíos de registro* (registry ships), 44–45, 49–61; as polycentric monarchy, 44; Portuguese New Christian bankers as royal financiers, 45–47; wars, 53, 58
Spinoza, Rachel, 89
stereotyping, 149–50, 154
Straus, Oscar, 27–28
Stuyvesant, Peter, 32
Suasso family, 75
subscription publishing, 201–11
suffrage. *See* voting rights
sugar trade, 3, 62–77, 82, 139
Sulzberger, Mayer, 273n22
Suriname: Ashkenazim in, 143; Dutch colonization of, 48; English colonization of, 70–71; Eurafrican Jews, 181, 188–89; free people of color in, 140; Jewish community, 27–28, 35, 39–40, *158*; Jewish slaveowners in,

150; political rights, 171; Sephardic merchants in, 71; Society of, 174; sugar trade, 76
Sur Israel (congregation), 92–93, 96
Sussman, Lance J., 199, 210
Sutcliffe, Adam, 37–39, 79–80, 227n71
Sutro, Abraham, 198
Symcox, Geoffrey, 159
synagogues: in Brazil, 1, 67, 69–70, 91, 93; in Jamaica, 125; in North America, 30, 36; sexual encounters in, 182–89

Tacky's Revolt (1760), 139, 148
taxes, 16, 18–19, 52, 60, 96, 142, 144–45, 161, 166, 170, 180, 183, 192–93, 241n52; *almirantazgo*, 51, 230n30; community, 87–89; on Jews, 142, 144–45, 161, 180, 252n4; slave trade, 94
tax farmers, 69–70, 93
Teixeira family, 75
Test and Corporations Act, 128
Thirty Years' War, 87
Time for Planting (Faber), 36
Tiribás, Victor, 3–4
Tobias, Sophia, 202
Toland, John, 122
tolerance: citizenship and, 171; early modern policies of, 43; in Europe, 160–61; as ideological framework, 229n6; in Jamaica, 142; in US, 30–31
toleration: in Brazil, 69; in British Empire, 28, 31, 106, 123; pragmatic, 43–49, 59–61, 229n6
Toleration Act (1688), 122
Touro Synagogue, 30
trade, 3, 27–28; Ashkenazi networks, 101, 105–6; British imperial expansion and, 99–115; ethnoreligious networks, 105–6, 247n26; free trade, 48, 51; goods, 56–57, 64–65; kinship networks, 59, 105, 247n26; non-Jewish partners, 105–6, 115; sociocultural, religious, and political entanglement in, 53–61; "trading diaspora" model, 79. *See also* contraband; *navíos de registro*; sugar trade
Trade and Navigation Acts (English), 72–74, 76
transnational history, 37
Trent, William, 106, 112–13
Trieste, *157*, 262n10

Trivellato, Francesca, 59
Trois-Rivières, Québec, 116–18, 127, 129, 131–32, 134
Tuscany, 166

United States: Constitution, 163, 171; Jewish community, 6, 100, 197–211, 271n6; political rights, 32, 123–24, 133, 170–71, 254n27; religious tolerance and liberalism, 30–31. *See also* American exceptionalism; American Jewish history; American Revolution; *specific states*
United States Jewry, 1776–1985 (Marcus), 32–33
Upper Canada, 129–30, 254n24
urban environments, 5, 14, 146–48, 154, *157*, 163
utility, 149–50

Vandalia, 113
Vatican Council, Second, 119
Vaugeois, Denis, 255n36
Velázquez, Diego, 16–17, 221n45
venereal diseases, 180, 186, 189
Venezuelan goods, 57
Venice, 14, *157*
violence: colonial, 79, 81, 97; inquisitorial persecution, 92, 96–97; against Jewish communities, 29, 142, 160; of slave trade, 94
Virginia, 111, 124, 133, *158*
voting rights: Canada, 253n24, 254n27; England, 253n24, 254n27; free people of color, 259n56; Jamaica, 124–27, 134, 144–46, 152–54, 253n18, 259n56; United States, 128–29, 254n27

Wagener, Zacharias, 94, *95*
Wallot, Jean-Pierre, 134
Walpole, Robert, 104
Walpole, Thomas, 113
Walpole Company, 113
Ward, Nathaniel, 123
Ward, Richard, 128, 255n29
Ward, Samuel, 128
wars: free people of color and, 145, 148–49; in Lower Canada, 127; trade and, 47, 53, 56–58, 68, 82, 99–115. *See also* Eighty Years' War; revolutions; Seven Years' War
Washington, George, 22–23, 30, 36, 114
Watson, Karl, 191

Watts, John, 104, 108
Western Design, 73, 237nn60–61
West India Company (WIC): creation of, 48, 68; Jewish merchants, 68–71; Jewish soldiers in, 4, 78–98; shares in, 89; slave trade, 48, 69–70, 72, 93–94, 95, 97; sugar trade, 65
West Virginia, 112
Whitehall Conference (1655), 119, 121
white supremacy, 137, 179, 191, 261n94
Wiernik, Peter, 29–30, 32, 34, 36
Willemstad, 66, 147

William III of England, 122
Williams, Francis, 146
Williams, Roger, 121, 123
Wise, Isaac Mayer, 6, 199
Wiznitzer, Arnold, 66–68, 236n49
Wolff, Aaron, 203–4
World War II, 29

Yerushalmi, Yosef Hayim, 220n30

Zapata, Pedro, 53
Zion in America (Feingold), 31

www.ingramcontent.com/pod-product-compliance
Lightning Source LLC
Chambersburg PA
CBHW031328230426
43670CB00006B/276